Donna Jean Troka, PhD
Kathleen LeBesco, PhD
Jean Bobby Noble, PhD
Editors

The Drag King Anthology

The Drag King Anthology has been co-published simultaneously as *Journal of Homosexuality*, Volume 43, Numbers 3/4 2002.

*Pre-publication
REVIEWS,
COMMENTARIES,
EVALUATIONS . . .*

" **A**LL UNIVERSITY COURSES ON MASCULINITY SHOULD USE THIS BOOK . . . challenges preconceptions through the empirical richness of direct experience. The contributors and editors have worked together to produce cultural analysis that enhances our perception of the dynamic uncertainty of gendered experience."

Sally R. Munt, DPhil
*Subject Chair, Media Studies
University of Sussex*

The Drag King Anthology

The Drag King Anthology has been co-published simultaneously as *Journal of Homosexuality*, Volume 43, Numbers 3/4 2002.

The *Journal of Homosexuality* Monographic "Separates"

Below is a list of "separates," which in serials librarianship means a special issue simultaneously published as a special journal issue or double-issue *and* as a "separate" hardbound monograph. (This is a format which we also call a "DocuSerial.")

"Separates" are published because specialized libraries or professionals may wish to purchase a specific thematic issue by itself in a format which can be separately cataloged and shelved, as opposed to purchasing the journal on an on-going basis. Faculty members may also more easily consider a "separate" for classroom adoption.

"Separates" are carefully classified separately with the major book jobbers so that the journal tie-in can be noted on new book order slips to avoid duplicate purchasing.

You may wish to visit Haworth's website at . . .

http://www.HaworthPress.com

. . . to search our online catalog for complete tables of contents of these separates and related publications.

You may also call 1-800-HAWORTH (outside US/Canada: 607-722-5857), or Fax 1-800-895-0582 (outside US/Canada: 607-771-0012), or e-mail at:

docdelivery@haworthpress.com

The Drag King Anthology, edited by Donna Jean Troka, PhD (cand.), Kathleen LeBesco, PhD, and Jean Bobby Noble, PhD (Vol. 43, No. 3/4, 2002). *"ALL UNIVERSITY COURSES ON MASCULINITY SHOULD USE THIS BOOK . . . challenges preconceptions through the empirical richness of direct experience. The contributors and editors have worked together to produce cultural analysis that enhances our perception of the dynamic uncertainty of gendered experience." (Sally R. Munt, DPhil, Subject Chair, Media Studies, University of Sussex)*

Homosexuality in French History and Culture, edited by Jeffrey Merrick, PhD, and Michael Sibalis, PhD (Vol. 41, No. 3/4, 2001). *"Fascinating . . . Merrick and Sibalis bring together historians, literary scholars, and political activists from both sides of the Atlantic to examine same-sex sexuality in the past and present." (Bryant T. Ragan, PhD, Associate Professor of History, Fordham University, New York)*

Gay and Lesbian Asia: Culture, Identity, Community, edited by Gerard Sullivan, PhD, and Peter A. Jackson, PhD (Vol. 40, No. 3/4, 2001). *"Superb. . . . Covers a happily wide range of styles . . . will appeal to both students and educated fans." (Gary Morris, Editor/Publisher, Bright Lights Film Journal)*

Queer Asian Cinema: Shadows in the Shade, edited by Andrew Grossman, MA (Vol. 39, No. 3/4, 2000). *"An extremely rich tapestry of detailed ethnographies and state-of-the-art theorizing. . . . Not only is this a landmark record of queer Asia, but it will certainly also be a seminal, contributive challenge to gender and sexuality studies in general." (Dédé Oetomo, PhD, Coordinator of the Indonesian organization GAYa NUSANTARA: Adjunct Reader in Linguistics and Anthropology, School of Social Sciences, Universitas Airlangga, Surabaya, Indonesia)*

Gay Community Survival in the New Millennium, edited by Michael R. Botnick, PhD (cand.) (Vol. 38, No. 4, 2000). *Examines the notion of community from several different perspectives focusing on the imagined, the structural, and the emotive. You will explore a theoretical overview and you will peek into the moral discourses that frame "gay community," the rift between HIV-positive and HIV-negative gay men, and how Israeli gays seek their place in the public sphere.*

The Ideal Gay Man: The Story of Der Kreis, by Hubert Kennedy, PhD (Vol. 38, No. 1/2, 1999). *"Very profound. . . . Excellent insight into the problems of the early fight for homosexual emancipation in Europe and in the USA. . . . The ideal gay man (high-mindedness, purity, cleanness), as he was imagined by the editor of 'Der Kreis,' is delineated by the fascinating quotations out of the published erotic stories." (Wolfgang Breidert, PhD, Academic Director, Institute of Philosophy, University Karlsruhe, Germany)*

Multicultural Queer: Australian Narratives, edited by Peter A. Jackson, PhD, and Gerard Sullivan, PhD (Vol. 36, No. 3/4, 1999). *Shares the way that people from ethnic minorities in Australia (those who are not of Anglo-Celtic background) view homosexuality, their experiences as homosexual men and women, and their feelings about the lesbian and gay community.*

Scandinavian Homosexualities: Essays on Gay and Lesbian Studies, edited by Jan Löfström, PhD (Vol. 35, No. 3/4, 1998). *"Everybody interested in the formation of lesbian and gay identities and their interaction with the sociopolitical can find something to suit their taste in this volume." (Judith Schuyf, PhD, Assistant Professor of Lesbian and Gay Studies, Center for Gay and Lesbian Studies, Utrecht University, The Netherlands)*

Gay and Lesbian Literature Since World War II: History and Memory, edited by Sonya L. Jones, PhD (Vol. 34, No. 3/4, 1998). *"The authors of these essays manage to gracefully incorporate the latest insights of feminist, postmodernist, and queer theory into solidly grounded readings . . . challenging and moving, informed by the passion that prompts both readers and critics into deeper inquiry." (Diane Griffin Growder, PhD, Professor of French and Women's Studies, Cornell College, Mt. Vernon, Iowa)*

Reclaiming the Sacred: The Bible in Gay and Lesbian Culture, edited by Raymond-Jean Frontain, PhD (Vol. 33, No. 3/4, 1997). *"Finely wrought, sharply focused, daring, and always dignified. . . . In chapter after chapter, the Bible is shown to be a more sympathetic and humane book in its attitudes toward homosexuality than usually thought and a challenge equally to the straight and gay moral imagination." (Joseph Wittreich, PhD, Distinguished Professor of English, The Graduate School, The City University of New York)*

Activism and Marginalization in the AIDS Crisis, edited by Michael A. Hallett, PhD (Vol. 32, No. 3/4, 1997). *Shows readers how the advent of HIV-disease has brought into question the utility of certain forms of "activism" as they relate to understanding and fighting the social impacts of disease.*

Gays, Lesbians, and Consumer Behavior: Theory, Practice, and Research Issues in Marketing, edited by Daniel L. Wardlow, PhD (Vol. 31, No. 1/2, 1996). *"For those scholars, market researchers, and marketing managers who are considering marketing to the gay and lesbian community, this book should be on required reading list." (Mississippi Voice)*

Gay Men and the Sexual History of the Political Left, edited by Gert Hekma, PhD, Harry Oosterhuis, PhD, and James Steakley, PhD (Vol. 29, No. 2/3/4, 1995). *"Contributors delve into the contours of a long-forgotten history, bringing to light new historical data and fresh insight. . . . An excellent account of the tense historical relationship between the political left and gay liberation." (People's Voice)*

Sex, Cells, and Same-Sex Desire: The Biology of Sexual Preference, edited by John P. De Cecco, PhD, and David Allen Parker, MA (Vol. 28, No. 1/2/3/4, 1995). *"A stellar compilation of chapters examining the most important evidence underlying theories on the biological basis of human sexual orientation." (MGW)*

Gay Ethics: Controversies in Outing, Civil Rights, and Sexual Science, edited by Timothy F. Murphy, PhD (Vol. 27, No. 3/4, 1994). *"The contributors bring the traditional tools of ethics and political philosophy to bear in a clear and forceful way on issues surrounding the rights of homosexuals." (David L. Hull; Dressler Professor in the Humanities, Department of Philosophy, Northwestern University)*

Gay and Lesbian Studies in Art History, edited by Whitney Davis, PhD (Vol. 27, No. 1/2, 1994). *"Informed, challenging . . . never dull. . . . Contributors take risks and, within the restrictions of scholarly publishing, find new ways to use materials already available or examine topics never previously explored." (Lambda Book Report)*

Critical Essays: Gay and Lesbian Writers of Color, edited by Emmanuel S. Nelson, PhD (Vol. 26, No. 2/3, 1993). *"A much-needed book, sparkling with stirring perceptions and resonating with depth. . . . The anthology not only breaks new ground, it also attempts to heal wounds inflicted by our oppressed pasts." (Lambda)*

Gay Studies from the French Cultures: Voices from France, Belgium, Brazil, Canada, and The Netherlands, edited by Rommel Mendès-Leite, PhD, and Pierre-Olivier de Busscher, PhD (Vol. 25, No. 1/2/3, 1993). *"The first book that allows an English-speaking world to have a compre-*

hensive look at the principal trends in gay studies in France and French-speaking countries." (André Bèjin, PhD, Directeur, de Recherche au Centre National de la Recherche Scientifique (CNRS), Paris)

If You Seduce a Straight Person, Can You Make Them Gay? Issues in Biological Essentialism versus Social Constructionism in Gay and Lesbian Identities, edited by John P. De Cecco, PhD, and John P. Elia, PhD (cand.) (Vol. 24, No. 3/4, 1993). *"You'll find this alternative view of the age old question to be one that will become the subject of many conversations to come. Thought-provoking to say the least!" (Prime Timers)*

Gay and Lesbian Studies: The Emergence of a Discipline, edited by Henry L. Minton, PhD (Vol. 24, No. 1/2, 1993). *"The volume's essays provide insight into the field's remarkable accomplishments and future goals." (Lambda Book Report)*

Homosexuality in Renaissance and Enlightenment England: Literary Representations in Historical Context, edited by Claude J. Summers, PhD (Vol. 23, No. 1/2, 1992). *"It is remarkable among studies in this field in its depth of scholarship and variety of approaches and is accessible." (Chronique)*

Coming Out of the Classroom Closet: Gay and Lesbian Students, Teachers, and Curricula, edited by Karen M. Harbeck, PhD, JD, Recipient of Lesbian and Gay Educators Award by the American Educational Research Association's Lesbian and Gay Studies Special Interest Group (AREA) (Vol. 22, No. 3/4, 1992). *"Presents recent research about gay and lesbian students and teachers and the school system in which they function." (Contemporary Psychology)*

Homosexuality and Male Bonding in Pre-Nazi Germany: The Youth Movement, the Gay Movement, and Male Bonding Before Hitler's Rise: Original Transcripts from Der Eigene, the First Gay Journal in the World, edited by Harry Oosterhuis, PhD, and Hubert Kennedy, PhD (Vol. 22, No. 1/2, 1992). *"Provide[s] insight into the early gay movement, particularly in its relation to the various political currents in pre-World War II Germany." (Lambda Book Report)*

Gay People, Sex, and the Media, edited by Michelle A. Wolf, PhD, and Alfred P. Kielwasser, MA (Vol. 21, No. 1/2, 1991). *"Altogether, the kind of research anthology which is useful to many disciplines in gay studies. Good stuff!" (Communique)*

Gay Midlife and Maturity: Crises, Opportunities, and Fulfillment, edited by John Alan Lee, PhD (Vol. 20, No. 3/4, 1991). *"The insight into gay aging is amazing, accurate, and much-needed. . . . A real contribution to the older gay community." (Prime Timers)*

Male Intergenerational Intimacy: Historical, Socio-Psychological, and Legal Perspectives, edited by Theo G. M. Sandfort, PhD, Edward Brongersma, JD, and A. X. van Naerssen, PhD (Vol. 20, No. 1/2, 1991). *"The most important book on the subject since Tom O'Carroll's 1980* Paedophilia: The Radical Case.*" (The North America Man/Boy Love Association Bulletin, May 1991)*

Love Letters Between a Certain Late Nobleman and the Famous Mr. Wilson, edited by Michael S. Kimmel, PhD (Vol. 19, No. 2, 1990). *"An intriguing book about homosexuality in 18th Century England. Many details of the period, such as meeting places, coded language, and 'camping' are all covered in the book. If you're a history buff, you'll enjoy this one." (Prime Timers)*

Homosexuality and Religion, edited by Richard Hasbany, PhD (Vol. 18, No. 3/4, 1990). *"A welcome resource that provides historical and contemporary views on many issues involving religious life and homosexuality." (Journal of Sex Education and Therapy)*

Homosexuality and the Family, edited by Frederick W. Bozett, PhD (Vol. 18, No. 1/2, 1989). *"Enlightening and answers a host of questions about the effects of homosexuality upon family members and the family as a unit." (Ambush Magazine)*

Gay and Lesbian Youth, edited by Gilbert Herdt, PhD (Vol. 17, No. 1/2/3/4, 1989). *"Provides a much-needed compilation of research dealing with homosexuality and adolescents." (GLTF Newsletter)*

Lesbians Over 60 Speak for Themselves, edited by Monika Kehoe, PhD (Vol. 16, No. 3/4, 1989). *"A pioneering book examining the social, economical, physical, sexual, and emotional lives of aging lesbians." (Feminist Bookstore News)*

Monographs "Separates" list continued at the back

The Drag King Anthology

Donna Jean Troka, PhD (cand.)
Kathleen LeBesco, PhD
Jean Bobby Noble, PhD
Editors

The Drag King Anthology has been co-published simultaneously as *Journal of Homosexuality*, Volume 43, Numbers 3/4 2002.

Harrington Park Press
An Imprint of
The Haworth Press, Inc.
New York • London • Oxford

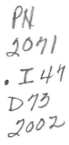

Published by

Harrington Park Press®, 10 Alice Street, Binghamton, NY 13904-1580 USA

Harrington Park Press® is an imprint of The Haworth Press, Inc., 10 Alice Street, Binghamton, NY 13904-1580 USA.

The Drag King Anthology has been co-published simultaneously as *Journal of Homosexuality*™, Volume 43, Numbers 3/4 2002.

The development, preparation, and publication of this work has been undertaken with great care. However, the publisher, employees, editors, and agents of The Haworth Press and all imprints of The Haworth Press, Inc., including The Haworth Medical Press® and Pharmaceutical Products Press®, are not responsible for any errors contained herein or for consequences that may ensue from use of materials or information contained in this work. Opinions expressed by the author(s) are not necessarily those of The Haworth Press, Inc. With regard to case studies, identities and circumstances of individuals discussed herein have been changed to protect confidentiality. Any resemblance to actual persons, living or dead, is entirely coincidental.

Cover design by Jennifer M. Gaska
Cover photography by Helen M. Harris <eleni_harris@yahoo.com>

Library of Congress Cataloging-in-Publication Data

The drag king anthology / Donna Jean Troka, Kathleen LeBesco, Jean Bobby Noble.
    p. cm.
    The Drag King Anthology has been co-published simultaneously as Journal of homosexuality, volume 43, numbers 3/4 2002.
    Includes bibliographical references.
    ISBN 1-56023-308-7 (alk. paper) – ISBN 1-56023-309-5 (softcover : alk. paper)
    1. Male impersonators. I. Troka, Donna Jean. II. LeBesco, Kathleen, 1970- III. Noble, Jean Bobby. IV. Journal of homosexuality.
PN2071.I47D73 2003
810.8′353–dc21
                                     2003001514

Indexing, Abstracting & Website/Internet Coverage

This section provides you with a list of major indexing & abstracting services. That is to say, each service began covering this periodical during the year noted in the right column. Most Websites which are listed below have indicated that they will either post, disseminate, compile, archive, cite or alert their own Website users with research-based content from this work. (This list is as current as the copyright date of this publication.)

Abstracting, Website/Indexing Coverage . . . . Year When Coverage Began

- *Abstracts in Anthropology* **1982**
- *Academic Abstracts/CD-ROM* **1989**
- *Academic ASAP <www.galegroup.com>* **2000**
- *Academic Search: Database of 2,000 selected academic serials, updated monthly: EBSCO Publishing* **1995**
- *Academic Search Elite (EBSCO)* **1993**
- *Alternative Press Index (print, online & CD-ROM from NISC) <www.altpress.org>* **1996**
- *Applied Social Sciences Index & Abstracts (ASSIA) (Online: ASSI via Data-Star) (CD-Rom: ASSIA Plus) <www.csa.com>* **1987**
- *This periodical is indexing in ATLA Religion Database, published by the American Theological Library Association <www.atla.com>* **1986**
- *Book Review Index* **1996**
- *Cambridge Scientific Abstracts <www.csa.com>* **1993**

(continued)

(continued)

(continued)

Special Bibliographic Notes related to special journal issues (separates) and indexing/abstracting:

- indexing/abstracting services in this list will also cover material in any "separate" that is co-published simultaneously with Haworth's special thematic journal issue or DocuSerial. Indexing/abstracting usually covers material at the article/chapter level.
- monographic co-editions are intended for either non-subscribers or libraries which intend to purchase a second copy for their circulating collections.
- monographic co-editions are reported to all jobbers/wholesalers/approval plans. The source journal is listed as the "series" to assist the prevention of duplicate purchasing in the same manner utilized for books-in-series.
- to facilitate user/access services all indexing/abstracting services are encouraged to utilize the co-indexing entry note indicated at the bottom of the first page of each article/chapter/contribution.
- this is intended to assist a library user of any reference tool (whether print, electronic, online, or CD-ROM) to locate the monographic version if the library has purchased this version but not a subscription to the source journal.
- individual articles/chapters in any Haworth publication are also available through the Haworth Document Delivery Service (HDDS).

ABOUT THE EDITORS

Donna Jean Troka, PhD (cand.), is in the Graduate Institute of Liberal Arts at Emory University in Atlanta, Georgia. Her work addresses issues of race, gender, class and sexuality in American Popular Culture. Her article "When We Were Kings: On Being a Midwestern Drag King" appeared in issue 12 of *Bitch* magazine, and her article entitled "'You Heard My Gun Cock': Female Agency and Aggression in Contemporary Rap Music" appeared in the Spring/Summer 2002 issue of *African American Research Perspectives*, a journal of the University of Michigan's Program for Research on Black Americans. Contact her at <donnatroka@hotmail.com>.

Kathleen LeBesco, PhD, is Assistant Professor of Communication Arts at Marymount Manhattan College. She writes and teaches about media and popular culture studies, as well as feminist and queer theory. She is co-editor of *Bodies Out of Bounds: Fatness and Transgression* (University of California Press, 2001) and the author of an essay commissioned by GLAAD (Gay and Lesbian Alliance Against Defamation) concerning fan discourse about gay characters on reality TV shows.

Jean Bobby Noble, PhD, is Assistant Professor of English at York University, teaches Cultural Studies at York University (Toronto), and is the author of *Masculinities without Men* (forthcoming Spring 2003 with UBC Press), a study of female masculinity and whiteness in twentieth-century fiction and popular culture. After working as part of the Fireweed "Trans/Scribes" guest editorial, Jean is also currently co-editing *Counting Past 2: The Making of a Transsexual/Transgender Arts Movement* with Toronto performance artists and activists Mirha-Soleil Ross and Trish Salah, as well as undertaking a new study of femme subjectivities.

The Drag King Anthology

CONTENTS

Introduction

Donna Jean Troka, PhD (cand.)
Jean Bobby Noble, PhD
Kathleen LeBesco, PhD

What kinds of inroads stand to be made by a collaborative, interdisciplinary project that claims drag kings as its focus? *The Drag King Anthology* was begun with many aims in mind: to create a dialogue about a type of performance overshadowed in both scholarly and popular writings by camp and drag queens; to showcase the amazing growth and development of drag king troupes and communities outside the well-known happening scenes of New York, London, and San Francisco; to complicate the easy understanding of drag kings as "female-to-male" performers or as simple "women doing drag"; to provide a forum for performers and fans to speak alongside scholars, instead of being spoken for like so many ventriloquists' dummies; to merge vectors of culture, race, ethnicity, gender, sexuality, feminism, popular culture, anthropology, sociology and cultural politics both *within* and *between* essays in order to create a conversation which bridges disciplinary borders; to document a fascinating end-of-millennium cultural moment, and to understand the motivation for this most recent drag king explosion in its historical context. We feel strongly that the works amassed before you in this volume effectively propel the fulfillment of our intentions and open new avenues for research and discussion, as well.

* * *

[Haworth co-indexing entry note]: "Introduction." Troka, Donna Jean, Jean Bobby Noble, and Kathleen LeBesco. Co-published simultaneously in *Journal of Homosexuality* (Harrington Park Press, an imprint of The Haworth Press, Inc.) Vol. 43, No. 3/4, 2002, pp. 1-12; and: *The Drag King Anthology* (ed: Donna Troka, Kathleen LeBesco, and Jean Bobby Noble) Harrington Park Press, an imprint of The Haworth Press, Inc., 2002, pp. 1-12. Single or multiple copies of this article are available for a fee from The Haworth Document Delivery Service [1-800-HAWORTH, 9:00 a.m. - 5:00 p.m. (EST). E-mail address: docdelivery@haworthpress.com].

Frequently, it is some combination of scholarly endeavor and personal experience that awakens individuals to the necessity of a project like this one.

Donna: I was initiated into male drag performance as an undergraduate at the University of Illinois Urbana/Champaign, where a group of friends often hosted theme parties. Invited to the "Crossdress to Get Laid" party, I attended dressed in trousers and a shirt, tie and vest, with my shoulder length hair parted to the side and pulled back in a ponytail. Interestingly, my understated performance of masculinity stood apart from many of the "knowing" hosts of the party, who parodied 1970s disco hypermasculinity. Tight polyester, loud print shirts, hairy chests, greasy hair, gold chains and big bulges carried the evening. I recognized that my own performance of masculinity was much less a stagy antic and more a part of my queer identity. The juxtaposition of my masculine image with the parodic hypermasculine images of my friends began to elucidate the vast spectrum of masculinities that can be and are performed and embodied.

Later, after beginning a Master's degree program at Ohio State University, I reconnected with my interests and curiosities about performing/embodying masculinity. An acquaintance with two other Women's Studies Master's students who planned to create a lesbian-run troupe that performed in male drag during "party" nights at a local bar paved the way for my stint with H.I.S. Kings of Columbus, Ohio, with whom I performed as d.j. love for nearly three years. The talent and passion of the drag king scenesters inspired and educated me while my studies helped me to develop a critical awareness of the cultural and political significance of my performances.

Bobby: I saw my first drag king show in a Toronto drag bar in 1995. While I have no aspirations to perform, that night I instantly became the Toronto drag kings' biggest fan, academic or otherwise. I certainly found the performances to be some of the most compelling I have ever seen and relegate them, with Rosenfeld (see chapter), to the terrain of illusion and magic. While I thoroughly enjoyed the show on stage, I also could not help take note of the impact the show was having off-stage, on the fans. My academic work up to this point had theorized female masculinity; what I was witnessing that night constituted one of the most entertaining and intriguing appropriations, stagings even, of gender, fantasy and desire I had ever seen. Indeed, it begged to be theorized because so much could be learned from it about how women, butches, trannyboys, femmes, and gender variant folks negotiate, resist, queer, pervert and articulate their own desires to be, to have, and to rearticulate the gendered and en-gendering environment we all inhabit. My desires were never to become a drag king; I leave that entirely to the experts. But as someone who has always found himself on the "/" between butch/female-to-male transsexual and, increasingly, as a transman, I recognized something about myself that night within the entirely new set of fantasies, desires and bodies that materialized in and around that stage. As an academic fan, I've been warmly received into drag king culture as friend of the kings. Our first adventure together was our trip to The First International Drag King Extravaganza in Columbus Ohio, 1999. At that time, I had been hanging with the kings for about two months. When I prepared to give the paper that is printed here, it became very clear to me that these same boys whom I had studied now constituted *my* audience. I confess experiencing a trepidation that day unlike any other I have experienced as a graduate student and now professor. The paper was very well received and what has emerged since is not only a wonderful "academic-performer" alliance, but deeply meaningful friendships. As a boy, I've never felt more deeply connected to boy-culture as I have with the kings and dedicate my work here to Zack, Carter, Flare, Christopher Noelle, Stu, Chris, Jesse James Bondage, Derk/Mann Murray, Moaner and Mitch . . . the Fabulous Toronto Drag Kings.

Katie: My fascination with drag kings stems from neither personal stage experience nor longtime fan loyalty, but from an interest in performances of corporeality that mark an individual as somehow different from culturally determined norms. My particular area of interest is in fatness, which overlaps and diverges from the corporeal performance of queerness in numerous ways. Earlier work of mine investigates the parallels between fat bodies and queer bodies, as well as between fat politics and queer politics (LeBesco 2001): one can "come out" as fat just as one can come out as queer (though ease of passing is one difference), and both types of bodies incur social stigma for their "abnormality" compounded by the extent to which their bearers are perceived to be willful agents of their own deviance. Drag kings, then, intrigue me. Like fat people, particularly fat women, drag kings take up much more space than they're supposed to, reappropriating power all the while. Drag kings wear their difference on their body in visually inescapable ways. One notable difference, though, is that for conventionally defined drag kings, the performance ends (at least to some extent) when the music dies down and the moustache comes off, whereas fat performance has more of an air of inevitability about it. Thus, I'm interested in expanding theory about the drag king in order to consider transgender performance in everyday life, where its power to explode cultural expectations seems to be more promising.

* * *

Just six years ago, there was a dearth of information about drag kings within the context of rich and nuanced queer and feminist scholarship. Where work about drag queens was abundant, drag kings were mentioned mostly in passing (if at all) prior to the late 90s. Very little work addressed women, or anyone for that matter, performing masculinity, but early work on butch-femme subjectivities did create an early intellectual space for work on drag kings. While the work of Judith Butler, Marjorie Garber and Esther Newton provided points of extrapolation for those interested in understanding drag kings, it was not until Judith Halberstam's 1998 work on "female masculinity" that kings were formally made the subject of any sustained focus. Even then, their exposure came at the expense of the fluidity of identity many of her subjects had worked hard to achieve.

In the very late 90s, more work appeared about women doing drag or drag king performances, and while most of it was journalistic (with only a smattering of scholarship), almost all was isolated and local, seemingly decontextualized from the emerging drag king phenomenon. H.I.S. Kings learned about troupes around the United States and Canada, but most academics, journalists, critics and filmmakers were still focusing on the holy triad of San Francisco, New York and London. It was not until the *First International Drag King Extravaganza* (IDKE), held in Columbus, Ohio in October 1999, that groups of people from North America and England came together to begin a dialogue about drag kings. Who are they? What do they do? What don't they do? How do they do it? How don't they do it? Why do they do it? With this weekend, the landscape of drag king performance began to expand from its heretofore narrow confinement; drag kinging seemed well suited to San Francisco, but what was it doing on the windy plains of Alberta, Canada? While a natural for New York, was kinging a political act of defiance in the rolling hills of western Pennsylvania? One intention of this anthology is to continue this work of expansion and dialogue. While the *Extravaganza* (IDKE 1) created a space for us, as editors, to come together and brainstorm, this collection helps to develop the discussion even further.

Beyond fostering and maintaining a dialogue about the performance/embodiment of masculinity, we editors are dedicated to presenting this dialogue as a mosaic. The mosaic analogy reflects our manuscript well, in that it contains shards of diverse viewpoints, disciplinary perspectives, topics, genres (scholarly prose, autobiographical narrative, and poetry), and formats of expression (written and photographic) arranged to create an aesthetic whole that is more than the sum of its parts. The authors of the chapters in the "King Me" section all work from a first-person perspective to explore their individual experiences as drag kings within the context of larger communities and questions about the performance of masculinity. k. bradford reveals inspiration for a female masculinity based on flashiness, fluidity, and working class misbehavior–John Travolta. In "Grease Cowboy Fever, or, the Making of Johnny T.," bradford contends that both stage and street drag performance successfully intervene in overdetermined systems of gender and desire, pushing "human behavior and erotics to a futuristic edge." Neeve Neevel, a.k.a. Pat Riarch, recounts hir journey from hir first sentence, a masculine self-declarative, to hir current drag king performances. Neevel's "Me Boy" recognizes kinging as simultaneously a rejection of "the authority relegated to the world of male duds and dicks," but also an opportunity to claim that power. Jay Allen Sennett and Sarah Bay-Cheng, in "I Am the Man! Performing Gender and Other Incongruities," question definitions of drag based on gender dichotomies. This joint essay by members of the transgendered community discusses "the ambiguous relationship between performing gender on stage and in everyday life, differences in audience expectations and the consequences of those reactions, and the possibility of doing transgendered drag."

Contributors to the "Drag King Scenes" section depict the goings-on in performance locales often far-removed from the trinity of New York, San Francisco, and London. Colleen Ayoup and Julie Podmore describe the locally specific codes of dress, performance styles and forms of masculinity of the Montréal-based Mambo Drag Kings in "Making Kings." They aim to understand "how the participants of the group interpret and experience kinging and its impact on their own gendered and sexual identities." In "Lesbian Drag Kings and the Feminine Embodiment of the Masculine," Steven Schacht explores the Imperial Sovereign Court of Spokane, Washington, attending to hierarchical relationships among court members. Schacht suggests that "as much as lesbian drag kings subvert existing gender hierarchies they also recreate them in the pursuit of exercising situational power." Jennifer Patterson elucidates the nature of the Washington, DC scene through interviews with several locally prominent kings in "Capital Drag: Kinging in Washington, DC." She celebrates the "safe, supportive environment in which lesbian performers and audience members can celebrate and explore their relationships to female masculinities and queer sexualities." Thomas Piontek interrogates and responds to Judith Halberstam's work on drag kings in his essay "Kinging in the Heartland; or, The Power of Marginality." Piontek expands beyond Halberstam's work on the thriving king scenes in large urban centers–New York, London and San Francisco–by theorizing Columbus, Ohio's own troupe, H.I.S. Kings. Piontek argues that H.I.S. Kings' function as an example of how cultural practices in the provinces may actually challenge, contradict or expand what is happening in the traditional cultural centers on the west and east coasts, in order to refute American cultural geographies which characterize large parts of the center as cultural wastelands. In "Walk Like a Man," Sheila Koenig unpacks "the potential of drag king performance as a tool of deconstructing gender." Against the backdrop of the Edmonton scene, Koenig discusses drag king performances as the praxis of queer theory and gender, speculating that such performances may be read to reinforce rather than subvert gender norms. She further examines the complexities of "passing" gender performances and the ways that these practices align or fail to align with performances intending to fail. In "Drag Kings in the New Wave: Gender Performance and Participation," Kim Surkan considers traditional and alternative ways of "doing drag," both performative and participatory, as a means of interrogating the proximity of king culture to academic theory, focusing on Columbus and Minneapolis communities. Through interviews and readings of new king aesthetics, her work explores "the relationship of butch-femme gender roles to drag as it has evolved from earlier critiques of king culture to the present day."

Chapter authors for the "Desire and the Audience" section investigate drag king performances from the perspective of the fan, interrogating the multidirectional workings of desire that accompany the construction of dynamically gendered selves. Ann Tweedy's poem "A Voice from the Audience" speaks of the erotic dynamics between a smitten fan and an artful drag king, illustrating the multidirectionality of desire. In "One Body, Some Genders: Drag Performances and Technologies," Alana Kumbier examines her own experiences as both drag king and drag queen against a background conceptualization of gender as the non-binary product of various social technologies and cultural artifacts. As both performer and fan, Kumbier argues for the effects of a heightened awareness of gendered subjectivity, desire, and relationship to one's body. Kathryn Rosenfeld's chapter, "Drag King Magic: Performing/Becoming the Other," "theorizes drag king practice through the lenses of alterity, liminality and performance theory, while attempting to complicate and reinvigorate discussions of identity raised by drag." The author explores the involvement of the concept of "the Other" in drag king performance, and forces confrontation with a complex field of desire as embodied by the king. Tara Pauliny, in "Erotic Arguments and Persuasive Acts: Discourses of Desire and the Rhetoric of Female-to-Male Drag," analyzes the performance of New York-based king Dréd, whose act she argues appropriates and embodies both dominant and subversive discourses as it makes rhetorical arguments about gender, masculinity, race, and desire.

In the "Theorizing Kings" section, contributors address some of the more difficult conceptual issues attached to the practice of performing masculinity. Jean Noble's chapter, "Seeing Double, Thinking Twice: The Toronto Drag Kings and (Re-) Articulations of Masculinity," theorizes Toronto drag kings as situated at the conjuncture of three intellectual currents: "theories of masculinity as one site of gender 'performativity'; the theatrical practices, relations and technologies known as 'performance'; and the imperatives of critical whiteness studies, to theorize these performances as interventions into and re-articulations of the operations of whiteness and gender." Noble ultimately argues in favor of the dialogic nature of drag king performances. Annabelle Willox investigates the difficult relationship of camp and drag performances in "Whose Drag Is It Anyway?" She reveals "why drag has a fundamentally different contextual meaning for kings and queens" by examining historical, cultural and theoretical similarities and differences between drag kings, butches, drag queens and femmes in the context of performances provided at the United Kingdom drag contest held in London. Finally, Vicki Crowley's essay, "Drag Kings 'Down Under': An Archive and Introspective of a Few Aussie Blokes," mines the issues of naming and personae evident in Adelaide's lesbian and gay cultural festival to argue for drag king performance as an important though contested site for dealing with race and racism, in that it "acknowledges histories and affirms subjectivity while disturbing and destabilizing absolute identity." With the entirety of this endeavor, we are then better equipped to contextualize and comprehend drag king performances, the audiences that watch them, and the literatures that inform them.

In the final section, "Picture This: King Photos," the work of photographers Pierre Dalpé, Stephanie Rogerson, Melinda Hubman and Aaron Kimberly handsomely illustrates the striking visual impact of drag king performance. Tania Hammidi's collage-style flyer for a drag king workshop also begins to speak to the increasing popularity of the drag king phenomenon.

This anthology is not only an interdisciplinary project, but also a project that creates a forum in which we can address three specific problems. First, we hope to address the fact that, historically, much of the writing on drag kings or women doing drag consists of academic "experts" speaking for performers/kings. We find this methodology problematic if it is not paired, in some way, with the opportunity for performers to speak for themselves. Often, in the social sciences, an expert will interview, analyze, and theorize about a subject or group of people without allowing room for the subject(s) to reflect on the analysis or even possibly contribute to the theorizing. With the pieces we have chosen for this anthoogy, we hope a more reciprocal and collaborative methodology becomes apparent. Furthermore, with this anthology, we hope to expand the category "expert" to include more people theorizing about the performance/embodiment of masculinity. With this expansion, we are then creating a richer and more complete narrative about drag kings. This expansion also helps us realize the multiple origins of and varied influences on drag king culture.

The second problem we hope to investigate is a lack of analytical diversity within academic writing on drag troupes and communities. Much of the work to date avoids theorizing the full spectrum of racialized identities performed, including performances of whiteness. Moreover, little work on drag kings to date really investigates class identity along with age (or disability, for that matter). While most work does address sexual and gender identity, these other axes of identity are ignored, overlooked or commented upon in a most cursory fashion. One might suggest the dearth of discussion of race, class and age among drag king theorists is directly related to the specific age, race and class composition of most North American troupes. Perhaps because a large portion of North American drag kings are young, middle class, and white—three categories that in our society are often seen as unmarked, neutral, and normal—theorists see no need to discuss issues of race, class or age; instead, discussions center on their gender and/or sexual identities. In addition, most of what has been written about drag kings confines itself to urban exemplars from the United States or Britain, with Canada functioning as the "exotic" and geographical other. Such a move leaves unexplored the performances of masculinity extant in most of the world. Along with uncovering the markedness of such categories of "white," "middle class," and "young," we hope to investigate why such normalization occurs within an often queer context as well as how some performers have begun to subvert such normalizing forces. Also important are the ways in which all kings perform, subvert and interrogate race, class, gender, ability, sexuality and body size. We offer the anthology as a forum for pondering such previously unaddressed issues. By embracing difference and diversity and by recognizing and questioning its absence, one can then increase the political potency of drag king culture.

Lastly, we hope that with this anthology we can continue to address the contentions within feminist movements about masculinity, especially as it coheres in and around drag kinging and drag king cultures. There is a history within feminist and lesbian-feminist theory of ambivalence or acrimony when it comes to either masculinity or gendered performances of desire. The authors of *The Joy of Lesbian Sex*, for example, write the following about butch/femme: "Back in the days when role-playing in the style of straight couples was more common, butch referred to the 'masculine' partner, femme to the 'feminine.' . . . Pathetically, this behavior was generally a parody of the worst heterosexual coupling: the butch stomping and hen-pecked, the femme kittenish and nagging . . . [both] . . . have rejected contemporary liberation movements . . . and find psychological and sexual satisfaction in passivity, submission and heterosexual game-playing" (Sisley and Harris 1977, 40, 65). Similarly, Monique Wittig characterized butch/femme subjectivity as "Tweedledum and Tweedledee." If wanting to become more 'feminine' was suspect, wanting to 'imitate' masculinity was jumping out of the frying pan and into the proverbial fire. "At least for a woman, wanting to become a man proves she has escaped her initial programming," Wittig writes, but wanting to become a man means acquiring "not only a man's external appearance but his consciousness as well, that is, the consciousness of one who disposes by right of at least two 'natural' slaves during his life span" (1992, 13-14). Drag kinging depends upon a gendering of desire; some feminist arguments that dismiss gendered erotic systems as "role-playing" argue repeatedly that lesbians who "imitate" men, either on or off the stage, are neither subversive nor avant garde. Instead, or so the argument goes, these performances of masculinity are an emulation of maleness and misogyny, undergirded by a secret desire for male power (Jeffreys 1993). While it is true that some drag king performances may perpetuate misogyny (among other things like racism and classism), and even go so far as to objectify women, this is a limited evaluation of the cultural work drag king performances accomplish. For some kings, performances of masculinity (and femininity) are a re-creation or de/re-construction of gender roles. Some kings investigate masculinity by exposing its performative nature, while others perform masculinity as a means of expressing themselves. Others again put the objectifying gaze defiantly on display. With this anthology, then, we complicate and broaden these debates about drag kings and gendered performances of desire within feminist movements.

Despite our intention to address many of the troubling issues surrounding drag king performance, we editors have stumbled across an important one of our own in creating this anthology. One of the most fraught issues has been managing the terminology we choose to use. The term "drag king" or "drag kinging" is easy to wield, but it lacks the cache of widespread familiarity. Much of the literature connected to the *Extravaganza* (IDKE 1) used the terminology "women doing drag" or "FTM" (female to male) drag. While these terms do encompass some of the performances, they ultimately exclude others, specifically members of trans communities. They also exclude those people who do not identify as "man" or "woman," "masculine" or "feminine" but perhaps as both or neither, maybe even as a part of a "third sex." However, as these essays suggest, those who perform on stage identify across the spectrum of sexual and gender categories. It becomes a challenge, then, to create a more inclusive language that recognizes and respects diversity of identity among performers. Our hope is that the word choices we have employed in *The Drag King Anthology* both reflect and construct a more affirmative reality for drag king performers of all stripes.

REFERENCES

Jeffreys, Sheila. 1993. *The Lesbian Heresy: A Feminist Perspective on the Lesbian Sexual Revolution*. North Melbourne, Vic., Australia: Spinifex.

LeBesco, Kathleen. "Queering Fat Bodies/Politics." Pp. 74-87 in *Bodies Out of Bounds: Fatness and Transgression*, eds. Jana E. Braziel and LeBesco. Berkeley: University of California Press, 2001.

Sisley, Emily L. and Bertha Harris. 1977. *The Joy of Lesbian Sex*. New York: Simon and Schuster.

Wittig, Monique. 1992. *The Straight Mind and Other Essays*. Boston: Beacon Press.

SUGGESTED FURTHER READINGS

Egan, Richard and Dave King, eds. 1996. *Social Aspects of Cross-Dressing and Sex-Changing*. New York and London: Routledge.

Ferris, Lesley, ed. 1993. *Crossing the Stage: Controversies on Cross-Dressing*. New York and London: Routledge.

Garber, Marjorie. 1992. *Vested Interests: Cross-Dressing and Cultural Anxiety*. Durham: Duke University Press.

Gardmer, Ralph Jr. 1997. "Drag Kings." *Penthouse* (February 1997): 84-87, 128.

Halberstam, Judith. 1998. *Female Masculinity*. Durham: Duke University Press.

———. 1997. "Mackdaddy, Superfly, Rapper: Gender, Race and the Drag King Scene," in *Social Text*, eds. A. McClintock, J. Munoz. (Fall 1997).

Hausman, Bernice. 1995. *Changing Sex: Transsexualism, Technology and the Idea of Gender*. Durham: Duke University.

Kroker, Arthur and Marilouise. 1993. "Finding the Male Within and Taking Him Cruising: Drag King for a Day." Pp. 91-97 in *The Last Sex: Feminism and Outlaw Bodies*, eds. A. Kroker and M. Kroker. New York: St. Martin's.

Meyer, Moe. 1994. "Fe/Male Impersonation: The Discourse of Camp." Pp. 130-148 in *The Politics and Poetics of Camp*, ed. M. Meyer. New York: Routledge.

Robertson, Jennifer. 1998. *Takarazuka: Sexual Politics and Popular Culture in Modern Japan*. Berkeley: University of California Press.

Rubin, Gayle. 1992. "Of Catamites and Kings: Reflections on Butch, Gender and Boundaries." Pp. 466-483 in *The Persistent Desire: A Femme-Butch Reader*, ed. G. Rubin. Boston: Alyson Publications.

Troka, Donna Jean. 2000. "When We Were Kings: On Being a Midwestern Drag King." *Bitch* 12: 42-47.

Volcano, del La Grace, and Judith Halberstam. 1999. *The Drag King Book*. London: Serpent's Tail.

Wheelwright, Julie. 1989. *Amazons and Military Maids: Women Who Dressed as Men in the Pursuit of Life, Liberty and Happiness*. London and Boston: Pandora.

ISSUES AND QUESTIONS FOR FURTHER CONSIDERATION

1. How can we better merge the "insiders" (drag kings and their supporters/fans) and the "outsiders" (academics/filmmakers/photographers/journalists who are reporting on them)?
2. How can we better unite the traditionally academic community and the general public; that is, how do we better create public scholarship on drag kings that is collaborative? How does one reach each community effectively?
3. What social and political movements influenced and helped shape drag king culture(s)?
4. What types of projects will foster further collective and collaborative work on drag kings and the performance of masculinity (and its relationship to the performance of femininity by women, men and those "in between")?

KING ME:
FIRST PERSON NARRATIVES

Grease Cowboy Fever;
or, the Making of Johnny T.

k. bradford, MA

SUMMARY. Through a mix of theory, memoir and performance narrative, this chapter examines the making of drag persona Johnny T. as part of a king movement where the dominant cultural paradigm of gender is reconsidered and remastered. As seen in *Grease, Saturday Night Fever* and *Urban Cowboy*, pop culture icon John Travolta's particular blend of 50s greaser, faggy 70s disco, and 80s country masculinities are shown to be prime drag king conditions, particularly for a dyke who came of age during the 70s Travolta fever. While drawing from personal experience as a king, current trends in the king movement, and gender theory, this essay calls into question the lines between performing masculinity on and off the stage, inviting us to see both the work and play, the parody and realness, the struggle and liberation that make up the transgressive world of drag kinging and gender variance. Drawing upon gender theorists Judith Butler and Judith Halberstam, gender is exposed as a social construction both produced and performed, and as such, drag kinging is framed as an arena where gender is reconfigured. *[Article copies available for a fee from The Haworth Document Delivery Service: 1-800-HAWORTH. E-mail address: <docdelivery@haworthpress.com> Website: <http://www.HaworthPress.com> © 2002 by The Haworth Press, Inc. All rights reserved.]*

KEYWORDS. Drag king, gender, queer, transgender, performance, feminism, liberation, social change, Travolta

---

[Haworth co-indexing entry note]: "Grease Cowboy Fever; or, the Making of Johnny T." bradford, k. Co-published simultaneously in *Journal of Homosexuality* (Harrington Park Press, an imprint of The Haworth Press, Inc.) Vol. 43, No. 3/4, 2002, pp. 15-30; and: *The Drag King Anthology* (ed: Donna Troka, Kathleen LeBesco, and Jean Bobby Noble) Harrington Park Press, an imprint of The Haworth Press, Inc., 2002, pp. 15-30. Single or multiple copies of this article are available for a fee from The Haworth Document Delivery Service [1-800-HAWORTH, 9:00 a.m. - 5:00 p.m. (EST). E-mail address: docdelivery@haworthpress.com].

Johnny T. is my main man, my primal and primary drag king persona.[1] Persona is not quite the word for it: yes, being Johnny T. involves taking things on (*and takin' em off too*, says Johnny T.) And he is a part, an expression that I move in and out of. But Johnny T. is not only a show I put on (*yeah, but I am quite a show, you gotta give me that*). He is not a male character I become now and again (*I do kinda come and go though, if ya know what I'm sayin*). He's no stranger who comes by only at night. Let's just say, Johnny T. does something to me: he's a chemistry, a fuel injection that sets me in motion. He brings up and out of my body gendered modes and erotics that are deeply–and on the surface–rooted in the subversive and transgressive tendencies I gravitate toward and groove on as a queer dyke. He is part of how I move in the world–he shifts me into a gear where I follow my instincts full-speed ahead. *You bet I do, they don't call me grease lightning for nothin'.* I have to give him that: he burns up a quarter mile.

GENDER INVERSIONS/INVERTED GENDERS

With Johnny T. there are many versions of T. For starters, T stands for testosterone, tranny, trouble, T-Birds, Travolta. *You're god damn right. Just ask anyone's around, they'll tell ya how many T's there are when it comes to me. Enough T's for the whole lot a ya's, I say.* You know what I say Johnny? T is for Turn it down. We're just getting started here–let me get back to my point. T for Travolta is the original derivation of Johnny's "T."[2] While Johnny T. is an evolving part of my identity and daily walk, with new acts, inventions and expressions always in the making, the original impulse and a continuing thread of Johnny T. is the performative ethos of John Travolta. Without a doubt, the draw of performing Travolta is his layerings–the multiple and varied genders he embodies and the range of personas/genders/erotics which I can draw upon and incorporate in the making of Johnny T. Johnny T. creates a slippage that reveals the reality (and fantasies) of the masculine in "woman" and the feminine in "man." He jumps at the chance to reinvent himself on new turf, which of course, is also what he offers me. We are a well-matched pair, Johnny and I. We bring out each other's best. *Don't you know it. One a the best things anyone evah told me was that I reminded them a one a those mirage trinkets, where ya know, you look at it one way and it's jesus and the next minute it's mary. They says to me, man: woman, woman: man, that's what I see when I look at you. A trick a the eye, I tell ya. Come a little closer and see whats ya sees.*

In his early years, Travolta was a walking display of testosterone (or, what is constructed out of testosterone). He played a range of masculinities, and for all of his hetero machismo, there was always a mix, a queering of the masculinity he represented. In fact, he seems more butch than macho—and I mean butch in the lesbian derivation of the term—because underneath the tough veneer you could almost see a woman (well okay, a fag). As Danny in *Grease* and Tony in *Saturday Night Fever (SNF)*, Travolta's swivel of hips, gyrating pelvis, flinging arms, faggy run, lilting voice and that underlying sensitivity combine with the distinctly Travolta butch strut and tough guy persona, transmuting his maleness into something subversively delicious. At times Travolta's characters go out of their way to prove they are "real men"—Tony trying to rape Stephanie in *SNF*, Bud hitting Sissy in *Urban Cowboy*, and Danny dumping on Sandy in *Grease*. Despite this compulsive drive toward misogyny, the line up of early Travolta characters is framed by the camp of his disco/country stage identities as well as the constant transmutation of masculine personas he undergoes in order to pursue his love interests and be the king of cool. Travolta's characters constantly criss-cross, backtrack and cut through the masculinities he sets up for himself so that we can't pin a singular heteronormative masculinity on him. One Travolta masculinity always upstages another. *Yeah, that Travolta ain't all he appears to be eithah. There's a lot to the man within the man, that's for sure.*

At the beginning of *Grease*, when Sandy shows up unexpectedly, Danny shows delight, his voice pitching high, his face lighting up with emotion. When Kenickie struts over and hovers disapprovingly, Danny suddenly drops his voice and puts on his macho cool. Sandy sees through his act and immediately asks, "What happened to the Danny Zuko I met at the beach?" He responds with, "I don't know, maybe there's two of us. Why don't you take out a missing persons ad? Check the yellow pages." Before running off, Sandy throws back at him, "You're a fake and a phony, and I wish I'd never laid eyes on you!" Up until the very end of the movie, Danny stages a split-masculinity. Like a jump-cut on screen, in *Grease* and *SNF*, Travolta jumps abruptly back and forth between up-classing himself to win a lady and out-cooling himself to impress the guys; he smoothes out or greases up his working-class masculinities accordingly. While Travolta's maleness may be assumed, his theatricality—all of the dressing up and changing roles and taking center stage—draws attention to the lines (and the holes) between maleness and masculinity. He self-consciously tries on and plays up various divergent masculinities, and as a result, the seams, the cut and paste involved in making a male masculine are revealed for what they are. This break in the construction of maleness and the conscious cultivation of a certain look, is one giant invitation to drag kings to jump in and play with our own versions, imitations and remakes of Travolta masculinities.

KING STRATEGIES AND FEMINIST APPROACHES

As the king movement expands, there is a proliferation of king cultures, communities and identities, as well as the goodies with which we make our gender. While drawing on age-old king accoutrements—facial hair, packages, bindings, costumes, names—kings are busy drumming up new methods and combinations of applying the goods, and we are all too proud to spread the wealth. *Oh yeah, that's the kind of spreadin' I like to see. Spread those royal jewels around, I say.* More than ever, it seems kings have a lot at our disposal to make of ourselves what we want. As opposed to drag queens, however, drag kings have historically found it a challenge to camp up the performance of masculinity. As Judith "Jack" Halberstam has observed, minimalism is often the rule of thumb, both in the get-up and the movements a drag king embodies (Volcano and Halberstam 1999, 35). Generally, there is less paraphernalia, less garb, less goo to put on and quite a lot to cover up in female-to-male drag performance. Kinging in a business suit seems inherently serious, refined, controlled and (on the surface) difficult to camp up. But there are ways to parody the stiffness, seriousness and constrained cockiness of white upper-class masculinities, thus creating vital, transgressive critiques of the ways wealth and privilege are performed, especially by white men.

When I wear a three-piece suit, I enjoy embodying and breaking out of "suit stiffness" with faggy flamboyancy, a mouthing off or a particularly cheesy move. The act of performing certain masculinities exposes how performative gender is to begin with; that is, there is nothing inherently or originally male about certain behaviors, attitudes or traits—they are simply marked as a male role and performed accordingly. As Judith Butler puts it, "In imitating gender, drag implicitly reveals the imitative structure of gender itself" (Butler 1999, 175). For me, the project and distinct pleasure of drag kinging is the act of revealing gender for what it is—something made up, produced—as we go about making our own mixes and variations of gender. Whether a woman-identified dyke or a tranny guy, as kings we actively dislodge masculinity from the apex of the hetero-hierarchy, showing how it is equally ours to claim from our diverse vantage points. *I ain't so sure about that. I kinda like havin a mountain or an apex or whatevah, so I can be king a the mountain–a course! Johnny Top, I tell ya.*

In recent years, camp has become a central vein in the production of king personas, performances and realities. Historically, the dyke community, equipped with lesbian feminist thinking and perspectives initiated in the 1970s, has tended to occupy the realms of serious critique. At times, it has seemed that camp, with all of its humor, lightness and parody, has been off limits–a muscle we have chosen not to flex due to the risks of minimizing harsh realities we live with. The 90s and millennium breed of dyke performers and drag kings, many of whom are busy repopularizing post-stonewall butch/femme identities and creating boyz/bois cultures,[3] have decidedly claimed the domain of camp as dyke turf. It is exciting that as a community we have an increasing range of strategies (and pleasures) at our fingertips. Rather than undoing the progress made by the women's movement, the move toward camp and parody can be an expansive and visionary one. While it requires a keen sense of irony to embrace and reclaim gender binaries, camp allows for new layers of complexity and possibility within the arenas of feminist critique and cultural production. It behooves feminism to view humor, exaggeration, pleasure and parody not as dismissive elements, but as tools that, while less straight forward and more circuitous, are vitally engaged in and contribute to critical thinking and social change initiated by women. While drag king performances are not inherently or necessarily transgressive, and some kings actively reassert misogynist roles and relations, when handled with a crafty, campy approach, kinging can take the sexism built into masculinity and turn it on its head (Volcano and Halberstam 1999, 41). As Judith Butler says, "Gender meanings used in drag are part of hegemonic, misogynist culture, they are nevertheless denaturalized and mobilized through their parodic recontextualization" (Butler 1999, 176).

Elvis and Travolta–two male pop figures who drip with camp–are popular king icons and personas. The raunchy looseness, the grease, the toughness and the foul mouths that make Elvis, Travolta and other campy drag king personas what they are, spring from the complexity of their working-class masculinities. They play up the stereotype of working-class "misbehavior," staging it to an extreme, while also assuming the expressive range that working-class culture allows working-class men. Along with the appropriation of Black culture and rhythm as initiated by Elvis, who became an icon for Travolta and others, the working-class "license to be bad" urged both of them to set the pelvis loose from the stiff hold of the white upper-class patriarchal complex. It is no surprise that many dykes, with our own set of raunchy proclivities and appetites, gravitate toward performing layered masculinities (often working class) that shake things up from the pelvis on out. *No shit, I like to shake it up–that's just how I do things. No goddamn shame in that, I tell ya. They'll try to trick you into shame, but here's what I say: shake it off. As long as you know you're shakin' ya shit, or shakin' shit up for the right reasons–that's all that mattahs.*

GENDER SCHOOL DROP-OUT

   John Travolta was a figure of great allure to me growing up in the 70s. For several years, at countless slumber parties, my friends and I obsessively performed *Grease*. I guess the all-girl, late night, impromptu space of gender performance got under my skin at the get-go. At the time, performing the bold and lewd butch moves of Danny and doing over-the-top renditions of Sandy's straight-girl femme allowed me to embody behaviors, sexualities and gender expressions that were off limits in my particular brand of waspy, New England, middle-class upbringing. Accordingly, I was not allowed to see *SNF*, but I danced incessantly in our back room to the Bee Gee's. I was also enthralled with hot pants Vinnie Barbarino, watching *Welcome Back Kotter* whenever I could. At the time, I was pretty clear that I wasn't "in-love" with Travolta like the rest of his fans; what I wasn't able to see then was that I wanted to *be* him–or my version of him. The 70s pulse of loose sex and sexuality was (and is) an ever-magnetic pull. As an adolescent girl, performing Travolta allowed me to temporarily enter the fantasy of embodying that pulse–an act that was risky, taboo and altogether vital and freeing for me as a girl and a dyke-feminist-to-be. Performing Johnny T. as an adult calls up a butch erotic that is distinctly 70s–at once, and with confidence, being totally in control and going to the edge of "losin' control"–an aesthetic and an erotic in which my body and I feel right at home.
   As friends of Johnny T. like to say, he knows how to cut a rug. Just as with Travolta, it's all about movement, about dancing his ass off. *Hey, don't be tradin' my ass away! It's one a my best pieces of equipment. I need it for a few things. Man, don't ask me to spell it out for ya's. I've*

said enough already! Johnny T. loves stitching together the best moves of Tony, Danny, Bud and even *Pulp Fiction*'s Vincent Vega (the only recent Travolta character who busts a move, and notably, the character through whom Travolta made his comeback). The music alone–*SNF*'s classic 70s disco, *Grease*'s 50s musical tunes with 70s overtones, the down-home country songs of *Urban Cowboy*–sets Travolta's rhythms and movement to an especially campy note. As much as his identity is pinned to being tough and in control, by unleashing his body, Travolta cuts up the performance of masculine restraint, using every ounce of his moving form to camp up and express his desire. And where Travolta left off, Johnny T. picks up the ball and runs with it. Johnny takes Travolta's camp and the faggyness he displayed but always kept under lock and key, and unleashes it. Johnny T. takes Travolta where he couldn't go. *You bet I do. I ain't afraid a nothin'. And that ain't all. I'll show you more than that.*

In both *Grease* and *SNF*, Sandy's and Stephanie's characters pale in comparison to Travolta, and the female leads actually function as foils to the homoerotic pulse between the boys. While the boy-girl pairs give the illusion of being the front-story, it is actually the boy-on-boy arena where Travolta generates his heat. The homo-heat between Danny and Kenickie and the pulse between Tony and the guys is the central nerve of the *Grease* and *SNF* narratives. When Danny or Tony struts his stuff for "the girl," the female figure is a stand-in, a buffer that masks the ever-present gaze between Travolta's character and the boys. At the disco in *SNF*, take note: for Tony's friends who are always on the side-lines, their pleasure is about watching Tony, not the girls. In *Grease* on Thunder Road, the boys strut their stuff and race their wheels for each other. Equipped with the homoerotics and gender-bending of a drag king, Johnny T. likes to pull out the stops with the boyz and also do re-makes of the Danny/Sandy and Tony/Stephanie pairs. Whether with a Kenickie remodeled in fag-drag or a line-up of kings, Johnny goes to town with his pack of boyz, reveling in the display of queerness set loose between the boyz. Where the boys on screen are never allowed such pleasure, with a host of kings and tranny guys, the queerness is not only freed up, but also multiplied by the many versions of masculinity at play.

Likewise, Johnny T. has found some stunning Sandys to partner up with–straight women, femme dykes, and a few kings in femme drag. With the butch/femme dynamics at play, the campy femme versions of Sandy really get Johnny–and the audience–stirred up. Sandy suddenly emerges from her paperdoll status into a woman who is real and pulpy and palpable. Where the classic Hollywood het version of *Grease* leans on Rizzo (though we love her!) to do the trick, a dyke, drag king remix of *Grease* at last gives us a Sandy to sink our teeth into. At the end of the movie, Sandy makes her own attempt remodeling herself to win over Danny; where Sandy leaves off, we get to pick up the job and do it right. *Man, that's all I was tryin' to get Sandy to understand. I shoulda had her talk to you–it woulda saved her a lotta trouble.* The act of freeing these characters from prescribed gender roles–letting Sandy be whatever version of femininity a performer brings forth, letting Danny and Tony have a range of sexual preferences–is pleasurable and liberatory for both performers and audience. *You bettah believe it. It's fun no mattah how ya slice it.*

Travolta's masculinities are often dished up with his diva, faggy, feminine flourishes. His characters cultivate masculine images with great care, relishing the process of getting done up. Danny is constantly combing his hair just so; at home, Tony is glued to his vanity mirror (grooming and staring, staring and grooming) and on the street he makes a ritual of checking out his reflection in windows; Bud is ever conscious of his appearance as a *real* cowboy. Travolta loves what is flashy: the blue polyester shirt he *must have* in *SNF*, the shiny red shirt in *Urban Cowboy*, his leather and another (!) pink shirt (with a tight suit, of course) in *Grease*. In *SNF*, Tony asks for an advance in his pay so he can buy the pink polyester shirt he covets in the opening scene. His boss preaches to him about college and saving money and the future. Tony says, "Tonight's the future." True to his campy heart and his working- class values, he knows what matters most is the pink polyester shirt on that Saturday night. With the specter of class assimilation always overhead and the resulting need to "fit in," Tony goes right for a shirt that makes him stand out. Tony, like Danny, is a package deal: along with the many insecurities underneath and conflicting needs to be seen in different ways due to gender- and class-pressures, they both do what it takes to command center stage. While the drive to be leader of the pack and the king of cool is loaded with both his talent and social pressures, Travolta's characters get strokes for his antics which only refuels his fire. *I like those strokes–just throw 'em my way. The more the bettah, that's my philosophy.*

ON THE STREETS, ON THE STAGE, ON THE ROAD

Because of the many vocabularies of Johnny T.–bodily, verbal, the get-up, the go-go, the groovin'–he invites me to king it up the way I like it: all flash, all thrusting pelvis, pure grease, pure disco. The Travolta conditions match my own gender variance and allow me to play out my multiple and mixed-gender proclivities and pleasures at different pitches and in different modes. My self-image as a dyke and my particular brand of gender variance are ever evolving, a process rather than any kind of a fixed identity. Identifying as butch for a number of years in the early 90s, I then entered a sort of androgynous zone for several years. I now embody a mix of femme, butch, transgendered and, of course, kingy elements of style, body language, appearance and attitude. I am engaged in creating a complex but clear articulation of multiple genders that feels altogether queer. My gender isn't fluid exactly–it feels more like quirky, bumpy clockwork with different gears that I engage in, shifting between innate/chosen and performed/naturalized genders. Johnny T. is one of the ways I do this, because Johnny T. crystallizes my brand of butchness encoded with femmey-faggy-tranny elements.

Whether on the stage or on the streets, Johnny T. is a filter, a mode that allows my gender variance to come into sharper focus, tighter action. During my daily walk, Johnny T. pops up at random or necessary moments. When I want Tony's particular Brooklyn fuck-you, his disco strut, his dare-devilesque instincts, when I want Danny Zuko's greaser sleaze, his dorkiness, his pelvic thrust, Johnny T. is right there where I need him. He's a useful guy. Gets me zeroed in on what counts. Between you and me, he's a high-maintenance guy, I can't have him around all the time. Although, more and more, he is an integrated part of my daily walk and my identity–he pops up when I am out doing errands and the assorted mundanities of daily life. With his newest speech pattern–a king lingo in the works, made up by and with the Chicago Kings–Johnny really likes to speak up. Johnny T. spruces it all up for me. *There's a hell of a lot more to make out of life, I say.* He reminds me that there is nothing like taking "normal" daily interactions and pushing them to unexpected edges. That there is a lot to do and undo, a lot to fuck with in public spaces that are loaded with social expectation and monotonous repetition. He reminds me that you just have to go get a rise out of all those passersby, push at their brains until there is room on their radarscreens for something else, something they are afraid of but secretly yearn for, something wild and unsure.

Without a doubt, Johnny T. is a man of the stage, and most often, that's where he drags me–to the center stage. Since our first show at the CoCo Club in San Francisco in 1998, Johnny has strutted his stuff at drag shows, theater spaces and impromptu performances in New York, Chicago, L.A., Columbus and Austin. When Del La Grace Volcano was in town for the Austin Gay and Lesbian International Film Festival in 1999, Johnny insisted on throwing Del a midnight masquerade drag show at my house–a sure thrill for Johnny and other Austin kings. Johnny T. always wants to take things further (well, let's be honest: he likes to take over, which quite often, I let him do). He begs me to push out, to take our gigs to new venues and audiences. We've been doing a lot of that lately. With fellow Austin kings, Johnny has been working to stir up the burgeoning king scene in Austin. And Johnny T. is becoming Johnny Traveler, Johnny Transit, Johnny Taking the show on the road, going to king events and shows around the country. Most notable was our recent virgin ride at the annual International Drag King Extravaganza in Columbus (IDKE3) hosted by H.I.S. Kings, which in its third year continues to be a groundbreaking, seminal event where king cultures and communities are forged.

After road tripping from Texas for twenty-four hours, traveling through various states and through Chicago to get there, Johnny felt he had truly arrived in a Kingdom. When he headed back on the road, hitching a ride with the Chicago Kings, he not only found a new voice, but a new family of kings that makes his heart sing. The experience of traveling in full Johnny mode and attending IDKE3 as the only king from Texas helped cement the newest version of Johnny T: Johnny Texas. After living in Austin for ten years, Johnny is helping me claim some of my Texas roots. With his Amarillo cowboy hat and his cheesy heart the size of Texas–*hey, I got some other things the size a Texas too*–Johnny has taken to performing his version of an *Urban Cowboy* Garth Brooks. This gypsy cowboy is out to show everyone a different side of Texas. *There's a whole lotta sides to it ya know. Just like Travolta and me–don't be limited by what you think you see. Lemme say it one more time: come in for a closer look.*

After a show, Johnny T. clicks into different modes. Sometimes he does his dance and heads off stage right away, all cool. Sometimes he stays–he likes to slink around in his sweat and his polyester, stay in the after-heat of strutting his stuff. I like it that way too. I ask him to stick around, so I can linger in my done-up Johnny T. In that hyped-up bad boy mode, I instigate from the package, the loud mouth, the dorky-cool. Sometimes Johnny peels out of his polyester jacket and shirt, does a tease-dance in his tank. He unbuttons the top of his pants, fiddles with the zipper (never undoing it all the way, just enough to show off some equipment). Johnny likes to get raunchy, but he's a guy, and as faggy as he might be in some ways, he's too macho to take off more than that. So once in a rare while, I choose to push Johnny T. and his masculinity past his comfort zone. (I think he enjoys it, but he'd never admit to it.) I get him to strip out of Johnny's faggy-butch mode and reappear in femme drag.

The thing of it is, stripping out of Johnny T.'s get-up and identity allows me to create a transgressive femme drag persona. Rather than showing off an inherent femininity, the process of performing butchness and switching to camped up femme drag stages the artifice of femininity. Femme drag (I can't quite say I am a drag queen) is an act, which sometimes feels as subversive and necessary to me as a gender variant dyke as do my drag king acts (although not quite as *bad*). I like to leave traces of my king on the same bodily surface where femme emerges, showing the seams of gender in the making. The layering involved in the butch-to-femme drag maneuver breaks down assumed gender relations; it allows me to perform exaggerations of femme in ways that are pleasurable and expansive to me. The potential of female drag queening/femme drag is often vastly unexplored and underrated; luckily, a host of bio queens across the country are taking this to task. To be able to parody and self-consciously play up femininity as females challenges the heterosexist construction of femininity from the inside out. In male-to-female drag queen performances, the parody of femininity is subversive, but can in ways leave sexism intact. As marginalized as drag queens are, and as much as they work against the grain of dominant gender systems, their maleness at least partially locates their parody of femininity in a set of relations built on sexism. The parody involved in dyke femme drag/bio queening cuts up essentialist gender assignments, exposing the randomness of that assignment system. *Yeah, they know how to cut a rug too. And they cut up a lot a other stuff–ya know that societal bullshit–at the same time. Queens of multi-taskin' I tell ya.*

THE POLITICAL RESISTANCE OF GENDER VARIANCE

I am not interested in a rigid, fixed gender paradigm but in recouping traditional gender relations, creating new ones and taking on extreme variations that crack open the prescriptions and strictures of that paradigm. Kinging is the staging of the reality that masculinity (and femininity) is elements you can paste on and play up, or conversely–cut out and pare down. The tools of drag (the accoutrements, the body language, the attitudes) are the very "flaws" of the straight gender system, and the performance of drag proves what a farce that system is. Drag kinging stages (and often parodies) the fact that there is nothing essential about gender and the tools drag kings and queens don that attach to the biological categories of male or female. As a drag king, you step into the seams of that binary system, bust open the constructs it is built upon, and create a rich, steamy world of excitement and desire where the terms of gender are reworked and reapplied in ways that make gender not just palatable but mouthwatering to many dykes, fags and trannys. Staging the genderfuck at play creates a political resistance that is part of the coup of drag; no matter how much we embody gender extremes or create our own binary relations, we refuse the slippage back into a binary gender system that doesn't account for us to begin with.

While some kings flaunt the seams of gender, other kings stage a "seamless" show–some of them being butches who pass on a daily basis (Volcano and Halberstam 1999, 36). Drag kinging in general, and the different approaches of drag kings, offends some butches and trannys whose versions of masculinity or femininity are naturalized; they might work at their gender, but the idea of gender being performed or parodied seems to contradict their daily struggle. What seems important here is that as dykes and trannys who drag king, we are clear and upfront about our differences and where the lines of our struggles and privileges intersect and diverge. The more we own up to our differences, the less we end up divided by the pitfalls of the very gender hierarchy we are working to undo. It is not an issue of certain kinds of drag kings being more authentic–it's that drag kings who live out the struggle of gender variance day to day need to have that reality understood rather than erased by their own community. While there are different meanings and realities involved, drag shows, drag on the streets and passing day to day are all ways that, as queers and trannys, we not only make visible but show off, with pride and pleasure, in spite of the dangers, our ingenious work at fucking with the established systems of gender and desire. Being seen by the world at large *and* by each other, whether through hostile or celebratory lenses, is part of the radical, risky work of creating gender difference and deviant desires. *You gotta show ya stuff off. Ain't no one else gonna get it out there for ya, not in your way at least. So go to town, I say.*

My gender variance is at play during the day in various ways. I have both passed and "been mistaken" on and off since 1991–for some years because of my buzzcut butch look and in recent years because of the intensification of my mustache, goatee and leg hair. More than ever, I throw mainstream onlookers into mass confusion. *Kinda throws me into mass confusion too. I don't know what to do with all that facial hair–I'm a clean-cut kinda guy.* This seems to be a result of my mixed gendered look: both my body type and the style I choose. In a lot of ways, I fit into society's idealized beauty standards–I am white, relatively tall and thin, have blue eyes, dirty blonde hair, high cheek bones and a strong nose. Yet, I have small breasts, prominent facial and body hair, and I dress and move like a dyke. No matter how much I femme it up (which I do sometimes), I rarely (if ever) slip over into a "pure" category of feminine. Because of my mixed gendered body/look, however, I am simultaneously assigned certain privileges and harangued (verbally and non-verbally) by the general public. It seems that on days when I look more femme because of my clothes or my stance, my mustache and beard are read as "artificial" entities that I don. Sometimes when someone is staring hard, I choose to accentuate a butch or femme part of me to further the transgendered image I send off. Whether this further confuses onlookers, I am not sure, but it is part of how, off stage, I choose to stage the complexity of my gender. Sometimes I confront people when they stare, to push their boundaries farther. To a degree, I enjoy the subversion (the disturbance!) I create. There is definitely play involved, but the element of humor and camp is essential–it is part of what keeps me from being driven crazy by the reductive gender boxes people constantly throw my way. But the work I do as a gender variant out on the streets is exactly that: work. I choose to do it because it feels necessary and vital; but often it is difficult, and often I feel vulnerable.

PUBLIC PLEASURES/COMMUNITY ACTS

Performing on stage as Johnny T. is a whole different story. On stage (whether a formal or impromptu stage), I find unstoppable pleasure in my masculinity and gender variance. Because of the safe, queer context, drag shows create a different set of social dynamics and possibilities than does passing as a man or standing out as a gender variant in daily life. When I king it up, I up the volume and the extremes of my gendered identities and erotics, which invariably involves upping the pleasure I feel in exhibiting gender variance. The stage is where I take the daily work, the daily acts of transgression, and throw it over the top, into something larger than life for an audience who not only "gets it" but revels in the spectacle of queer, perverted bodies. The subversion of cross-dressing is charged with the erotic power and pleasure of crossing established gender lines, the political resonances of daily slippage and the risks of pestering, disgust, violence and blindness. A lot of what makes a drag king show what it is, is the audience. With drag kinging, audience is community–a community with a range of histories, realities, meanings and fantasies, that recognizes, validates and celebrates your act. The fact that drag king audiences bring to bear daily contexts and struggles as well as a penchant for subversive pleasure is what allows me to let go for a moment, and go full into the pleasure of performing. *Losin' control is as important as keepin' your cool. There's a right moment to lose control. You just gotta have a feel for it.*

As Johnny T., I get totally charged up by and in charge of my body, my movement, my multiple–*and multiplyin!*–desires. Johnny T. knows how to strut his stuff, how to make his moves, electrify both himself and his audience. As the Bee Gee's say, "Night fever, night fever, we know how to do it." Without a doubt, Johnny T. is all about exhibiting sexual self-confidence. He revels in his erotic pulse and the pleasure it evokes among his peers and/or audience. Johnny T. understands that desire is bigger than getting someone in the sack–it's about being so fully in the erotics of your body that you want to feel the charge of your desire out in the world, to feel how it pulses in and against other people, generating a heat that comes back to you. Johnny T. is electric, he's greased lightning because he's magnetic, because he throws his hot stuff around and demands that you throw hot stuff back at him. His erotic fuel is that reflection, that pulse coming right back to start him up all over again. *We know how to do it.*

For me, that's what drag is about: the full-on, no-stops embodiment and exhibition of subversively gendered desire–desire not just as I-want-to-fuck-you or be-fucked, but a more expansive, public state of desire, something elastic and electric, something you are constantly tuning in to and reproducing–multiplying, like Danny Zuko's "chills"–with the aid of a "power supplying" audience. Making our deviant desires public is a fundamental operating principle of queer and trans movements and communities; rather than holing up our desire in heteronormative homes, we use public space and create alternative public arenas to bring alive our realities and our fantasies. We make desire public property. This is our revolutionary work: we put our bodies on the line to enact queer and trans visibility and to forge new social spaces and relations in a rigid, role-bound society.

Drag kinging is part of a series of public acts where queers and trannys stage a range of butch identities, female masculinities, male femininities and other gender variations between and beyond. Drag king shows are ultimate public events because, despite differences, a collective enterprise transpires between the kings and the audience. Since a queer/tranny audience brings a historical and daily context to bear, the audience plays an active part in bringing alive the subversive desires on stage, and the public goods offered up are all the more theirs to devour if they wish. The elements of gender, sexuality, style and desire are compressed, intensified and exaggerated into pure pulse, and put on display as one tight and feverish package for the audience to mouth up. *No joke, you bettah mouth me up.*

As dykes, our choice to king it up and create arenas for drag king culture is a political, liberatory move with deep resonances for shaking up outdated, oppressive gender systems and sexual codes, as well as our own potential for power. Queers and trannys do more than survive (and live) at the margins of society; through the exaggerations, perversions and transmutations we create, we push human behavior to a futuristic edge. Drag kinging produces new erotics, new genders, and new forms and modes of power. Johnny T. allows me to push to that edge of invention. I tell him I hope he keeps me at the edge of my seat for a long time to come, to which he can only reply: *You won't be sittin' in any seat at all. We'll be burnin' up that quarter mile.*

NOTES

1. Johnny T. would like to thank—from the bottom of his Texas sized heart—the host of folks who, through their critical thinking, inspiration and support, contributed to the writing of this essay: Emily "Rocco" Cohen, Kathleen McLaughlin, Liza "Leo" Travis, Liz Cohen, Julie Gozan, Maggie Jochild, Cameron Scott, Del LaGrace Volcano, Meg Chilton/Jeff Stroker, and the Chicago Kings.

2. In this piece, Travolta refers to John Travolta himself, whereas Johnny T. indicates the drag king persona I create. More specifically, when I discuss Travolta, I draw upon several key characters he played in his early years as well as the overall essence/sensibility/style/identity/culture he projected. Likewise, Johnny T. usually draws heavily from the characters Tony and Danny and Bud. But in the bigger sense, Johnny T. is a composite of my own personae mixed in with John Travolta's moves, gestures, attitudes and voice as conjured through my particular lens, sensibilities, aesthetics, politics.

3. The terms "boyz" and "bois" are used to represent subversive masculine identities claimed by dykes, trannys and kings, as opposed to the term "boy" which, unless stated as "tranny boy," refers to biological gender.

REFERENCES

Butler, Judith. 1999. *Gender Trouble*. New York: Routledge.
Halberstam, Judith. 1998. *Female Masculinity*. Durham: Duke University Press.
Volcano, Del LaGrace and Judith Halberstam. 1999. *The Drag King Book*. London: Serpent's Tail.

SUGGESTED READING/VIEWING LIST

Books:

Butler, Judith. 1999. *Gender Trouble.* New York: Routledge.
Halberstam, Judith. 1998. *Female Masculinity.* Durham: Duke University Press.
Volcano, Del LaGrace and Judith Halberstam. 1999. *The Drag King Book.* London:
   Serpent's Tail.

Magazines:

Kingdom, The International Drag King Magazine published by Carlos Las Vegas and
   Ken Las Vegas; contact: kingdomidkm@yahoo.ca or geocities.com/kingdomidkm.

Films:

By Hook or By Crook, by Harry Dodge and Silas Flipper
Third Antenna, Directed by Freddie Fagula and Hellery Homosex; contact:
   thirdantenna@hotmail.com.
XY: DRAG, by Robin Deisher

QUESTIONS FOR DISCUSSION

1. In what ways does drag kinging overturn sexist and heterosexist constructions of gender? Does it create social change? How is kinging a feminist project?
2. What freedoms does kinging and king culture create? Who does this reach, and not?
3. How and when do king performances reinscribe sexist roles and relations? What kind of critique exists around this dynamic?
4. How central is camp to drag king culture? What is its function? What does it allow?
5. How do the different folks who converge on a king stage– butches, femmes, dykes, trannys–form overlapping and diverging king identities, cultures, communities?
6. What are the different king identities and realities represented offstage versus onstage?
7. How are king shows more than shows–how are they sites of community? What is being forged? For whom?
8. Is drag kinging a gender revolution that can eventually reach a mainstream audience–gay or straight? What possibilities for change exist in that arena?
9. How is the production and consumption of public pleasure a radical act for women, feminists, queers, trannys?
10. Where is your king? How might he speak, move, interact, think? Are king identities for everyone?

Me Boy

Neeve "Amy" Neevel

SUMMARY. Neeve provides an overview of hir personal and political motivations for drag performance as Pat Riarch. Initially based in a discussion of hir youth's gender game, s/he proceeds to elucidate hir location of adult playmates in the gender-bending/drag king community. *[Article copies available for a fee from The Haworth Document Delivery Service: 1-800-HAWORTH. E-mail address: <docdelivery@haworthpress.com> Website: <http://www.HaworthPress.com> © 2002 by The Haworth Press, Inc. All rights reserved.]*

KEYWORDS. Drag king, gender, feminism, gender performativity, transgender, female masculinity, transfeminism

"Me boy." Neevel family lore names this as my first "sentence." Already used to my unique sense of self, my mother replied in a straightforward manner: "Why do you want to be a boy, Amy?" The events that spurred such prophetic grammar were clear enough: my dad and brother had just departed for an exciting day of world philosophy and playground discourse, respectively. I wanted a piece of the action. Weary of hanging out at the local high chair, I answered with a girl-child's keen insight: "Boys go bye-bye."

I do not doubt that I am who I am today because of my mother's acceptance of my youth's gender questions. She simply looked at me, grabbed the implications of my statement and said, "Girls go bye-bye too." We went to the park. Later, we stopped by my mom's part-time job, where the story was recited and co-workers demonstrated "what

[Haworth co-indexing entry note]: "Me Boy." Neevel, Neeve 'Amy'. Co-published simultaneously in *Journal of Homosexuality* (Harrington Park Press, an imprint of The Haworth Press, Inc.) Vol. 43, No. 3/4, 2002, pp. 31-37; and: *The Drag King Anthology* (ed: Donna Troka, Kathleen LeBesco, and Jean Bobby Noble) Harrington Park Press, an imprint of The Haworth Press, Inc., 2002, pp. 31-37. Single or multiple copies of this article are available for a fee from The Haworth Document Delivery Service [1-800-HAWORTH, 9:00 a.m. - 5:00 p.m. (EST). E-mail address: docdelivery@haworthpress.com].

girls did too." Nonetheless, their phraseology was not completely convincing: what was this "too" all about? Why were my actions "in addition" to those of the male species? These elder apologetics could not disprove my innate sense that the boys had it good.

And so, throughout my youth, I was entranced with all things male (with a few hard, fast, pointed exceptions). In first grade, I beat up boys that teased my girl friends and was eventually initiated into one of the boy gangs. In second grade, I convinced my mom that a jean jacket, wrangler cords and cowboy boots was the only acceptable outfit. Ever. In third grade when I started developing breasts, I bemoaned the fact that people would think I was a girl. To my chagrin, my mother declared "Well, Amy, you are a girl." One summer, I convinced a new pal of my desired identity, finally daring to answer that stale question, "Are you a girl or a . . . ", with: "boy." This clandestine operation succeeded for a month as I assured Brad's mother that my parents were Eastern Europeans and that Amy was a perfectly acceptable name for a boy over there. During that time, I craftily plotted the theft of my brother's underwear, and proudly strutted around bare-chested with toothpick in mouth. Fearing discovery, I casually mentioned to my mom that if Brad asked her if I were a boy or a girl, she didn't really need to tell him because he already knew the answer. Ultimately, Brad's older brother unveiled my "passing" status. While Brad came over later that day, wanting to go catch butterflies, we were both awkward and suddenly unsure of each other. I never saw him again.

In fourth grade, I became obsessed with the fur I would never obtain. I drew beards and chest hair on all of my male action figures. I meticulously added mustaches, goatees and stubble to the faces of male models in those dense Sears-Roebuck catalogues; upon completion, I quizzed my parents as to the models' natural state of facial hair. Well-studied in my craft, I often fooled them. Buckling to social pressure in fifth grade, I started dating boys. Fortunately, Matt, my "boyfriend" of a year and a half, was convinced that our relationship would be much better if I were a boy, because then I could sleep over. It was at this time that male rock stars became my idols. I wallpapered my room with *Teen Beat* shots of Duran Duran, Corey Hart, The Police, and Wham! Upon receiving a horrible perm from my mother, my only condolence was a friend telling me that it made me look a lot like John Cougar Mellencamp. These men weren't my crushes; they were my crash course in successful masculinity. In sixth grade, I latched on to the "tie craze," demanding that my father teach me every style of knot and convincing my mother that ties were the ultimate accoutrement to any outfit. Always. By seventh grade, it became evident that the best way to a girl's heart was friendship, not male posturing, and so I collapsed into discussions of boys, Bennetton and blends of nail polish. Clearly, this was the only way to get invited to those coveted sleep-over parties. By the time I left that haze and became a fresh "youngwoman" in high school, I was all that I knew I could be: a dyke, passionate about all things "woman" and curious about most things "male." Now, I steadily return to the meaning of my youth, having found promise in my young passions, having found identity in my six-year-old's sense of the world. And so, the sage of my childhood, with the distinct wisdom of origin, has helped discern my most modern identity: gender outlaw.

This identity has obviously resulted in loss. Around the time that penises and vaginas began defining social circles, I lost my best friend. I began to sense that I wasn't as welcome as I used to be: no longer invited to all the kickball and basketball games, no longer asked to romp with "the boys" into the summer nights. One day I asked Mike, "Do you think you'll be able to be my friend next year?" Mike somberly responded "I'm not sure."

As I reflect on this gender journey, I am left puzzled by my young mind. At a time when I was more concerned with road construction than social construction, more in tune with making gender performative (read: cowboy boots and boxing gloves) than critiquing what was gender normative, I obviously had an inherent sense of our world's dualistic nature. I knew that there were choices to be made, and I was willing to duel over which path would be mine. Whether my young soul was shaped by a stubborn political subconscious or some sort of innate psychological inclination, I'm not sure. Today, however, I am sure that my political *consciousness* and my *personal* inclinations collude in one destiny: drag kinging.

In donning drag attire, I arouse my youth's ambitions and quell kid fears. This time I know that lip-syncing, mirrored swaggers, and meticulously drawn beards are not for want, rather they are for desire, meant to satisfy my masculine wiles and beguile the willing audience. While I have learned to critique the authority relegated solely to the world of male duds and dicks, my inner boy still revels in the experience of claiming that power. In designing the acts, however, I refuse to be lost in that thrill.

Instead, I savor the titillation of challenging the archaic. Within the Drag Kingdom, I experience political power, that which is traditionally defined as male and that which I claim as a feminist, in the context of social parody. The brilliance of parody is that it always glimmers with elements of truth. Therefore, in being ridiculous, I am also able to ridicule the more insidious aspects of "masculinity." As a male gigolo, a closeted priest, a gun-toting southerner or a rock-star slave to the music industry, I aim to strip, literally and figuratively. I aim to strip male "prowess" of its appeal.

I aim to strip institutions of repressive dogma. I aim to strip down to my vinyl pants. With these goals in mind, I have created a drag identity that is universally understood; an identity we are all familiar with. I am the thread with which we are forced to weave our lives, I am: Pat Riarch.

Pat's gender critique is best embodied in acts that embrace our most base human commonalities: humor and sex. When Pat uses his drag king powers in the form of a male gigolo, 70s star Paul Anka serenades the scene and Pat praises the multitude of women who are "Having My Baby." During this number, three pregnant women make their way to the stage, one a beaming ex-wife with a child support statement in hand, next a gum-snapping Catholic school girl who refuses to have an abortion, and third a defeated depressive clad in a bathrobe and carrying her constant accoutrement, a whiskey bottle. As this occurs, Pat croons, in full, hairy-chested seventies attire, "You're having my baby, what a wonderful way of saying how much you love me, you're having my baby, what a lovely way of saying what you're thinking of me." It is readily apparent that Pat is more enthusiastic about the spreading of his seed, than the imminent new lives. Well practiced in narcissism, Pat is oblivious to his girlfriends' distaste and discomfort. These women almost appear forced to sing their bit of the song: "I'm a woman in love and I love what it's doing to me, I'm a woman in love and I love what's going through me" (at which point the housewife grabs her hand bag and throws up). As the song ends his arrogance is very clear, the finale involves Pat dispersing small sperm, each individually signed, to the audience.

"Father Figure" features Pat incarnate as a closeted gay priest. As George Michael's sultry song fills the candle-lit space, Pat enters, regaled in a priest's collared gown. He slowly approaches the altar and places a holy book down on the holy pedestal. Gazing towards the sky, towards his Lord, Pat begins the tale of his turmoil: "That's all I wanted something special, something sacred–in your eyes, for just one moment to be bold and naked at your side." As this verse ends, the altar boy (a.k.a. Rey CruitHer), clad in a white robe, approaches the priest to retrieve the holy book and walks away from Pat. They are formal with one another, yet the music shows hidden tensions. "That's all you wanted, something special, someone sacred–in your life just for one moment to be warm and naked at my side." The song progresses and subtle moments of eye contact between Pat and Rey signify a mutual attraction, "sometimes I think that you'll never understand me, but something tells me together we'd be happy." Unable to face his passions, Pat retreats in his painful frustration, croons "oh baby, I'd love to be your daddy" and is subdued by a musical interlude.

In these moments, Rey opens the holy book and a gay male porn magazine falls out from between the pages. Initially shocked, he also reveals a fascination, a curiosity, a passion. The interlude ends with Rey making love to the porn magazine. However, he soon becomes conscious of his wayward activity and, appalled with himself, violently discards the magazine, in favor of a sign reading "It is an abomination." As this happens, Pat resumes his story, lamenting: "that's all I wanted, but sometimes love can be mistaken for a crime." Reaching towards Rey, Pat pleads "that's all I wanted just to see my baby's blue eyes shine, this time I think that my lover understands me, if we have faith in each other then we can be strong." During this time, Rey's confusion is evident. Ultimately, with a dramatic turn in the music, Rey abandons the abomination sign and faces Pat who assures him that "I will be your father figure." Trembling, he approaches Pat, who, with a passionate gaze, kneels Rey down and serves him communion, singing: "If you are the desert, I'll be the sea, If you ever hunger, hunger for me." At which point, Rey's mouth lustily tears the bread out of Pat's hand.

Pat then raises Rey up, takes his altar boy robe off and appreciates his new lover clad in tight black clothing and a dog collar. All the while, Pat is singing "so when you remember the ones who have lied, who said that they cared, but then laughed as you cried, beautiful darling, don't think of me." Maintaining intimate eye contact, Rey turns around and again kneels before Pat, "because all I ever wanted, it's in your eyes baby," he then lifts up Pats robe and proceeds to give him head. The audience is privy to Rey's head under the robe moving back and forth. As the music comes to a climax, so does Pat, "just hold on, hold on, I won't let you go, my baby."

Emboldened, Rey CruitHer strips Pat of his robe, revealing a tight vinyl outfit. Completely transformed in their gay male regalia, they are free to explore one another. As the song and the sex ends, Rey is in a submissive position while Pat stands above him, promising "I will be your father, I will be your preacher, I'll be your daddy . . . " As the music fades, Pat and Rey come together in stance, join in the holy cross across their chests and end in prayer position with heads bowed.

Obviously, Rey and I focus on creating narrative pieces that explore the underpinnings of male power and sexuality. Pat hopes to make people aware that within his culture, power is a tool used to control individual's thoughts, actions and desires; and that honest, vulnerable expressions of sexuality are considered a dangerous means of losing control. Pat aims to expose his power structure as a system wedded to rigid codes that limit acceptable expressions of sexuality, particularly male sexuality and sensuality. Our performances try to illuminate what Audre Lorde terms the power of the erotic, or the idea that power is not about control but rather the courage to relinquish control and experience a full range of human desires and possibilities. Ultimately, Rey and I strive to summarize patriarchy's effect on human society and sexuality in five-minute pop song digests.

The first time we performed the Father Figure act, I was given my greatest king compliment: "You made me wet." Drag acts that spur laughter and a sense of eroticism (a gender-bend-over, if you will) are often most subversive because, ultimately, these visceral reactions allow for a virtual understanding of gender theory. If an individual is turned *on* by a dyke-in-drag-representing-a-fag fucking another dyke-in-drag-representing-a-fag, traditional norms of gender and attraction have a greater chance of being turned *out*. If someone can laugh at the restraints of masculinity, they are implicitly placing gender roles under some degree of scrutiny. Really, the best theoretical lens is still the eyeball and the emotional filters that address images before us. The Drag Kingdom provides us with the (eye)balls to distort gender templates and refocus our visions. As this happens gender bending becomes less of an individual feat and more a form of community activism; together, through laughter and libidinous acts, we are bending society's notions towards a more honest understanding of gender.

As Pat, I am allowed access into many other realms of existence: taxi drivers in New York listen to me, straight men in New York ignore me, gay men everywhere hit on me and beautiful young college dykes pay me to practice the application of my youth's craft: beards. These college drag king workshops are amongst my most rewarding king experiences. During the workshops, I ask participants to think of one instance in which they strongly remember feeling "gendered" by an event, by another individual, or by themselves. Many young women recall instances of being mistaken as a teenage boy and scolded in the women's restroom. Others relate how their more "traditional" gender traits have restricted them. In examining the tradition of gender, we list terminology that reflects gender in some way, e.g., sissy, tomboy, chick, pretty, soft, butch. I then ask them to define their particular gender identity. I often hear replies similar to: "I used to be a boy-girl, pretty chick, but now I think I'm more of an androg, long-haired tomboy."

After this process, we begin playing with the idea of space, particularly gender's effect on how we stand in, utilize and move through personal and public spaces. As a part of this critique, each individual strikes a pose that reflects their internal masculinity. This exercise guarantees an element of shyness and giggles. Nonetheless, by the time we are prepared to design drag personas, the group has attained a much greater confidence in gender play. Having created drag names, such as Semen Freud and Sir Lanceislong, it is then time to don the appropriate attire. I am continually amazed at the revolutionary effects of spirit gum. I have seen a shy, quiet young woman transform herself into Rico Suave and strut the stage that night in a steamy rendition of "I Want Your Sex." I have seen a sweet dyke become a fifty-year-old biker daddy who, lost in his character, head butted the stomach of a six-foot-four male friend during a pseudo dining room brawl, in the process breaking every dish that had been on his tray. Essentially, I would say that the results are always akin to a gaggle of lesbians in a pet store: very furry and very fanatical.

Past workshop participants often write to share news of their drag king achievements; some have won local drag king contests, others have attended proms and formal events in drag, and a few are considering becoming full-time "drag kings." Whatever the accomplishment, it is obvious that drag kings are encouraging women, and men, to embrace themselves and each other in a new "fashion." As I witness this growth and the power of performance, I am proud to serve and spread word of the almighty Kingdom.

It is evident, now, that I had many compatriots in my youth's gender game. Having endured the teasing and taunting that all too often accompanies difference, I am relieved to have finally found my playmates. I am relieved that all of us, having endured the gender regime, are vindicated in claiming our rightful thrones as agents of social progress, as royalty, as drag kings.

"Pat Riarch and Rey CruitHer, a.k.a. Neeve "Amy" Neevel and Sarah Kowal"
[Samantha Farinella, photographer]

"I Am the Man!"
Performing Gender and Other Incongruities

Jay Sennett, MA

Sarah Bay-Cheng, PhD
Colgate University

SUMMARY. The following essay details the genesis of the performance "I Am the Man" for the First International Drag King Extravaganza. In it the authors explain both their autobiographical performances and the relationship between their drag performances and transgender theory by linking Shakespeare to queer theory and by overlapping their personal narratives. *[Article copies available for a fee from The Haworth Document Delivery Service: 1-800-HAWORTH. E-mail address: <docdelivery@ haworthpress.com> Website: <http://www.HaworthPress.com> © 2002 by The Haworth Press, Inc. All rights reserved.]*

KEYWORDS. Halberstam, transgender, drag, performance, Shakespeare, transsexual, gender, autobiography

Transsexuality is a response to the dream by forcing back, even abolishing, the frontiers of the real.

–Catherine Millot

[Haworth co-indexing entry note]: " 'I Am the Man!' Performing Gender and Other Incongruities." Sennett, Jay, and Sarah Bay-Cheng. Co-published simultaneously in *Journal of Homosexuality* (Harrington Park Press, an imprint of The Haworth Press, Inc.) Vol. 43, No. 3/4, 2002, pp. 39-47; and: *The Drag King Anthology* (ed: Donna Troka, Kathleen LeBesco, and Jean Bobby Noble) Harrington Park Press, an imprint of The Haworth Press, Inc., 2002, pp. 39-47. Single or multiple copies of this article are available for a fee from The Haworth Document Delivery Service [1-800-HAWORTH, 9:00 a.m. - 5:00 p.m. (EST). E-mail address: docdelivery@haworthpress.com].

39

TRANSGENDER PERFORMANCE AS DRAG

In queer subculture and mainstream popular culture alike, drag is often considered a temporary, performed presentation of the self. For example, in her book *Female Masculinity* Judith Halberstam defines the drag king as "a female (usually) who dresses up in recognizably male costumes and performs theatrically in that costume" (1998, 232). Despite a detailed examination of the complexities and paradoxes of performing masculinity, Halberstam's reliance on a stable, definable body "underneath" the drag king performance remains essential to her definition of drag.

While drag may disturb our notions of gender and encourage slippage between two gender identities, at its core drag performance relies on the existence of a permanent, fixed and biologically determined "body" beneath the trappings of drag. But what happens to our understanding of drag if we assume that the body is not fixed, but is in fact constructed by performance and the audience expectations of that performance? What happens to a definition such as Halberstam's when the "usually" female performer is replaced by another gender; when a male performs as a drag king? Can such a performance even be considered drag?

Using Judith Butler's claim that gender is a copy with no original, our performance of "I Am the Man" at the *First International Drag King Extravaganza* (IDKE) in Columbus, Ohio sought to disrupt the notion of drag as the performance of a fixed-body-as-gender into multiple unstable possibilities. Rather than use drag to reinforce the notion of a "real" or "true" body underneath the performance, our drag portrayals attempted to deny the audience knowledge of which of us had what body, or even the assurance that a definable body existed. We attempted to make our cross-dressing a cross-identity exercise. We used each other's identity as the temporary persona. In other words, Jay played Sarah and Sarah played Jay. Within these portrayals, we made no assumptions of how either of our bodies was supposed to look or act. Rather, we were as true to the text as we could be, and we coached each other on the visual and aural appearance of each other's role.

As such, "I Am the Man" represents an initial attempt to discover what transgender drag might look like. We tried to blur the distinction between our performance of gender on stage and our performance of gender in daily life. Seeing Jay on the street, little about his physical appearance suggests he had been born female. Facial hair, a strapping 6'2" frame, and a low voice all reaffirm the message communicated by his clothes that Jay is a man, albeit a man with a flamboyant sense of dress. Conversely, little about Sarah can be readily identifiable as definitively male. She has a low voice, but too high to pass on the phone. Physically smaller with rather delicate hands and an impossibly feminine first name, Sarah's much more conservative men's style rarely convinces the casual observer of an absolute man. However, the limitations of Sarah's male impersonation do not always make her recognizable as a woman either.

As part of our preparation, we spent hours of rehearsal discussing how we moved through the world, how people read us on the street, and how linguistic imperatives such as "he" and "she" neither encompass nor encapsulate our trans bodies. Who are we really, we pondered? Butches? Drag kings performing all day, all the time? Female-bodied men? Theory provided a useful point of departure. To return to Halberstam, her theory divides the broader spectrum of female masculinity into three distinct categories: the drag king, the male impersonator, and the drag butch. She writes:

> Historically and categorically, we can make distinctions between the drag king and the male impersonator. Male impersonation has been a theatrical genre for at least two hundred years, but the drag king is a recent phenomenon. Whereas the male impersonator attempts to produce a plausible performance of maleness as the whole of her act, the drag king performs masculinity (often parodically) and makes the exposure of the theatricality of masculinity into the mainstay of her act. Both the male impersonator and the drag king are different from the drag butch, a masculine woman who wears male attire as part of her quotidian gender statement. Furthermore, whereas the male impersonator and the drag king are not necessarily lesbian roles, the drag butch most definitely is. (232)

Despite the care with which Halberstam creates these distinctions and definitions, gaps and overlaps remain. Most days Sarah falls under the category of drag butch with the occasional foray into male impersonation depending on the audience, and the odd bit of self-depreciating humor a la the drag king. Jay, for his part, exists completely outside these three categories. Or, rather, he performs all three simultaneously. Perhaps he is a male impersonator, except that part of Jay *is* male. Too, Jay can play the flamboyant dandy at the drop of a well-tailored hat. But much of his performance depends on the audience present. For still others he performs the drag butch. The role of the audience is particularly relevant to the fluctuation of these categories. Jay, sans breast binder, recently happened upon a group of young people. The gawking and giggling began. As Jay quickly moved to enter the safety of his home, one of the youths declaimed, "That's a woman on my life!" The longer Jay lives as a man, the less he believes in gender outside of his daily performance.

No matter how differently we look from each other, however, we both feel caught in the middle of the gender lines. Though we always part ways at the public restroom, our lives have followed similar courses. We studied the same magazines for cues about how to be male, learned from our fathers (both of whom are gay) about an exclusive world of men, and followed feminine women as our romantic ideals. Though we express it differently, we have been playing in male drag for most of our lives.

In our performance, we attempted to explore our individual performances of maleness and masculinity, while at the same time challenging the gender assumptions that usually support the performance of drag. In other words, we attempted to do drag without cross-dressing. To do this we not only cross-dressed, but also cross-acted. Jay wrote text that reflected a theatrical version of his experience as a transgendered /transsexual man. Sarah wrote text that represented her history of gender ambiguity and confusion. We then performed each other's texts, and eventually merged the two stories into Act I, scene v from Shakespeare's *Twelfth Night*. In this way, we did not assume a fixed body beneath our roles, but rather assumed the "real" body of the other. We thus approached our performance as a cross-*identity* piece instead of the more conventional cross-dressing.

SHAKESPEAREAN DRAG

Our interest in Shakespeare emerged out of both the Elizabethan cross-dressing performances and the more specific use of cross-dressing and identity confusion evident in many of the comedies, Of particular interest to us was the exchange between Viola and Olivia in *Twelfth Night, or, What You Will*. The parallels between the modern day drag king and the impersonations of Shakespeare's heroines seemed particularly relevant to the gender issues we wanted to explore. The scene we performed occurs early in the play as Viola, dressed as a man, woos Olivia on behalf of Viola's master, Orsino. Shipwrecked in Illyria, Viola has adopted the persona of a man to survive in her new environment. Though Viola is herself in love with Orsino, she agrees to court the fair Olivia on his behalf. Unfortunately, Olivia falls in love with Viola in her male persona of Cesario. All is resolved at the end when Viola's twin brother arrives, enabling Olivia to easily transfer her homoerotic attachment to a more appropriate mate. The scene we performed highlights Olivia's mistaken attraction for Viola and Viola's sense of displacement in the erotic relationship. We chose this scene in particular because it highlights the complications of gender as performance not only for one's gender definition, but sexual orientation as well.

Within this context of cross-identity, we sought to perform what seems natural (Jay's male identity, Sarah's in-between identity) as façade. For Jay, our intention was to explicate the lack of preparation for Jay's gendering as a man. As he writes, "How does a thirty-five-year old man who played as a tomboy, bled like a girl, reared as a lady, fucked like a stone butch lesbian, and dresses like a dandy become a man?" To perform Jay's persona, Sarah wore a fake mustache and adopted exaggerated macho gestures. Sarah-as-Jay-as-facade highlights a felt truth for Jay. He will not lie about his past girl/woman/lesbian/stone butch self. Medical authorities prefer that Jay, himself, believe that he has never been anything but a man, that he was raised erroneously as a woman. Indeed, in the words of Kate Bornstein, "[Transsexuals] are labeled as having a disease for which the only therapy is to lie, hide, or otherwise remain silent" (1994, 62). Jay's openness about his past was a major part of our performance work together. Indeed, it seems ideal. For it is in the context of "drag" that the definitions, visual cues, and mental assumptions that the average viewer has of Jay as a man can be best challenged.

This awareness of Jay as a performing "man" was an integral part of our work. Constructed as alternating monologues, Jay's language was performed by Sarah. Thus, the following speech, though directly Jay's experience, was spoken by Sarah in "drag":

> But the me the world sees is not the me who sees the world. Don't get me wrong. I am a man . . . a white man . . . a white heterosexual man. Your eyes tell you that. My look is unassailable. But am I man?
>
> The first time I took off my shirt at the public pool, I knew everyone would see the truth . . . but of what? A woman with whiskers, broad shoulders, a nice looking package and hair, hair, every-

where hair; or a man with bigger tits than average and a great bathing suit on?

Because the drag act is performed by a woman who is recognizably female, the artificiality of the "act" is highlighted. Even with a fake mustache and tie, Sarah's appearance as a man is hardly "unassailable." But the simultaneous presence of Jay who–despite being dressed in an ill-fitting, Catholic school girl's uniform–does look unassailably male, draws attention, not only to Sarah's performance as Jay, but also to Jay's performance as man in girl drag (Is Jay a drag queen or female impersonator or neither?) and highlights Sarah's in-between reality as a woman performing masculinity performing drag. Eventually all of these complications coalesced into a fundamental question regarding the notion of a "real" body underneath Sarah's pants or Jay's skirt.

Interspersed within Sarah's performance as Jay is Jay's performance of Sarah through a monologue detailing teenage love. The subject of the monologue is a girl who mistakenly believes Sarah, the object of her affection, to be male. As Jay (as Sarah) recounts:

> When I was fifteen, I found true love. The most lasting perfect love, that every teenager hopes to find, and I did. Me! Trouble is, she thinks I'm a guy. I keep pretending . . . and hiding the fact that I attend an all-girls Catholic high school.

From this beginning, Jay quickly segues into a high school recitation of Viola's monologue from Act II, scene ii of *Twelfth Night*. In preparation for the monologue, Jay remarks on the similarities between Viola's being mistakenly viewed as a man, and consequently being made (unwillingly) into the object of Olivia's affection, and the drama of a high school crush. "Funny how a guy in the 17th century could have such a clear understanding of me and my situation, while my best friend ignores my little incongruities." Once the perimeters of the high school crush are established, Jay moves into Viola's monologue.

In this new context, Viola's monologue takes a new understanding of double entendre. When Jay, dressed as he usually is, states "I am the man! If it be so, / Poor lady she were better love a dream" he comments not only as Viola, a woman dressed in men's clothes, but also on his own status as a man who possesses male secondary sex characteristics, but not the primary "real" body, i.e., the phallus. The monologue further comments on Sarah's ambiguous relationship to masculinity and her stated gender as opposed to others' assumptions of her gender orientation.

AUTOBIOGRAPHICAL DRAG

Jay-as-Sarah-as-Viola's reading begs the question of how deep drag goes. Is it only in clothes, hairstyle, and glued on facial hair? Or, does it extend to hormone treatment and some surgery as well? Is Jay's body itself drag? Within the context of the performance, these questions remain unanswered. Even within the original Shakespeare, Viola, herself in love with her master on whose command she is sent to woo Olivia, cannot uncover the solution to her own convoluted gender identity. In Shakespeare's original text Viola laments:

> How will this end? My master loves her dearly,
> And I (poor monster) fond as much on him;
> And she (mistaken) seems to dote on me.
> What will become of this? As I am man,
> My state is desperate for my master's love;
> As I am woman (now alas the day!),
> What thriftless sighs shall poor Olivia breathe!
> O time, thou must untangle this, not I,
> It is too hard a knot for me t'untie. (1989, 350)

For our performance, however, we changed a few of the lines, although we kept the text in iambic pentameter.

> How will this end? Poor she that dotes on me.
> What will become of this? As I am a man,
> My state is desperate for another's love;
> As I am woman (now alas the day!),
> What thriftless sighs shall poor Olivia breathe!
> O time, though must untangle this, not I,
> It is too hard a knot for me t'untie.

By the conclusion of the monologue, Jay has emerged as his male self and Sarah has been buried under a pile of feminine accoutrement. Once the gender switch is complete–Jay has moved from female to male, Sarah from male to female–they begin to play the roles of Viola-as-boy (Jay) and Olivia (Sarah) in their first meeting in Act I, scene v. Buried under the skirt and wig, Sarah adopts a falsetto voice, highlighting the contrivance of the performance of femininity while Jay affects an exaggerated masculine physicality, as a former woman, now a man. The disguise goes deeper than most drag, but is arguably still a creation within the context of the performance. In other words, the performance of both Jay's male body and Sarah's female body are both reduced to merely layers of creation without a stable foundation. Though both appear to be playing themselves (Sarah *is* a woman and Jay *is* a man), the exaggeration of the masculinity and femininity draws attention to the artificiality of gender performance. The inversions of performance finally climax in the moment that Olivia/Sarah reveals her face, formerly hidden behind the wig. Her revelatory line reads: "We will draw the curtain, and show you the picture. Look you, sir . . . Is't not well done." What is revealed, however, is Sarah's face still created to look male, including a mustache. Thus, the vision of Olivia, of feminine perfection, is marred by the presence of facial hair. Upon seeing this Viola/Jay responds, "Excellently done, if God did all," which of course, can be taken as an insult, both to Olivia commenting on her facial hair, and to Sarah commenting on the artificiality of the facial hair. Clearly, one can see by looking at Sarah's face that God did not "do all." Sarah, with a novelty store mustache and spirit gum, did at least part. Similarly, Jay does all with hormones, and still others have plastic surgeons do all while still others do all through voice lessons and body movements. God or nature is irrelevant to gender. The transgendered body only provides canvas, not the art.

Theoretically, separating trans performance from drag or assuming a fixed body beneath a performance or gender remains problematic. One must be sensitive to the individual performer's preference for definitions and biological determinism. Not every drag king considers herself to be transgendered. Many transmen would consider the term drag king derogatory or mocking. Finally, scores of genderqueer people believe in only two genders while scads more do not. But barring the individual's preference and scientific belief system, one can see the places of obvious overlap between Halberstam's drag king, male impersonator, and drag butch, and the problem of assuming that a fixed body exists underneath the performance. These spaces of overlap, ambiguity, and ambivalence gliding, sliding and interpenetrating around a whirling, changing, transforming body became a "truth" we wanted to perform. Since we live this dervish dream every day, performing in front of a crowd of screaming dykes and kings felt like a vacation.

REFERENCES

Bornstein, Kate. 1994. *Gender Outlaw: On Men, Women, and the Rest of Us.* New York: Routledge.

Halberstam, Judith. 1998. *Female Masculinity.* Chapel Hill: Duke University Press.

Millot, Catherine. 1990. *Horsexes: Essay on Transsexuality.* Brooklyn, New York: Autonomedia.

Sennett, Jay and Sarah Bay-Cheng. 1999. "I Am the Man! Performing Gender and Other Incongruities." Unpublished script.

Shakespeare, William. 1989. *Twelfth Night, or, What You Will. The Unabridged Shakespreare*, eds. William George Clark and William Aldis Wright. London: Running Press.

ON LOCATION: DRAG KING SCENES

Making Kings

Colleen Ayoup, BA, BFA

Independent Filmmaker

Julie Podmore, PhD

John Abbott College

SUMMARY. Due to a general lack of representation of female masculinities within the North American media, most urban drag king cultures
have evolved in isolation from each other. As a result, drag kings tend to
develop locally specific codes of dress, performance styles and forms of
masculinity. This chapter describes the case of a group of Montréal drag
king performers, The Mambo Drag Kings (MDKs). It is based on interviews that were conducted for Colleen Ayoup's film *Kings* (2001), a
short documentary that explores kinging by examining the development
of this specific group of performers. We present excerpts from our discussions regarding the relationships between everyday gender identities,
lesbian sexuality, and performing as a king in a society that is fundamentally based on an asymmetrical sex-gender system. While the chapter does
highlight these theoretical concerns, the focus is on how the participants of
the group interpret and experience kinging and its impact on their own
gendered and sexual identities. *[Article copies available for a fee from The
Haworth Document Delivery Service: 1-800-HAWORTH. E-mail address:
<docdelivery@haworthpress.com> Website: <http://www.HaworthPress.com> © 2002
by The Haworth Press, Inc. All rights reserved.]*

[Haworth co-indexing entry note]: "Making Kings." Ayoup, Colleen, and Julie Podmore. Co-published
simultaneously in *Journal of Homosexuality* (Harrington Park Press, an imprint of The Haworth Press, Inc.)
Vol. 43, No. 3/4, 2002, pp. 51-74; and: *The Drag King Anthology* (ed: Donna Troka, Kathleen LeBesco, and
Jean Bobby Noble) Harrington Park Press, an imprint of The Haworth Press, Inc., 2002, pp. 51-74. Single or
multiple copies of this article are available for a fee from The Haworth Document Delivery Service
[1-800-HAWORTH, 9:00 a.m. - 5:00 p.m. (EST). E-mail address: docdelivery@haworthpress.com].

KEYWORDS. Drag kings, lesbians, performance, sexuality, masculinity, documentary film, Montréal

INTRODUCTION

In 1996, a loosely connected group of lesbians living in the Plateau Mont-Royal District of Montréal came together to discuss a drag performance for an upcoming lesbian fund-raising event. The performance would be a lip-sync and dance interpretation of "J'attendrai," a 1970s hit by the French pop-star Dalida. The piece was intended to launch *Le Boudoir*, an annual lesbian formal cabaret night and fund raising event for *Diver-Cité* (Montréal's gay pride organisation). Over the course of a few weeks, the choreography was laid out and at least twenty hours of practice went into perfecting a three-minute number. On the night of the performance, the MC for the evening had memorized all of Dalida's lyrics, had her hair and make-up done, and was donning a gold-lame dress and high heels. She was escorted onto the stage by a chorus line of lesbians sporting absurd forms of facial hair and dressed haphazardly in suit jackets and ties gathered from second-hand stores and neighbourhood closets. Although they stumbled through the number missing steps and staring at their feet, the audience found the performance endearing. This three-minute performance marked the inception of an amateur drag king performance group now called *The Mambo Drag Kings* (MDKs).[1]

Over the past five years, the MDKs have been a central project in both of our lives. It is not simply a political, theatrical or theoretical project. It has shaped our social networks, provided important personal challenges, and led us to reconsider our own gender identities. Each of us has been involved in this project in different ways. Julie Podmore (Julien St-Urbain) is an original member and perennial figure in the chorus line of the MDKs. Colleen Ayoup is a filmmaker who has video taped every performance of the group since 1997 as well as some rehearsals, make-up sessions, and other events. In April 2001, she completed the film *Kings* (Ayoup 2001) in which she explores the act of kinging by focusing on the evolution of the MDKs.

The interviews conducted for *Kings* are the focus of this chapter. We will focus on the MDKs' reflections on drag, gender, sexuality, representation and performance and, ultimately, on politics. We do not attempt to present a sophisticated theoretical argument about drag kings and kinging, but rather to provide an account of what enticed a group of Montréal lesbians to become drag kings and what it means to them.

THE MAMBO DRAG KINGS

At first, the MDKs had no official members and the configuration of the group was based on availability and drawn from friendship networks. The troupe continued to perform annually for *Le Boudoir* and branched out to create shows for other lesbian events. During this phase, various forms of performance, musical themes and icons of masculinity were explored. What began as a social activity among friends became more serious by 1998. A relatively permanent group of performers had been established that now had a well-developed repertoire. By this point, the group also had established relationships with three local choreographers.[2] Although the lesbian club scene and benefits for the gay and lesbian community have always been the primary venue for the MDKs, by 1998 the group was also performing in large queer nightclubs and at drag balls. Their largest venue was *Mascara,* an outdoor drag ball for Montréal's gay pride week in August, 1998 where they performed for a mixed audience of 8,000 people. Soon the repertoire of their activities included experimenting with other forms of performance such as modelling men's swim suits for a local gay magazine (*Fugues* 1998), ushering at an AIDS memorial service, and discussing the topic with the media (Todd 1999b).

Unlike most other drag king performers, the MDKs always perform as a group and place great emphasis on dance, theatricality and interpretation. Their pieces are usually organized around a lead performer ("male" or "female") who lip-syncs for the audience and is backed-up by a chorus line of kings. The pieces never involve the direct impersonation of male icons. Most of the acts are loosely interpretive and the focus is on creating their own distinctive atmosphere. This is done by using theme songs from films (i.e., James Bond's *Goldfinger*), the hits of male sex symbols (i.e., Tom Jones' "It's not unusual"), or French and English retro-pop music with lyrics that allow for a play on gender (i.e., Sylvie Vartan's "Comme un garçon"). Other musical pieces have also been chosen simply for stylistic reasons (i.e., John Paul Young's "Love is in the air"), for their kitsch character, and because they permit the group to romance and flirt with their audience.

The MDKs are relatively distinct both in terms of their performance as a group[3] and the characteristics of the women who participate. They display a uniform aesthetic, with each performer wearing a variation on a central theme. Their specific aesthetic is inspired by swing, lounge and whatever suits, ties and brightly coloured shirts can be found. While drag kings elsewhere often simulate drag queen performance in the sense that they generally lip-sync and often impersonate the singer as a solo act, the MDKs never perform on an individual basis. From the beginning, the MDKs have balked at the notion of being a collective, but the group focus is central to their project and performance. After more than five years of choosing and developing pieces, practising and exploring masculinity together, the MDKs have become a very tight social network. The group dynamic is especially central to the development of the individual gender identities among the participants as they explore and witness shifts in how they integrate masculinity into their everyday lives. It functions as a "brotherhood," with high levels of camaraderie. Practices and meetings are important social events, if not more important than the actual performances. Overall, the project of the MDKs has brought large challenges for each individual participant, whether it is confronting self-consciousness, developing coordination or learning how to work within a tight-knit group.

Formed on the basis of social networks, the group is relatively uniform in social and cultural terms. Although the participants range in age from 25 to 38, they come from a social network of lesbians who are students or in the early stages of their careers and are living in the Plateau Mont-Royal District of Montréal. The group is an important project and social network, but being a drag king is not the central focus of any of their lives. They are all pursuing careers in fields ranging from business and the arts, to counselling and academia. Their places of origin range from Montréal and its outlying regions, the rest of Canada, the United States and France. The ethnic origins and mother tongues of the participants include French, Québécois, German, Italian, English and Chinese. Although some have French as a mother tongue and many are bilingual, the group primarily speaks English, which is very significant within the context of predominantly French-speaking Montréal. Their audience is usually Francophone, which makes it necessary to emphasize dance and body movement. When choosing music and developing pieces, they cannot always rely upon American or English-language popular icons without losing or alienating the audience. Finally, the everyday gender identities of the MDKs are wide-ranging. Most would probably characterize themselves as "soft butches," but being a "butch" is not a prerequisite for the group. Discussions regarding gender identity within the group, moreover, often highlight differences among the participants rather than producing a sense of "sameness."

KINGS, THE FILMS

This chapter focuses on interviews with Colleen Ayoup for her documentary film on the MDKs. In this section, Colleen describes how she became involved in the project and why she felt it was important.

In 1997, I was asked to videotape one of the first Mambo Drag King performances at the Mississippi Club during Montréal's gay pride week. Although I was not eager to be a slave to the camera all night long, I agreed, and not long after I pressed "record" it struck me that this was an important and exciting event. It was important not only to the lesbian audience that evening, but to queer history and lesbian visibility within the queer community.

Soon thereafter, I began documenting as many group gatherings as I could—including rehearsals, performances, photo shoots, etc. . . . with the expectation that some day I would find the means to compile a short video on the topic of drag kings. In 1999, I decided to work on this project during my final year in Film Production at Concordia University. The result was Kings *(Ayoup 1999), a twelve-minute documentary that included interviews, footage from performances, and dramatizations. Although the video had a number of technical shortcomings, this short piece attracted considerable attention at feminist and "queer" film and video festivals, and led to two television interviews (Todd 1999a; Todd 1999b).*

Due to all the attention that the first cut of Kings *(Ayoup 1999) received,[4] I decided to improve upon the imperfections, and expand the theoretical questioning within the interviews. A deeper exploration of kinging in the video has largely been inspired by discussions with the MDKs. The members are outspoken, sharp-minded women who share an eagerness to engage, criticize, and contemplate issues surrounding gender identity and their roles as drag kings. Although the group began on a whim, struggles to find a common direction soon led to questions regarding gender, drag and performance. At the end of the 1990s, some materials and reflections on the subject of drag kings were published, which fur-*

ther inspired and fuelled my enthusiasm for the topic. Perhaps the most influential was Judith Halberstam's (1998) Female Masculinity. *Halberstam's work provided a much-needed theoretical framework for my project and informed my line of questioning during interviews. Del LaGrace Volcano's photographic collection also inspired me to continue with my project, and reminded me of the necessity to make drag kings a visible part of queer culture (Volcano and Halberstam 1999).*

With the help of the National Film Board of Canada, an extended version of Kings *(Ayoup 2001) was released in 2001. It includes new imagery along side of the old Video 8 footage of performances, and more in-depth dialogue sequences with eight members of the group. During the first edit, I was struck by the richness of the interviews. It became rapidly apparent that reducing six hours of tape into approximately 20 minutes would be heartbreaking. What follows is an account of some of the many interesting discussions that I recorded during interviews with the MDKs in January, 2000.*

DEFINING DRAG

The gender identities of the participants in the MDKs are diverse. Each individual's involvement with the group, their experiences with performing, and interpretation of "drag" varies to a significant degree. Although each participant described "drag" as a "performance," the extent to which they considered "masculinity" to be a performance varied from person to person. Halberstam (1998, 246-255) has developed a very thorough taxonomy of drag king identities. These include "drag butches" and "female pretenders," as well as women who use "male mimicry," "denaturalized masculinity" or "butch realness" in their performances. We can find elements of each of these personae among the MDKs. We are, however, hesitant to impose them. In what follows, we let each of the MDKs describe drag in their own words.

For Sailor Saul (Sarah Gibson), Tommy Boy (Cindy Mancuso) and Félix Le French (Isabelle Saillard), performing in male drag is an opportunity to proudly express themselves and their masculinities. Performing masculinity is a realm of comfort for these kings. In everyday life their masculinity is often a source of scorn, but on stage they are respected and admired. As Saul states:

I get mistaken for a boy or for a man all the time in my life but it's always with hostility and onstage I'm able to carry it off and it's honoured and it's fun. However, that's not true for everybody in the group and I think that some of them would like to go a "cheesy" route, caricatures, . . . and I like that to a certain extent but there's always that part of me that says, " . . . wait, you can't go that far with the joke," 'cause there's something real about it for me. So, that can be a source of tension.

What does it mean, therefore, to parody masculinity onstage if the performance does, in fact, offer a source of comfort? Tommy offered the following:

I think for Sarah [Saul] and myself, . . . being in drag is really just expressing a part of ourselves, so to take that further, to make fun of it [masculine aesthetic] we're making fun of ourselves in a way. I think we have a bit of pride about not doing that and I think for other people, they're like, "C'mon, let's make it more drag, a bit more like how the drag queen's would do it," and we kinda hesitate 'cause it's a part of us that we take pride in, [pride] in how we look.

Phil LeRupp (Johanne Cadorette), whose daily aesthetic is generally more "feminine," is one of the MDKs that experiences kinging differently from Saul, Tommy and Félix. She plays a unique role in the troupe because, in addition to her drag king role, she also performs "female" characters. Her ideal performance of masculinity is a more embellished version of the drag king aesthetic:

I think during [drag king] events it's fun to play with ideas [of drag]. Like, sometimes I will dress like a real "cheese ball" kind of guy, with a polyester shirt, greasy hair, and a big chain . . . I like that, but I won't necessarily go onstage with the MDKs like that 'cause it would break the uniformity of the group's "look," if you will.

For Phil, dressing in male drag is not an opportunity to feel comfortable and honoured, but rather a moment to explore another aspect of her persona. "I feel more coquette in drag than when I'm in an evening dress. I don't know why, [but] I'm more capable of flirting or [expressing] the 'pig man' in me [when I'm in male drag]."

Not all of the MDKs have such polarized experiences of drag king performance. Gender identity for Jimmy (Jeannie Jay), Julien St-Urbain (Julie Podmore), Max A. Million (Cathrin Winkelmann) and Zack Attack (Andrea Kwan) is more fluid than it is for the others in the group. This middle sub-group perhaps represents the majority within the MDKs, but defining their approach to drag is difficult. This is because they fall somewhere in the middle of two extremes, in which a variety of identities are subsumed into one category. They do, however, share two primary characteristics. First, masculinity, femininity and all of their various mutations are performed interchangeably in their everyday lives. Secondly, although each takes pride in their masculinity, kinging is primarily a playful performance. Their performances are not, however, any less political than the others. For lesbians with more fluid identities kinging can be about adopting a momentary concrete gender identity. As Zack suggests, this can also be a subversive act:

> For me it's almost an act of rebellion, you know? To be a drag king and to do this is an act against people deciding that I am a certain way [such as not being butch enough]. . . . So, I think that being a drag king and playing with that is a really important part of deconstructing the kinds of identities that are placed on us.

Despite the above variations, all of the participants (except for Phil) shared a similar interpretation of the performance of femininity. To dress in "female" clothing was also perceived as a form of drag and, in most cases, represented an even greater extreme than the performance of masculinity.

LESBIAN KINGS

Halberstam (1998, 232) has argued that perhaps the only form of female masculinity that is implicitly lesbian is the "drag butch," "a masculine woman who wears male attire as part of her quotidian gender expression." According to her analysis, there is no necessary relationship between drag kings and lesbian sexuality. Among the MDKs, however, the distinction between the "drag butch" and the "drag king" is less clear. In this specific case, the expression of a lesbian sexuality is central to their performances and the ways in which masculine clothing and accoutrements are fetishized. Their reflections on the topic of sexuality, moreover, often confounded drag kings, transgendered women, and drag butches. Although most did not identify with these other categories, they still believed that their motivation to be a drag king stemmed from their sexuality.

In fact, the interpretation of how sexuality relates to the act of kinging sparked little enthusiasm or discussion during the interviews in comparison with most of the other questions. It almost seemed that the question was too obvious to answer. Most of the MDKs thought that a lesbian sexuality was implied by kinging although there was some recognition that it was not a necessary prerequisite. As Max stated, "I think that in being a drag king sexuality is implicit. . . . I've never known a drag king that wasn't a lesbian. And I think that sexuality is a big part of being a drag king." The gap between a theoretical recognition that there is no necessary relationship between sexuality and gender and their own experience of an implicit sexuality behind kinging, therefore, indicates that this relationship is not so straightforward. The MDKs' individual motivations for performing as drag kings, however, provide some resolution to this dilemma. For Julien, for example, being a drag king was simply an extension of exploring her sexual identity as a lesbian, specifically exploring the possibility of female masculinity afforded by a lesbian identity. She described this experience:

> [F]or me it's totally related to sexuality in the way that I would never have questioned gender identity . . . if I wasn't a lesbian to the same extent that I do; I would not have had that freedom . . . part of being a lesbian for me was getting out of . . . a narrowly defined gender identity and being able to explore a much more complex identity for myself in terms of gender and that's part of what the drag king thing is too.

While kinging is often treated as a form of representation, a performative act to be analysed and interpreted, it is in the links to the personal that we find the lesbian drag king. Drag kings give expression to forms of desire that exist within lesbian cultures. The most obvious among these is butch-femme desire. Not all of the participants in the MDKs identify with butch-femme desire and the group plays with a range of sexual dynamics in their performances, but the most predominant sexual dynamic performed by this group is butch-femme. As previously mentioned, some of their acts involve mixing gender roles whereby Phil performs a leading female role and the remaining MDKs perform as her male chorus line. For these pieces, Phil's female persona is the object of their desire. Zack offered the following insight into the importance of these types of performances:

I feel very much that that's [a butch-femme dynamic] where the level of appreciation comes from within the lesbian community because it's public admission of a butch-femme relationship within the lesbian community . . . and people can be more comfortable with that by saying, "oh yeah, that's me onstage" . . . It's not really a parody . . . it becomes a celebration which is what I feel it is sometimes. So to have that "feminine" element within the performances really speaks to a whole other reality–then it's really not only about playing with masculinity so much as it's about describing a lesbian life.

The MDKs do not always simply "describe a lesbian life" by extending a butch-femme dynamic. Other sexualities–even other expressions of lesbian sexuality–are expressed in their performances. They perform mimicry of gay male sexuality and heterosexuality that stems from a lesbian perspective as well as "butch-on-butch" expressions of desire. For example, when Phil is dressed in a ball gown and backed by a chorus line of men, some of the kings have described this as a parody of heterosexuality. Although it may appear to be an extension of a butch-femme dynamic, the opposition of male and female is also intended to mimic heterosexuality as the kings dance with their diva, try to romance her, and carry her on and off the stage. Kinging, therefore, provides more than a venue to parody masculinity. With or without a female opposite, the MDKs provide caricatures of heterosexual masculinity through their interactions, behaviours and aesthetic. An all-male chorus line of handsome fellows provides opportunities to express a "butch-on-butch" erotic, but it also lends itself to gay male play. As Julien remarked, "I think that we like the sort of homosocial element of all being men together when we do stuff like kissing each other as men and dancing, waltzing together, and so we like to play with all of that and mix it all up, . . . mix up sexuality as well as gender." Although there is certainly a critique of masculinity occurring within the MDKs, the moments when they dance or flirt with each other as men add another layer of sexuality to the performance that attracts a larger "queer" audience.

KINGS ONSTAGE

The primary (and very loyal) audience of the MDKs has always been lesbians; lesbians at community benefits, lesbians in bars, and lesbians attending women's cabaret nights. As the only formal drag king act in Montréal, the MDKs can always be assured a great reception in any of these venues. But, do lesbians accept drag kings uncritically, even if they are giving expression to something deeply relevant to lesbian culture and desire? As performers, the MDKs sense the reactions of the audience, and are often intensely aware of their reception. With lesbian audiences, the reception is generally very positive. The troupe has a sense of reflecting something back to their audiences, of inspiring people to join in by wearing drag to their shows and events and even providing an erotic image to Montréal lesbians. Despite the amateur character of the performances, the audiences are extremely encouraging and the group has even acquired a bit of local fame.

Kinging does not, however, always translate across cultures, generations or gender identities within the "lesbian community." Age and political ideology often have a strong effect on the reception of the MDKs by lesbians in Montréal. For example, kinging is sometimes interpreted as an uncritical celebration of masculine values and ways of being. As Max remarked,

> I think some women think we're trying to . . . model ourselves after men, or our objective is to *be* men which in my case, it's not, and I really don't think that's the case for anyone in the group. But, I mean for people coming out of the 70s–that whole generation–I can see where drag king culture might be offensive to them. For people trying to move away from male culture and male values . . . maybe they think we're idealizing certain male values.

Max highlights a generational perspective on kinging that has been shaped by feminist ideology. She speculates that the rejection of kinging by older lesbians might represent a generation gap between queer lesbians (even queer feminist lesbians) and lesbian feminists that strive to reaffirm "women's values." Phil, on the other hand, links the discomfort with kinging among older lesbians to their experiences during a more gender-polarized era. Although Phil was hesitant to generalize, she observed, "I have often found that with lesbians that are a little older and who have perhaps, at a particular moment in their own lives, needed to dress to pass as male in order to survive, it is probably less funny to watch us do this onstage and to . . . take all this [cross-dressing and performance] so lightly." Similar comments were also made about transgendered people, who have often had negative reactions to the MDKs' portrayal of masculinity, especially when it involves a parody of a masculinity expressed through female bodies.

Perhaps the second largest audience outside of the mainstream for the MDKs has been gay men. Their reception by this audience seems to be highly contextual. In camp situations, such as within a drag show or during a lesbian-dominated event, the MDKs have been well received (if not admired) by gay men in the audience. In gay male spaces where masculinity dominates and is eroticised, however, they do not always fit the bill. Zack recalls discomfort during an appearance of the MDKs in a local queer bar:

> I know we did one show at UNITY and there was a lot of gay men there and that was not so cool at all. Mind you, I think it was a certain brand of gay man . . . I just remember looking out and seeing a whole bunch of like really buff, really hot looking trendy guys [who seemed to be] thinking, "What the hell are they doing?"

Zack's feelings about that event were shared by all the kings. "The gay men were looking at us as if we were extraterrestrials," remembers an outraged Félix. In a place where buff male dancers usually occupy the stage, perhaps the drag king provides too much parody of the actual object of desire and cannot be a substitute for a "real" man. While some men might appreciate the king for the camp character of his performance, the expression of a gay male sexual dynamic through kinging may not always be legible in a sexually charged, gay-male space. However, there is some play between drag kings and drag queens within these contexts. The reactions of drag queens fall into a different category, as Julien explained,

> If we look enough like the Village People or we look sexy enough in our suits then they [the drag queens] will flirt with us and they'll flirt with the notion that we might really be men and play with that. Drag queens always flirt with me in a club when I look like that so, there's a whole lot of camp going on there, like all this gender inversion–that's really kinda fun.

Because they are not "real" men, the drag king shares a camp camaraderie with drag queens.

The MDKs have rarely performed for an audience with a large proportion of heterosexual spectators except on television. The group has received some positive if puzzled feedback regarding a short journalistic portrait shown on a program called *Eros* on the Life Network (Todd

1999b). Their relationship to the media and to live audiences highlights the difficulty of performing female masculinity in a heteropatriarchal society. While drag queens are often perceived as "representing" gay male culture in the mainstream media, drag kings are a much less visible and more indirect representation of lesbian culture in the public eye. Other authors have remarked on the "invisibility" of female masculinity and drag kings in contemporary society (Halberstam 1998; Volcano and Halberstam 1999). This invisibility highlights the "actual" gender of the drag king (i.e., the fact that they are women who are performing masculinity). On this theme, Julien makes an important observation: "I think that in our culture if you're making fun of masculinity, it's pretty bold, it's pretty unusual and sometimes we get pretty negative reactions because of that." Interviews with the MDKs further suggest that the invisibility of drag kings may be linked to a public distaste for "butch realness" as described by Halberstam (1998). While images of super models and starlets in male drag have made the pages of leading fashion magazines, few masculine women in drag have been embraced by the mass media. Tommy describes the absence of butch images in mainstream portrayals of male drag:

> I can see this magazine type, taking off her hat to reveal long hair. . . . I think it's just more acceptable, it's just more palatable to see a beautiful woman where the femininity that we look for comes through despite the clothes. It's still acceptable and it's still attractive to men who are seeing this, therefore, it's acceptable. But, the minute the woman loses her femininity in the clothes and then all of a sudden becomes androgynous and people aren't able to figure out or see the femininity or see what they want to see, then it becomes disturbing . . . it crosses almost into the offensive for some people.

Both drag queens and feminine "male impersonators" have received significant media attention precisely because of the centrality of femininity to their performances. As Phil pointed out, "I think it's always been more acceptable to laugh at what's feminine than to laugh at the masculine. . . . I don't think that the world at large is ready for a ridiculization or even an interpretation of masculine. I think it is still very threatening to conceive of a woman borrowing masculinity as an identity." Simply put, Julien states: "In a patriarchal society, it's much easier to make fun of femininity."

KINGS AND QUEENS

Discussing "drag kings" with individuals who are unfamiliar with the term usually requires a long explanation that begins with, "Well, you know what drag queens are, right? Well, drag *kings* are women who dress . . ." This type of comparison can be quite tedious and reduces what kinging involves and represents into a simplistic dichotomy. It seemed vital during the interviews to create a forum in which the MDKs could discuss the uniqueness of kinging, but we did explore the differences between kings and queens as a means of taking the dichotomy apart. According to the interviews, one of the primary differences between kings and queens was the gender that each is performing in a heteropatriarchal society. In a society where femininity is constructed as excess and masculinity as neutral, the two are clearly not parallel. The political and performative elements are very different. First, as Tommy argued, the performance of masculinity involved in kinging is a specific political act:

> I think there is something very acceptable about making fun of women. I say making fun, I can appreciate drag queen shows. I can appreciate the humour in it and I don't necessarily take offense to it but . . . there's always that element. . . . You can poke fun of women, you can make fun of their bod[ies], the way they look the way they speak, it's always been there and I think that's why it's been more accepted, but to impersonate a man? . . . I don't know that that's very entertaining for most people.

As Tommy suggests, the performance of masculinity by women, even when done as a parody, does not have the same effect on the audience. Certainly, North American mainstream society is not only less familiar and less comfortable seeing women claim a masculine subject position, but also less willing to see masculinity be deconstructed and exposed as a performance. This is primarily because of the way in which the attributes of each gender are constructed in heteropatriarchal societies. Performing masculinity, therefore, is not only a different political act, but it also involves the performance of a set of gender attributes that are more restrained and subdued. Phil describes the differences between kings and queens in these terms:

> Drag queens do not imitate women. It's a whole other world. It's a whole other universe of gestures, another language that exists in-

dependently of the feminine reality. . . . With a drag king . . . we practically have to erase our feminine traits and over that create masculine traits that are not exaggerated.

Among MDKs, each person's need to "erase" femininity and "create" masculinity varies. For Phil, whose daily persona is identifiably feminine, the acquisition of "masculine" gestures for a performance requires a conscious removal of one gender identity in order to replace it with another. For others in the group, whose everyday identities integrate more masculinity, the erasure of feminine traits requires less effort. In this case, there is an emphasis on highlighting pre-existing masculine traits.

Perhaps due to the camp nature of drag established by drag queen performers, the MDKs have had lengthy discussions regarding how the performance of masculinity and femininity differ. The asymmetrical relations between masculinity and femininity in heteropatriarchal society mean that masculine and feminine drag are constructed differently. If feminine excess is central to the drag queen's performance, a naturalized masculinity would be its binary opposite. Apart from facial hair, therefore, it is not always apparent what other attributes would emphasize "the man." As Saul explained: "[I]t's complicated because we don't tend to think of masculinity as performed at all; we tend to think of it as neutral and I don't think it is. . . . In fact, I think that our performances prove that masculinity is just as performable and performed as femininity." This is where kinging needs to be recognised as independent from the more visible drag queen. Julien remarks: "I don't think that [kinging] is really camp, but I think that what is important about what we do . . . is that it is exposing that masculinity is constructed. That's the bottom line for me; that's what's interesting about it."

This distinction between the genders has implications for the ways in which the MDKs perform drag and create their pieces. First, the MDKs rarely perform over-the-top kinging. They are a dapper group of guys who have progressively perfected the "realism" (gravitating toward "butch realness") of their facial hair and movements over the years. Secondly, they do not imitate or emulate male performers directly. Instead, they use songs and images to create their own atmosphere during their performances. Their pieces are more reinterpretations than imitations. As Tommy explained,

some of the drag queens here in Montréal, who do Céline Dion for instance, I mean they *do* Céline Dion–from the hair to the way she dresses, to the mannerisms, everything. We don't really take it to that point, it's more than just the person, it's the ambiance that we create. It's about an illusion. It's not about imitating a particular performer.

Tommy lip-syncs to Tom Jones songs, but she does not wear tight, flared, clinging polyester pants, nor does she flaunt heaping curly chest hair or apply a heavy five-o'clock shadow. Instead, she prefers a pair of black tailored wool pants, a white dress shirt (opened at the collar) and takes pride in a simple goatee. She completes her look with a spruce pair of shades. This is how she feels sexy and how she makes the ladies swoon!

The MDKs not only avoid impersonation; their icons are also less established. Icons of masculinity for this group range from hypermasculine to "butch," and from androgynous woman to pretty-boy. The types of "men" that the MDKs identified with were also popular androgynous figures. On a personal level, Félix chooses androgyny as an ideal. She stated, "If I was a man I would be like Johnny Depp. I find he has style, a masculine and feminine side that I like and that I find interesting." When asked who their drag king icons were, Jimmy and Max provided a wide selection of gender identities. Jimmy said, "Elvis, and ah, the Village people–which is funny isn't it? And then personally, my drag king icon, k. d. lang!" Instantaneously, Max jealously exclaimed "I was just going to say that!! . . . but I think in terms of our group, I certainly don't think we have icons . . . in our group we go with more a style of music and the ambiance that surrounds that . . . whether it be something Tom Jones like, or from women too like Dalida." Overall, the MDKs enjoy playing with images of the crooner aesthetic, but have no admiration or emotional link to these figures or any desire to embody their masculine identity.

The difficulty in comparing drag queens and drag kings also stems from the "actual" gender of the performers. While drag queens have certainly posed a challenge to gender systems, "essentialist" feminists have rarely seen them as political figures who are involved in a meaningful deconstruction of gender. Perhaps due to the longstanding relationship between feminism and lesbian politics, there continues to be a tendency among lesbians to idealize kings along essentialist lines. While, on the one hand, they are appropriating masculine values and attributes, they are, on the other hand, seen as the "true gender radicals" because they are "women" challenging a patriarchal gender system by appropriating male power. A dialogue between Max and Jimmy indicates that Max sees kinging as a project that can have feminist implications:

Max: I think different from drag queen culture, drag kings are still women, and if your perspective is, if you're a feminist, lesbian feminist, whatever, and you really truly believe that women are still struggling against the patriarchy, I think this is just one more step in terms of finding a voice, creating subjectivity, I mean, it's challenging gendered systems . . .

Jimmy: Well, why can't we say that drag queen culture challenges gendered systems?

Max: It does challenge gendered systems, but it's still men doing it, and men are still part of the patriarchy.

The practice of appropriating, even momentarily and with some irony, a masculine subject position, however, gives kings a very uncertain ground within feminism. While the queen's performance of "femininity" is often seen as misogynist, the king's is conversely misinterpreted as an idealisation of masculine attributes and patriarchal values. Rather than dismissing either category, however, a comparison of the two requires great sensitivity to the gender relations that make kings and queens (both in and out of drag) very different political identities.

CONCLUSION

At the end of each interview the MDKs were asked how they felt about discussing theoretical ideas surrounding drag king culture. Julien instantly expressed that she was not comfortable doing so because being a part of the MDKs is what she does for pleasure. Zack's motivations for kinging were the opposite. Zack stated that what she enjoyed about kinging was the opportunity to theorize about gender within this project. Although kinging is primarily a social activity for the MDKs, something that these kings do purely for fun, they were extremely articulate when reflecting on its meaning, building connections between theories of gender inversion, camp and female masculinity and personal experience. In part, this was also a result of the interview process. The interviews were conducted by an insider who is close to the group and the making of the film became an integral part of the development of the MDKs over the years. Some said that because of this approach, they were less suspicious of how they would be characterized and more willing to be honest about their feelings.

This chapter has two objectives, both of which have involved "making kings." It describes the creative project of a group of lesbians who formed a drag king performance group. It also describes the process of creating a documentary film that uses the MDKs to understand more broadly the figure of the drag king. The most important result of the chapter, however, is that it provides readers with the perspectives of the performers on what kinging means to them, how it relates to the expression of their sexuality, how they relate to their audiences, and their perceptions of drag queens. The objective has been to highlight the distinctive expression of women doing male drag in a society organized around asymmetrical gender relations. Our broader goal was to make use of these perspectives to highlight the nuances of contemporary gender transformations. We often see these shifts in terms of the "vanguard," drag kings living in centres of artistic expression such as New York and London. In contrast, there is really no drag king "scene" in Montréal. The MDKs perform for a small community-based audience in which they are a queer oddity and a treat. This is why, when the film *Kings* was first shown outside of Montréal, we were unsure of its reception. We were surprised at how well it was received and how often it was solicited for queer festivals and even mainstream media. The response from the media was somewhat unexpected, but not all that surprising since drag kings are considered a novelty for heterosexual curiosities. The response from queer festivals, however, was rather remarkable since we assumed that there would be many more films about drag king performers on the circuit. The response to the film from these quarters seemed to reinforce the fact that images of drag kings are much needed and sought after within the queer community. We hope that the film and this short text can provide more visibility for drag kings, but also images that connect drag kings to the everyday lives of lesbians. We also hope that lesbians elsewhere might see themselves in the MDKs. So many women have approached the MDKs after shows expressing the desire to be drag kings and join the group. There is a strong untapped desire among many lesbians to explore their own masculinity and perform it on stage. We hope that the story of how these women formed the MDKs will reach the drag king in others who have never thought that they could be in the spotlight.

NOTES

1. Since 1998, the primary participants in the MDKs have been Johanne Cadorette (Phil LeRupp), Sarah Gibson (Sailor Saul), Andrea Kwan (Zack Attack), Jeannie Jay (Jimmy), Cindy Mancuso (Tommy Boy), Julie Podmore (Julien St-Urbain), Isabelle Saillard (Félix Le French), and Cathrin Winkelmann (Max A. Million).

from Boudoir

2. The MDKs have worked with three Montréal choreographers: Caroline Boll, Natalie Morin and Mireille Painchaud. Caroline Boll has not only choreographed most of the numbers, she has played a much larger role in the group. While developing numbers with the MDKs, Caroline has coached the group on performance, and helped each individual participant to develop a character and to express their own masculinities through body movements.

3. A survey of *The Drag King Book* (Volcano and Halberstam, 1999) indicates that some other drag king performers do group acts (i.e., The Dodge Bros.) and that kinging often emanates from a network of people or friends that develop their king personae, even in duos. It is more typical, however, for drag king acts to emphasize the individuality of the performers and their characters (i.e., the performers at Club Casanova in Manhattan, New York). In this paper we emphasize the group character of the MDKs because they always perform together and their drag king identities do not really extend beyond this group.

4. *Kings* (1999) has been shown at the following film and video festivals: *The Lux Cinema's Drag King Video Festival*, London, England (June, 1999); *Out on Screen*, Vancouver, Canada (August, 1999); *Image & Nation Gay and Lesbian Film and Video Festival*, Montréal, Canada (September, 1999); *Groupe Intervention Video (GIV) Video Festival*, Montréal, Canada (October, 1999); *herland*, Calgary, Canada (October, 1999); *Centre de production video et photo Daimon*, Hull, Canada (October, 1999); *Lesben Film Festival Berlin*, Berlin, Germany (October, 1999); *Inside Out*, Toronto, Canada (May, 2000).

from Boudoir

"Felix"

"Group Portrait"

"Jimmy"

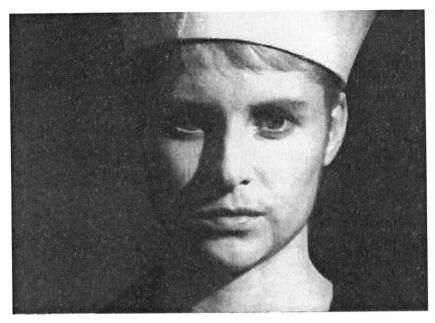

"Saul"

REFERENCES

Ayoup, Colleen. 1999. *Kings*. Montréal. 12:00 Minutes.
_____. 2001. *Kings*. Montréal: Groupe Intervention Vidéo. 21: 39 Minutes.
Fugues. 1998. "Mambo Drag Kings." (Summer).
Todd, Travis. 1999a. Interview with Colleen Ayoup. *CityMag*. Canal Vox. (19 September).
_____. 1999b. Interview with The Mambo Drag Kings. *Eros*. Life Network. (12 November).
Volcano, Del LaGrace and Judith Halberstam. 1999. *The Drag King Book*. London: Serpent's Tail.

Lesbian Drag Kings
and the Feminine Embodiment
of the Masculine

Steven P. Schacht, PhD

Plattsburgh State University of New York

SUMMARY. Part of an ongoing ethnography of an imperial sovereign court I am undertaking, this chapter explores the world of the lesbian drag king and the gendered performance she undertakes in this realm. Taking a relational, situational approach to understanding gender, the lesbian drag queen of the court is also examined in terms of how "her" image and actions give gendered meaning and confer import to the lesbian drag king. Note is also made of lesbian court members' often contradictory gendered relationships with the gay men in this setting: gay drag kings and gay drag kings. Although embodying a masculine persona in image and action has enabled some lesbian drag kings to successfully challenge the often sexist actions and reign of the gay men of the court, it has also resulted in some lesbian drag queens being subordinated in the process. Thus, as much as lesbian drag kings subvert existing gender hierarchies they also sometimes recreate them in the pursuit of situational power. *[Article copies available for a fee from The Haworth Document Delivery Service: 1-800-HAWORTH. E-mail address: <docdelivery@haworthpress.com> Website: <http://www. HaworthPress.com> © 2002 by The Haworth Press, Inc. All rights reserved.]*

[Haworth co-indexing entry note]: "Lesbian Drag Kings and the Feminine Embodiment of the Masculine." Schacht, Steven P. Co-published simultaneously in *Journal of Homosexuality* (Harrington Park Press, an imprint of The Haworth Press, Inc.) Vol. 43, No. 3/4, 2002, pp. 75-98; and: *The Drag King Anthology* (ed: Donna Troka, Kathleen LeBesco, and Jean Bobby Noble) Harrington Park Press, an imprint of The Haworth Press, Inc., 2002, pp. 75-98. Single or multiple copies of this article are available for a fee from The Haworth Document Delivery Service [1-800-HAWORTH, 9:00 a.m. - 5:00 p.m. (EST). E-mail address: docdelivery@haworthpress.com].

KEYWORDS. Lesbian drag king, lesbian drag queen, doing gender, gender as performance, imperial sovereign court, embodiment, masculinity, femininity, gay drag kings, gay drag queens

Similar to numerous fundraisers held throughout the year, tonight is an Emperor and Empress Scholarship Show, sponsored by the Imperial Sovereign Court of Spokane (ISCS). Emceeing the event are two gay drag queens, Tina Louise Sapphire Dior (Empress XXIV), Paige DeMonet Sapphire Rockafellar (Miss Debutante XIX), and myself (somewhat holding the appointed title of "the token straight man of the court" given to me by various members of the setting). Like almost all court shows, performers this evening include an array of gay drag queens, gay drag kings, and lesbian drag queens[1] lip-syncing and performing their favorite songs for tips (typically single dollar bills) with all monies collected being donated to the given fund raiser event ($622 is raised tonight for the ISCS Scholarship Fund). The audience is also made-up of numerous other non-performing gay and lesbian kings and queens with over a dozen straight women and men (all students of mine) also in attendance. Although several spirited performances have already been staged, many eagerly await Donna's number, as she has promised it will be a special one. Prior to all performers taking the stage, one of the emcees announce their entrance, often trying to put an affirming, personal touch on the performer's introduction. Tina announces Donna.

> *Tina:* Ladies and gentlemen, I kind of like bribed, I pleaded, and finally went to the girlfriend for this next number. I said if this girl doesn't sing, you ain't giving it up. . . . So obviously you gave it up. . . . Didn't you?

Lori, Donna's girlfriend–a very feminine and culturally attractive lesbian drag queen–sitting in the audience, and appearing quite embarrassed, sheepishly nods yes.

> *Tina:* Good for you! Ladies and gentlemen, this is a dedication from one lover to another, to Lori from Donna, because she thinks you're cute as a button. And you are! Ladies and gentlemen, please welcome His Imperial Majesty, the Panda Bear Emperor herself . . . please welcome the Baby Butch Emperor, Donna.

Enter Donna to the stage wearing tight fitting Levi jeans, held up by a thick black belt replete with a large buckle, red western shirt with tight fitting black t-shirt underneath (it appears she has taped her breasts), and cowboy boots. Donna, with her short feathered back hair and smaller but muscular frame, in appearance and demeanor, looks more like a well-groomed young man in his early twenties than a grandmother in her late thirties (which she is). A song by a male country artist blares in the background.

Donna: "Love is unconditional . . . you will always be the miracle that makes my life complete." Immediately after lip-syncing a line or two, Donna picks up a dozen red and white roses and brings them to Lori in the audience and additionally gives her a kiss. After returning to the stage, she receives tips from nearly twenty people. When taking the money, instead of dropping her head in deference, like some gay drag kings and lesbian drag queens often do, she looks the given individual right in the eyes, and takes the money out of her/his hand firmly almost like a handshake. Towards the end of her routine, she tosses the money she has collected onto a speaker, turns, stares at Lori and assertively gestures to her with one finger to come up to the stage. She draws her hand down across her lower face, like a man feeling his whiskers, bends down onto one knee, and then pulls Lori up to her to give her a passionate kiss. This, combined with audience members clapping loudly, ends her performance. Thereafter, Donna tips all the remaining performers with Lori as her consummate escort and leaves later that evening with her securely in tow–Lori tightly holding Donna's arm–as they walk out the door.

The immediate response of most societal viewers of this or similar gender bending scenes is one of puzzlement, confusion, and, in extreme cases, anger and hatred.[2] How is it that girls can be boys and boys can be girls so easily? In the hegemony of present dichotomous gender outlooks where seemingly everyone must be male or female, how is it that individuals such as Donna are apparently both yet neither? Why would anyone want to be both a man and a woman? Why do images of butch and femme seemingly appear better together than separately? The court and its multifarious gendered cast offer many suggestive answers to these questions (Schacht 1998).

This chapter examines my ethnographic experiences in the ISCS as a complete participant in the setting.[3] While I have previously written several pieces about the gay drag queens and, to a lesser extent, the gay drag kings of the court (Schacht 2000; in press a & b), this chapter specifically explores lesbian drag kings and their contextual contrast, the lesbian drag queen, as without "her," "he" would have little meaning in this setting.[4] In the section that follows, I review some of the growing body of literature on "doing gender," which promotes the idea that the categories of male and female are largely, if not entirely, social performances, and the few pieces that have been written specifically about drag kings. Special attention will be paid to how the lesbian drag kings of the court both support and contest present understandings of doing male drag. Next, I explore the ISCS and its gendered expectations. The two sections that then follow analyze the lesbian drag king and "his" signifier, the lesbian drag queen. A section follows this that describes a performance number by both lesbian kings and queens that highlights the tenuous basis of the lesbian drag king's superiority in this context. The chapter ends by noting the promise and limits of the transgressive role the lesbian drag king plays in the court and the larger society.

GENDER IMPERSONATION AND THE DRAG KING

Such acts, gestures, enactments, generally construed, are *performative* in the sense that the essence or identity that they otherwise purport to express are *fabrications* manufactured and sustained through corporeal signs and other discursive means. That the gendered body is performative suggests that it has no ontological status apart from the various acts that constitute its reality. (Butler 1990, 136)

And if butchness requires strict opposition to femmeness, is this a refusal of an identification or is that an identification with femmeness that has already been made, made and disavowed, a disavowed identification that sustains the butch, without which the butch qua butch cannot exist? (Butler 1993, 115)

Increasingly, various gender theorists are conceptualizing the social constructs of male and female as nothing more than performances, based on imitative forms of behavior for which there are no original scripts, relationally played out in front of an audience of gendered others (Butler 1990 & 1993; Connell 1995; Garber 1992; Lorber 1994; Schacht 1996; West and Zimmerman 1987). This approach argues that what it means to be a "man" or a "woman" is often best understood in terms of what one is not supposed to be–the "opposite" sex, typically defined by the dominant culture as what one can not be–as "the thou shalt not's" of life are always more powerful than the often far more numerous "thou shall's" in defining social behavior (Schacht 1998). Thus, much of successfully performing being a "real" man is scripted in terms of never acting like a woman (no sissy stuff) while, conversely, being a "real" woman means never acting like a man (no butch stuff).

These relational contrasts of being, of course, have no meaning without social interaction, as it is through the collaboration with gendered others that we come to view and experience ourselves as men and women. The terms "male" and "female" are largely meaningless in and of themselves and can only be fully understood when considered simultaneously. Thus, as much as the saying goes that "behind every successful man is found a good woman," every "good" woman must have a man to be a "successful" woman. The "successful" performance of gender, then, is conceivably always dependent on a relational contrast. As this applies to the topic at hand, to successfully perform being a man means not only undertaking a set of prescribed masculine behaviors, but also having women present (in image or body) to demarcate what one is not (Schacht 1996). As I will demonstrate later in this paper, this performance-based model of gender works well when exploring the world of the lesbian drag king and their gendered contrast, the lesbian drag queen.

Although women have a long and rich past of donning male attire and convincingly passing as men (Thompson 1974; Wheelwright 1989) and the notion of butch women–both lesbian and straight–has received a fair amount of research and theoretical attention (i.e., Dover 1989; Faderman 1991; Gremaux 1994; Nestle 1992) the notion of the drag king is quite recent. While the term "drag queen" has been in circulation for untold years, and is very much part of mainstream society's lexicon, the term "drag king" is not widely used or recognized. In fact, in writing an earlier piece on the court (Schacht 1998) I used the term "drag king" to theoretically conceptualize both gay male and lesbian masculine-appearing personas in the setting, but had never seen it used in any previous literature or context.[5] Finally, in the summer of 1999 I read Judith Halberstam's wonderful book *Female Masculinity* (1998) and was pleased to see her not only using the term as a research construct, but her additionally noting the emergence of the drag king in various club scenes in New York City and San Francisco in the mid-1990s. Although still far from being a common term, as evidenced in this anthology, the drag king appears alive, well, and here to stay.

So what exactly is a drag king? Volcano simply defines a drag king as "Anyone (regardless of gender) who consciously makes a performance out of masculinity" (Halberstam 1999, 16). This definition very much applies to the lesbian drag kings of the court and their gendered activities in the setting (and would also equally apply to the gay drag kings). Halberstam further refines this definition to differentiate between types of drag kings where "a female-identified Drag King will be 'he' onstage and in costume, but 'she' offstage [while] a transgender Drag King will be 'he' on- and offstage" (Volcano and Halberstam 1999, 8). As I will demonstrate shortly, this definition does and does not apply to the lesbian drag kings of the court, as they are more "she-he's" onstage and "she's" offstage, and yet are conspicuously masculine in appearance and demeanor in almost any setting they find themselves. Moreover, although they recognize and treat their drag personas as performances, the consistency of their actual mannerisms and appearances indicate a different form of masculine embodiment and identification than just the terms "he" or "she" represent, regardless of which stage they are on. Thus, as will be demonstrated in later sections of this paper, defining who and what a drag king is, is probably a far more complicated enterprise than just the simple terms "he" and "she" suggest.

AN IMPERIAL LAND OF KINGS AND QUEENS

The ISCS is one of 57 imperial court chapters located throughout North America (and now England) that make up the Imperial Court System (recently renamed the International Court System). The Imperial Court System (ICS) was founded by gay activist Jose Sarria in 1965.[6] As such, the ICS is one of the first (and oldest) formally established gay, lesbian, bisexual, and transgendered (glbt) grassroots activist groups in the world. The ISCS itself has existed for over 25 years, and is reported to be the second oldest ICS chapter in the Pacific/Inland Northwest, and the first gay, lesbian, or transgendered organization in Spokane. The stated purpose of the ISCS, as written in its detailed and rather extensive by-laws (that are quite similar to those of other ICS chapters), is to function as a "non-profit charitable organization . . . for the common good and general welfare of the Gay community, friends and residents of Spokane and the Inland Northwest, and the United States of America." Accordingly, shows sponsored by the group during fiscal year 1995/96 raised over $35,000 for various local AIDS-related community groups; i.e., Children With AIDS, The Spokane AIDS Network, and The Inland Northwest AIDS Coalition. The court also maintains a Disaster Fund from which members can draw limited monies

($100) for medical or personal emergencies. Reflecting the ISCS's charitable commitment to the larger community, the group annually raises money (over $2000 during fall of 1997) for and personally distributes Thanksgiving and Christmas baskets of food for low-income people in Spokane. It also awards three to four $500 to $750 college scholarships to needy individuals at the yearly coronation ball. Members of the court, the larger gay community, and residents of Spokane are all eligible to receive food baskets and scholarships. Thus, the group's activism is directed both towards issues largely specific to the group and social problems experienced throughout the community.

While the court's contributions to the local gay and larger straight community are quite notable, the charitable emphasis of the group perhaps provides an even more important service to its members. In a society that often tries to oppressively deny the existence of gay and lesbian individuals, the ISCS serves as a structural arrangement that bestows upon its members feelings of respectability, affiliation, affirmation, friendship, and in some cases, experiences of interpersonal power. One of the formal ways in which this is accomplished is through elected and appointed official titles (i.e., empress and princess, princess and prince) that confer significant group status. Since only a limited number of people can be titleholders at any given time, beyond group membership, formal affiliation is also made available through the use of "family" last names. For instance, there are over 125 Kennady Smith's on the West Coast with a gay drag king named Eunice being the matriarch of the family. In total, the court provides almost exclusively gay and lesbian members an established, formal yet quite affirming venue and safe haven for publicly "coming out,"[7] a place where significant friendships and "families" are constructed and nurtured, and ultimately a context where gay and lesbian identities are normalized and celebrated (Troiden 1988; Herdt 1991; Murray 1991; Nardi 1992; Kaufman and Raphael 1996; Weston 1997).

In the ISCS, like all the courts I am familiar with, the gay drag queens are seen as the group's best performers and its rightful leaders.[8] In the role of reigning or past empress, the queens of court are responsible for the planning of all sponsored shows, with the best emceeing these events. While they take center stage, gay drag kings play a supportive, often behind-the-scenes role. Serving as dressers (personal attendants who help their chosen queen change outfits), seamstresses (doing almost all the beadwork and sewing of gowns), stage-hands (responsible for the assembling and taking down of stages for more extravagant events), and escorts (almost like a prop) when tipping other performers, in both image and behavior (albeit inverse to the dominant culture), gay drag kings are very much the drag queens' subordinates.

While the lesbian drag kings of the court also play similar supportive, secondary roles in the setting, such as stagehands and escorts, as will be demonstrated, they are far more likely to contest the drag queens' otherwise omnipotent contextual power. Part of this may be a function of the increasing numbers of lesbians, proportionately speaking, involved in the group's activities. Due to many gay men of the court dying from AIDS in previous years, their numerical losses have largely been made up with lesbians, especially lesbian drag kings. Thus, while at one time gay drag queens were estimated to make up over fifty percent of the group's membership, today they barely account for one third of the group's members, with lesbians as a group now making up nearly fifty percent of the court's ranks. I believe much of the lesbian drag kings' contesting of power, however, has to do with their embodiment of masculine outlook and their according perceptions of what sorts of relationships are appropriate: superior to others and certainly not subordinate to anyone, even though they often are treated this way by gay men, especially gay drag queens.

THE LESBIAN DRAG KING AND "HIS" TETRARCH

Lesbians now constitute nearly fifty percent of the active membership of the court. In their actions and presentation of self, the vast majority of these participants (close to seventy-five percent) I consider lesbian drag kings. Similar to the gay drag kings, who often appear as some gay macho clone (Levine 1998), lesbian drag kings have adopted very masculine-appearing styles of dress and personal mannerisms. Short, feathered back hair is by far the most frequent hairstyle sported. Apparently seen as more appropriate for the queens, both gay and lesbian, no makeup of any sort is used by the kings. The most typical attire for informal occasions includes blue jeans, cowboy boots, leather pants and jackets, and tight fitting western shirts. For more important functions, like the "men" of the court, lesbian drag kings don tuxedos (often covered in beads or rhinestones) and other formal male attire. From just their appearance, one could easily mistake several of them to be "real" men if one was not told otherwise.

Lesbian drag kings also carry themselves and act in a stereotypically masculine fashion. Broad, almost swaggering, steps are taken when walking, legs are never crossed but instead comfortably spread apart when seated, and by far the most popular beverage is a beer drunk out of a long-neck bottle. Most speak in a deeper, more authoritative voice. Often with their lesbian drag queen girlfriends in tow or on their arms, they very much act like "the man" with their partners. Most songs selected for their lip-syncing routines are from male (often country) and lesbian singers (such as Melissa Etheridge) and are performed with obvious masculine gesture. In general, both performing or simply interacting in the context, they very much exude an unfaltering type of confidence—sometimes almost cockiness—that is most frequently associated with men in the dominant culture. The description of Donna's performance at the beginning of this paper is quite prototypical of lesbian drag kings in both appearance and demeanor.

Most, if not all of these lesbians also "wear" their masculine appearance and demeanor in other public contexts. This is very different from the gay drag queens who only appear as women for shows. Of course, the gay drag kings also wear masculine attire outside of the court setting, but as I have reported previously (Schacht 2002), their mannerisms often change and become quite effeminate (some appearing like the stereotypical limp-wristed gay man) whereas the lesbian drag kings are quite consistent with their masculine presentation of self. Also unlike the gay drag queens, who make up names for their female personas, lesbian drag kings, onstage and offstage, always go by their given female names. Finally, it is worth making note that, while almost all the gay drag kings have mustaches (typically quite thick) or short, well-groomed beards, and dissimilar to drag kings reported elsewhere (Volcano and Halberstam 1999), I have never seen a lesbian drag king in the court setting ever appear with any facial hair.

Seven of the past twenty-four emperors have been lesbian drag kings and several have also held lesser "male" titles (such as Prince and Mr. Wrangler) in the court. As such, in both appearance and status, lesbian drag kings, like the "men" of the court, also fulfill the function of being relational signifiers of the gay drag queens (Schacht 2000; 2002). And while they are not as fully immersed in this role in the sense that they do not serve as dressers or sew outfits, lesbian drag kings are still expected to escort gay drag queens to tip other performers and also are responsible for an array of behind-the-scenes activities (such as building stages, selling raffle tickets, or being door attendants) for which very little formal recognition is given.

Unlike the gay drag kings, however, who are after all gay men, lesbian drag kings (and lesbians in general) often are treated in quite sexist, sometimes even outright misogynist ways. Perhaps like gay men in general (Miles and Roffes 1998), many men of the court hold a strong "ick" outlook on anything associated with lesbian sexuality or "real" women's bodies. This repulsion often is used as a reason for the lesbians' second-class treatment by the gay men of the court. For instance, during one conversation I was having with a couple of men about what a "bitch" the bar owner Sharon is (their viewpoint, not mine), one of them gleefully recounted how he had once witnessed her have her period and "bleed like a pig" right through her white jeans for all in the bar to see. On another occasion, during a fund raiser for a former emperor, Carla, held to cover some of her expenses for breast cancer treatment (although $4000 was raised, she has since passed away), many of the gay men expressed their displeasure at the stage and bar being taken over by lesbians. Moreover, this is the only show I have ever attended where lesbian energy far outweighed the typical gay male energy present. Constant eye rolls and comments about too many "smelly fish" being present were repeated throughout the show. As will be discussed in the below descriptions of three lesbian drag kings, many of these attempts at subordination by the gay men are contested, with varying degrees of success, and have resulted in the creation of a lesbian tetrarch of sorts within the larger court context.

Donna

In many ways, Donna could be considered the quintessential lesbian drag king of the ISCS. As described at the beginning of the paper, she is quite boyishly masculine in appearance and demeanor both inside and outside of the court setting. Donna is a grandmother in her late thirties and has a good paying job as a car detailer for an employer who is quite supportive about her being an open lesbian and her court activities. Until very recently, she was involved with Lori (to be described below) who is a lesbian drag queen; they were once considered one of the ideal couples of the group. She has been active in the court for over ten years and twice held the title of emperor. Accordingly, her official title is "His Most Imperial Sovereign Majesty, The Double Crowned Silver Panda Bear Emperor XXI [and XV] Baby Butch, Donna."

Her title also very much reflects her ambivalent feelings about her gendered outlook. On one hand, she very much enjoys holding the title of emperor, replete with its "his most sovereign majesty" status, as it is symbolic of her high standing in the court. In both image and gesture, her well-groomed look is very befitting of the lofty masculine title she holds. On the other hand, Donna entirely thinks of herself as a lesbian woman. Or, as she stated to me, "It feels right to hold the emperor title. I'm not one of those drag queens who insists on being called 'she.' I'm a lesbian woman and a she." In a sense, like the next two lesbian drag kings to be discussed, I believe Donna's gendered embodiment is that of a she-man—she very much thinks of herself as a woman yet convincingly appears and acts in a decidedly masculine manner. Stated slightly differently, Donna is undertaking a form of the feminine embodiment of the masculine.

A self-identified woman who embodies a masculine outlook often takes a transgressive approach to the world. Unlike traditional images of women, the lesbian drag king is a woman who is not going to take shit from anyone, someone who is always going to give her opinion on matters, whether asked or not, and in extreme cases, kick your ass if you get in her way. In other words, "I am a lesbian woman, proud of it, and do not ever cross me or I will put you in your place." In a context where the gay drag queens reign supreme, as one might guess, this often leads to the lesbian drag kings challenging the court leadership, and inevitable conflict results. Sometimes this is accomplished through subtle actions, like Donna often refusing to call various queens "she" or by their "girl" names. Other times it is done in a more confrontational manner, like one time Donna nearly getting into a physical fight with one of the gay drag queens (both were thankfully restrained before anyone could get hurt), threatening to not only "kick 'his' ass," but saying "I wish you all would just die from AIDS."

In fact, because of obvious subversive actions such as these on Donna's part, she was arrested during the Gay Spokane Dinner awards one year (1997) in front of all present that evening. It was rumored that one of the more powerful queens in the court had conspired with another lesbian drag king and had a criminal background check done on Donna where they discovered an outstanding warrant from years before.[9] The very public arrest was supposed to embarrass Donna in hopes that she would then resign from the court. As one might expect of a lesbian drag king, however, she did not resign as reigning emperor and instead undertook further actions—convincingly donning drag queen attire during one show as if to mock the queens—to undermine certain gay drag queens' authority in the court. In the end, the conflict was resolved with some of the involved parties becoming friends with Donna (in my viewpoint, as a way to coopt her growing power in the court with her becoming a lieutenant of sorts to a powerful gay drag queen). Regardless, I can personally say that Donna is one individual who I would never want to wrong or have angry at me.

Virginia Bixler Kennady Smith

Virginia has been involved in the court for nearly 10 years and is a former emperor titleholder (XVII). She lives with her partner Kari (a lesbian drag queen described below), Kari's teenage son, and her own mother. Virginia is in her late 30s and a successful lawyer who has started her own firm. In contrast to the boyish muscularity of Donna, Virginia looks more like a gay "bear," minus the possible facial hair (Kelly and Kane 1998). With short, cropped hair, large framed glasses, and always wearing masculine-appearing pants and shirts (for court shows she almost always wears a tuxedo), she very much looks like a slightly overweight but nevertheless well-groomed businessman. Her accordant mannerisms are decidedly masculine but softer than the almost hyper-masculine gesture of some other lesbian drag kings. She almost seems "daddy" like, as she always comes across as kind and understanding but confident that she knows what is best for everyone and is ultimately in control of the situation. It is more than apparent that she enjoys playing the role of former emperor, with all its masculine trappings, but she is still very much a self-identified lesbian woman.

Prior to Virginia (and Kari) largely withdrawing from court activities in 1998 (and now being only marginally involved in the group),[10] she wielded considerable influence in the ISCS. While assuredly some of this might have been because of her outside professional standing, much of her power was the result of aligning herself with one of the more powerful gay drag queens of the court (and like Donna, becoming a lieutenant). This allowed her to oversee most of the activities of the lesbians of the group, and on occasion, even challenge some of the gay men of the court. Although never officially stated as such, under the tutelage of a particular gay drag queen, Virginia at one time was one of the most powerful lesbians of the realm. Her masculine image and demeanor were quite consistent with her lofty station in the group.

Sharon Wilson

In her late 40s, and very much appearing like the stereotypical older butch lesbian; i.e., short hair, no make-up, and always wearing masculine-appearing attire which is often quite casual (t-shirts and jeans), Sharon is without question the most powerful lesbian in this context. She has been involved with the court almost since its founding, is a past emperor (III), and is the first woman to hold an elected title in the ISCS. On the rare occasion that she performs at a court function, she always dons a tuxedo or leather pants and a vest. Although her past contributions as a court member are significant, the majority of her power comes from the fact that she owns the bar, Pumps II,[11] where almost all of the court's functions except the coronation ball are held.[12] As she ultimately decides when (both days and hour) shows will be held in the bar, this has caused considerable conflict with various court members (especially gay drag queens) over the years.

In recent years she has decided to try to limit the number of court fundraisers to one Friday or Saturday night a month, as she feels holding more shows than this hurts her business (in particular, the growing numbers of lesbians who frequent her bar). She does allow for shows to be held nearly any other night of the week, makes exceptions for annual events that involve using the bar on multiple nights (e.g., coronation weekend, in-town and out-of-town shows, and the Gay Spokane Pageant), and her bar is where monthly court meetings are held. Nevertheless, I have listened to many of the gay men of the court vehemently complain that "she is nothing more than a bitch who hates gay men," "she is trying to make Pumps an exclusively lesbian bar," and "she is trying to put the court out of business." Threats have been made to move the court to one of the other two gay bars in Spokane, both of which are ill-equipped to hold big court shows like Pumps II does. While Sharon has been able to significantly increase the number of lesbian patrons coming to Pumps, she is still dependent on court members for their business, as some of the bigger annual events draw extremely large crowds, often with many other out-of-town courts in attendance. Thus, a tenuous relationship exists between her and the court with neither party appearing too much like the other but each knowing that their existence is dependent on the other.[13]

However, as Sharon is typically only marginally involved (or interested, as best I can tell) in the court's activities; other than when shows will be held, she really does not exercise any other power in the group. As long as she stays in the back bar area with her other older lesbian friends, beyond a cordial "hello" or short visit, she is largely ignored by most of the gay men. Conversely, as long as the court continues to bring in paying customers, they will be welcomed on her terms. These "terms" have and potentially will continue to challenge the gay drag queens' otherwise nearly omnipotent power in the court context.

Lesbian Tetrarchs

Several lesbian drag kings of the court have developed strategies to challenge the gay drag queens' (and gay drag kings' to a lesser extent) authority in the setting and/or to thwart unreasonable demands or subordinating actions by the gay men in general. To successfully do this often means that they must employ masculine power tactics, which results in their exercising authority in the setting themselves. For Donna, this is found in her "don't mess with me or I will beat your ass" outlook. Virginia was able to exercise power in the setting by aligning herself with existing male authority, while Sharon invoked economic power–"I own the bar." Their approaches to doing power are quite consistent with the masculine images they have created and nurtured in the court setting.

Masculine image and demeanor alone, however, are insufficient for doing male power. Masculinity always demands that there are dominants and subordinates, as doing superiority is impossible without someone being subordinated in the process (Stoltenberg 1998). In a very real sense, the number of subordinates a given superior has is a direct measure of her/his power. Thus, as one would expect, Donna, Virginia, and Sharon all have (or had) significant followings in the context. There are several lesbians and a few disenfranchised gay drag queens in the court who are vehement Donna supporters. Virginia had the support of several lesbians and the blessings of a powerful gay drag queen. Sharon, the most powerful of the three, has scores of lesbian friends and bar patrons, many who resent court shows being held on their night out, who will come to her support at a moment's notice. These subordinates are expected and do support their given leader whenever conflicts arise with the gay men of the court. Thus, much of a lesbian drag king's power comes from their subordinate rulership–their tetrarch–of other lesbians. Without it, the lesbians would be almost powerless in dealing with the gay men of the court.

For a lesbian drag king's image to ultimately be complete, however, similar to the successful businessman's wife, a contrasting image of feminine beauty must be present to fully attest to "his" standing and import: the "prettier" this feminine image is, the "realer" the masculine becomes. Like Donna's performance description offered at the beginning of this chapter, the following section on the lesbian drag queens starts with a description of Kari's (Virginia's partner) performance at this same show.

MY FAIR LADY

Tina: This next performer has done an absolutely incredible, incredible job in my book. Ah, she only asked me one thing when I asked her to be Crown Princess, and that's we become friends. And we have gone way beyond that. I consider this person to be my confidant and I absolutely love her. She has something she wants me to read.

Tina picks up a card previously written by Kari from the podium and begins to read it.

Tina: I want to thank everyone for coming to last weekend's show. I am going to do a song I got cookie dough on.

Tina has started to have a puzzled look on her face, but then smiles, and puts down the card and continues.

Tina: Oh, last weekend she wanted to do this number but got cookie dough on it. And she got it off. Thank god Kari.

Carrie is known for distributing her homemade chocolate cookies to appreciative court members prior to shows. Tina picks up card and resumes reading it.

Tina: Rick [a male who is the reigning Crown Prince], I'm glad you are here. This song's for you. Love you. Ladies and gentlemen, please welcome Her Most Imperial Crown Princess . . . Ladies and gentlemen, Kari Bixler Kennady Smith.

Enter Kari to the stage wearing a black satin sequined gown, black boa, black high heels, and a sparkling necklace and matching dangling earrings. Her back-combed hair is done-up into a loose bun on top of her head with ringlets hanging on the sides of her face. She also has bright red nails and lipstick on, combined with noticeable eye shadow and base makeup. In the background a song by a female performer is being played.

Kari: "I believe in love . . . I believe in dreamers . . . I believe in mom and dad . . . I believe in miracles . . . And I believe in you."

Frequently sashaying back and forth and tipping head from side-to-side, she lip-syncs the words to this song in a feminine manner very similar to how a gay drag queen might perform it. When taking tips from audience members she curtseys and bows her head, with eyes down turned, in apparent deference. She ends her performance by looking into the video recorder, smiling, and rolling her eyes in a seemingly cutesy fashion.

Feminine-appearing lesbians in this context are somewhat of a rarity. Most lesbian drag queens are partners of prominent lesbian drag kings, few perform (most just attend shows to support their partners), and only a handful have ever held court titles: (two princesses, one enchantress, and a couple of lesser titles). Their corresponding influence on the court's activities is extremely limited. I would speculate that this is partially the result of only the gay drag queens being seen as the rightful heirs to images of traditional (and quite sexist) feminine beauty in this context; e.g., skinny but shapely legs and torsos combined with large (albeit fake) breasts and round (often padded) hips. Ironically, in both the court and other drag settings, many men's bodies often seem better suited for realizing these idealized and quite sexist standards of feminine beauty. As this is the real estate upon which they exercise power, they are quite protective over whom they will allow on their turf.[14]

Nevertheless, lesbian drag queens also subscribe to conservative ideals of feminine beauty in that they tend to have longer often permed hair and paint their nails; wear make-up, dresses and gowns, and high heels; speak in higher pitch voices; and sit, walk, and in general carry themselves in a "ladylike" manner. As reflected in Kari's description, using songs by female recording artists, their lip-sync performances–always using songs by female recording artists and hyper-feminine gesture–often tend to be quite similar to those staged by gay drag queens. The following descriptions of Kari and Lori are offered to further highlight the gendered roles that lesbian drag queens play in the context of the court.

Kari Bixler Kennady Smith

In her mid-30s, Kari has been involved in the court for nearly 10 years. She has held the appointed Crown Princess title and holds the Enchantress VIII title (the latter gives her voting privileges in the College of Monarchs and is a status just below that of empress and emperor). Although sometimes employed as a part-time nurse's aide, with her partner's financial means, she is able to be largely a stay-at-home mom caring for her son and Virginia's aging mother. In some ways, she could be viewed as the quintessential housewife of a bygone era in both image and family role.

As already noted, Kari's image is decidedly feminine. This is true in both the context of the court and all other public settings. Regardless of the occasion, whenever I have seen Kari in public settings she always has carefully applied makeup, nicely done hair, always wears notice-ably feminine attire, and is conspicuously hyper-feminine in demeanor. Moreover, she very much plays the traditional feminine role of perpet-ual supporter and helper not only to her partner, but also to many of the gay men in the court. This has earned her many appreciative friends. As reflected in the description above, much of this appreciation is ex-pressed for the subordinating role she plays in relation to others: Kari was Tina's appointed Crown Princess.

In sum, like Lori discussed next, and once again unlike the gay drag queens, there is an obvious consistency to Kari's femininity. She is the consummate and well-liked (especially by the gay men of the court) supporter, helper, and subordinate. In image and activity, she props up the significance and import not only of her partner, Virginia, but also of other "superiors" in the court.

Lori Olson Lake Kennady Smith

In her late 20s, Lori is a newcomer to the court. She was largely intro-duced to the ISCS activities through her partner, Donna, who was at the time (1996-97) holding the title of emperor for the second time. Lori is a very culturally attractive woman, and a definite "catch" for any lesbian drag king (or straight man, for that matter). Regardless of the setting, Lori's hair and make-up are always meticulously done while her clothes, typically designer labels, are very feminine. During the early days of her court participation she was often quite shy and appeared to try to be inconspicuous in the setting. Over time, and perhaps as a result of supporting Donna through the aforementioned conflict, she very much subsumed a place in the court and was subsequently appointed a Crown Princess.

What is perhaps truly unique about Lori is that in her image at least, she can compete with many of the drag queens over who is fair-est-in-the-land. At formal court functions her tight-fitting designer gowns are comparable to those worn by the gay drag queens, and once appointed Crown Princess, she always seemed to wear her tiara and other sparkling accoutrements to all shows. Once the above discussed Donna conflict was resolved, she too became friends with one of the most powerful gay drag queens in the setting, and as a result, I would speculate her otherwise unacceptable image was tolerated by others in the court.[15]

While Lori embraced her esteemed role in the court–in a sense, al-most starting to truly act like one of the gay drag queens–this eventually created conflict in her relationship with Donna. Moreover, Lori had a good-paying job at the local power company and, thus, was not financially dependent upon Donna. This past year Lori and Donna broke up and Lori has since moved to Seattle. Perhaps not that surprising, Donna's power in the court is reported to have diminished significantly since then. Early signs of this can be seen at Lori's Crown Princess Presentation (performance) at the 1998 coronation. I have included this last description of the setting as I believe it highlights recognized power dynamics in the group and just how tenuous they can be between the lesbians of the court.

The Lesbian Drag Queens Strike Back: A Tenuous Inequality

Three couples of lesbian drag queens and lesbian drag kings (one of each in each couple) slowly dance to the pleasant ballroom sounding music in the background. This image of harmony is quickly shattered as a new song begins. The three lesbian drag queens abruptly break away from their respective partners, take center stage, and in an alternating fashion, start to lip-sync the following verses.

> *Song Verses:* Don't tell me what to do. Don't tell me what to say. And when I go out with you, don't put me on display. You don't own me. You don't own me. You don't own me [the last three verses are lip-synced as a chorus by all three]. (*You Don't Own Me*, 1964, words and music by John Madara and David White)

While all three of the lesbian drag queens in this number are to a certain extent their usual feminine selves in appearance, and Lori is even wearing her tiara, they are also wearing leather pants and vests, and in a sense, usurping the typical attire worn by kings of the court. The three lesbian drag kings are all wearing jeans, baseball caps, and t-shirts. Donna and another lesbian drag king's t-shirts have in bold letters the following message, SHE-MEN, WOMENHATERS, which can be easily seen by all present. After a few verses of the above song, the three lesbian drag queens return to their partners and escort them off the stage to a table in the audience. Their performance of the above song continues for several more minutes. Once the song ends and they have left the stage, the three lesbian drag kings quickly retake the stage and start taking bows for the laughing and applauding audience.

While this number was obviously staged by six willing participants (and previously practiced) who were all having fun, it also illuminates the tenuous inequality that exists between the lesbian drag kings and their queens. In masculine image and demeanor, the lesbian drag kings often attempt to commandeer a position of superiority over their partners. Thus, while lesbian drag kings are often held in high regard for using their masculinity to fend off the subordinating actions of some of the gay men, when this same interpersonal way of being is applied to their lesbian drag queen partners, it often is resented and challenged. It is ironic that, like the lesbian drag kings, the lesbian drag queens in this number themselves borrowed images of masculinity—leather pants and vests—in an attempt to subvert a preexisting masculine form of power being exercised.

THE TRANSGRESSIVE POSSIBILITIES AND LIMITS OF THE LESBIAN DRAG KING

Drag king performances, however, provide some lesbian performers (although all drag kings are by no means lesbians) with the rare opportunity to expose the artificiality of all genders and all sexual orientations and therefore to answer the charge of inauthenticity that is usually made about lesbian identity. (Halberstam 1998, 240)

In this sense, it is important to note that it is the lesbian *phallus* and not the *penis* that is considered here. For what is needed is not a new body part, as it were, but a displacement of the hegemonic symbolic of (heterosexist) sexual difference and the critical release of alternative imaginary schemas for constituting sites of erotogenic pleasure. (Butler 1993, 91–emphasis in the original)

While the court always tries to maintain a public image of solidarity, veiled beneath this collective portrayal of oneness is a setting where conflicts over who will and will not exercise power in the group frequently occur. In some ways, the court is like a family (replete with shared last names) where brothers and sisters fight, and although some of the battles can be ruthless, there is still a strong sense that she might be a lesbian (or gay man) but should an outsider fuck with them, everyone will be in your face. Spatial boundaries such as this—outsiders versus insiders—very much demonstrate the court to be a community; a safe haven of sorts where gay and lesbian individuals can "come out" and such identities are honored and celebrated (Murray 1991).

Nevertheless, much of the conflict within the court is the result of the gendered roles various parties play and the prescribed behavior individual actors perceive to be affiliated with such statuses. The lesbian drag king uses images and actions associated with the masculine to challenge attempts of subordination by the gay men (especially gay drag queens) of the court. Without question, when a given lesbian drag king is successful in exercising masculine power against the gay men of the court, in both image and action, male power is revealed to be nothing more than a farcical performance that really anyone can undertake. This, per se, is obviously quite transgressive.

As I have written elsewhere (Schacht 2000; 2002), however, the gay drag queens also successfully demonstrate being a "woman" as nothing more than a performance, yet I have concluded that their actions are far more customary than subversive, as they are still men using women (images of them applied to themselves) to exercise male power over subordinated others. As a result, the gay drag queens most typically try to do power over others. Obviously lesbian drag kings also try to exercise power over other lesbians but to effectively challenge the authority of gay men calls for a different approach to doing power. Stated in slightly different terms, for one to successfully exercise masculine authority, others must be continually subordinated in the process while to successfully challenge masculine authority (power-over), parties must join together. Thus, as already noted, external, power-over threats to the court are met with a united "us," power-with response, while internal conflicts involve a whole different set of "us" and "them" outlooks and corresponding "with" versus "over" ways of doing power called for.

Unfortunately, much of the lesbian drag king's power, in both image and practice, is predicated in other lesbian women's subordination (and sometimes even that of gay men). Yes, the lesbian drag king sometimes does do power-with other lesbian women, as cooperative efforts are always necessary to challenge existing authority. Yet the most successful still utilize their lesbian drag queen partners as a prop to attest to the import of their masculine image. Like Virginia and Donna, once power is realized (sometimes as lieutenants of sorts to the more powerful gay drag kings) they seem to become more disposed to using it to subordinate others. As evidenced by Lori's princess performance, some of the lesbian drag queens resent and challenge the lesbian drag kings authority (although they, too, appear to be using images of masculinity to this end). Thus, in the final analysis, while I very much respect and applaud the courage and prowess of the lesbian drag king, it truly saddens me that it appears that sometimes the only way that the oppressed can experience affirmation, status and esteem in the hegemony of our present hierarchal society is by finding someone else–another group in the matrices of categorical inequality–to oppress.

Despite the seriousness of the roles gay drag queens and lesbian drag kings earnestly play, there is still a mocking, sometimes campy, basis to their performances. As previously discussed, the gay men often make fun of the lesbians, and although I have been less privy to their comments, lesbians frequently make fun of the gay men. The difference between these otherwise similar utterances is that one kind reifies women's subordination, whereas the latter type questions male dominance. Insomuch as the lesbian drag king is making light of the artificialness of masculinity and questioning men's perceived superiority, they are very much subversive, transgressive agents of gender.

NOTES

1. This conceptual framework of types of drag in this context is more fully discussed in Schacht (1998). Some descriptions of the lesbian drag kings and lesbian drag queens in this chapter are taken from this earlier piece. Parts of the "setting" section and my endnoted (#3) role in it are taken from Schacht (2000).

2. In many of my classes I have shown a video recording of this very night's activities, and these have all been very typical responses, the more angry ones often directed at Donna's performance in particular.

3. I have been involved in the ISCS since 1994. My most active involvement in the group was from 1995-96 when I was a core member of the group. My specific participation in the ISCS has been in the form of emceeing a show for the group, performing in over 30 shows as a male (and once, during an annual event called Turnabout, in female drag) attending over seventy-five different shows and ten monthly court meetings, serving as a dresser and attendant to various gay drag queens during many shows, and walking with the court at several out-of-town coronations and balls. My participation was further augmented by my spouse (at the time) and I holding and attending numerous parties, dinner parties, meals out, and nearly daily telephone conversations with core members of the court. We were also responsible for bringing nearly two hundred different students and other straight and gay friends to various court events. While it took nearly a year to establish the necessary rapport to become fully immersed and accepted in the setting, from a period of October 1995 to October 1996, I spent anywhere from 10 to 40 hours per week with various court members. This resulted in several hundred pages of field notes (taken after shows and interacting with court members), one five-hour, tape-recorded depth interview, dozens of written documents distributed at various court functions, over 400 photographs of participants, and nearly 50 hours of videotape taken at shows. Thus, the ethnographic observations offered in this paper are based upon a confluence of personal experiences, snapshots, tape and video recordings, and written documents generated by the group.

4. My initial research focus in the court was largely directed at the gay drag queens and, to a lesser extent, the gay drag kings. This limiting focus is very much found in my early field notes, and given the often androcentric focus of the group, also reflected in the videotapes given to me, as notwithstanding coronation, I have found that performances by lesbians often have been omitted on these recordings. Nevertheless, over time I did grow close to several lesbians in the group, and towards the end of my most active involvement in the court (1996-97), increasingly started (and have continued) to take notes about their activities in the group and the various sentiments they have personally shared with me. In sum, I feel fortunate that I was able to overcome my own shortsightedness and start to recognize and appreciate the important activities of the lesbians of the court. Hopefully this paper is one way to start to make up for this early bias on my part.

5. My usage of the term drag king was an attempt on my part to come up with an equivalent category to the drag queens in the court setting, and in no way reflects the argot of the setting, as members of the ISCS use gendered titles–empress/emperor, princess/prince, etc.–to designate the gender persona of the given individual.

6. For a wonderful biography about Jose Sarria, see Michael R Gorman's (1998) *The Empress Is a Man: Stories from the Life of Jose Sarria.* Unfortunately, this text only has a very limited discussion of the ISC and, beyond newspaper articles, is the only published source I have found that even discusses the court system and its variously gendered participants.

7. Performing for the first time and holding a title are often framed as "rites of passage" in the court. For a more detailed discussion of the importance of "rites of passage" in lgbt communities see Herdt (1991).

8. For more detailed discussions of how the gay drag queens create positions of authority and exercise masculine power in the court, see Schacht (2000; 2002).

9. Although I could name people's names here, beyond the rumors that circulated thereafter, I have no way of proving this statement. Moreover, as I have various court members read everything that I write about the setting, I do not want to rekindle old battles.

10. When she left the court she sold many of her beaded jackets and tuxedos to several gay drag kings, all of whom were quite happy to have her expensive and handsomely attractive attire as their own.

11. Pumps II is a very clean, well-kept bar and restaurant with a large stage made for performers and people wishing to dance, an expensive lightening and sound system replete with a DJ booth, a large backroom that can serve as a dressing room, and patio out back used by many in the summer months.

12. Prior to 1995, she owned another somewhat run down bar called Pumps where most court functions were also held.

13. Most of the conflict between Sharon and the court is kept behind-the-scenes, while in more public settings, an image of partnership is maintained. The more public the setting, the more cozy this relationship appears. Thus, at large yearly events, such as coronation, where many out-of-town guests will be in attendance, many awards are bestowed upon Sharon and Pumps II for their continued support of the court and, in return, she makes sure all the right people are tipped and always has the staff at Pumps II put on some fun production number in honor of the court.

14. In all drag contexts that I have been involved in where gay drag queens perform, societally attractive "real girls," whether lesbian or straight, are frequently made to feel unwelcome, and in extreme cases, treated in a belittling misogynist manner. For a more detailed discussion, see Schacht (2002).

15. Several court members during this time privately expressed to me their negative feelings about Lori's appointment as Princess and the subsequent role she came to play in the court. As I was largely absent from the setting, and most of this information was given to me via e-mail, I think it is best to speculate here and not try to offer any definitive explanations.

REFERENCES

Butler, Judith. 1990. *Gender Trouble: Feminism and the Subversion of Identity*. New York: Routledge.

_____. 1993. *Bodies That Matter: On the Discursive Limits of "Sex."* New York: Routledge.

Connell, R.W. 1995. *Masculinities*. Berkeley: University of California Press.

Dover, Holly. 1989. *Gender Blending: Confronting the Limits of Duality*. Bloomington: Indiana University Press.

Faderman, Lillian. 1991. *Odd Girls and Twilight Lovers: A History of Lesbian Life in Twentieth Century America*. New York: Columbia University Press.

Garber, Marjorie. 1992. *Vested Interests: Cross-Dressing & Cultural Anxiety*. New York: Routledge.

Gorman, Michael R. 1998. *The Empress Is a Man: Stories from the Life of Jose Sarria*. New York: Harrington Park Press.

Gremaux, Rene. 1994. "Woman Becomes Man in the Balkans." Pp. 241-281 in *Third Sex, Third Gender: Beyond Sexual Dimorphism in Culture and History*, ed. Gilbert Herdt. New York: Zone Books.

Halberstam, Judith. 1998. *Female Masculinity*. Durham: Duke University Press.

Herdt, Gilbert. 1991. " 'Coming Out' as a Rite of Passage: A Chicago Study." Pp. 29-67 in *Gay Culture in America: Essays from the Field*, ed. Gilbert Herdt. Boston: Beacon Press.

Kaufman, Gershen and Lev Raphael. 1996. *Coming Out of Shame: Transforming Gay and Lesbian Lives*. New York: Doubleday.

Kelly, Elizabeth A. and Kate Kane. 1998. "In Goldilocks's Footsteps: Exploring the Discursive Construction of Gay Masculinity in Bear Magazines." Pp. 66-98 in *Opposite Sex: Gay Men on Lesbians, Lesbians on Gay Men*, ed. Sara Miles and Eric Rofes. New York: New York University Press.

Levine, Martin P. 1998. *Gay Macho: The Life and Death of the Homosexual Clone*. New York: New York University Press.

Lorber, Judith. 1994. *Paradoxes of Gender*. New Haven, CT: Yale University Press.

Miles, Sara and Eric Rofes, eds. 1998. *Opposite Sex: Gay Men on Lesbians, Lesbians on Gay Men*. New York: New York University Press.

Murray, Stephen O. 1991. "Components of a Gay Community in San Francisco." Pp. 107-146 in *Gay Culture in America: Essays from the Field*, ed. Gilbert Herdt. Boston: Beacon Press.

Nardi, Peter M. 1992. "That's What Friends Are For: Friends as Family in the Gay and Lesbian Community." Pp. 108-120 in *Modern Homosexualities: Fragments of Lesbian and Gay Experience*, ed. Ken Plummer, 108-120. New York: Routledge.

Nestle, Joan, ed. 1992. *The Persistent Desire: A Femme-Butch Reader*. Boston: Alyson Publications.

Schacht, Steven P. 1996. "Misogyny On and Off the 'Pitch': The Gendered World of Male Rugby Players." *Gender & Society* 10: 550-565.

_____. 1998. "The Multiple Genders of the Court: Issues of Identity and Performance in a Drag Setting." Pp. 202-224 in *Feminism and Men: Reconstructing Gender Relations*, ed. Steven P. Schacht and Doris W. Ewing. New York, NY: New York University Press.

_____. 2000. "Gay Female Impersonators and the Masculine Construction of Other." Pp. 247-268 in *Gay Masculinities*, ed. Peter Nardi. Newbury Park, CA: Sage.

_____. 2002. "Turnabout Gay: Drag Queens and the Masculine Embodiment of the Feminine." Pp. 155-170 in *Revealing Male Bodies*, ed. Nancy Tuana et al. Bloomington: Indiana University Press.

_____. 2002. "Four Renditions of Doing Female Drag: Feminine Appearing Conceptual Variations of a Masculine Theme." Patricia Gagne and Richard Tewksbury (eds.) *Gendered Sexualities* issues for *Advances in Gender Research 6*: 157-180. Elsevier Science Ltd.

Stoltenberg, John. 1998. "Healing from Manhood: A Radical Mediation on the Movement from Gender Identity to Moral Identity." Pp. 146-160 in *Feminism and Men: Reconstructing Gender Relations*, ed. Steven P. Schacht and Doris W. Ewing. New York: New York University Press.

Thompson, C.J.S. 1974. *The Mysteries of Sex: Women Who Posed as Men and Men Who Impersonated Women*. New York: Causeway Books.

Troiden, Richard R. 1988. *Gay and Lesbian Identity: A Sociological Analysis*. Dix Hills, New York: General Hall, Inc.

Volcano, Del LaGrace and Judith "Jack" Halberstam. 1999. *The Drag King Book*. London: Serpent's Tail.

West, Candace and Don H. Zimmerman. 1987. "Doing Gender." *Gender & Society* 1: 125-151.

Weston, Kate. 1997. *Families We Choose: Lesbians, Gays, Kinship*. New York: Columbia University Press.

Wheelwright, Julie. 1989. *Amazons and Military Maids: Women Who Dressed as Men in the Pursuit of Life, Liberty and Happiness*. London: Pandora Press.

Capital Drag:
Kinging in Washington, DC

Jennifer Lyn Patterson

University of Maryland

SUMMARY. Through individual interviews with three DC drag kings and detailed, first-person accounts of their performances, I examine the role the kings play within the lesbian community at Club Chaos in Dupont Circle. My interviews address how and why the kings started performing, how their drag characters relate to their everyday personalities and experiences as lesbian women, why performing in drag is important to them, why drag performances are important to the women who attend their shows, and how gay men and drag queens have responded to their performances. My descriptions of the kings' performances, the audience response, and the atmosphere they create at the club reflect my viewpoint as a lesbian audience participant who has much appreciation for drag queens and much curiosity about the burgeoning drag king scene. I conclude that drag kings provide a valuable service to lesbian communities by creating a safe, supportive environment in which lesbian performers and audience members can celebrate and explore their relationships to female masculinities and queer sexualities. *[Article copies available for a fee from The Haworth Document Delivery Service: 1-800-HAWORTH. E-mail address: <docdelivery@ haworthpress.com> Website: <http://www.HaworthPress.com> © 2002 by The Haworth Press, Inc. All rights reserved.]*

KEYWORDS. Drag, gender, king, lesbian, masculinity, performance, queer, sexuality, Washington

[Haworth co-indexing entry note]: "Capital Drag: Kinging in Washington, DC." Patterson, Jennifer Lyn. Co-published simultaneously in *Journal of Homosexuality* (Harrington Park Press, an imprint of The Haworth Press, Inc.) Vol. 43, No. 3/4, 2002, pp. 93-123; and: *The Drag King Anthology* (ed: Donna Troka, Kathleen LeBesco, and Jean Bobby Noble) Harrington Park Press, an imprint of The Haworth Press, Inc., 2002, pp. 93-123. Single or multiple copies of this article are available for a fee from The Haworth Document Delivery Service [1-800-HAWORTH, 9:00 a.m. - 5:00 p.m. (EST). E-mail address: docdelivery@haworthpress.com].

Drag kings are some of the newest gender performers to sprout from queer culture, but interpretations of their performances stem from research that has been conducted for over a quarter of a century. Building on Esther Newton's groundbreaking article "Role Models," scholars have elaborated how homosexual cultures in particular value camp, which Newton defines as explorations of incongruity through theatricality and humor (1972, 23-4). Sue-Ellen Case, extrapolating from a localized study of Lois Weaver's and Peggy Shaw's performance of *Beauty and the Beast*, theorizes lesbian camp in her landmark manifesto "Toward a Butch-Femme Aesthetic." Case argues that through role-playing, a strategy of appearances, the butch-femme couple gains radical agency "free from biological determinism, elitist essentialism, and the heterosexist cleavage of sexual difference" (1989, 304-5). Her stance is liberationist, as her butch-femme couple evades claims to truth about gender realities. Newton later takes Case to task for neglecting to contextually historicize her theorization of a butch-femme aesthetic, for not analyzing how the roles function within lesbian lifestyles (Newton 1996, 64-5). Subsequent analysts of lesbian gender have been more careful to base their assertions upon observations of relationships within and among communities. For instance, Judith Halberstam undertook broad studies of different cultures of drag king lesbian camp and dyke and FTM transgenderism, examining the infinite permutations of masculinity as manifested in the female body (Halberstam 1994; Halberstam 1998; Volcano and Halberstam 1999). Working from Case, Halberstam's project is also liberationist, as she claims, "there is some relation between performing masculinity and diminishing the natural bonds between masculinity and men" (1999, 150).

Within the drag king culture of Washington, DC, female masculinities are more than just visual, stylistic presentations that work politically to dissolve associations of masculinity with men. As scholars have noted of butches (Cvetkovich 1998; Feinberg 1993), the DC kings have emotional and social investments in their characters, and spectators have emotional, visceral reactions to their performances. The DC drag kings have worked to create an atmosphere in which people receive female masculinities much more favorably than in any other public, social space I have ever encountered. Their performances provide forums in which lesbians can act out and interact with fantastic masculinities, examine their responses to different female masculinities, and experience firsthand the varying relationships between different gender roles and sexual desires. The DC drag kings are not merely masquerading;

kinging is an intimate part of their lives as lesbian women involved in a community of other lesbian women.

CHAOS

April 5th, 2000. Several months ago, I learned that on the first Wednesday of every month, the DC drag kings perform at Club Chaos. As an avid drag queen fan, I am eager to attend this month's drag king show. I want to see how drag king performances differ from drag queen performances and how the audience responds to the kings.

I board the Metro with my friend, Bunny. On our way to Dupont station, we gab about drag. Drag queens have long been synonymous with celebrations of queer sexuality for me. As a closeted lesbian teenager growing up in southern West Virginia, I had my introduction to drag queens at Miss Helen's Shamrock Lounge. PFLAG, SMYAL, and Lambda societies do not exist in rural West Virginia, so the gay bar is the only place sex and gender minorities can meet and be completely uninhibited about our lives and supportive of one another. The Shamrock was open only on the weekends, but it was a mecca for queers within three hours driving distance of Bluefield, the tenth largest city in the state. Semiannually, the Shamrock hosted queens from throughout Appalachia. It was the only time more than twenty people showed up to the club on the same evening. The queens brought festivity and positive energy to the Shamrock. They displayed what I most feared straight people might see in me; they paraded themselves shamelessly in all their genderqueer glory. They rocked the house, and everyone went home happy.

When I went away to college in Huntington, a city on the Ohio River near the tri-state intersection, I fell in love with the queens at the Driftwood. Sick to death of trying to achieve both a normatively feminine and markedly lesbian appearance, the Driftwood drag queens inspired me. I was tired of pitying myself because my arms were too flabby, my waist too thick, my gait neither graceful nor commanding. The list of flaws continued ad infinitum. I wanted to flaunt my unique femininity as fearlessly as the queens flaunted theirs. Stephanie St. Clair was one of the most elegant queens I had ever seen. When she took the stage, all eyes were on her. I wanted to be as comfortable with my body as Stephanie appeared to be in hers. I shed my flannels and baggy jeans and began to wear dresses and makeup to the club. With each incarnation, Ivana Hump showered me with compliments and hugs. When I shaved my head, leaving only two blue curls at the top of my forehead, she declared, "Oh girl. I just *love* your new do," and smothered me in the folds of her soft flesh. For the first time in my life, I felt sexy in my skin. I did what I wanted with my body.

I think about the queens back home as Bunny and I walk down Q Street to its intersection with 17th Street, and I begin to wonder if the kings will live up to my high expectations. Descending the stairs to the nightclub's entrance, I am taken aback by the number of women loitering about the doorway. Sandwiched between JR's and Windows 2.0, whose patrons are primarily gay men, Club Chaos is a restaurant by day and caters to a predominantly male crowd as well. As we pass by the women at the door and enter the club, Bunny remarks, "They're not charging a cover?" Surveying the crowd, I reply, "Looks like they'll make plenty of money on drinks alone."

By ten o'clock, women pack the club. The only men in sight are the polite gentlemen working behind the bar and a handful of presumably gay men scattered throughout the room. The same Madonna videos run simultaneously on television screens from all corners of the club. Although the crowd is mostly young and white, every element of lesbian subculture is present at the club. Bunny and I strike up a conversation with Terri, a blonde butch with flattop hair. She rests her forearms on the bar, a non-alcoholic beer between them. The club is warm from all the body heat, but she still wears her leather biker jacket. A slim punk girl, tough and weighed down in chains dangling from her waist, weaves in and out of the sea of assorted ballcaps, dreadlocks, buzzcuts, and long teased femme hairstyles. The club is so crowded that I have to worm my way between groups of people to queue up for a shot at a toilet.

The kings mingle with the audience until King Ken waves them to the wall near the DJ booth. Terri, Bunny, and I have strategically situated ourselves near them. The crowd joins us, forming a semi-circle around the kings. Their stage, the dance floor, is level with the rest of the floor space in the club. Some of the women lining the stage sit down on the floor. The performance space is intimate.

Drag King Ken calls us to order. His voice is smooth and suave, deep and sexy as his saunter. Everyone listens up. The spotlights spark off the flecks of glitter in his hair and on his red velvet suit jacket. He is packing something fierce in his skin-tight leather pants. He has the universal sex appeal of a dignified, effeminate bisexual man.

As Ken steps back towards the wall, the "James Bond" theme wafts out of the loudspeakers. King Hunter peeks around the corner of the DJ booth and executes a forward roll, throwing himself over his shoulder. He pops up crouched in the middle of the stage. He wears a tuxedo, and he wields a large, black hairdryer in his hands. Whoops, laughter, and clapping accompany him. The energy level of the crowd soars. Hunter opens the show with a castrated James Bond, his lethal weapon a mere appliance, and I am all smiles. (See Figure 1).

FIGURE 1

Flyer created by Kendra Kuliga

HUNTER

May 3rd, 2000. Act Three. The kings place two chairs, one on either end of the stage, in preparation for Hunter's appearance this evening. A femme sashays out, sits in one of the chairs, and immediately crosses her legs. Dressed in a tight, short-sleeved shirt and mini-skirt, she chews gum vigorously and glowers at the audience. She's so surly, I can't help but chortle.

A king wearing a gray wig, dark business suit, tie, and wide-framed plastic eyeglasses steps out onto the stage. Several women in the audience begin to chant, "Jer-*ry*! Jer-*ry*! Jer-*ry*!" The crowd immediately roars with laughter, hoots, and applause. The Stringer King bows to each corner of the room, "Thank you, thank you. Hi, and welcome to the show."

King Stringer explains the premise of the show, "Billie Jean has something she wants to tell her boyfriend Hunter. Let's meet Hunter." Hunter swaggers out onto the stage and plops into his chair. He slides down far into the chair, legs spread-eagle and arms crossed over his chest. He sports a blue baseball cap, turned backwards. A mustache frames his mouth and joins up with his goatee, and black suspenders hold his pants up a little too high on his gut. He wears an unbuttoned blue workshirt over a dirty V-neck T-shirt, and a vacant, slightly insolent expression. Hunter is the epitome of male realness. If he walked off the stage and out into the streets, no one would think he was a woman.

Billie Jean explains that she is pregnant with Hunter's child. Hunter hops out of his chair, hollering at her with the ferocity of a newly caged animal. He adamantly denies paternity. The audience boos and chuckles. Hunter shouts back at us, "Yeah, yeah. You don't know nothing about me!" The DJ begins the number, Michael Jackson's "Billie Jean." Hunter knows all of Jackson's signature dance moves, and he works out each of them expertly. He keeps a straight face while lip-synching the lyrics, even though the audience is alive with laughter. In a single performance, Hunter manages to parody two types of people who are already parodies of themselves: Jackson, who plays with his own race and gender, and the young, sensationalized middle-American youth, who play out their stock dramas on the Jerry Springer show.

May 10th, 2000. Hunter's performance impressed me so much that I introduced myself to him after the show and asked if he would concede to an interview. I explained that I wanted to learn about how he started kinging and why he continues to perform regularly. Today, I meet Hunter for the first time as Erin Hunter, a twenty-three-year-old white lesbian. Erin's personality and appearance is very different from Hunter. Her hair falls in short dark curls trimmed close around her neck and ears. A rugby player, her body is stout and muscular. She dresses smartly in a striped T-shirt and knee-length shorts slung low about her hips. One of her eyebrows is pierced with a small silver ring. Because she appears to be so strong and sturdy, she might be intimidating to a stranger, but her personality is soft and kind. She is an energetic ham.

Over dinner at a pizza parlor, Erin lists the many reasons why she does drag. She likes being the center of attention, being creative with her performance, having fun, and entertaining the audience. Hunter is entirely Erin's own creation. She chooses the music, brainstorms the background stories that underlie Hunter's lip-synching acts, and coordinates Hunter's costumes, gestures, and movements. Erin explains how Hunter has evolved, "Hunter isn't totally defined yet. He started out being a frat boy, and I think that's still essentially who he is, kinda cocky frat boy, 'life's a party' kinda thing. And also very interchangeable because he's just playing around."

Newly crowned Capital Pride King 2000 during DC's annual Pride Week festivities, Hunter is a dynamic character. Another of Hunter's performances I saw, set to Soft Cell's "Tainted Love" and "You're My Obsession," involved a flirtation between Hunter and another king. In contrast with Hunter's hokey version of the Jerry Springer show, Hunter's "Tainted Love" escapades had hot and heavy sex appeal. At first, Hunter and the other butch king circled around one another, checking each other out while playfully pretending to rough each other up. During the second half of the performance, a femme joined them onstage and competed with Hunter for the other king's attention. The act was both a steamy play of gay male eroticism and a thoughtful challenge to the butch on butch taboo still upheld in some factions of the lesbian community, in which feminine women are expected to desire and date more masculine women.

In talking to Erin, it becomes clear that she does not relish some of the social constraints often paired with gender labels and identity categories like butch and femme or man and woman. Her rebellion against gender norms of behavior is apparent in her genesis as a drag king:

> I went to school at Bryn Mawr, and we had this thing called Hell Week, which is kind of like a rush week, but it's a small school so the whole campus is involved in it. And there are performances where there's a stage in the middle of the cafeteria, and all the freshmen have a Heller, which is a sophomore that has them do

things on stage, you know, has them perform or whatever. And there's also dorm dress-up days, and the dorm that I lived in was supposedly a brothel, so we were supposed to be the whore-court, but me and a couple of friends didn't really have any whore clothing, so we were like, "Ooo! We'll be *pimps*!"

She continues through my laughter, "So we dress up as pimps and we decided to have a pimp strut that night on the stage. And so we did that, and then me and one or two other people kept it going." Erin resumes her story after the server brings our drinks:

I know it wasn't really to the express purpose of drag. It was, I don't know, it was somehow tied into Bryn Mawr traditions. And then my senior year we had a drag ball, where we had drag queens come up and we had an amateur competition that the drag queens hosted, and my friend Carolyn and I entered that. We were the Blues Brothers, and we ended up winning. So then, we performed our number at a place in Philly.

Erin's story is particularly remarkable, because she did not realize she was a lesbian when she began to perform in drag. Raised in a small town in northwestern Pennsylvania, Erin admits, "I was definitely sheltered growing up and when I got to school, I was a little homophobic even." She came out as a bisexual during her sophomore year of college. When she graduated from Bryn Mawr, she began to identify as a lesbian, although she emphasizes, "I guess I'm a lesbian, but, I dunno. I hate to close myself off just because of somebody's gender." Erin's drag history suggests that her desire to king developed separately from her lesbian identity.

Erin has an intimate relationship with her character, Hunter. She considers Hunter a part of her personality that she normally tames rather than a composite of other performers' styles:

I don't know that I have had any real drag king or drag queen influences. Yeah, I guess it's all kind of fashioned after when I did the whole pimp strut thing, in the persona that I picked up there. I just think it's funny how when a woman pretends to be as big an asshole as a man can be, women totally love it! It's really funny! Like I just got done being totally cocky, and I'm like, "Hey, you want me," you know. And so they're like, "Yes, we do!" [laughter] I don't know, it cracks me up. I guess also my drag persona is like a part of my own self that doesn't come out all that often? . . . But you know, it *is* there and I like bringing it out. So yeah, I guess it is just a different part of me. It's a different side of me.

Later, she reiterates how she uses drag as an opportunity for self-exploration and assertive flirtation:

For me, it's bringing out a part of my personality. It's like a total exaggeration of that. And I really don't act the way that my drag persona does. It's different. It's like I feel different when I'm in drag too. When I'm actually performing I can stare women in the eye and just look them up and down and have no problems. Even when I'm *in* drag and not performing, I still have more of that. But like, dude. I don't make the first move! Like I don't even [laughter] want people to come to *me* you know. Maybe I'll look at them, but that's a big thing for me. . . . But when I'm in drag, I can. I can do that.

Erin's trepidation about flirting outside of costume surprises me, because Hunter is fearlessly sexual and confident. For Erin, kinging transforms her personality:

When I'm in drag, I do get a slightly different attitude. And when I take it off at night and I look in the mirror, it looks weird. Originally, when I first put it on, I'm like, "That looks so weird," but then by the end of the night, when I take it off and it's gone, I really feel like I've just changed inside. . . . And I'm like, "what happened?" you know. But then I wake up the next day and I'm fine again.

Erin Hunter is a superb entertainer, but for her, the performance is much more than an act. Hunter is Erin's alter ego.

In part, kinging seems to help Erin become more comfortable with the aspects of her personality and appearance that are socially perceived as typically masculine. Although Hunter is comfortable with his masculinity onstage, Erin is more ambiguous about her reactions to how people receive her masculinity offstage. She has been mistaken for a man in her everyday life, and her emotions surrounding these experiences seem to be largely negative. When I ask if she has ever tried to pass for male during her everyday life, she remarks,

I'm not really into passing in public. I mean, I am female and I'm happy being female. I'm not saying that because I have anything against anybody else, but because I know that there's a thing in the drag king community or whatever where you know. Like, "Are you trans?" I've had people ask me. For me it is pretty much a performance. And I think it might be funny to go out and try to pass, but I don't know. I guess cause people look at the way I look, like I get mistaken for a man a lot anyway.

She continues to speak over my interjection, "No way!":

Oh yeah. The whole like, "This is the *women's* room?!" ... But being called sir all the time if I go into stores or restaurants, so [laughter] I guess I'm saying I don't feel like I need to try any harder, and if someone calls me, "ma'am," right away, I'm like, "Oh, they're so *nice!*"

Although I am surprised that some people take Erin for a man, I can relate to what she is saying. I have been mistaken for a man, and every time it happened, I felt disappointed and slightly agitated. In queer spaces, our gender difference is celebrated, but in day-to-day life, it is often ridiculed or misunderstood. I ask Erin, "Is it a pain in the ass if people think you're a guy?" To which she answers:

It depends on my mood, really. Sometimes I really just think it's funny, and other times I'm like, "Couldn't you just take time to *look* at me first, before you like assume my gender?" I don't know. I think that I definitely have a woman's face. But you know, it's just amazing how people'll be like, "Oh, short hair, broad shoulders. *Man.*" So, I don't know. It doesn't really bother me, but if I let it bother me, then I'd be bothered a lot of the time, so. I don't know.

I learn in my conversation with Kimberly Keese, who performs as Peter Dicksen, that Erin is not the only king who has been misperceived as male and who kings in order to explore her relationship to masculinity.

PETER DICKSEN

April 5th, 2000. Act 2. The DJ throws on the latest trendy pop song, "The Bad Touch" by the Bloodhound Gang. Peter Dicksen struts out on the stage dressed like a young, pretentious science nerd, clad in a lab coat and clutching a clipboard. His long blonde hair is pulled back in a loose ponytail, and he carries himself vainly, his nose in the air. As the lyrics begin, Peter wanders around the stage taking notes and studying the audience as if they are specimens, scrunching up his lips and brow and scratching his head. When the music breaks into the comic refrain, "You and me baby, we ain't nothing but mammals, so let's do it like they do on the Discovery Channel," Peter begins to dance awkwardly. His knees are completely stiff as he rocks back and forth in a circular stepping motion, pointing his finger out at the audience and nodding his head to the beat. The woman beside me is cracking up, guffawing into her hand.

Halfway through the number, a femme woman steps out of the audience onto the stage. Dressed smartly in a business skirt, slightly revealing white top, and heels, she looks secretarial. Her glasses have slid down a little low on her nose, and as she steps past Peter, she stares brazenly into his eyes over the top of her glasses. Jaws drop throughout the audience. When Peter throws off his labcoat, the woman beside me hollers, "Whew-hoo! The geek's gonna get some!"

Sure enough, Peter ends the number by banging the femme obscenely. Their mock fucking is so aggressive, the femme's skirt slides way up over her thighs. If Peter were a different character, the scene would seem sexually hostile and disturbing, but by creating himself as the paradigm of the socially backward man we all secretly pity and adore and by engaging the femme in consensual seduction, the entire audience is on his side. We behave completely indecorously as Peter carries on with the femme. Women hop up and down with their arms up in the air, egging him on. A couple across the semi-circle from me dances so closely they swap breath, barely rubbing against each other. Hips swing all over the room, and a few women step into the stage space vying for a go at Peter. Bunny slings her arm over my shoulder and kisses me. The mood in the club is positively orgiastic.

May 12th, 2000. Kimberly Keese's handshake is firm and reassuring when I meet her for the first time. She is a thirty-nine-year-old white woman who describes herself as "politically lesbian, but personally much more than a lesbian." Peter Dicksen is her stage name. Her mellow posture and casual attire, consisting of khakis and a T-shirt advertising an ice-cream parlor, reflect her laid-back, easygoing personality. Throughout our conversation, she is completely comic and candid.

Kimberly grew up in Washington Grove, a small suburb of the District near Gaithersburg, Maryland. She has been in the DC drag king scene since 1997, when she handled technical work and video production for the second drag king show held in DC, which was organized by the Lesbian Avengers as a fund-raiser. Shortly afterward, she and a few other Avengers founded Puss N' Boots Productions, a company dedicated to organizing area drag king events. In February 1998, Puss N' Boots put on their first production at the Hung Jury, a downtown club off of Pennsylvania Avenue which caters to lesbians on Friday and Saturday nights. Peter Dicksen performed for the first time during the show. His act included all five women in the company. With his chest bound, Peter came out onstage wearing only a mustache and his BVDs. The women slowly dressed him to the tune of ZZ Top's "Sharp Dressed Man." The show was so successful that it packed the Jury to capacity. The bouncers had to turn many people away at the door.

Since the first show at the Jury, Puss N' Boots has staged seven other drag king shows in DC. Kimberly confides that Puss N' Boots tries to draw an older crowd of lesbians than those who attend the shows at Chaos, which Kimberly says "is just like its name. It's chaotic. . . . People used to always complain about how late the show was, how loud the place was. Some people wanna come and sit down and watch the performance." Currently, Puss N' Boots consists of Kimberly, Merle Hooker, and Holly Foglebach. Both Merle and Holly perform for the company as well, as Miss Baby and The Reverend respectively. Miss Baby, master of ceremonies for the 2000 DC Pride Parade, introduces herself as "the world's first female-to-female transsexual." Kimberly describes Miss Baby, "What Merle does is she is a man. . . . She's a woman who is [laughter] a man dressing up as a woman. She dresses up as a drag queen. And she *does*, she does it really well. She's done a lot of stuff with drag queens and she often gets mistaken as a man within the drag queen scene." The Reverend appears as the name suggests. Holly dresses in Protestant drag.

Like Erin, Kimberly is often mistaken for a man. She recalls, "I have pretty much all my life been mistaken for a man. Not all the time. But my brother and I are two years apart, and we look very much alike, and often when we were younger, we were either mistaken for twin girls or twin boys." It used to bother Kimberly when people mistook her gender, but she does not have a problem with it anymore. She likes to "keep 'em guessing."

Kimberly also has an intimate relationship with her stage character. She says when she stepped out onstage for the first time, "It was like I was whole. Once I step onstage, it all clicks." When I ask Kimberly why she does male drag, her response implies that kinging comes naturally to her: "There's something about the gender play with it. I guess I consider myself butch. I mean everybody else does. [laughter] Although I've had a hard time sort of taking that label on. For a long time that word had really negative connotations for me." Like Erin, Kimberly seems uncomfortable with the prescriptive nature of gender labels, and she kings in order to manifest the masculine aspects of her psychology and appearance. Kimberly uses drag as an opportunity to enhance her appearance in a manner which best suits her, incorporating elements of men's dress:

> I've always been interested in that play with gender. I think the drag king performances, I'm realizing now that it gives me an opportunity to dress up the way I really feel comfortable dressing up. I'm not much of a formal dresser, and I haven't worn a dress in a *really* long time. . . . But I do love dressing up. But I've never been comfortable with all the stuff which is typically female or women's clothes as far as formal wear. And so I love suits. I love all the accouterments that come with men's suits, like handkerchiefs or the ties. I have loads of ties. . . . I love getting all that stuff. You know, "I've gotta get a tie clip!" I had to get cufflinks for that shirt. So I was like, "Yeah! Cufflinks! Whew!"

Later in the interview, she relates her stage performance to her evolving sexuality:

> You know, when I first started dating Margie. We've been dating for two years now. I remember telling her that I liked women in skirts. And she was kinda taken aback by it, and I was like, "Oh. Was that a bad thing to say? Is that wrong to want?" It's like, "I don't want you all the time in skirts, you know. You can wear whatever you want to." And . . . what we've done since we've been together, I think it has a lot to do with what I've been doing with drag kings. We've really both explored. I've explored more of my butchness, and she has explored more of her femmeness. She's become more comfortable with that, and I've become more comfortable with, I mean I'm still not sure about that word, but I know what that means to people, and I fit in that.

For Kimberly, like Erin, kinging serves as an avenue for sex and gender exploration. Kimberly even confides to me that her lover Margie played the femme in Peter's staged science experiment.

Kimberly also notes that drag king performances serve a similar purpose for the audience. It gives them an opportunity to sort out their relationships to masculinity:

> I think that it gives a certain amount of validity or acclamation to . . . butch and femme. I think that drag kings can be really sexy performers. And I think that in the early feminist movement, the feminists, not just the feminists but a lot of lesbian feminists, didn't wanna have anything to do with anything that was male or masculine. . . . And I think the drag king thing allows women to be attracted to that maleness or that masculinity. I mean, I don't think it's about being attracted to *men*. I don't think it's about wanting to *be* a man. It's about exploring your masculinity and how that works in sexuality and attraction. I think it gives women a chance to whoop and holler at a sexy man that you know is a woman. It's like a woman being all sexy like that you know.

As an audience member, I concur wholeheartedly with Kimberly's remarks. With his "The Bad Touch" number, Peter staged a pornographic scenario in which we audience members were encouraged to imagine ourselves as either Peter, the man, or the femme. Both characters were equally seductive. The fact that women in the audience joined Peter on stage, trying to get him to dance with them, is evidence that Peter excited them. Peter elaborates on the phenomenon:

> I know that for me, when I do a performance, I see a woman up onstage who's dressed in a little short skirt and a revealing blouse or whatever, I get, I'm excited by that. . . . I love that interaction, if I do something kinda sexy . . . or when people get all excited. . . . So that's what I get out of the performances, and I think that is the same for the audience. It's like, it's OK to go "woo-woo," you know, "good looking woman in man's clothing."

Moreover, Kimberly remarks that the masculinities drag kings assume and their viewers interact with are not always realistically male or even butch masculinities:

> Being butch, I suppose, helps you in drag, but it doesn't have to be butch to be drag. In fact, there are several New York kings who are not butch. I don't think Will Dewar is necessarily butch, or even Dred. I don't think she's all that butch out of character. She's a

fabulous male illusionist. She's a fabulous *performer*. . . . I think that for me, I can't answer it for anybody else because you know not all drag kings are butch. But I think it helps me, because I think I kind of naturally move in a sort of masculine way. And I'm more comfortable in male clothing.

As both Kimberly and Erin consider themselves sex and gender female, both women use kinging in order to explore and demonstrate their unique varieties of female masculinity. Peter and Hunter are not imitating men; they are manifesting masculinity in a female body. They celebrate queer masculinities.

Kimberly cites King Ken as an example of one DC king who succeeds admirably at queering masculinity:

> I remember really being *totally* inspired by Kendra's performance. She was so smooth, and so slick, and so sexy, and was like, "Wow yeah! That's great!" . . . I think Kendra's got this really interesting look, but I don't think she looks like a man. I think she's got this whole, you know, doing this whole gender thing. . . . What Kendra does is she brings you into the illusion that she is trying to create. You know she is not a man, but the way she performs and the way she looks and how she dresses herself up, you participate in her illusion. . . . There's just something about her. It's sexy, and it just brings you in.

KING KEN

May 3rd, 2000. Act 1. George Michael's "Outside" pours from the sound system. Five drag kings file onto the stage. They stop before the wall encasing the DJ booth, and they turn their backs to the audience. Each of them unzips his own pants and stands as if pissing up against the wall. The stage is set–a public men's room. Cackles ripple through the audience. I whistle through my fingers at the kings.

King Ken exits the DJ booth and strides into the bathroom. He wears a long, black, British-style jacket split up to his thighs in the back, button-fly leather pants, and a loose scarf around his neck. His smug, tightlipped smile is thinly veiled by a slim mustache on his upper lip and a small divot of hair between his lower lip and his chin. All the kings swivel their heads towards him, and then self-consciously return their focus to their pants and the task at hand. Ken moves slowly, lacing himself closer and then farther away from the kings. They take turns glancing slyly over their shoulders at him.

Facing the audience, King Ken stops beside Juan Moorehead, the third king down the line. Ken quickly forms a vulvate shaped frame with his hands, placing the tips of his index fingers beside each other as well as the tips of his thumbs. As the music breaks a heavy beat, he frames Juan's ass with his hands. With the fall of the next beat, leaving one hand at Juan's ass, Ken pulls his other hand back in the shape of a gun and points directly at Juan's asshole. He nods at the audience with a knowing grin. Juan looks over his shoulder at Ken in mock surprise. The audience roars to life and begins to hurl wads of money at the stage.

Like Hunter's drag, Juan Moorehead's drag is realistically male; however, Juan's drag is totally serious and completely butch. He is the stoic military man. Decked out in camouflage pants, leather army boots, bomber jacket, and mirrored sunglasses, he trudges around the stage with absolutely no expression on his face. Conversely, King Ken plays the suave gay man out to find the best cut of meat. He parades his sexual conquest by alternating his attention to Juan with crooning to the audience. A professional seducer, he is the ladies' favorite. He goes after what he wants, and he gets it. The crowd adores King Ken.

Ken works Juan all over the stage, maintaining physical, if not emotional and mental, distance from Juan through most of their racy performance. The sexual tension between them is palpable. Near the end of the act, Juan plants his hands firmly on Ken's pelvis. Juan bites his lower lip and pretends to sweat it out on Ken's ass. Momentarily bent over and taking it like a real man, Ken smirks at the audience and winks. As the act draws to a close, Ken reciprocates the gesture, fucking Juan from behind.

May 11th, 2000. Kendra Kuliga meets me for coffee. As she coasts up on a mountain bike, I realize she is very tall. A twenty-six-year-old lesbian, Kendra is a photographer by profession. She has worked for the *City Paper* and the *Washington Blade*, the District's general free weekly and GLBTQ weekly. Currently, she is a photographer for *Metro Weekly*, a free DC GLBTQ party journal. A series of her photographs, "Housemate Hook-up," was published in the February edition of *On Our Backs*, a popular lesbian sex magazine. She leans over the table, thumbing through her scrapbook of photographs she has taken of drag kings. She thinks through her words carefully and delivers them slowly in a low, soothing voice.

Like Kimberly, Kendra is a native of the DC area. Starting when she was fifteen and continuing throughout her high school years, she spent her free-time videotaping herself singing and lip-synching other people's songs in her basement. She says, "It's amazing what happens when you're bored out of your mind in Gaithersburg, Maryland. . . . I never thought it was gonna end up like this."

Kendra performed before an audience for the first time in 1996 at the first drag show organized in DC. The show was the brainchild of Cheryl Anne Spector, who had seen some drag kings in New York and thought holding a drag king contest in DC would be a good way to raise money for the local Lesbian Avengers. Kendra won the contest hands-down, tens across the board. She performed at the Avengers' second show the following year and has performed regularly ever since at venues as diverse as Puss N' Boots Productions shows, the First International Drag King Extravaganza in Columbus, Ohio, and DC clubs like Millennium, the Nation, and Remingtons, which typically sponsor only drag queens.

Kendra is the linchpin behind the Chaos drag king events. After she performed at the 1999 Capital Pride, the owner of Chaos approached her and asked if she would like to hold a show at his club. Kendra seized the opportunity, because as she says, "Puss N' Boots kept the drag king thing alive here in DC and did a lot of stuff, you know. But the thing that I felt was lacking was that there was no regular gig." On October 22nd, 1999, she staged the first Chaos show. It was so successful that the owner asked her to organize a monthly show.

Kendra also performs regularly at Chaos. Her persona, King Ken, has metamorphosed into a gender ambiguous character over the past year. Kendra describes her first performance at Chaos:

> I started toying with the idea of ambiguity . . . I opened the show doing "Sweet Dreams" as a guy mouthing women's words, you know Annie Lennox, and then after about a minute and a half of "Sweet Dreams," I switched right into "If I Was Your Girlfriend" by Prince. And then I revealed that I'm a woman. I had a bustier, you know, my breasts are huge, and yet I was singing a man's song, but I was a woman, kind of.

In another Chaos act, King Ken dressed in Louis XIV drag, flamboyant French Baroque period attire replete with white makeup, wig, puff pants, and fleur-de-lys. King Ken's signature style of confounding gender assignation serves as evidence that, as Kimberly notes, kinging is not always about realistic male illusion.

As a supplement to the regularly scheduled shows, Kendra has also convinced drag kings from other cities, like Lizerace and the Backdoor Boys from New York and D'Angelo from Baltimore, to perform at

Chaos. In addition to organizing the performers and MCing the events, Kendra photographs the kings and designs the signs and flyers advertising the shows.

Despite her hard work, Kendra is very humble as she speaks about her dual role as performer and promoter. Her main motivation seems to be altruistic. She credits Chaos for paying for all the advertisements and all the performers, and she states, "I definitely am evolving as a performer, but I thank Chaos for that opportunity, because it's making me deal with it much more often." Furthermore, she expresses her appreciation for the other drag kings: "I'm very grateful that people are giving their time to do it." She seems to be more concerned with promoting the other drag kings than with self-promotion, as she has turned down invitations to appear on national television. When I ask her what personal satisfaction she derives from kinging, she replies:

> I've been asking myself that question actually. Cause it's a lot of work. Just keeping on top of things, not letting people forget that I'm interested in them, and always reminding people, "Hey, you know, I'm out there for you, and if you wanna talk about drag kinging, if you wanna perform, I can put you on no problem."

She adds that her motivation for drag kinging is idealistic, because it provides a much needed service to DC lesbians: "It's giving women another opportunity to express themselves, as well as another venue of entertainment for lesbians."

Indeed, Kendra seems to be a mother hen for the burgeoning drag king community in DC. In addition to being an inspirational performer, Kendra encourages the kings to develop their own unique, individual stage presence:

> With the DC kings, because we're starting, we don't really know what we are. And as a promoter, I suppose I don't really wanna form anybody's opinion on how they should perform it. I don't wanna guide anybody into an idea of what drag king is. I'm really curious what people come up with every show, and I wanna see how it grows as a community. . . . I mean I've always felt, I guess because everybody's different, everybody does it for different reasons, you know. . . . From a performer's standpoint, I always felt like I needed room to grow and decide what it is to me. And I felt that wasn't being encouraged. There was becoming a very fine line of what drag kinging was supposed, was expected to be.

In my interview with her, Erin confirms Kendra's supportive role in the drag king community and open-mindedness about how drag kings should perform:

> Another thing that I like that Kendra's doing with Chaos is harboring a sense of community with the drag kings. I feel very encouraging of them, and I feel like they're very encouraging of me when we go on, and I really like that. I know I've heard that with some of the drag queens, they can be kind of catty, you know? I'm not about that.

The audience also benefits from Kendra's asking the kings to encourage one another. The Chaos king shows feel more like pep rallies gone raucous than competitions. The audience response is always appreciative and respectful, never judgmental.

Overall, Kendra's relationship to drag queens is healthy. She expresses gratitude for the support she has received from the majority of the DC queens, the Chaos queens in particular. Also, she implies that drag kings can learn a lot about costume and artifice from the drag queens, admitting, "I think that's one thing that drag kings can pay more attention to is their presentation. Cause drag queens have that down." On the other hand, she expresses her distress about some negative feedback she has received about drag kings from a few of the local drag queens:

> Recently, I've just [laughter] been challenged with the idea of "what is drag kinging," you know. Or "should drag kings be taken seriously." And I've been getting this more on the drag queen front. There's been talk that drag kings really aren't . . . just that drag kings are amateurish and don't really know what the hell they're doing and shouldn't be really revered or taken seriously like the queens.

A few local queens suggested to Kendra that one of the Chaos kings' flaws is that they are not realistically masculine enough. Supportive of each king's individual expression of masculinity, Kendra argues that the goal of drag, both queening and kinging, is not necessarily illusion:

> This is my big thing, when that was questioned, that drag kings aren't real enough, they're just girls with facial hair, I said, "Why should men be the ones to decide how a drag king should be?" you

know, based on the queens. Why is that the stick to be measured by? Like, why is it about illusion? Why is it about packing in such a way that your whole appearance looks as such that you could be mistaken as a man? And I said, "All right, I'd *really* like to see a drag *queen* be mistaken as a woman."

Indeed, I think now of Lisa Castillo, one of only two drag queens I've known who could pass for a woman, the other being Miss Baby, of course. For the longest time, I thought Lisa was just another lesbian who hung out at the bar, but when I saw her perform, a friend told me she was a man, that she was taking female hormones and preparing to surgically alter her anatomy. I never really believed that Lisa was a man, though. Kendra adds,

> I mean, I think there's a very small percentage, like maybe five-percent, who could actually pass. But then again, one has to question: are they taking hormones? Are they physically altering themselves? Because it's skin quality, and it's not so much how much makeup you put on at all, because I think the more makeup you put on, the more drag queenish you look. You know, people can't help their bone structure.

I interrupt her with laughter, thinking again of Miss Baby, who manages to pass for a man in women's clothing by donning fancy sequins and caking on the Maybelline. Kendra continues, "I mean there's so much going on there you know. I think it's bullshit about the illusion stuff. I mean it's like, 'Yeah, in a room full of men, sure you're the closest thing to a woman, but you're still a man' [laughter]."

Kendra believes the antagonism of this particular set of queens towards the kings stems from an "old boys' club" attitude about what makes a good drag performer:

> I think there is a bit of a, what is it called when men don't allow women into their space? . . . I think that's what I was getting from the queens. You know, it's interesting. They're emulating women, yet they're not giving respect to women. It's interesting, and I'm kind of getting wakened up to that idea, with drag queen shows not opening their doors to kings as of yet.

Although some drag queens belittle drag kings, their attitudes do not reflect those of the larger gay male community. The gay men at the Chaos shows seemed to love the kings, and several men tipped them. I chatted with a man just before one of the Chaos shows, and he raved about the kings. Erin remarked, "Last time, I had a gay man tell me that he worshipped me. Then, he bought me a drink." Similarly, Kimberly stated, "I had a couple of comments from men who say, 'I'm *so* tired of the drag queens. This is so much fun!'" Of the separation of drag queen and drag king events, Kendra thinks, "It's a problem, and I'd like to see more kings get in, and I think the men, the male's response to it, like actual gay men who see it, love it. And some of them think it's even more innovative and more exciting than the queens." Clearly, the segregation of drag kings from drag queens is certainly not due to lack of interest within the gay male community.

Kendra is impassioned when she discusses her encounter with the drag queens who responded negatively to the DC drag kings. She feels the queens can learn a lot from the kings:

> I think when the Backdoor Boys performed here at Chaos last Saturday night, the drag queens were paying attention, because the response to the Backdoor Boys was so overwhelming that you would have to be stupid if you ignore why people responded to it the way it was, you know, with the dance they did. I mean drag queens would come out and maybe get maybe five dollars. The Backdoor Boys came out, and it was like fifty, sixty dollars every time they came out. They just were getting money thrown at them, you know. And I mean, yeah. One could say it was novelty, and people just loved it, and they got all emotional, and they started throwing money at them, but also it was really well done.

As a fan of both drag kings and drag queens, it occurs to me that arguing whether and why queens are better than kings is ridiculous and self-defeating. The queens' unease with the kings reminds me that sexism is alive and well within the gay community, and the segregation of drag queens from drag kings results in more divisions between male, female, and transgendered queer people. Nevertheless, while I agree with Kendra that the segregation of drag shows according to sex is a problem, the sex segregation contributed to the initial formulation of a uniquely lesbian drag in DC and the creation of a supportive space in which women can explore their queer masculinities.

COMMUNITY SERVICE

I know something about my appearance is either not quite feminine or not quite straight enough. I know, because I have been addressed as "Sir" and "Son," and because I have passed men walking down the street who holler "Dyke" or "Lezzie" back at me from a safe distance. I know, because straight people are constantly advising me on how to improve my appearance, usually cloaking their criticism with a backhanded compliment, like "you'd look so pretty, if you'd . . ." I admire and appreciate the kings at Chaos for teasing out the queer bits of themselves and presenting them to us as treasured gifts. They are sexy, fun, and proud of their queer difference.

The drag kings fulfill an emotional and social need for themselves and for their lesbian audience. The crowd at the Chaos king shows is more rambunctious and involved in the performance than any other drag audience I have witnessed in the past. Kendra, Kimberly, and Erin each cited showmanship and entertainment value as the most important drag king qualities. For them, the illusion of male realness is either secondary or unimportant to their performance. Their primary goal is to please the audience. By offering money and applause, we audience participants demonstrate our gratitude to the kings and encourage the sexually volatile performances.

I believe the most important function of kinging is the service it provides to the lesbian community involved in the shows. Kendra summarizes the important role kinging plays in empowering the audience and the performers and fostering a sense of lesbian community:

> Oddly enough, just with the drag king thing, even though it's not really related to representing the lesbians of the community, 'cause they're made up as drag kings, that's giving them an opportunity to express themselves one more place. And it's kind of like . . . it is helping the cause, you know. It's one more women's event that women are attending that women are enjoying that is making women feel more comfortable with themselves, and as a result, maybe gives them strength to move on to bigger things. I think as a lesbian growing up and coming out in this community, every time there's a lesbian party even, where I can meet other lesbians and dance with other lesbians and look at other lesbians, that's self-affirming, that's empowering. And then you move on and start finding your own niche, start throwing your own parties, inspiring other lesbians. I think the first step is getting people comfortable with themselves, providing safe spaces.

Flyer from Club Chaos courtesy of the author
Flyer created by Kendra Kuliga

I know exactly what she means. Growing up in West Virginia, Miss Helen's Shamrock Lounge was my only safe space, the only place I could go to talk to other gay people and be assured that I was not alone in my queer love. Kendra and the Chaos kings have created a similar space in DC. Whereas the queens back home celebrate queer femininities, the DC kings parody, exaggerate, and celebrate butch, gay male, and female masculinities. They stage lesbian fantasies, affirming sex and gender difference and fostering public displays of appreciation for queer sexualities and masculinities. The kings help alleviate the anxieties of lesbian participants like me, whose queer genders and sexualities are challenged in our everyday lives. They encourage women to embrace the masculinity and queer sexuality within themselves.

REFERENCES

Case, Sue-Ellen. 1993. "Toward a Butch-Femme Aesthetic." Pp. 294-306 in *The Lesbian and Gay Studies Reader*, ed. Henry Abelove, Michele Aina Barale, and David M. Halperin. New York: Routledge.
Cvetkovich, Ann. 1998. "Untouchability and Vulnerability: Stone Butchness as Emotional Style." Pp. 159-69 in *Butch/Femme: Inside Lesbian Gender*, ed. Sally R. Munt. London: Cassell.
Feinberg, Leslie. 1993. *Stone Butch Blues: A Novel*. Milford, CT: Firebrand.
Halberstam, Judith. 1994. "F2M: the Making of Female Masculinity." Pp. 210-28 in *The Lesbian Postmodern*, ed. Laura Doan. New York: Columbia UP.
_____. 1998. *Female Masculinity*. Durham: Duke University Press.
Newton, Esther. 1972. "Role Models." Pp. 14-29 in *Margaret Mead Made Me Gay: Personal Essays, Public Ideas*. Durham: Duke University Press, 2000.
_____. 1996. "Dick(less) Tracy and the Homecoming Queen: Lesbian Power and Representation in Gay Male Cherry Grove." Pp. 63-89 in *Margaret Mead Made Me Gay: Personal Essays, Public Ideas*. Durham: Duke University Press, 2000.
Volcano, Del LaGrace and Judith Halberstam. 1999. *The Drag King Book*. London: Serpent's Tail.

BIBLIOGRAPHY OF SUGGESTED FURTHER READINGS

Atkins, Chloe. 1999-2000. "Drag Kings and More." *RFD* 26, no. 2 (Winter): 33-40.
Cleto, Fabio, ed. 1999. *Camp: Queer Aesthetics and the Performing Subject*. Ann Arbor: University of Michigan Press.
DC Drag Kings. Home page. Chaos drag kings. 10 January 2002. Available online at <http://www.geocities.com/dcdragkings/>. Gives information about upcoming performances, explains the group's function, offers biographies, photographs of the kings, and links to other worldwide drag king sites.
Dobkin, Alex. 1999. "Pirates, Anarchists, and Drag Kings." *Off Our Backs* 29, no. 10 (November): 15.
Dyer, Richard. 1991. "Believing In Fairies: The Author and the Homosexual." Pp. 185-201 in *Inside/Out: Lesbian Theories, Gay Theories*, ed. Diana Fuss. New York: Routledge.
Garber, Marjorie. 1992. *Vested Interests: Cross-Dressing and Cultural Anxiety*. New York: Routledge.
Kat, Johnny. 2000. "Interview." *Play: The Paper* (DC) (April): 6-7.
Kingdom: International Drag King Magazine. Home page. Carlos Las Vegas and Ken Las Vegas (a.k.a. Drag King Ken), eds. 10 January 2002. Available online at

<http://www.geocities.com/kingdomidkm/>. Explains organizational structure, provides mission statement, calls for contributors, writers, and volunteers, retail and contact information, links to other drag king sites.

Kuliga, Kendra. 2000. "Diary of a King." *Women in the Life* 10, no. 5 (September): 6-8.

Maltz, Robin. 1998. "Real Butch: The Performance/Performativity of Male Impersonation, Drag Kings, Passing as Male, and Stone Butch Realness." *Journal of Gender Studies* 7, no. 3 (November): 273-86.

Smyth, Cherry. 1998. "How Do We Look? Imaging Butch/Femme." Pp. 82-9 in *Butch/Femme: Inside Lesbian Gender*, ed. Sally R. Munt. London: Cassell.

Volcano, Del LaGrace. 2000. *Sublime Mutations: Bodies of Work 1990-2000*. Tubingen: konkursbuch Verlag Claudia Gehrke.

Wiltz, Teresa. 2002. "Grrrls II Men: Drag Queens Are Out. Drag Kings Rule, and Club Chaos Is Their Local Dominion." *Washington Post* (January 9th): C01.

LIST OF ISSUES AND QUESTIONS
FOR FURTHER CONSIDERATION AND ANALYSIS

1. In general, how do other audience participants respond to the Chaos drag king performances? Why do they attend the shows? What do they think of the performances? How do the performances affect them?
2. How do audience participants, African-American audience participants in particular, respond to performances in which white kings parody famous African-American men or lip-synch to their music, e.g., in which a white king dresses as Sisqo and lip-synchs "The Thong Song?" Are such performances a type of blackface? Do they reinforce visual stereotypes of blackness? Are such performances meant to be flattering, a type of impersonation or identification, as is often the case in drag queens' impersonations of female celebrities? Is the effect the same when a black king parodies a famous white man?
3. How are drag kings received outside the context of lesbian bar cultures?
4. What social and historical circumstances surround and account for the sudden upsurge of drag king cultures?
5. In general, are drag kings more intimately connected to their onstage personalities than drag queens? Like kings, do drag queens also regard their stage personas as alter egos, or do queens consider their performances to be acting and impersonation rather than manifestations of parts of their own personalities?

Kinging in the Heartland;
or, The Power of Marginality

Thomas Piontek, PhD

Ohio State University

SUMMARY. Theorizations of the drag king phenomenon and definitions of "the Drag King" thus far have relied almost exclusively on Judith Halberstam's description of the drag king scenes in New York, London, and San Francisco. In order to expand the scope of the investigation of drag king culture and as an example of the range of drag kings and drag king acts that have developed across the U.S. and across the world, this article focuses on H.I.S. Kings, a group of women, who have been performing in Columbus, Ohio since 1996. By infusing drag with a dose of theory, which is always tempered by their outrageous sense of humor, H.I.S. Kings have developed what arguably is one of the most interesting varieties of kinging, an approach to the genre of the drag show that Halberstam's model cannot account for. Unlike kings in New York, for example, H.I.S. Kings frequently utilize the supposedly gay male form of camp in their performance of multiple masculinities and femininities, and they create innovative ensemble numbers that engage the racial and gender politics of drag. The example of H.I.S. Kings calls into question any theorization of the drag king phenomenon that ignores cultural developments in the heartland by focusing exclusively on cities traditionally considered the centers of queer culture. *[Article copies available for a fee from The Haworth Document Delivery Service: 1-800-HAWORTH. E-mail address: <docdelivery@haworthpress.com> Website: <http://www.HaworthPress.com> © 2002 by The Haworth Press, Inc. All rights reserved.]*

[Haworth co-indexing entry note]: "Kinging in the Heartland; or, The Power of Marginality." Piontek, Thomas. Co-published simultaneously in *Journal of Homosexuality* (Harrington Park Press, an imprint of The Haworth Press, Inc.) Vol. 43, No. 3/4, 2002, pp. 125-143; and: *The Drag King Anthology* (ed: Donna Troka, Kathleen LeBesco, and Jean Bobby Noble) Harrington Park Press, an imprint of The Haworth Press, Inc., 2002, pp. 125-143. Single or multiple copies of this article are available for a fee from The Haworth Document Delivery Service [1-800-HAWORTH, 9:00 a.m. - 5:00 p.m. (EST). E-mail address: docdelivery@haworthpress.com].

KEYWORDS. Camp, drag king, drag queen, femininity, gender, H.I.S. Kings, masculinity, Midwest, performativity, race

Unlike his "counterpart" the drag queen, the drag king is a relatively new addition to queer culture. Much of what we know about this phenomenon we owe to the work of Judith Halberstam (1997; 1998; 2001; Volcano and Halberstam 1999), who thus far has dedicated a book and several essays to her ongoing investigation of female drag. Combining detailed textual readings and empirical research, Halberstam (1997; 1998) considers drag king performance within the broader framework of "female masculinity," which she argues is not some bad imitation of virility but the staging of hybrid or minority genders. Thus, her work introduces us to an exciting development in lesbian culture while at the same time making an important contribution to the debates in queer scholarship about the performativity of gender.

Because Halberstam is the most prolific of the handful of academics who have analyzed the drag king phenomenon, her work assumes a highly representative character, so that anyone who writes about drag kings must engage her work. Therefore, it is all the more regrettable that Halberstam's work suffers from one highly consequential limitation: it focuses exclusively on the drag king scenes in New York, London, and, to a lesser extent, San Francisco. One wonders why Halberstam made these specific choices. Is it because she believes the phenomenon under investigation is limited to these particular places? In an essay she wrote for *The Drag King Book*, Halberstam confirms this suspicion when she asserts that "the Drag King lives in the cities that never sleep [New York, London, San Francisco]" and "thrives on the varied queer nightlife" of these cities (Volcano and Halberstam 1999, 64). Her essay seems to suggest that, since there is no "varied queer nightlife" outside of these three centers of urban queer life in the U.S and the U.K, there are no drag kings anywhere else either.[1] Drag kings, we are led to assume, need big city energy like they need the air they breathe.

However, in a recent interview with Annamarie Jagose for the e-journal *Genders* (http://www.genders.org/g29/g29_halberstam.html), Halberstam surprises her readers by declaring, "by far the most exciting drag king scene in the United States is in the Midwest in Columbus, Ohio where the H.I.S. Kings perform monthly for huge screaming audiences of fans." As it turns out, Halberstam has known about H.I.S. Kings at least since February 26, 1998, when–on the occasion of presenting her research on the drag king scene in New York at the Ohio State University–she met several of the local performers (most of them in full drag) at her talk and at a reception following her presentation. In spite of this fact and in spite of her unequivocal endorsement of the Columbus troupe, H.I.S. Kings do not figure at all in Halberstam's theorization of the drag king phenomenon, which to this day continues to focus exclusively on "cities that never sleep"–without paying attention to performers who are kinging in the heartland.

In an American context, Halberstam's focus on urban cultural centers such as New York and San Francisco as the only dwelling places of "the Drag King" may be understandable, for as far as the American cultural landscape is concerned, we have grown accustomed to the assumption that in the U.S. cultural production is limited to the Coasts. The fact that we consider Los Angeles/San Francisco and New York/Washington the country's cultural centers, in turn means that we frequently think of large parts of the country as a cultural wasteland. This mind-set has also had a distinct effect on the way we think about national queer culture, which has traditionally been associated with the gay meccas of New York, Los Angeles, and San Francisco. William Spurlin takes issue with this assumption in the introduction to a collection of essays by gay and lesbian writers and artists who have lived in the heartland, polemically entitled "What?! Queers in the Midwest?" He argues that, while mainstream media like the *New York Times* have reported that "issues of gay identity and activism have been slowly moving over the past two decades *from the East and West coasts to the heartland*" (emphasis added), gay and lesbian scholarship has not "adequately reflected and chronicled this significant geographic shift." Spurlin quite rightly insists that, "for many lesbians and gay men living in Michigan, Ohio, Wisconsin, Minnesota, Missouri, Illinois, Nebraska, and Kansas, the Midwest–the heartland–is a significant vantage point from which to create as authors, poets, artists, intellectuals, and cultural workers" (1996, xi). H.I.S. Kings, I maintain, reflect this significant geographic shift in queer culture and do their part to put the heartland on the map.

The fact that Columbus is unlike New York City hardly comes as a surprise, and consequently we may be tempted to regard this difference as yet another instance of the heartland trailing the Coasts in terms of culture. Instead, I hope to show how at least one drag king company is performing in ways that encourage us to revise Halberstam's theories of drag king performance as well as the categories she develops to describe the drag kings she encountered. Because she focuses on her favorite three cities, Halberstam misses variations and inventions within the drag king phenomenon and develops her model of *the* Drag King without considering what arguably are some of the most interesting varieties of kinging. By focusing on the Columbus troupe, I do not make any claims for the exclusivity of H.I.S. Kings' approach to drag; rather, I use the Columbus troupe as a counter-example to Halberstam's model so as to challenge the generalizations she makes about "the Drag King." I want to suggest that we read H.I.S. Kings as an example–and a very encouraging one at that–of how cultural practices in the heartland actually challenge, contradict, and expand what is happening in the traditional cultural centers on the West and East coasts, an example, if you will, of kings in the heartland reshaping our idea of "the Drag King" and of the margins redefining the center(s).

* * *

How do H.I.S. Kings differ from other drag king scenes? The shows and competitions Halberstam (1997; 1998; 1999) describes in her work mostly consist of individual acts dedicated to the performance of what she calls "female masculinity." There is very little interaction among individual acts or, particularly in New York City, between white drag kings and kings of color. H.I.S. Kings, however, decidedly perform as a group rather than grooming individual stars. The troupe has always been racially mixed and performances frequently cross racial boundaries. Last but not least, H.I.S. Kings shows are not limited to performances of female masculinity but also include complex commentary on the construction and performance of femaleness, since members of H.I.S. Kings also perform a variety of femininities. Through their approach to the drag performance–including the ensemble character of their shows and the deliberate crossing of racial and gender lines–H.I.S. Kings manage to forge connections between popular culture, subcultural styles, and theoretical discourses. H.I.S. Kings' shows, I argue, not only reflect current debates about the performativity of gender in feminism and queer theory; they also complicate them in productive and entertaining ways.

To begin with, H.I.S. Kings shows are not merely a compilation of single drag king performances; they are carefully crafted theatrical productions, framed by the performances, announcements and commentary of emcee extraordinaire, Lustivious de la Virgion (Si'le Singleton). Furthermore, individual drag kings perform a number of different roles, lip-synching to a wide variety of music ranging from Garth Brooks to Ricky Martin, in the case of Derrick (Ivett Domalewski); from Mimi, the hyper-feminine heroin addict in the rock musical *Rent,* to one of the Backstreet Boys, in the case of dj love (Donna Troka). Another aspect of H.I.S. Kings performing as a group is their ensemble pieces: H.I.S. Kings frequently delight their audiences with performances by musical groups, duets, reenactments of musical numbers from films and musicals as well as theatrical interpretations of songs, which performers working on their own simply could not pull off. Interestingly, the showcase at *The Third International Drag King Extravaganza,* held in Columbus, Ohio, in October 2001 featured ensemble numbers by drag troupes from other cities, including Santa Barbara and New York. This demonstrates that the theatrical approach to drag king performance is not limited to H.I.S. Kings. Furthermore, it suggests that the drag scene in New York City is different today from the one Halberstam observed in the mid-1990s. Perhaps three drag king conferences have inspired drag kings throughout the country to theatricalize their act. This kind of "cross-fertilization" could be considered one example of how the heartland is helping to redefine kinging all around the country. In any event, ensemble numbers broaden the scope of the drag act and allow performers to comment on the gendered dimensions of the popcultural phenomena they take on in some of their numbers.

In their interpretation of the Backstreet Boys' popular song "Everybody (Backstreet's Back)," for instance, H.I.S. Kings reconfigure the phenomenon of boy bands–all male musical groups whose primary appeal is to straight teenage girls and (unofficially) to gay men. The H.I.S. Kings' version of the Backstreet Boys produces the familiar frenzy in the audience, albeit with one significant difference: everyone in the band and virtually all members of the audience are women. The playfulness onstage also inspires a kind of audience participation as some audience members play girly girls to the "boys" onstage. Regulars at these shows in particular delight in performing for/to the performers and many come dressed for the occasion in extremely feminine and sexy outfits. The familiar audience reaction and the number of female spectators handing dollar bills and small gifts to the "Backstreet Boys" from both sides of the stage add to the "realness effect" of the Kings' performance. The femininity of the fans and their stereotypically female behavior accentuate the masculinity of the performers.

What I'm calling "realness effect" here should not be confused with reality, for neither drag kings nor drag queens are about imitating reality. As LaMiranda (Guillermo Diaz), the protagonist of Nigel Finch's movie *Stonewall* puts it: "I'm a drag queen, baby, I don't do reality" (1997). A drag queen's stylish and stylized femininity usually looks more believable when seen next to the mundane masculinity of a man, even the always already suspect masculinity of a gay man. H.I.S. Kings utilize and play with this convention in a number in which Lustivious, the troupe's emcee, performs as a drag *queen*. I'll have more to say about Lustivious and the phenomenon of the female drag queen later; right now, I'd like to focus on the way that a male audience member handing dollar bills to the drag queen performing on stage creates what I call a realness effect. The audience member's masculinity seems to enhance the illusion of femininity created by the performer onstage. The irony here, however, is that the supposed audience member turns out to be David (Sumira Pruitt), one of the Kings, whose masculinity is performed, as is Lustivious' femininity, although she seems to have an ontological claim on femininity by the mere fact of her "being"–though not necessarily performing herself as–"woman" offstage. In other words, what I call "realness effect" is here achieved by one illusion of reality propping up another, two illusions reinforcing each other to create an effect of realness.

In interesting ways, H.I.S. Kings' performance of the popular band changes the Backstreet Boys from an object of teenage girl crushes or gay male fantasies to an object of lesbian adoration and approval; it appropriates the Backstreet Boys–a boy band and an icon of straight girl (and gay male) culture–as a phenomenon in lesbian culture. Importantly, however, in this case the female fan's relationship to the pop icon is not limited to the fantasy of *having* the Boy(s)–the crush or the sexual fantasy–but also entails the added dimension of *being* the Boy. Kinging thus puts an entirely new spin on another crossdresser's famous maxim, "Don't dream it, be it,"[2] and recommends itself as a sure way not merely to ascertain female pleasure but to double it.

While in their rendition of the Back Street Boys, H.I.S. Kings put a subcultural spin on a popcultural phenomenon–the boy band–more frequently popular culture draws on subcultural influences. Thus, Halberstam (2001) analyzes the influence of drag king satire on the depiction of masculinities in such film comedies as *Austin Powers: International Man of Mystery* (1997; dir. Jay Roach) and *The Full Monty* (1997; dir. Peter Cattaneo). H.I.S. Kings have lampooned both of these movies in several numbers over the years. Their tongue-in-cheek rendition of the famous striptease scene from The Full Monty has long been an audience favorite, and one of the most prolific Columbus Kings, Toe B. (Heidi Madsen), who specializes in representations of what we might call "awkward masculinities," has portrayed Austin Powers in some of her most popular performances. We can only guess how a reading of these acts might have influenced Halberstam's analysis, but unfortunately her most recent essay on the drag king phenomenon makes no mention of H.I.S. Kings' ensemble number from *The Full Monty* or of Toe. B.'s various renditions of *Austin Powers.*

The Full Monty, the 1997 surprise British film hit, focuses on the lives of five men who try their luck as strippers when they find themselves unemployed and on the dole. Much of the film's humor is predicated on the discrepancy between the buff bodies and stereotypically good looks of professional male strippers such as the Chippendales and the rather average bodies and unconventional good looks of the struggling amateurs. The film's dramatic tension owes everything to the build up from the initial idea to the hilarious auditions, the sometimes tumultuous rehearsals, and finally to the big night when they promise to "take it all off." The film does not deliver on this promise, freezing the image just as the five men are about to reveal their "manliness," avoiding full frontal nudity in favor of a shot of their naked behinds, presumably to maintain the film's PG rating which certainly contributed to its highly profitable run in the U.S.

Considering this background, I was quite surprised that H.I.S. Kings chose this very scene from the film as an ensemble number for their Valentine's Day extravaganza entitled "Boys on Film" (February 13, 1999). After all, they would neither be able to simply freeze the image, nor would they be able to deliver on the promise that the striptease and Tom Jones' soulful rendition of "You Can Leave Your Hat On" make. But deliver they do! As the Kings take off their police uniforms, they reveal body suits that look more like long underwear than the real thing–and quite intentionally so. The effect that they're after in this number is not realness or mimicry but the hyperbole of an exaggerated and hence denaturalized maleness. Toe B., one of the Kings in this number, makes this quite clear as he takes off his shirt to reveal a chest hair toupee of truly gigantic proportions.

Roland Barthes denounces striptease, which promises nudity but usually doesn't deliver on that promise, as a "mystifying spectacle" in which "evil is *advertised* the better to impede and exorcise it." The function of the striptease, Barthes claims, consists in "inoculating the public with a touch of evil, the better to plunge it afterwards into permanently immune Moral Good: a few particles of eroticism, highlighted by the very situation on which the show is based, are in fact absorbed in a reassuring ritual which negates the flesh as surely as the vaccine or the taboo circumscribe and control the illness or the crime" (1972, 64). The stripper's G-string becomes a sign for the structure of containment to which Barthes refers in this passage, for it usually signifies the very end of the striptease. This final revelation in a strip show tends to be quite anticlimactic–it simply can't live up to the expectations built in the course of the striptease. That's why this moment is frequently cut short, giving the audience at best a very brief peek at what has been promised all along, or more likely withholding the ultimate revelation altogether–as is the case in the film version of *The Full Monty*.

H.I.S. Kings interrupt this inherent logic of the striptease as Toe B. and the others take off their bright red G-strings and bashfully cover their manliness with their police hats. When the Kings raise their hats in unison, however, they go further than their counterparts in the movie by revealing gargantuan phalluses made of stuffed fabric, replete with fake pubic hair. Far from shying away from the "moment of truth" then, H.I.S. Kings do deliver and deliver more than any biological male could hope to. What is particularly interesting about this scene is the way in which the attribution of female lack according to which woman = man – penis is countered by the excess of the grossly exaggerated male members, which the strippers expose to the audience as they walk off the stage.

Toe B. seems to have a particular knack for exposing the awkwardness of the male body, whether in his rendition of *Austin Powers* or in another performance in which he answers the question of just what a Scotsman wears underneath his kilt by repeatedly lifting the fabled garment to expose an appendage similar to the one he and his mates sport in the *Full Monty* number. Toe B.'s solo performance as well as the *Full Monty* number demonstrate that H.I.S. Kings refuse to accept the limits imposed by biology and the body by privileging an extravagantly exaggerated and comical version of masculinity over a realistic representation. This allows H.I.S. Kings to expose the hyperbolic way in which males usually speak of their bodies as well as their assumption that the bigger the penis, the more sexually potent, powerful, and masculine the man. If it is true that size matters, it is certainly noteworthy that, without attempting to imitate reality, the H.I.S. Kings end up producing a copy that is actually bigger (and hence better?) than any original.

Halberstam (1997, 116) argues that "camp has not worked for 'kings' and that therefore different systems of humor and different circuits of performance and theater must be corralled in order to make the king role interesting." The *Full Monty* number, however, obviously calls into question her assertion that, while it has always been an important part of gay male culture, camp has not worked for kings. In this context it is particularly interesting that Halberstam (1997, 116) defines camp as an "ironic gender practice within which gender traits are exaggerated for theatrical and often comic effect," which, I would argue, is exactly what happens in the case of H.I.S. Kings' rendition of *The Full Monty* and "The Scotsman." These and similar H.I.S. Kings numbers contradict the notion that camp "tends to be the genre for an outrageous performance of femininity . . . rather than outrageous performances of masculinity" (Halberstam 1998, 237). I'm not denying the obvious asymmetry between male and female impersonation. However, it needs to be pointed out that drag queens–or gay men, for that matter–do not have a monopoly on camp. So, let me answer the question "Can drag kings do camp?" with another question, made famous by Eve Sedgwick, "Does the pope wear a dress?"[3]

The same kind of irreverent attitude H.I.S. Kings display in liberally utilizing the supposedly gay male form of camp in their drag king performances also characterizes their approach to the issue of race. One characteristic of the New York drag king scene on which many observers have commented is the racial segregation of public lesbian space. As Halberstam (1997, 119) observes, "A split between clubs that attract white lesbians [in the East Village] and those which draw lesbians of color [in midtown] does linger on." Halberstam notes that none of the kings she spoke to were willing to address the issue of racially split lesbian spaces. Perhaps this reluctance to deal with the politically and emotionally charged issue of race also helps to explain the New York kings' anxiety about cross-ethnic performances. As understandable as these trepidations may be in some cases, occasionally they assume comical proportions. This is made painfully obvious in a short film by Lucia Davis (1999), which introduces the kings of New York to a wider audience. In one segment of her film Davis documents one of the rare occasions during which New York drag kings actually work together to stage numbers by various musical groups. When no more than three African American kings can be found for a rendition of a song by the Jackson Five, the three choose to perform as a trio, the Jackson "Five," rather than having non-black kings join them as Jackson brothers four and five. Apparently, the playfulness the kings exhibit in their performance of masculinity does not extend to the problematic of race, where authenticity seems to be the name of the game instead.

This contrasts sharply with the modus operandi in Columbus, where H.I.S. Kings frequently cross racial and ethnic lines in their performances, with Asian kings performing black masculinities, black kings performing white masculinities, white kings performing Latino masculinities, and so on. H.I.S. Kings' cross-racial acts and their willingness to directly address the issue of race in their performances may be attributable to a number of factors. To begin with, the smaller number of local lesbian bars and venues for drag performers may make racial segregation less feasible in Columbus than in New York. Or perhaps it is the fact that both H.I.S. Kings and the production company they formed, Fast Friday Productions, have been racially mixed from their inception that makes race less of a divisive issue in the Columbus scene. In any event, it is apparent that kings in the heartland are not necessarily subject to the same laws that govern the drag king scene in big cities such as New York. Perhaps the lack of racial tensions constitutes one way in which it may be beneficial to be on the margins of national queer culture, for ironically it allows H.I.S. Kings to address the issue of race in their performances, which are playful, provocative, and politically astute at the same time. In other words, the fact that race is less of an issue for kings and their audiences in Columbus allows H.I.S. Kings to make it more of an issue in some of the innovative numbers they stage.

H.I.S. Kings' rendition of the 1997 hit song "We Trying to Stay Alive" by hip hop artist Wyclef Jean (1997) provides a particularly instructive example of the kind of work this crossing of racial boundaries makes possible. In this song, Wyclef samples the Bee Gees' 1970s disco anthem "Staying Alive." Unlike a cover version of a particular song, which usually does not acknowledge the original it appropriates, sampling pays tribute to the music being cited by incorporating pieces of the original into the new composition so that the original piece of music can usually be identified and attributed to a specific performer. Because the new context has the potential to change the meaning of the song being sampled, it could be argued that sampling creates a new work altogether rather than merely copying previous music. In their performance of "We Trying to Stay Alive," H.I.S. Kings playfully utilize this blurring of the boundaries between "original" and "copy." While the rap part of the song is interpreted by a white King, the sample of the Bee Gees' song is delivered by three black Kings. This scenario, it could be argued, turns on its head the reality of the American music industry, which has been characterized by the appropriation of black styles–for example in music and fashion–by white artists and (eventually) white audiences. Unlike sampling, a technique pioneered by African American hip hop artists such as Wyclef and the late Notorious B.I.G, the traditional expropriation of black music by white artists rarely acknowledges original sources or compensates originators. In the H.I.S. Kings' performance, sampling can be read as a potential reversal of or, at the very least, an ironic commentary on the racial politics of cultural appropriation.

In spite of this apparent fluidity, however, it needs to be pointed out that "the performance of whiteness by a black king and the performance of blackness by a white king have very different meanings and resonances" (Halberstam 1997, 125). This seems especially true in the economic context of a music industry characterized by the appropriation of black musical styles by white artists from Elvis to the Rolling Stones to Madonna. Therefore, it comes as no surprise that predominantly white audiences tend to be accepting and even appreciative of white Kings performing musical numbers by black artists, whereas black Kings performing songs by white singers occasionally meet with quite a bit of resistance.[4] This fact may well explain why African American Kings are, for the most part, less inclined to cross racial lines in their performances than their white colleagues.

As Richard Dyer (1997) argues, whites take up the position of ordinariness, belonging to what they think of not as a particular race, just the human race. It is this apparent unremarkability of whiteness coupled with its assumed representativeness–being no race and every race at the same time–that allows white kings to cross racial lines with ease while black kings, whose racial difference is clearly marked, are expected to respect racial boundaries. Consequently, there seems to be a much lower incidence of African American Kings performing the music of white artists than there is of white Kings performing black music. This imbalance, however, is due to the "invisibility" of whiteness described by Dyer and not, as Halberstam (1997, 116) claims, the fact that "white masculinity remains a somewhat difficult object of parody." For as we have seen, H.I.S. Kings parody a wide variety of masculinities, including white masculinities. Nonetheless, the fact remains that H.I.S. King audiences seem to accept parodies of white masculinities–the kind we see in H.I.S. Kings' version of *The Full Monty* and "The Scotsman"–more readily if they are performed by white Kings.

In addition to the variety of masculinities they perform, some members of H.I.S. Kings have also distinguished themselves through their captivating performances of femininity. Thus, Baby T (Donna Baladad), an Asian member of the Columbus company, on one occasion presents himself as a suave gentleman singing about his desire to "Kiss the Girl," but in a different number acts upon his desire to *be* the girl. In the dance that Baby T and his Caucasian partner Reardon (Jacci Morrison) perform to the theme song from *Dirty Dancing*, Baby T's femininity is set off by Reardon's masculinity, already well-established in a previous number, in which he performs as a man and quite rightly declares that he's just "Too Sexy." Reardon's "masculinity" offsets Baby T's "femininity" and bolsters the illusion of sexual difference their number creates.

The representation of masculinity and femininity in this act, however, is complicated by a number of factors. For one thing Baby T's performance queers both the character played by Jennifer Grey in the movie and her relationship with the Patrick Swayze character by making theirs an interracial affair and thus undercutting the representative character of white heterosexuality.[5] More importantly perhaps, Baby T's carefully crafted femininity–the girlish pink of her dress, the hair cut, the demure facial expression, the red lips, and the bobby socks–are undercut by a physical marker that seems to contradict this construction of femininity: Baby T's tattoos. One of the modes of drag king performance Halberstam (1998, 260) distinguishes is "layering," which she defines as a recognizably "male role [being] layered on top of the king's own masculinity." This definition may be helpful for kings who exclusively perform masculinity, yet it seems entirely too limited for an analysis of Reardon and Baby T's performance, for it does not describe the ways in which all gendered performances–including the performance of femininity–may in fact be layered.

In Baby T's case tattoos are a signifier for a more masculine kind of femininity and thus alert us to the fact that in this particular case *femininity* is layered on top of the performer's own female masculinity. This becomes especially clear at the moment during their dance when the tattoos Reardon and Baby T sport on their upper arms are at approximately the same height. This creates a visual parallel, which on a symbolic level suggests a kind of similarity between the two dancers, a similarity that undercuts the appearance of sexual difference on which the performance of heterosexuality is based, and thus calls into question the "naturalistic effects of heterosexualized genders" (Butler 1991, 21). I'm not suggesting that a performance should be a seamless act or that Reardon and Baby T fail because their performance is not seamless. On the contrary, I agree with Halberstam (1998, 260) that "the permeable boundaries between acting and being" help expose the artificiality of conventional gender roles. However, we need to add one important point here: a drag king may expose the artificiality of conventional gender roles not only through his performance of masculinity but just as effectively, if not more effectively, through a performance of femininity.

In much of her work, Judith Butler has challenged the normative relations between sex, gender, and desire–the belief that there is first a sex that is expressed through a gender and then through a sexuality. Gender, Butler argues, is a regulatory fiction that naturalizes heterosexuality (for instance, as the logical outcome or the epitome of proper sexual identification and appropriate gender expression). Thus, to be male = to act masculine = to desire women, while to be female = to act feminine = to desire men. In other words, real men and real women are heterosexual. As an alternative, Butler explores how the deconstruction of normative models of gender legitimates gay and lesbian subject-positions and proposes a definition of gender as "performative." While Butler is interested in all performativities that displace the law of the sex/gender system, she focuses on drag, which offers a useful cultural model for deconstructing the substantive appearance of gender by exposing its constitutive parts. Drag, according to Butler (1991, 21),

> is not the putting on of a gender that belongs properly to some other group, i.e., an act of *expropriation* or *appropriation* that assumes that gender is the rightful property of sex, that 'masculine' belongs to 'male' and 'feminine' belongs to 'female'. There is no proper gender, a gender proper to one sex rather than another, which is in some sense that sex's cultural property.

H.I.S. Kings' performances of different kinds of femininity and different kinds of masculinity demonstrate that, as Butler argues, "drag enacts the very structure of impersonation by which *any gender* is assumed" (21)–including, one might add, the performance of femininity by women.

H.I.S. Kings' African American emcee extraordinaire, who occasionally performs as King Luster, more frequently delights audiences as Lustivious de la Virgion. Lustivious is what one might call a "female drag queen": she presents a construction of femininity, which is "relayed through a gay male aesthetic" (Halberstam 1998, 240). A recent example of the influence of a gay male aesthetic on the cultural construction of femininity is the description of Monica Lewinsky's nemesis Linda Tripp as "looking like a badly made up drag queen" as well as the rejection of this characterization as "an insult to drag queens everywhere." The implication here is clear: Tripp's performance of femininity appears to be lacking when compared to the more successful performance of the drag queen.[6] H.I.S. Kings, the name of the ensemble, read as a possessive rather than an acronym, interpellates the performers as "his" Kings and puts their performances of masculinity in relation to the emcee's performance of femininity. This in turn suggests that Lustivious is not a woman or performing herself as a woman; she is a female drag queen, a woman pretending to be man, pretending to be a woman.

Lustivious drives home this point most forcefully in a number based on a song by the artist formerly and once again known as Prince. Lustivious performs as a drag queen up to the point where she wipes off her feminine makeup and dabs her face with black shoe polish to suggest sideburns, a goatee and a mustache. Just as Prince poses the all-important question "Do you want him or do you want me?" Lustivious concludes her transformation by ripping off her wig and exposing her/his bald head. The choice of music and the sexually ambivalent persona of the artist already introduce the theme of gender ambiguity.[7] The question "Do you want him or do you want me?" is equally ambivalent, for the assumption of a heterosexual scenario here depends entirely on the presupposition that the speaker is male and the addressee of the question female. The performer's application of black shoe polish, on the other hand, is reminiscent of vaudeville entertainers blackening their faces before a performance in a minstrel show. The layering of blackface on a black face, however, problematizes the construction of race and racial identities at the same time as her/his performance calls attention to the construction of gender and the ways in which gender performances are always inflected by race.

As a final point, it is important to note that the removal of the wig, rather than producing the certainty and clarity that the taking off of a disguise is supposed to provide, complicates matters even further. This indeterminacy distinguishes the King's disclosure from that of the drag *queen*, who at the end of a performance frequently reveals the man underneath. This subcultural convention has been taken up in a popcultural context by Blake Edwards' film comedy *Victor/Victoria* (1982) in which Julie Andrews plays Victoria, a gifted soprano who can't find work in prewar Paris until a gay friend convinces her to audition for a nightclub gig as a female impersonator. Playing a woman pretending to be a man pretending to be woman, Victor ends all of his cabaret performances by ostentatiously removing his wig–a gesture greeted by the audience's expressions of disbelief and delight. As Chris Straayer (1992) so persuasively argues, "Ending 'his' female impersonation act with a double negative, Victor/Victoria collapses these generic gender conventions of short hair and removal of the wig to 'expose her (male) disguise as real.'" The problem, albeit a temporary one, is that because of this revelation Victor drops out of the heterosexual economy by no longer being available as a suitable object of desire for King Marchand, the

Chicago gangster played by James Garner. The rest of the film is focused on Marchand's attempt to reveal Victoria's true identity as a woman in order to legitimize his heterosexual pursuit of her. The case of Lustivious, however, is not that simple. Her performance contests the notion of a temporarily concealed female subject that can be revealed and recuperated within the heterosexual economy. Unlike Victor/Victoria, Lustivious is not a temporary transvestite but a crossdresser whose performance of gender is layered with her performance of queerness and race. This performance negates gender fixity and promotes sexual unfixedness.

The queering of gender categories is also at the very heart of a performance by Toe B., in which he comes onto the stage dressed in cowboy fag drag,[8] including chaps and a Stetson, and dances to the Shania Twain song "I Feel Like a Woman," which interestingly enough is being interpreted by a male voice. (H.I.S. Kings' former musical director Julia Applegate informed me that her mixer allows her to electronically alter the pitch of someone's voice, a technological legerdemain that makes it possible to let Shania Twain both sound like a man and feel like a woman.) Toe. B. proceeds to strip and at one point puts on lipstick with the help of a mirror. As he takes off his hat to reveal long blonde hair (a wig)[9] and tears off his shirt to expose a rhinestone-studded bra, the music changes to the original female version of the song. In the course of his presentation, Toe B. takes us from fag drag to transgender drag and finally to female drag, and in the process demonstrates that there are no "direct expressive lines or causal lines between sex, gender, gender presentation, sexual practice, fantasy and sexuality" (Butler 1991, 25).

In contrast to the fluidity of Toe B.'s gender performance and others I've described above, Halberstam (1998, 232) defines a drag king in a surprisingly fixed way as a female "who dresses up in recognizably male costume and performs theatrically in that costume." Considering the multiple ways in which H.I.S. Kings perform gender, this definition seems much too limiting. If one were to apply this definition to the performance by Toe B. described above, for instance, it would mean that at one time during his act he stops being a drag *king* and–by way of extending Halberstam's argument–becomes a drag *queen*. Perhaps the focus on female masculinity in general is too limiting, as H.I.S. Kings make visible not only the part that masculine women have played in the construction of modern masculinity but also the part that lesbians and butch women have played in the construction of femininity.

* * *

Through tours of the United States and Canada and three international drag king conferences, H.I.S. Kings have shared their style of kinging with kings and audiences across the U.S. and beyond. In the process they have clearly proven that the drag king scene in a Midwestern city such as Columbus is not any less exciting simply because its queer nightlife is less varied than that of, say, New York. On the contrary, the Columbus company puts on a show that is anything but provincial. What they might be lacking in "big city energy"–however we may define that–they more than make up for in theoretical sophistication and originality. More importantly, however, the example of the H.I.S. Kings demonstrates that any theory of drag king performance that focuses exclusively on the traditional cultural centers on the West and East coasts will likely miss some of the most interesting varieties of kinging.

Kinging in the heartland is not a limitation. Quite the opposite. It is precisely H.I.S. Kings' location on the margins of national queer culture that allows them to push the boundaries of drag, most noticeably when it comes to the issues of race and gender. The New York drag king scene is characterized by the racial segregation of the public lesbian space in which drag performances take place; thus New York kings are reluctant to deal with the politically and emotionally charged issue of race. The relative absence of such racial tensions in the Columbus scene goes a long way towards explaining the lightheartedness with which H.I.S. Kings approach the issue of race and the racial politics of drag. H.I.S. Kings have the freedom to make race an issue in some of the innovative numbers they stage, thus infusing the drag king performance with theoretical reflection and political commentary.[10]

The Columbus company's approach to gender politics is characterized by a similar blend of originality and playfulness. H.I.S. Kings' hyperbolic performances of masculinity, which exaggerate gender traits for their theatrical and comical effect, are remarkable for at least two reasons. On the one hand, these performances disprove the dictum that camp only works for the outrageous performance of femininity by staging a uniquely lesbian version of camp; on the other hand, they help to make white masculinity, which heretofore has been considered impervious to satire, a frequent and productive object of parody. Yet it is by performing a range of femininities in addition to a wide variety of masculinities that H.I.S. Kings challenge what is perhaps the most limiting definition of the drag king as a theatrical male impersonator. H.I.S.

Kings demonstrate that a drag king may expose the artificiality of conventional gender roles just as effectively by layering a female role on top of the king's female masculinity. By assuming female as well as male roles, H.I.S. Kings drive home the point that any gender is (a) drag and emphasize the idea that "gender confusion" is not only, as Kate Bornstein (1998) so eloquently puts it, "a small price to pay for social progress" but also highly entertaining.

Most importantly perhaps, the example of H.I.S. Kings suggests that it may be time to abandon the project of defining "*the* Drag King" altogether and focus instead on describing and theorizing the range of drag kings and drag king acts that have developed across the U.S. and across the world. This special volume dedicated to the exploration of drag king culture is, I believe, an important step towards providing us with a more inclusive answer to the question "What is a drag king?" In any event, the example of the Columbus Kings reminds us that any theorization of a national queer phenomenon such as kinging will necessarily be deficient if, at the expense of the heartland, it focuses exclusively on places like New York, or if it falsely assumes that what holds true for queer culture in urban centers also applies to what is happening in the heartland.

NOTES

1. Fortunately, this assertion has recently been challenged by an event that demonstrates that "the Drag King" also lives in small towns and cities, both in the U.S. and abroad. The *First, Second,* and *Third International Drag King Extravaganzas* (IDKE), which took place at the Ohio State University in 1999, 2000, and 2001 respectively, brought drag kings from two-dozen U.S. states and several Canadian provinces to Columbus, Ohio. Granted, we may not count Columbus among the "cities that never sleep," and yet these extravaganzas–part academic conference, part drag kingdom science fair, and part drag king showcase–proved in a most impressive manner that, contrary to what Halberstam suggests, there is queer culture in the heartland; there is a drag king scene in the Midwest. All three *International Drag King Extravaganzas* were arranged by members of H.I.S. Kings, a troupe of about 20 drag kings, who have been organizing drag shows and "dragdoms," amateur drag king showcases, in Columbus, Ohio, since 1996.

2. The reference is to Frank N. Furter, the "sweet transvestite" in *The Rocky Horror Picture Show* (Sharman, 1975).

3. Sedgwick (1990, 52) uses this rhetorical question to comment on the fact that while many of the most centrally canonical figures in the Euro-American tradition were homosexual, literary analysis has traditionally paid little attention to questions of same-sex desire. Hence the project of queering the canon of Euro-American literature

entails making homosexuality a salient category of literary scholarship rather than merely inserting homosexual writers into that canon:

Has there ever been a gay Socrates?
Has there ever been a gay Shakespeare?
Has there ever been a gay Proust?
Does the Pope wear a dress?

4. During a plenary session at the first IDKE, October 16, 1999, Maxwell (Shani Scott) of the H.I.S. Kings talked frankly about his experience "doing white music" as an African American King. According to Maxwell, he has no qualms about doing Billy Idol simply because he likes Idol's music and persona. While he prides himself on getting Billy Idol's moves and facial expressions–including his trademark sneer–"just right," he admits being taken aback by the audience's reaction: "It was as if they were saying 'Why the f*** is he doing a *white* artist?'"

5. Jennifer Grey's claim to representativeness is of course already compromised by the fact that the character she plays in the movie is Jewish. The presence of an interracial couple, however, seems to complicate matters even more than the movie character's ethnicity.

6. This joke works on least two levels. On the one hand it deconstructs the substantive appearance of gender by suggesting that femininity can be performed, to varying degrees of success, by anyone, no matter what their gender. On the other hand, the misogynistic implication of this joke is that men simply are (or make) better women.

7. As Bette Midler (1985) says about Prince in one of her comedy routines, "Maybe it's just me, but when there's a sex symbol, I'd like to know the sex of the symbol."

8. Halberstam (1998, 253) defines "fag drag" as a form of gay male masculinity that references gay male sex play, such as the "Castro clone" or a Village People type of hypermasculinity.

9. In this context it is interesting to note that the longhaired wig which here signifies femininity, in a different context may well signify masculinity, for example in a number in which King Andy (Alyson Mann) performs "Give It Away" by the Red Hot Chili Peppers, a band which is known as much for the long hair of its male members as for their music.

10. In addition to their career in lesbian entertainment, most of the H.I.S. Kings are also (current or former) students of Women's Studies, which certainly contributes to the theoretical sophistication of their shows. This is not, of course, to suggest that graduate school is the only way to attain theoretical sophistication. In fact, just as one can be a feminist without being Women's Studies student, so some very provocative theoretical work is being done by H.I.S. Kings who are not associated with the university.

REFERENCES

Barthes, Roland. 1972. *Mythologies.* Translated by Annette Lavers. New York: The Noonday Press.

Bornstein, Kate. 1998. "My Gender Workbook." Reading at An Open Book, Columbus, Ohio. 5 February.

Butler, Judith. 1991. "Imitation and Gender Insubordination." Pp. 13-31 in *Inside/Out: Lesbian Theories, Gay Theories,* ed. Diana Fuss. New York: Routledge.

Davis, Lucia. 1996. *Kings of New York.* Produced and directed by Lucia Davis. 6 mins. Esoterikpix. Videocassette.

Dyer, Richard. 1997. *White.* New York: Routledge.

Finch, Nigel. 1996. *Stonewall.* Directed by Nigel Finch. 99 min. Strand Releasing/BMG Entertainment. Videocassette.

Halberstam, Judith. 1997. "Mackdaddy, Superfly, Rapper: Gender, Race, and Masculinity in the Drag King Scene." *Social Text* 52-53 (1997): 104-31.

_____. 1998. "Drag Kings: Masculinity and Performance." Pp. 267-78 in *Female Masculinity.* Durham: Duke University Press, 1998.

_____. 2001. "Oh Behave! Austin Powers and the Drag Kings." *GLQ: A Journal of Lesbian and Gay Studies* 7.3: 425-52.

Midler, Bette. 1985. *Mud* Will *Be Flung Tonight!* Atlantic 81291-2. CD.

Sedgwick, Eve Kosofsky. 1990. Pp. 154-64 in *Epistemology of the Closet.* Durham: Duke University Press.

Sharman, Jim. 1975. *The Rocky Horror Picture Show.* Directed by Jim Sharman. 100 min. Videocassette.

Spurlin, William J. 1996. "Introduction: What?! Queers in the Midwest?" Pp. xi-xxv in *Reclaiming the Heartland: Lesbian and Gay Voices from the Midwest,* eds. Karen Lee Osborne and William J. Spurlin. Minneapolis: University of Minnesota Press.

Straayer, Chris. 1992. "Redressing the 'Natural': The Temporary Transvestite Film." *Wide Angle* 14:1: 36-55.

Volcano, Del LaGrace and Judith "Jack" Halberstam. 1999. *The Drag King Book.* London: Serpent's Tail.

Wyclef Jean. 1997. *Wyclef Jean Presents the Carnival Featuring the Refugee All Stars.* Sony/Columbia B000002BV3. CD.

Walk Like a Man:
Enactments and Embodiments
of Masculinity and the Potential
for Multiple Genders

Sheila "Dragon Fly" Koenig, BA

SUMMARY. With this chapter, I explore the potential of drag king performance as a tool of deconstructing gender. I begin with a brief examination of the ways that gender is constructed as natural through the repetition of a set of norms, noting the pervasiveness of these norms and their location at the center of cultural imagination. I then turn to the idea of drag as a practice of subverting these norms through breaking their repetition. I argue that drag king performance, through its failure to approximate the "natural male," draws attention to the very constructedness of the category, and thus of all naturalized categories of gender. Using the budding Edmonton drag king scene as a case example, I discuss some of the ways that drag kings take queer theory and gender deconstruction out of the classroom and into practice. I speculate as to the effectiveness of such practices in the realm of queer theory, pointing to the ways that these performances may be read to reinforce rather than subvert gender norms. I also look at the complexities of "passing" gender performances, such as transsexual or transgendered practices, and the ways that these practices align or do not align with performances intending to fail. I propose that the emergence of these practices is in itself a beginning step toward a reevaluation of normative gender, and toward a radical reinvention of new gender possibilities. *[Article copies available for a fee from The Haworth Document Delivery Service: 1-800-HAWORTH. E-mail address:*

[Haworth co-indexing entry note]: "Walk Like a Man: Enactments and Embodiments of Masculinity and the Potential for Multiple Genders." Koenig, Sheila "Dragon Fly." Co-published simultaneously in *Journal of Homosexuality* (Harrington Park Press, an imprint of The Haworth Press, Inc.) Vol. 43, No. 3/4, 2002, pp. 145-159; and: *The Drag King Anthology* (ed: Donna Troka, Kathleen LeBesco, and Jean Bobby Noble) Harrington Park Press, an imprint of The Haworth Press, Inc., 2002, pp. 145-159. Single or multiple copies of this article are available for a fee from The Haworth Document Delivery Service [1-800-HAWORTH, 9:00 a.m. - 5:00 p.m. (EST). E-mail address: docdelivery@haworthpress.com].

KEYWORDS. Drag kings, queer theory, gender, transgender, Edmonton, Fly Bastards, lesbian, sexuality, male impersonation, performativity

What are you, a Boy or a Girl?
-Folk saying

You could say I'm one inevitability of a post-modern anti-spiritualist acquisitive culture.

—-Kate Bornstein

We live in a society in which we cannot ignore gender; its force is felt everywhere; institutions are designed around it. From the moment a child is born and the pronunciation is declared, "It's a _____," the performance begins. Judith Butler maintains that all of gender is a performance, designed to reinforce the categories of "man" and "woman" as dictated by heteronormative, patriarchal culture (Butler 1991). Through this performance, the two sexes are held up to be original and thus natural, and, conversely, yet simultaneously, are revealed to be a construction. However, acknowledging the constructed nature of gender does not lead to an ability to simply escape the whole gender system, as has been attempted by some early radical lesbian feminists. Gender is a very pervasive institution that precludes any notion of an objective outside analysis of it. We are all implicated in gender; the extent to which we reinforce or subvert boundaries set up surrounding gender turns on the extent to which we "pass" or "fail" in our own performance. Performing gender with the specific intention to fail, then, is a practice of resistance. Drag performances can act in such a way. Although drag king performances have only recently begun to receive any critical attention, I would suggest that such practices work in various ways to challenge boundaries surrounding the categories of "man" and "woman," destabilizing the implied "originality" of these categories and the centrality of maleness to cultural subjectivity.

GENDER PERFORMATIVITY AND SUBVERSION

The Gender Cycle: Imitation and Repetition

Judith Butler's "Imitation and Gender Insubordination" marks one of the first and most detailed explorations of gender as the product of its own repeated performance. She points to all of gender as a performance, a sort of drag. Rather than an imitation of some pre-existing gender, drag can be seen in this way to encompass the way that any gender is played out:

> Drag constitutes the mundane way in which genders are appropriated, theatricalized, worn, and done; it implies that all gendering is a kind of impersonation and approximation. If this is true, it seems, there is no original or primary gender that drag imitates, but *gender is a kind of imitation for which there is no original*; in fact, it is a kind of imitation that produces the very notion of the original as an *effect* and consequence of the imitation itself. (Butler 1991, 21)

Gender, then, is a performance which works to solidify the notion of its originality. It is a form of boundary policing; it proclaims its own authority as original, and thus dubs any performance contrary to its specific designations "Other," "imitation," "failure," etc. Interestingly, it is precisely this designation of "Otherness" upon which heteronormative gender structures are dependent in order to prove their "originality." Thus, in a sense, by its self-proclamation of originality, heteronormative gender reveals itself to be constructed.

Nonetheless the construction of gender is extremely pervasive; one cannot simply remove oneself from the system of gender duality. Many early radical feminists have attempted such strategies of resistance. Monique Wittig's paper "The Straight Mind," for example, endeavors to create a distinction between "woman," or the gendered female constructed within heterosexual institutions, and "lesbian," or the autonomous female who lives outside of heterosexual institutions, and thus outside of gender. She maintains that "woman" is defined only in her relation to, or rather her difference from, man, the norm. Thus a lesbian, because she refuses to be defined only in terms of her Otherness, ceases to be woman:

> Frankly, [the question of what is woman] is a problem that lesbians do not have because of a change of perspective, and it would

> be incorrect to say that lesbians associate, make love, live with women, for "woman" has meaning only in heterosexual systems of thought and heterosexual economic systems. Lesbians are not women. (Witting 1992, 32)

Lesbians, separated from their relation to men, jump the gender ship, so to speak, and exist outside the constraints of gender. Wittig seems to ignore the various new constraints that such strategies as separation in turn create.

Although I see value in creating new spaces for different genders and sexualities, I find her argument problematic for various reasons. First, rather than to present a challenge to any existing categories of gender, she simply creates a third category in which to escape the bonds of the first two. In order to maintain such a category, boundaries are immediately set up surrounding what constitutes a "lesbian." The exclusion of various women is a foregone conclusion. I would argue that this is precisely the downfall of radical lesbian separatism: the policing of boundaries that simply cannot be sustained. That such boundaries can be set up at all assumes a vantage point, presumably outside the gender system, from which a subject can presume to judge what is excluded from and included within "lesbian." This is the second problem I identify within Wittig's argument. Gender is an institution around which our society is structured in intricate ways. There is no "outside." Wittig's "lesbian" is defined by her rejection of men; thus she is as wrapped up in gender as any prior category. Stepping outside of gender is not an option.

As Butler notes, gender "is a *compulsory* performance in the sense that acting out of line with heterosexual norms brings with it ostracism, punishment, and violence" (Butler 1991, 24). Failure to approximate the norms set up within heteronormative gender may result in various punitive measures enacted upon the transgressor. Such policing ensures that the performance will be repeated, and will gain more power in its claim to originality through its repetition. Yet, as we have already established, the constructedness of heteronormative gender is revealed in this very claim. As Butler states, "Heterosexuality is always in the process of imitating and approximating its own phantasmic idealization of itself–and *failing*" (Butler 1991, 21). It is in the gaps, the failures of heteroperformativity to approximate itself, that the "originality," the "naturalness," of heteronormative categories of "man" and "woman" are challenged.

The Project of Drag: Disrupting the Repetition

Thus the project of drag as a subversive practice is to fail. Rather than an attempt to step outside of heteronormative gender practice, drag is a practice which is immersed in gender. It is the hyperbolic enactment of gender, aimed at exploding boundaries surrounding gender norms by highlighting their absurdity. Drag attempts to reveal the constructedness of gender, to interrupt the cycle of repetition that gives power to the proclamation of "originality" that heteronormative gender assumes. As Butler notes, "Queer appropriation of the performative mimes and exposes both the binding power of the heterosexualizing law *and its expropriability*" (Butler 1993, 22). Drag performance is a practice of caricaturing the norms set up around gender while blurring these norms, creating ambiguity in which gender then can be questioned and disrupted.

Most of the work that has been done addressing drag, including the work of Judith Butler, tends to focus on drag queen performances. I would suggest that there are various reasons for this, not the least important being the spectacularity of femaleness. It has been argued that drag queen performance receives more attention than drag kinging because the former is viewed as more transgressive due to its apparent measure of downward mobility. Enacting womanhood is enacting a desire for lower status, and thus directly challenges norms surrounding what is "appropriate" desire. However, I want, for now, to move away from explanations that turn on desire. Drag is not necessarily an expression of desire for a body that one does not inhabit. Such explanations conflate drag with transsexuality, and these two, however linked, are certainly not the same thing, as I will discuss later.

Rather, I point here to the visibility of femaleness. Although Monique Wittig's analysis is fraught with problems, she does make a valid point regarding gender: "men are not different, whites are not different, nor are the masters" (Wittig 1992, 29). Maleness is an aspect of transparency in our culture. Women, as other-than-men, are marked by their Otherness, and are thus watched more carefully than men. Race, class, language "differences" (i.e., differences from the "original" white, male, bourgeois, anglo/euroamerican) further mark bodies and spectacularize them. Our bodies are read in various ways, at every moment. Drag queens, then, are looked upon as women's bodies are looked upon, and through their failure to approximate conventional femaleness, elicit a more vocal response. The watching of women's bodies as a cultural practice makes the drag queen body more visible than that of the drag king.

Redirecting the Gaze: Drag Kings and the Art of Hyperbole

The project of drag king performance, then, differs somewhat from that of the drag queen. While queens draw attention to the conventions of "womanness," exposing the spectacle to be a construction of cultural imagination, kinging directs its attack at the *spectator*. Drag kings redirect the gaze toward the conventions of maleness, thus making a spectacle of the position which has been constructed as "transparent." This notion of transparency, as Maria Lugones outlines it, marks a vantage point from which "Otherness" can be judged as such:

> Thickness and transparency are group relative. Individuals are transparent with respect to their group if they perceive their needs, interests, ways, as those of the group and if this perception becomes dominant or hegemonical in the group. (Lugones 1994, 474)

Maleness in heteronormative culture becomes a criterion for transparency, along with whiteness, Englishness, middle-classness, etc. As Wittig has pointed out, gender is something which belongs to women; it is the marker by which women are distinguished as "Other."

Thus the hyperbolic enactment of masculinity, seen to be a transparent property of maleness, is resistant in that it spectacularizes the transparent. Drag king performance takes and exploits markers of "masculinity" to the point that these markers become visible as constructions. Edmonton drag king Little Vinnie describes his character as a parodic embodiment of an archetypal masculine figure:

> He's a sleaze, really. He's like a used-car salesman, you know, polyester suit and all. He picks his teeth with his tongue and puts one over on you. He's smooth, kind of creepy, I wouldn't look twice at him, he might get the wrong idea. He's the stock incompetent mobster in a Hollywood movie, really sleazy and silly. Fine to laugh at, but you don't want to get to know him. (Author interview 2000)[1]

Vinnie brings to stage the rudeness, crudeness, and bad-dudeness that we have come to associate with masculinity; his audiences associate this guy with stock movie characters and used-car salesmen, both well-known constructions of masculinity. Except that the construction is made atypical by its performance, on a stage, in exaggeration, and by a woman. Through his imitation of, yet failure to approximate entirely, norms of masculinity, Little Vinnie brings the audience to gaze upon the typical gaz*er*. His act works to queer the centre by making what is typically thought of as the centre a rather queer thing to see.

What I refer to as hyperbolized performance of masculinity, however, is not necessarily an acting up, so to speak; in fact, it is more of a tuning down. As we have already discussed, women are seen as more spectacular than men. Enacting maleness, then, requires a stripping down of sorts. As Judith Halberstam notes, "The art of the male impersonator relies upon understatement and cool macho rather than theatricality and histrionics" (Halberstam and Volcano 1999, 35). The theatrics of a drag king's stage show are not found in grandiose gestures or bright lights and music. Rather, the act is a restriction of action. As Edmonton king Muff E. Oso explains, "It's amazing how much differently you move and take up space when in drag. Men don't move! You have to tone it down, point a finger or clench a fist when your female persona might have wanted to shake her hips or wave her hands in the air. You have to minimize everything." Pelvis Parsley, fellow Edmonton king, asserts that

> men don't move because they don't have to. They take up twice the space that women do, and then some. When I'm a boy, I don't have to wave my hands because with the simple addition of facial hair and a pair of boots I have doubled in size! Muff's clenched fist is a subtle but powerful action that works to assert a wider circle of personal space that goes with being male.

Part of the dramatization of masculinity, then, is the enactment of subtlety; drag kings emphasize the understatement of the male body.

DRAG AND FTM: ALLIANCES AND CONFLICTS

Queer Theory vs. Identity Politics: Critiques of Butler and Halberstam

However, FTM performance is not necessarily encapsulated in the theatrics of a drag king show. There are various approaches to female masculinity, and varying degrees to which enactments of female masculinity are invested in gender systems. Thus far I have spoken only of the ways that hyperbolic enactments work to reveal masculinity as a construct to be exploded. In fact the varying ways that female masculinity is enacted often conflict with and directly challenge one another. As Halberstam notes,

> Some butch Drag Kings might accuse the femme Drag Kings of not being real and of just playing; some transgender Drag Kings highlight the difference between their real moustaches and the fake facial hair of the other kings; some female-to-male transsexuals see the whole Drag King scene as a trivialization of the gender issues they face on a daily basis. (Halberstam and Volcano 1999, 36)

Indeed, literature on drag kings (of which there is very little), butch lesbian identities, and FTM transsexual and transgendered experience are fraught with opposing views, both between groups and among members of each. The extent to which any of these practices can be aligned is dependent on context.

I will not attempt to create some sort of continuum between drag and transgendered practice; any suggestion of a flawless alliance would be both naïve and presumptuous on my part. The most I can do is to suggest that some practices of drag hold continuities with some practices of transsexuality. Along these same lines there are also vast discontinuities. I have based much of my discussion of gender performativity on the works of queer theorists such as Judith Butler and Judith Halberstam, both of whom, I should note, have been highly criticized by members of transsexual, transgendered, and/or "transgressively gendered" groups.[2] Indeed, both theorists tend to speak over the experiences of many people within these groups, producing theories which inadequately address the real effects of gender on such people.

Butler's discussion of drag focuses only on the enactment of heterosexual gender categories, ignoring the ways that drag can expose "Gender" to consist of many genders. That is, she does not consider the existence of multiple genders or sexes. She argues that "[t]he critical promise of drag does not have to do with the proliferation of genders, as if sheer numbers would do the job, but rather with the exposure or the failure of heterosexual regimes to ever fully contain their own ideals" (Butler 1993, 26). Her analysis precludes the creation of alternative genders; Butler assumes that drag is, as Chapman and Duplessis note, "*only* a representation of gender norms" (1997, 178). Drag, according to Butler, is an imitation of heterosexual gender norms which works to point out their own imitation of themselves. It does not challenge the duality of gender; it does not sufficiently acknowledge the spaces created for new genders, or transgenders, to exist.

Likewise, Halberstam has theorized female masculinity in such a way as to erase any particular experience of transsexuality with her work "F2M: The Making of Female Masculinity." She states that

> [w]e are all transsexuals except that the *trans* becomes less and less clear (and more and more queer). We are all cross-dressers but where are we crossing from and to what? There is no "other" side, no "opposite" sex, no natural divide to be spanned by surgery, by disguise, by passing. . . . The breakdown of genders and sexualities into identities is in many ways, therefore an endless project, and it is perhaps preferable therefore to acknowledge that gender is defined by its transitivity, that sexuality manifests as multiple sexualities, and that therefore we are all transsexuals. There are no transsexuals. (Halberstam 1994, 212, 226)

Unlike Butler, Halberstam does assert that there can be many genders, sexes, sexualities, etc. However, in her assertion that all gender is transgender, she negates the notion of a particular transsexual experience. As Chapman and Duplessis argue, her argument is "a sweeping statement that sweeps transsexuality as a specific social struggle under the carpet" (Chapman and Duplessis 1997, 178).

Thus, theorizing drag, FTM transsexuality, butch subjectivity, female masculinity, etc., is tricky business. Queer theory is one of the many approaches, but has yet hardly scratched the surface of what sorts of alliances, and disalliances, can be made among these very different groupings. The implications of trans-gendered identities (and I hyphenate this word to highlight the many variations of "trans" that all of these gender performances entail) in any discussion of drag become very important; however, it is all-too easy (and all-too-often done) to speak for and about transsexuality without acknowledging, or, even worse, by incorrectly appropriating, the experience of transsexual people. I cannot assume to speak about such experience. I have experienced drag as a performance, yet neither can I assume to speak for drag kings. I think it is safe to assume that there will be no unifying theory. There is the further risk of *over*theorizing, of ignoring the ways that discussions of gender transgression can become so bound up in theory that new boundaries are created which counter any attempts at political alliance between drag and transgendered practice.

Common Enemies: Resistance as a Point of Alignment

For theories can bend as well as genders; in theory and in practice, there are places where these different gender blends intersect, working with one another to displace the centrality of heteronormative gender categorization. Chapman and DuPlessis write:

> transgender self-definition is about gender definition in public, collective, and coalitional forms. Because of its embodied resistance to prescribed gender roles, transgender and transsexual politics can join transgressively gendered people, lesbians, and feminists in a communal challenge to the effects of sexual dimorphism. Together, as transsexuals, transgenders, feminists, lesbians, queers, we can counter the violence–both physical and epistemological–of heterosexism. (Chapman and Duplessis 1997, 181)

In their trans-aggressive call-to-arms, Chapman and DuPlessis point to one factor that unites all transgressively gendered people, be they drag kings, lesbians, straight butch women, transsexuals, etc.: difference. This difference manifests itself in a multiplicity of ways. Embodiment, sexuality, histrionics, identities, all become important in marking and creating difference. Drag, with its parodic representation of gender "norms," reveals the mechanics of what constitutes a not-so-original gender construction. In the context of the Edmonton drag king scene, this difference has become a driving force of performance. As Pelvis Parsley notes, "becoming a man was at first, for me, just something fun to do. To be honest, I always look 'like a boy,' whatever that means; I never get out of a public washroom without some bruises on my femme ego. Dressing femme has always felt like drag. So this was just another drag, another body to inhabit. It's nice to be mistaken for a man when you're trying to be." Parsley's adoption of "another drag" leads to the creation of new genders to embody. He also notes the change in his own perception of masculinity: "I went from seeing this as a switch from one gender to another to seeing it as a fluidity of genders. There isn't one 'masculinity' to perform, there are so many genders to play with." Parsley's experience with drag has led him to reject a binary gender system in favor of a more fluid, malleable model.

Muff E. Oso also sees his male embodiment as a liberating space, particularly in the sense that it frees the "man within" that, when in female persona, Muff is not allowed to manifest:

> I was a moderately feminine woman with no interest in [doing drag]. I was attracted to the aesthetic and the performance of it all, the makeup, the binding of breasts, the clothes, the sock in the crotch, basically the artistic process of creating a character. One afternoon I was making mustaches for the boys and I tried one on to make sure it was the right size, what happened next is what I refer to as my sex change. It was like looking in the mirror and slowly dropping every attachment to my female features. I started gluing on huge porkchop sideburns and a soul patch to go with my leatherman mustache. I created Muff E. Oso that day, he is a tough urban cowboy/trucker with a heart of gold.

In Muff's case, the theatrics of maleness created a new masculinity as a sort of counter-identity to his "moderately feminine" day-to-day existence. Drag king performance then can be an outlet for differences from the stipulations of assigned gender roles.

Of course the transgression of such roles has a cost, and it is perhaps in the high stakes of gender transgression that alliances between the many practices can and must be made. Pelvis Parsley asserts that his understanding of drag has evolved since his first performances:

> I was a transgendered five-year-old. I wanted to be a boy because then it would be alright to like girls. Then I discovered lesbianism, which was still 'bad' for a little Catholic girl, but then I started to like being bad, and I still do. But there are consequences. Edmonton is a small city in a very conservative province of Canada. I remember one night I went straight from a show to a fast food pizza joint and was scared out of my wits by the stares and murmurs I received. We've all heard about Brandon Teena; many of us have had our own threats. I see that my drag, even though it is momentary and showy, is still received in similar ways that transgender is read. Gender benders are presumed to be acting as something we are not. Well, I was a drag king, that was my gender that night. I wasn't acting like anything else. But I was being hated for it.

Drag king performance, for Parsley, has become its own gender, or series of genders, which are to be valued as such, just as FTM gender is to be valued. The similarity is, once again, found in the transgression of cultural norms surrounding gender. Embodiment, then, becomes a point of alliance. Whether it is the "masculine" appearance of a butch female, or the surgically altered body of a transsexual man, or the spirit-gummed moustache on a drag king, a body that resists the "standard" of heteronormative gendered bodies is once again a point of united difference, and a site of empowerment.

Nonetheless I cannot so easily argue that mutual difference from heteronormative gender can so easily lead to an alliance between drag and FTM transgendered practice. If performance of gender, construction of body, and presentation of identity can only be considered resistant to the extent that they are read as in opposition to conventions surrounding gender, or to the extent, as I have mentioned, that they fail to reiterate the norms set up within heteronormative gender construction, then what do we do with performances that intend to "pass"? I have opined that if a performance "passes," either through sufficiently approximating a norm to be taken for "real," or through sufficiently approximating the norms surrounding "Otherness" to be easily rejected and dismissed, the performance may then work to reinforce rather than resist existing gender norms. I think then that I should qualify this notion of failure. The FTM transsexual who passes and identifies securely as a man may still enact a sort of failure to embody gender norms, not through a trans-identification or through flawed performance, but through a radicalization of gender practice. Here I am talking about a sort of infiltration of manhood, through which by approaching manhood with a knowledge of what it has been to be a woman (at least in body) and to be excluded from manhood, he can redefine what "man" entails. Thus he is failing to conform to a predetermined category of "man." He may not even intend to reinvent manhood in such a way; in some ways, the act of becoming a man physically and accepting this transition emotionally is already radicalizing manhood, since the basis for heteronormative gender categorization is the body into which he has been born. Thus, although I do not see an easy and uncomplicated alliance between FTM transgendered practice and drag, I do see both as acts of resistance that are subversive in their failures to fully approximate heteronormative gender categories.

CONCLUSION: PUTTING THEORY INTO PRACTICE

The question now becomes this: how do we enact a united front of resistance based solely upon our various differences from "the norm"? Especially when there are so many differences between "us"? How do we move beyond personal manipulations of gender norms to open spaces for others to create and inhabit new genders? Here is where the literature becomes very quiet. While various theorists suggest the possibility of alliance along the lines of difference, very few offer any tangible practices through which such difference can be enacted in order to unanimously overturn heteronormative gender. Our differences, in and of their own very existence, are not enough to affect any real change; were they, heteroperformativity would not be sufficient to suppressing and appropriating them.

I suppose that part of the answer (and I will not attempt to outline a complete answer, as I think such a venture is yet out of the question) lies in the emergence of such literature in recent years. Although theorists vary in scope and focus, and even directly conflict with one another, battle one another, appropriate and expropriate each other's work and experience, the visibility that such work brings to issues of drag king performativity, transsexual experience, female masculinity, butch subjectivity, and the multitude of sexualities and genders being articulated helps to bombard existing systems of gender construction with counter-subjectivities. Bodies are being revealed for their mutability, gender for its unstable position between essentialist and constructionist definitions. I see such expansion in this theoretical field as a beginning of sorts to bring such different resistances together in ways that, although they do not always agree, do engage with one another meaningfully to uproot accepted norms surrounding gender. Theory alone, of course, is a privileged pursuit and more work must be done before any significant, allied resistance can be formed, but this is a beginning.

And the growing practices of female masculinity is another beginning. Pelvis Parsley sees the Edmonton scene "as a way of putting theory into practice. And putting practice back into theory, really. Taking on male personas has become far more than a performance for me, it has become a way for me to shift all of those rigid boundaries and overcome the fears I have of masculinity–my own masculinity and that of men I have feared." The embodiment of these fears has led to a breakdown of their construction. Little Vinnie refers to his performance as "being a character that I am afraid of, that I don't like, and making fun of it. Then it becomes something I can contain in a safe space." Muff E. Oso furthers this sentiment by explaining how this safety allows audiences, as well, to alleviate their fears of masculinity:

> I have my big porkchops on and I walk up to an older butch, you know she's been the butch for twenty or thirty years, and I make some kind of sleazy come on, tell her how cute she is, the whole thing, and if I were some guy on the street, she would either knock

me flat out or run away, well, this one, she'd probably knock me flat, but I'm not some guy on the street, and it's all in good fun, and she knows she can giggle and be a girl for five minutes and laugh out loud at the whole game of it. It is a game, and it's one from which a lot of queer people have been, to a large extent, excluded. This way, we're included and we can laugh at how ridiculous it is. I think that humour is political.

By Muff's account, drag king practice is a way of playing with all of the norms surrounding gender, not only those of male/female, but those of butch/femme, trans/nontrans, etc. The practice of drag comes closer to making alliances between gender transgressions than most existing theory.

And these practices and theories comprise a promising start. For the collective and continual bombardment of heteronormative gender structures with the very question "Well, how do you explain this?" is certainly the precursor to our own suggestions toward new explanations. Through such work as I have discussed here as well as a growing body of exploration, both at the theoretical and practical level, of the subjects and subjectivities that gender can hold, we are attempting to carve out not one subjectivity, but a multiplicity of subjectivities which, in their refusal to be defined solely within terms of heteronormative gender boundaries, work to queer these very boundaries, to render them unstable, and to disrupt the effectiveness of their categories. As I have noted, the subversive act of gender turns on its failure to approximate such categories; and again I qualify that failure here. It is not simply a failure, but a blatant refusal to accept that two original sexes are the basis for any gender analysis that disrupts the claims that heteronormative gender structure hold on notions of "originality" and "authority." In this refusal, this qualified failure, the gaps are formed in which new subjectivities, new experiences of gender, new spaces are created to inhabit.

NOTES

1. Interview with The Fly Bastards, July 19, 2000. The Fly Bastards is an Edmonton-based drag king troupe. All further quotes from The Fly Bastards come from a group interview with the author and members Muff E. Oso, Little Vinnie, and Pelvis Parsley, on July 19, 2000.

2. The term "Transgressively gendered" is coined in Bornstein 1995, 13.

REFERENCES

Bornstein, Kate. 1995. *Gender Outlaw: On Men, Women, and the Rest of Us.* New York: Vintage.

Butler, Judith. 1993. "Critically Queer." *GLQ* 1, 1: 17-32.

_____. 1991. "Imitation and Gender Insubordination." Pp. 13-31 in *Inside/Out: Lesbian Theories, Gay Theories,* ed. Diana Fuss. New York: Routledge.

Chapman, Kathleen and Michael DuPlessis. 1997. "Don't Call me *Girl*: Lesbian Theory, Feminist Theory, and Transsexual Identities." Pp. 169-185 in *Cross-Purposes: Lesbians, Feminists, and the Limits of Alliance,* ed. Dana Heller. Bloomington: Indiana University Press.

Cromwell, Jason. 1999. *Transmen and FTMs: Identities, Bodies, Genders, and Sexualities.* Chicago: University of Illinois Press.

Feinberg, Leslie. 1998. *Trans Liberation: Beyond Pink and Blue.* Boston: Beacon.

Halberstam, Judith. 1998. "F2M: The Making of Female Masculinity." Pp. 211-226 in *The Lesbian Postmodern,* ed. Laura Doan. New York: Columbia University Press.

_____. *Female Masculinity.* 1998. Durham, N.C.: Duke University Press.

Halberstam, Judith and Del LaGrace Volcano. 1999. *The Drag King Book.* New York: Serpent's Tail.

Lugones, Maria. 1994. "Purity, Impurity and Separation." *Signs* 19, 2: 458-479.

Stone, Sandy. 1991. "The *Empire* Strikes Back: A Posttranssexual Manifesto." Pp. 280-304 in *Body Guards: The Cultural Politics of Gender Ambiguity,* ed. Julia Epstein and Kristina Straub. New York: Routledge.

Wittig, Monique. 1992. *The Straight Mind and Other Essays.* Boston: Beacon.

Drag Kings in the New Wave: Gender Performance and Participation

Kim Surkan, PhD (cand.)

University of Minnesota

SUMMARY. In an examination of Midwestern drag king performers and communities that have emerged since the study by Volcano and Halberstam of king cultures in London, New York, and San Francisco, this article considers traditional and alternative ways of "doing drag," both performative and participatory, as a means of interrogating the proximity of a "new wave" of king culture to academic theory. Tracing the evolution of drag king performance in the Twin Cities from the 1996 workshop by Diane Torr to the formation of two distinct king troupes in the late 1990s demonstrates a particular trajectory in kinging that reflects a new consciousness and enactment of gender theory through artistic praxis. Participation plays a key role in breaking down the distance between spectator and performer in venues such as the *First International Drag King Extravaganza* in Columbus, Ohio, and Melinda Hubman's art installation "Performing Masculinities: Take a Chance on Gender" in Minneapolis. By engaging the "audience" in drag, the *Extravaganza* "Science Fair" successfully referenced drag kings' shared history with early American freak shows in a clever and critical way. Moving beyond the contest framework of early king shows, new drag king troupes like Minneapolis' Dykes Do Drag are "mixing it up" in an attempt to complicate notions of butch/femme gender roles, sexuality, and drag stereotypes.

[Haworth co-indexing entry note]: "Drag Kings in the New Wave: Gender Performance and Participation." Surkan, Kim. Co-published simultaneously in *Journal of Homosexuality* (Harrington Park Press, an imprint of The Haworth Press, Inc.) Vol. 43, No. 3/4, 2002, pp. 161-185; and: *The Drag King Anthology* (ed: Donna Troka, Kathleen LeBesco, and Jean Bobby Noble) Harrington Park Press, an imprint of The Haworth Press, Inc., 2002, pp. 161-185. Single or multiple copies of this article are available for a fee from The Haworth Document Delivery Service [1-800-HAWORTH, 9:00 a.m. - 5:00 p.m. (EST). E-mail address: docdelivery@haworthpress.com].

161

KEYWORDS. Drag king, masculinity, butch, transgender, gender fluidity, identity, performance, participation, freak, disability

Contemporary drag kings (as opposed to the male impersonators who preceded them in Western culture by at least a century) have been around longer than most people think; Del LaGrace Volcano recalls having seen a drag king perform for the first time in 1985, but kings certainly did not enjoy widespread popularity until the late 1990s (Volcano and Halberstam 1999, 10). Despite some appearances of kings on American television talk shows, most drag king shows are still staged at queer nightclubs and performance venues, where they play to primarily lesbian audiences. Yet some kings are breaking out of this trend, bringing male drag into the public eye through photography, open air performance, and new variations on participatory modes of kinging such as workshops and contests.

In their 1999 *Drag King Book*, Del LaGrace Volcano and Judith "Jack" Halberstam document the urban drag king cultures of London, New York and San Francisco, three cities in which king communities thrived at the end of the twentieth century. Since they began their initial research, more drag king troupes have sprung up in other urban areas across the Midwest. In locations like Columbus, Ohio and Minneapolis, Minnesota, a new wave of drag kings has emerged. Not surprisingly (and due, in large part, to the 1998 contribution of Halberstam's *Female Masculinity* as well as *The Drag King Book*), there has been corresponding academic interest from the two large research universities in each city, both of which offer graduate programs in feminist studies. This essay considers traditional and alternative ways of "doing drag," both performative and participatory, as a means of interrogating the proximity of king culture to academic theory. The Columbus and Minneapolis communities exemplify variations on the performances and contests featured in London and on the coasts of the United States. Often the kings reflect and respond to popularized theories of female masculinity and the performativity of gender, seeking new alliances between artistic, academic and bar communities.

The most obvious instance of this alliance-building can be seen in *The First International Drag King Extravaganza* (IDKE), sponsored by H.I.S. Kings of Columbus, Ohio, in 1999. The weekend-long event drew 200 participants from the U.S., Canada and the U.K., featuring a combined program of discussions, performances, workshops and academic presentations. In framing the conference, organizers Donna Troka (dj love) and Julie Applegate (Jake) sought to make a connection between their interests in performance, production and the academic study of drag. In their letter of introduction to IDKE participants, they wrote: "We wanted to create a space that would encompass as many aspects of women doing drag as possible. This meant drawing together performers, theorists, fans, activists, photographers and all those that straddle and move through those categories" (Applegate and Troka 1999).

The IDKE gave participants several opportunities to explore different aspects of performing masculinity, both on- and offstage. The integration of performers and theorists at the conference opened new avenues of dialogue, illustrating the ways in which kings were responding to and testing the limits of conceptualizations of gender. In a similar vein, this chapter is a consideration of this intersection of theory and practice in more detail; I have tried to examine particular definitions of drag and gender performativity through specific examples of king performance, photography, and participation.

THEORY MEETS PERFORMANCE, AND VICE VERSA

Many claims have been made about drag and its potential to disrupt the binary gender system and the corresponding distribution of power along gender lines. That these claims have been just as widely contested points to a central dispute about the fluidity of gender and what it means to be "liberated" from gender roles prescribed by society. Judith Butler's theory of gender performativity has been integral to this debate, creating its own form of gender trouble in the wake of her argument that "the inner truth of gender is a fabrication," since gender is externally produced "through corporeal signs and other discursive means. Because the gendered body is performative, she argues, "it has no ontological status apart from the various acts which constitute its reality" (Butler 1990, 136).

Drag, then, is described by Butler as a parody of "the notion of an original or primary gender identity," rather than an *actual* original. As parody, drag has subversive potential in the sense that it calls attention to the fiction of gender: "In imitating gender, drag implicitly reveals the imitative structure of gender itself–as well as its contingency" (Butler 1990, 137). However, in her subsequent book *Bodies That Matter*, Butler cautions against viewing drag as *inherently* subversive, suggesting "that drag may well be used in the service of both the denaturalization and reidealization of hyperbolic heterosexual gender norms" (Butler 1993, 125). It is worth noting here that Butler's use of the term "drag" is primarily in reference to female impersonation, a point that Halberstam seizes upon in *Female Masculinity*. Citing Butler's inclusion of "cross-dressing" and "butch-femme identities" in addition to "drag" in her description of gender parodies, Halberstam questions Butler's tactic of positing gay male drag and lesbian butch-femme roles as equivalent parodies. The emergence of drag king culture, Halberstam suggests, complicates theories of gender performance by offering a female-to-male parody apart from butch-femme lesbianism, which historically never functioned as parody within butch-femme bar culture.

Halberstam defines a drag king as "a performer who makes masculinity into his or her act," noting that there is a particular and complex relationship between "the butch role" recognized by the lesbian community and female-to-male drag (Volcano and Halberstam 1999, 36). She divides kings into two "sub-types" in relation to this role–the "butch" king and the "femme/androgynous" king, and observes that the performance of masculinity differs in each case:

> The "butch" Drag King performs, we might say, *what comes naturally*, and s/he celebrates her masculinity or distinguishes between her masculinity and male masculinity . . . the "femme" Drag King or "androgynous" Drag King assumes her masculinity as an act. S/he understands herself to be engaged in some kind of parody of men and s/he leaves her masculinity behind when she takes off the fake hair and the boxers and the chest binding. (Volcano and Halberstam 1999, 36, emphasis mine)

Halberstam's "butch" king depends on a prior female masculinity that accrues to the butch "naturally" and lends authenticity or realness to the king's act, particularly in a drag contest setting. The category "butch" is curiously opposed to a conflation of "femme" with "androgyny" in the non-butch king; these two categories are consolidated by virtue of their lack of masculinity prior to their appearance onstage.

Applying categories of "butch" and "femme" to drag performers is valuable in that it allows for a way to discuss the stakes and the outcomes of performing masculinity on differently gendered bodies. The limits of its usefulness inhere in the limits of the binary upon which it is predicated–how much masculinity is required to be counted as butch? Is androgyny ever masculine? When are male drag kings butch, or femme? What is clear is that framing an analysis of drag kings in terms of "butch" and "femme" is predicated on an assumption that such a distinction can be made–that each person has a relatively stable gender identity that fits into one of these two categories. This is a move away from a utopian understanding of gender as fluid and malleable, a position Halberstam finds of dubious value:

> In opposition to many contemporary popular discussions of gender, I see Drag King theater not purely in terms of the fluidity of gender which, supposedly, opposes the conservatism of rigid and set gender expressions. Indeed, I challenge the notion of gender as fluid and as simply some kind of recreational pursuit or as no more than a choice between different wardrobes. (Volcano and Halberstam 1999, 39)

This sentiment echoes Butler's clarification of the relationship between her theory of gender performativity and drag. The two, she writes, were never intended to be construed as equivalent:

> If drag is performative, that does not mean that all performativity is to be understood as drag. The publication of *Gender Trouble* coincided with a number of publications that did assert that "clothes make the woman," but I never did think that gender was like clothes, or that clothes make the woman. (Butler 1990, 231)

The corresponding assertion (and subsequent denial) that "clothes make the man" is behind some of the controversy in drag king history, most notably in the response to participatory workshops that explore drag as an experiment in "passing."

DIANE TORR'S "DRAG KING WORKSHOP" AND THE POLITICS OF PARTICIPATION

The most famous example of participatory drag is unarguably the "Drag King Workshop," created by performance artist Diane Torr in 1989. The workshops, presented by Torr in cities all over the world, are participatory events in which women put on male drag and practice behaviors and gestures associated with masculinity with the intent of going into public space at the end of the day to pass as men. Torr's workshops have been widely publicized, receiving a steady stream of media attention, much of it based on the autobiographical experiences of journalists who participated in the project. With a background in dance, theater and performance art, Torr has been experimenting with alternatively gendered performances since 1978, and her theatrical training informs her approach to and philosophy of drag. Of her own performance piece *Drag Kings and Subjects*, Torr writes:

> I was interested in re-inventing the erotic, questioning notions of sexual identity and conveying the fluidity of gender. As a woman taking on male characters my working focus was to understand the physical–how the male body carries weight differently, nuances of gesture and motion, ways of looking, how the gaze is directed, creating new facial expressions, and so on–all the subtle characteristics that go into the creation of a separate identity. (Torr)

It is this insistence that gender is fluid that Judith Halberstam finds contentious in her study of female masculinity, an argument she reads as a denial of the realities of many people's lives. Halberstam cites transsexuality as a counterexample of gender fluidity, remarking that "The very existence of transsexuals suggests that for many people, gender is far from fluid and to represent its ideal state as fluid is to implicitly critique people who feel unable for what ever reason to hop back and forth between masculinity and femininity" (Volcano and Halberstam 1999, 80).

The sticking point about gender fluidity seems to be in regard to the ease with which people can alter their gender expression and the relationship of that expression to their sense of identity. If what we mean by saying gender is "fluid" is simply that one can willfully slide from one end of the gender scale to the other, the stakes and the consequences are radically different for the actor or drag performer than for the gender deviant. In the above quote, Halberstam invokes the transsexual as a case in which the individual actually finds sex to be more mutable than gender and chooses sex reassignment surgery as the only viable means of establishing congruence between gender expression and sexual identity.

It is important when considering gender fluidity to make a distinction between acting and real life. The very definition of acting is located in the transformation of the "real" actor into the fictional character being played. The fact that theater is a profession at all indicates that such transformations are never easy; in fact we judge the quality of the acting in terms of "realness." An actor playing a role must be able to convincingly "become" the person he or she is portraying–and that role might traverse the boundaries of age, race, gender or any other number of characteristics. Would we therefore say that age or race is fluid? Fluidity is bounded by audience (or societal reception of the performance) on one end, and the performer's own sense of identity in relationship to the performance on the other. If the performance fails to persuade–i.e., if the performer is "read"–then gender is not perceived as fluid. But we might also conclude that as long as the performer maintains the self-awareness of the performed identity as foreign, neither can gender be understood as fluid in that case. Ultimately, the drag performance is the creation of a convincing illusion rather than a transformation.

The greater the disparity between the actor's "original" identity and the presentation of the character, the more challenging the role is understood to be. Such was the case when Hilary Swank received the Academy Award for Best Actress for her performance in the role of the transgendered youth Brandon Teena in Kimberly Peirce's 1999 film *Boys Don't Cry*. Media coverage of Swank's nomination and subsequent selection by the Academy emphasized her "real-life" femininity in contrast to the boyish Brandon she played on screen. This coverage accomplished two things: the establishment of Swank's performance as superior acting, and the alleviation of cultural anxiety about cross-gendered performance.

Halberstam observes a similar pattern in the media accounts of Torr's Drag King Workshops, finding that:

> In the popular press Torr's workshop tends to be written up as consciousness-raising with a twist, and inevitably the female journalists who enroll in the workshops describe the experience in terms of a reconsolidation of their femininity and their resolute heterosexuality. (Volcano and Halberstam 1999, 79)

Consequently, she argues, the workshops do not ultimately challenge the binary gender system; rather, they reinforce it, creating a safe playground for experimenting with gender. At the end of the day, the women return to their original femininity, and order is restored. This scenario is a far cry from the representation of queer drag king culture Halberstam and Del LaGrace Volcano seek to chronicle in *The Drag King Book*, and Halberstam draws a sharp line between the two, writing that "the workshop is a small part of a larger social reconsideration of gender meanings, but it is not an original site for Drag King culture in the way that Torr claims" (Volcano and Halberstam 1999, 83).

Although Torr may be at times overstating the liberatory aspect of her drag king workshops, Halberstam is perhaps too quick to dismiss them entirely. Her critique of the workshops is predicated on the assumption that the majority of participants are straight feminine women, which in Halberstam's view places them well outside the queer scene she delineates for king culture. Furthermore, she questions why non-normatively gendered women would even be interested in the workshops, and what they could hope to gain from them:

> Torr claims that all kinds of women take her workshops, lesbians and transgenders in addition to the usual curious straight participants. But it is more difficult to determine what the appeal of this exercise might be to women who regularly pass (deliberately or not) as men or who experience their everyday gender expressions as ambiguous. (Volcano and Halberstam 1999, 79-80)

Despite the volume of press coverage of the workshops by straight female journalists, the fact remains that Torr's project also made a splash in the queer community. One notable example of this was the inclusion of both the performance *Drag Kings and Subjects* and the "Drag King Workshop" as part of a March 1996 art event called *Genders That Be* at Intermedia Arts in Minneapolis, Minnesota. Billed as "a series of visual and performance art events by transsexual and transgender artists," *Genders That Be* was scheduled to coincide with the 1996 International Foundation of Gender Education (IFGE) conference, and included transgendered artists Kate Bornstein, Loren Cameron, Steven Grandell, and Jordy Jones.

Curator Eleanor Savage described the aim of the program in an interview with Jayne Blanchard of the *St. Paul Pioneer Press*:

> "My interest in pulling together the series stems from issues of discrimination and bigotry," says Savage. "I wanted to create visibility, to challenge the notion that transgender people are perverted or unnatural." (Blanchard 1996, 1E)

Founder of the monthly Twin Cities' dyke performance cabaret *Vulva Riot*, Savage found that there was a profound lack of understanding in the lesbian community about transgender issues. "I had run into a lot of prejudice and bigotry directed toward transgender people, so my interest was in furthering the conversation," she explained. "[*Genders That*

Be was] a way of trying to educate people, and I guess my approach to everything is through artists" (Savage 2000).

As part of that educational process, *Genders That Be* defined transgender broadly as "anyone who transgresses gender," and that prompted Savage to include Torr's workshop in the program. "We were trying to at least capture in some way the drag king/drag queen part of the spectrum, in addition to the people who identify as transsexual," Savage said. Clearly, in this context the Torr workshop was intended to appeal to a much broader range of people than Halberstam is willing to allow in her critique. Furthermore, the subsequent emergence of the Twin Cities' first drag king troupe (the Club Metro Kings) the following year seems to bear out Torr's claim that her workshops launched king communities and culture in many cities.

BUTCH/FEMME AND DRAG KING AUTHENTICITY

The controversy surrounding Torr and the subversive potential of her workshops points to an underlying tension between so-called "butch" and "femme" kings, specifically in relationship to questions of authenticity, performance quality, and transgression. There is a tendency on the part of performers, contest judges and audiences to equate the offstage butchness of a king with authenticity onstage. The more masculine the performer's everyday gender presentation, the more theoretically transgressive the performance is understood to be, since the cultural anxiety surrounding gender deviance is not allayed by a return to femininity; the drag is never entirely removed. These elements of drag king performance are further complicated by issues of race, in the sense that butch/femme identities have different valences in different cultural contexts.

Halberstam opens *The Drag King Book* with both an admission and a disclaimer: on one hand, she states that she and Volcano embarked upon the project with an overt bias toward privileging butch (and transgender) kings; on the other, she cautions against using authenticity as a primary means of judging king performance:

> Some butch Drag Kings might accuse the femme Drag Kings of not being real and of just playing; some transgender Drag Kings highlight the difference between their real moustaches and the fake facial hair of the other kings; some female-to-male transsexuals see the whole Drag King scene as a trivialization of the gender

issues they struggle with on a daily basis. In fact, realness or authenticity is not the best measure of Drag King status, and we can only measure realness in terms of each king's investment and each audience's response. (Volcano and Halberstam 1999, 36)

However, the fact remains that all too often—and particularly in contest settings—audience response is based on perceived realness, with the result that people who can (and often do) pass in real life tend to come out on top, even in the absence of any sort of prepared act. Maureen Fischer, otherwise known as Mo B. Dick, describes this phenomenon in an interview with Volcano and Halberstam:

> I have been to some [contests], at the HerShe Bar for example, which were awful because the women entering them wouldn't do anything, they just walked up on stage and it was like a beauty contest or a popularity contest: if the crowd liked you or your look, you won; if they didn't, you lost. . . . It's the crowd's definition of realness because very often the winners were not even Drag Kings to my mind. . . . I think they are just very butch women. (Volcano and Halberstam 1999, 111-112)

This result is precisely what the organizers of the *First International Drag King Extravaganza* sought to avoid by planning a showcase instead of a contest for the performance element of the weekend. The aim of the Ohio conference was to be as inclusive as possible, allowing for many different variations on king performances, and placing the emphasis on performance quality rather than realness. Inclusivity and performance quality are two aspects of kinging that are also reflected in the examples of drag king art and performance I investigate further later in this chapter.

What Volcano and Halberstam actually found was that many of the "butch" kings they sought out resisted being categorized in that way (Volcano and Halberstam 1999, 41). The fact that many kings did not unproblematically affiliate with butch identity offstage indicates that the relationship between butchness and king performance is ultimately a complex mapping, one which, it turns out, has everything to do with the cultural context in which the king is performing. Halberstam and Volcano describe three very different queer communities in their study of drag kings in London, New York and San Francisco; the definition of "butch" and even "drag king" seems to vary in each geographic location, as well as along race, class and generational lines.

The bias toward privileging masculine kings situates them not only as more authentic but also as more transgressive. This viewpoint extends beyond critical response to Torr's workshops and the king contests; it is evident in critiques of non-contest performances as well. A primary example can be seen in reactions to performers whose drag act involves some form of strip tease, *when the king is stripping off male drag to reveal a feminine presentation underneath.* Halberstam raises the issue of stripping in the interview with Fischer, saying:

> I have seen quite a few acts now where Drag Kings strip down at the end of their act and transform themselves back into women. I personally don't find this act very interesting, it's too obvious, I suppose, and again it seems to reinforce a certain anxiety about asserting one's femininity. (Volcano and Halberstam 1999, 111)

Perhaps we should ask here *whose* anxiety is at stake–the personal anxiety of the individual drag king, or a greater cultural anxiety about sex/gender congruity? It seems unlikely that a performer choosing to be in the spotlight in male drag would strip out of anxiety about that performance.

Fischer also dismisses the drag strip act, saying, "It's too easy to strip and be a girl, for God's sake, you're a girl every day: the Drag King persona is quite difficult to take on and maintain, and somehow the strip act diminishes that effort" (Volcano and Halberstam 1999, 111).[1] But Volcano points to the crux of the issue:

> The strip confirms what the mainstream media wants to stress, that is, that underneath we really are all girls, pretty girls, and therefore we're acceptable, it's only legitimate, in other words, to drag up if underneath you are pretty. But what if you're not a pretty girl, what if you are a butch dyke? (Volcano and Halberstam 1999, 112)

This last question was in fact taken up in an interesting way by Sile Singleton, the emcee of the Drag King Showcase in her performance as Lustivious de la Virgion. Singleton's drag persona has two faces: Lusty, an over-the-top drag queen; and Luster, the king underneath. As Lusty, Singleton emceed the entire show, opening with a duet with the very masculine drag king Maxwell (Shani Scott). At the very end of the evening, Lusty removed her wig to reveal the "true" identity of the bald butch Luster, who at that moment looked so very male it became hard to register the significance of the move. What at first seemed to be simply a drag queen taking off a feminine exterior to reveal the male underneath, on second glance was seen to be a performance with yet another layer: butch female masculinity performing male performing femininity. The unmasking was further complicated by race, as Singleton's platinum blonde wig stood out as a signifier of white femininity, Lil' Kim style, against her own identity as an African American and the close proximity of Scott's performance of black masculinity.

In Lusty's performance, the strip act does not reassuringly confirm a normative gender identity underlying the drag. Instead, it demonstrates that there is no easy equation between having a female body and being "a pretty girl," as Volcano suggests–or even being feminine at all. Furthermore, it simultaneously disengages masculinity from the male body through the revelation of the drag king at the core of a series of layers. Both of these outcomes result in a sophisticated queer performativity, calling into question assumptions about not only the relationship of sex to gender, but of how race and sexuality factor into the ways in which bodies are read onstage.

As drag king performance continues to evolve into what I am characterizing as a new wave of kings, many performers are complicating the equation of butch authenticity with drag realness from early contest days. Variations on the drag strip act and other onstage gender transformations within king shows go beyond the simple reversals predicated on binary conceptions of sex and gender to create new gender configurations and new contexts in which to understand them. By responding to and revising what has come before, drag kings are creating new performance aesthetics that can be seen as practical applications of theoretical promises familiar to queer theorists, such as the disruption of "obvious categories (man, woman, latina, jew, butch, femme), oppositions (man vs. woman, heterosexual vs. homosexual), or equations (gender = sex) upon which conventional notions of sexuality and identity rely" (Hennessey 1993, 964). In addition to the evolution of king performance, there has also been further experimentation in the *process* of gender transformation, going beyond the participation model of the Torr workshops to create new environments in which to perform masculinity. The remainder of this chapter is a consideration of a series of performance and participatory examples of kinging that, I argue, are part of a new wave in the king phenomenon.

MIXING IT UP: TWIN CITIES DRAG PERFORMANCES

In the Twin Cities area of Minneapolis/St. Paul, Minnesota, there are currently two distinct drag king performance troupes in operation: the Metro Kings and a group of cabaret-style performers called Dykes Do Drag. The former is a group performing every other week on a regular basis at Club Metro, a venue catering to lesbians, but which also draws a significant number of gay men to its dance floors. Metro King acts are generally lip-synched solos, duets, or group numbers involving audience interaction in the form of tipping performers in exchange for a dance or a kiss. Many of the Metro Kings have a great fan base in the Twin Cities lesbian community; their stage names turn up in personal ads in local queer publications and GLBT readership surveys (Renaud and Peterson 2000).

In 1998, University of Minnesota undergraduate women's studies students Nikki Kubista and Erin Ferguson capitalized on the popularity and the spectacle of king performance in their successful bid for the offices of Minnesota Student Association president and vice president. Running on a feminist, anti-racism and GLBT rights platform, Ferguson and Kubista organized a drag performance featuring several Metro Kings in front of the student union as a way of increasing visibility and name recognition for their campaign.

The outdoor show drew a crowd of 400 onlookers just days before the election, a number just less than the total number of votes Kubista and Ferguson received to win the race.[2] "Racism, sexism and homophobia are a big drag," read signs facing the audience, displayed in promotion of the Kubista/Ferguson ticket (*The Minnesota Daily* 1998). The openly lesbian candidates strategically used drag kings and queens as signifiers of their stand against discrimination in general, and their celebration of alternative gender expressions and sexualities in particular. In an election known for its typically low turnout, the drag performance was a cultural production designed to galvanize the queer vote.

In February 1999 a new drag king troupe called Dykes Do Drag held a debut performance at the Bryant-Lake Bowl, a lesbian-owned bar and bowling alley that also houses a small stage. Performer Heather Spear curated the event, drawing together a new group of acts created by local dancers and performance artists. The Bryant-Lake shows differ from those at Club Metro in that they are ticketed events in which audience participation is limited, usually involving minimal tipping. Spear describes her intent in terms of creating an evening of "really strong performance quality, as well as continually playing with who's in drag, and what kind of drag they're in . . . it's women as men, women as women, men as women, mixing up the drag" (Spear 2000).

That emphasis on mixing it up is evident in the acts Spear performs in her own drag persona, The Gentleman King. Spear's stage name reflects her interest in exploring the trope of the gentleman rather than creating a particular character. To further that end, she selects numbers by lesser-known performers, "so they don't necessarily have a particular physical style or particular image that everyone would call up when they hear those songs" (Spear 2000). Appearing in a suit with very little facial makeup (sideburns but no mustache or goatee), Spear relies on past training in dance and movement to convey the Gentleman King's masculinity. His debut performance was a solo lip-synched to Leonard Cohen's "I'm Your Man," a song which created an interesting juxtaposition between Spear's androgynous look and Cohen's ultra-masculine baritone voice. The lyrics added to the appeal of the selection for Spear, reflecting the shifting identity of the drag performer: "If you want a lover / I'll do anything you ask me to / And if you want another kind of love / I'll wear a mask for you . . . Here I stand / I'm your man" (Cohen 1989).

The song goes on to position the singer as a versatile subject capable of many different personas: "If you want a boxer / I will step into the ring for you / And if you want a doctor / I'll examine every inch of you / If you want a driver / Climb inside / Or if you want to take me for a ride / You know you can / I'm your man" (Cohen 1989). Spear says she "liked the very obvious play in choosing a song titled 'I'm Your Man,'" adding "if you think about the lyrics, it's also saying, 'I'm whoever you want me to be.' So I'm playing with that–as a woman I can be that man" (Spear 2000).

A subsequent duet between Spear and fellow performer Sarah Gordon culminates in a gender role reversal to the tune of "Baby, It's Cold Outside." Spear, dressed in a tuxedo, begins by attempting to seduce Gordon, who faces away from the audience for most of the number, offering a view of her backless silver evening gown, shoulder-length wig, and fur-wrapped shoulders. During the course of the song, the performers reverse the scripted seduction, with Gordon removing Spear's jacket to reveal a bustier beneath the tuxedo, then turning to reveal her face–which is that of a drag king, complete with facial hair.

This example shares some elements of the drag king strip act discussed earlier, in that Spear's female form is revealed. However, in the context of a duet based on heterosexual seduction, the revelation of the "gentleman's" female body beneath the tuxedo is actually the unmasking of lesbian desire rather than the restoration of gender congruence and heteronormativity. Furthermore, the simultaneous reversal of the object choice from high femme to gender freak adds another layer to the performance. In the end we are left with something entirely queer in its clear expression of desire between two persons of indeterminate gender.

Perhaps the most complex, layered performance by Spear is her solo to "I Wish You Were a Girl," by openly gay singer/songwriter Ryan Olcott of the Minneapolis band 12 Rods. The Gentleman King, decked out in his signature blue suit, holds a red rose for the duration of this song–twirling it, playing with it and ultimately eating the petals when he is not lip synching. "The concept of the song is that the singer has a male friend who is gay, and there's definitely some attraction there, but the singer is not entirely comfortable with it," Spear explains. Confronted with homosexual desire, the singer's response is to wish for a transformation to heteronormativity rather than a denial of his feelings: "I wish you were a girl / A girl who is soft as silk / But silky from the inside out" (Olcott 1998). As in "I'm Your Man," the lyrics suggest a certain amount of versatility on the part of the singer, or at least a willingness to consider a different kind of desire: "Don't get me wrong, / I like you anyway / I'll be with you today / You can show me your way" (Olcott 1998).

Despite this concession, the singer establishes himself as primarily heterosexual in the chorus through his avowal that things would be better if his friend were female: "Cause if you were a girl (oh) / Nothing would seem to matter / (cause) if you were a girl (oh) / I wouldn't really care" (Olcott 1998). His solution posits the singer's own gender identity as stable; *he* has no desire to be a girl, and this is what makes the song such a fascinating and successful choice for a king performance. The singer's insistence on reconciling his desire for his friend by altering the friend's sex has the effect of highlighting his own threatened masculinity, throwing it into center focus and thereby making it more easily performed.

Furthermore, when Spear performs the song, the homophobia in the lyrics becomes ironic, since the audience knows that the performer is not actually a straight man at all, but in fact a "dyke doing drag." The stability of *lesbian identity* is also called into question in this performance, since the object of desire is problematically male. Spear acknowledges that sexuality functions as a key element in each of her drag performances:

I think that in some underlying sense in all of those pieces there is lesbian desire. . . . I think too, that in performing this king and putting together these shows, a lot [of my motivation] has been exploring myself, my ideas of desire, and who I want to be in the world. (Spear 2000)

In many drag king performances, lesbian desire complicates the picture, producing a particular layering effect that works against the collapse of gender and sex into a single, masculine/male entity. Kinging occupies a space somewhere in between passing and the everyday performance out of drag, and it is precisely the ambiguity of that location that makes the king available as an object of lesbian desire. He is masculine but not male, a queer object choice that begins to break down the historical lesbian feminist association of the masculine with the systematic oppression of women.[3] Finally, in an era described as a celebration of a "butch/femme renaissance,"[4] it is becoming permissible for women to express desire for female masculinity without being branded a traitor to feminism, lesbianism, or both. Venues in which drag kings perform have been instrumental in providing safe spaces for both the performance of alternative genders, and the corresponding expressions of desire for and from those gendered positions. In addition to traditional stage performances and king contests, participatory events such as the Science Fair at the First International Drag King Extravaganza (IDKE) and *Performing Masculinity: Take a Chance on Gender*, an installation by Twin Cities artist Melinda Hubman employ drag to create permissive spaces that allow for gender experimentation outside the lesbian bar scene.

PERMISSIBLE SPACES: THE POLITICS OF PARTICIPATION

The Science Fair

The First International Drag King Extravaganza (IDKE) included its own form of a how-to-be-a-king workshop as part of the conference program. Dubbed the "Science Fair," the event consisted of a series of booths, or stations–each one dedicated to a different aspect of female-to-male gender transformation for the stage. Participants learned how to choose appropriate men's clothing, walk "like a man," bind their breasts, apply facial hair with spirit gum, and create a fake penis out of a jock strap holding a condom filled with hair gel. In contrast to the Torr workshops, the Science Fair did not include any vocal training, an indication of its emphasis on the stage context of the drag king (who usually lip syncs)–as opposed to the workshop participants' attempts to pass in real life.

The Science Fair was several things at once: a practical exercise in the mechanics of body modification, a permissive and friendly space in which to experiment with gender expression and gender bending, and a spectacle in its own right. Its carnival-like atmosphere can be read as a queering of historical freak shows, which "were often presented as educational or scientific exhibits" and frequently included gender deviants such as bearded women (Bogdan 1996, 25). The particular history of enfreakment as it relates to female masculinity and the medicalization of gender deviance makes the inclusion of the Science Fair in the Columbus *Extravaganza* a fascinating example of the complex relationship between contemporary king culture and the history of cross-gendered performance.[5]

Freak shows, dime store museums, and vaudeville shared a moment in time prior to television and radio, in which live entertainment played a far greater role in American culture than it does today. Early male impersonators such as Annie Hindle and Ella Wesner were part of a community of performers in the late-nineteenth century who took their variety acts on tour, traveling to theaters and music halls across the country, and even the world (Rodger 1998). These cross-gendered vaudeville performances differed from the freak shows going on in circuses, carnivals, and dime store museums, in that they were billed as acts by women performing as men, rather than "real" freaks of nature such as hermaphrodites or bearded women.

Despite this distinction, there is much to suggest that the gender-bending exhibits in freak shows were no less performative than the male impersonators of vaudeville. As Robert Bogdan points out in his article, "The Social Construction of Freaks":

> In a strict sense of the word, every exhibit was a fraud. . . . Showmen fabricated freaks' backgrounds, the nature of their condition, the circumstances of their current lives, and other personal characteristics. The accurate story of the life and conditions of those being exhibited was replaced by purposeful distortion designed to market the exhibit, to produce a more appealing freak. (Bogdan 1996, 25)

One can only imagine, then, that backstage things looked remarkably similar—costumes, crepe hair, makeup and props being common to all forms of theater, including the carnivalesque freak show, the vaudeville stage, and of course the contemporary drag king performance. Considering this historical context, then, in its behind-the-scenes focus on male impersonation, the IDKE Science Fair can be seen as a reenactment of the age-old construction of masculinity for the stage.

While on one hand, the "Science Fair" was engaged in the practical demonstration of the "science" of gender performance, on the other, the event's title resonated in a broader way with the intersections between science, gender and body studies. This connection between science and the study of bodily difference has been most clearly articulated by disability studies scholars in relationship to freakery. For example, in her book *Extraordinary Bodies*, Rosemarie Garland Thomson observes a progression in the historical relationship between enfreakment and the scientific, noting that

> Although scientific and sideshow discourses had been entangled during the freak show era, they diverged toward opposite ends of a spectrum of prestige and authority as time went on. . . . By the mid-twentieth century, physicians and scientists, rather than the public and the entrepreneur, governed the production of freaks. (Thomson 1996, 75)

This shift in the cultural production of freakery coincides neatly with the rise of sexology as an area of scientific study in the nineteenth century, providing a medicalized discourse with which to classify and contain gender deviance. The "science" of sexology combined biomedical studies of the anatomical body with the psychological study of sexuality in an attempt to explain non-normative gender presentation and sexual "perversion."[6] The differently gendered freaks, along with their counterparts with disabilities, were added to the growing list of new medical specimens to be studied.

In *Exile and Pride*, activist and essayist Eli Clare comments on the parallel histories of disabled and queer people in terms of their equally conflicted relationships with the medical establishment:

> I think it no accident that I've paired the words *queer* and *freak* in this examination of language, pride, and resistance. The ways in which queer people and disabled people experience oppression follow, to a certain extent, parallel paths. Queer identity has been

pathologized and medicalized. Until 1973, homosexuality was considered a psychiatric disorder. Today transsexuality and transgenderism, under the names of gender dysphoria and gender identity disorder, are considered psychiatric conditions. (Clare 1999, 96)

Perhaps because of its claim to be a showcase of the "real" (as opposed to the officially performative nature of the vaudeville act), the freak show was a place of convergence of these two groups–transgendered and disabled people–under the single rubric "freak." Unfortunately, it was neither a positive nor enduring point of connection, as the venues started to disappear toward the middle of the twentieth century.

As the scientific pathologization of freaks and gender deviants began to take hold, the public display of these "extraordinary bodies" in freak shows declined.[7] In *Exile and Pride,* Eli Clare explains the trend in terms of a new deference to medical authority that recast disability as tragedy instead of novelty:

> The decline of the freak show in the early decades of the 20th century coincided with the medicalization of disability. As pity, tragedy, and medical diagnosis/treatment entered the picture, the novelty and mystery of disability dissipated. Explicit voyeurism stopped being socially acceptable except when controlled by the medical establishment. (Clare 1999, 84)

However, as Garland Thomson argues, after the turn of the century there was a sort of crossover period marked by a considerable overlap between freak shows and scientific discourse:

> In the transition period, scientists raided freak shows for observations and specimens and refereed sideshow debates, while the freak show exploited scientific rationalization to authenticate its exhibits. (Thomson 1996, 75)

The participation of scientific and medical "experts" in the authentication of freak exhibits had the added effect of officially delineating the distinction between the normal and abnormal, marking a comfortable distance between the paying audience and those displayed in freak exhibits.

Whereas nineteenth century freak shows depended on this sharp distinction between the "normal" rubes and the freaks they paid to see, the participatory nature of the IDKE Science Fair eliminated the distance between audience and performer. What was being "sold" was not the spectacle of gender deviance, but rather the apparatus of masculinity, as the kings "manning" each booth hawked their wares: Ace bandages and jock straps, crepe hair and spirit gum. Catering to the would-be drag king, the Science Fair was a freak show turned on its ear, a carnival that transformed each participant into a performer ready for the stage. The event was also unique in that it reached across the divide between performers and the academics interested in reading them, thereby reversing the notion of expertise and the corresponding power dynamic between the two groups. The "science" in this case was disseminated by the research subject, rather than the other way around. Kings with performance experience modeled the various physical accoutrements of masculinity, each demonstrating by example the mad science of gender transformation.

"Performing Masculinities: Take a Chance on Gender"

A second variation on a participatory drag king event also incorporates drag king models as a means of encouraging spectators to wear drag themselves. In a multi-media art installation titled "Performing Masculinities: Take a Chance on Gender," artist Melinda Hubman created an interactive environment designed to encourage viewers "to become a part of the work . . . [thus enabling them] to explore constructions of gender on both individual and social levels" (Hubman 2000a). Hubman juxtaposed process and product in her work, creating a "scene" based around the familiar bathroom mirror–in front of which, she specified, people regularly begin each day, "creating their gender expression" (Hubman 2000b).

In fact, there were two mirrors in the installation–a real mirror, which participants used to try on their own brand of masculinity using makeup and props provided by Hubman; and a constructed "mirror" over a sink that was actually a composite series of black and white photographs, each depicting a fragmented shot of an indeterminately gendered body. Hubman's photographically constructed mirror was based on a concept of the way the mirror is used:

> I imagined what happens when I'm in front of a mirror: I never think of one big fluid scene, but a lot of different images, where you check your hair, or you look at your eyes. . . . I got the idea to put a bunch of black and white images together that are going to blur gender lines, using biological women in the act of performing

a masculine or male gender—a lot of ambiguous, androgynous images, and then giving it the mirror look by putting the lights around it, the movie-star style. (Hubman 2000b)

Hubman heightened the gender ambiguity of the images by cropping in on portions of the body that are gender-cue locations, but ultimately denying the viewer enough of the image to provide a conclusive identification. Standing in front of the mirror, the viewer could see portions of the jaw, mouth, ears. In several instances, Hubman deliberately supplied contradictory information in her photographs:

> I have a couple of armpit shots, and those are on people who didn't shave, so that was interesting, because they had really feminine arms, but then they had these hairy armpits, which I think could very easily throw off a viewer. . . . I just wanted to mix it up so that the participant in the installation didn't know exactly what they were dealing with right away, which led them hopefully to think about why we always have to put someone in a category, and why we have to know if that's a woman or a man in that picture. (Hubman 2000b)

Standing before the "mirror," the viewer was confronted simultaneously with a set of ambiguous images and the societal imperative of gender assessment. Hubman further complicated the scenario by implying that these images were *reflections*, implicating the viewer/participant as a potential source of that image. "Like the camera, the mirror is supposed to speak the truth," she said. "I wouldn't have done [the installation] without using mirror shots . . . it's like taking everything society has taught you, and that's the defining moment, when you're standing in front of the mirror" (Hubman 2000b).

In addition to problematizing the "truth" of gender reflected in the mirror, Hubman allowed participants to control the photographic gaze by providing a Poloroid camera for people visiting the installation to capture and keep their own images. The photographs became artifacts documenting each individual's performance of masculinity, revealing what the participants thought masculinity looked like as they consciously constructed and recorded it. In the "Performing Masculinities" exhibit, participation extended beyond the role of performer in the experiment of gender transformation to situate the art installation visitor as an observer and an artist as well.

To encourage viewers to "take a chance on gender" and actively participate, Hubman mounted portraits of three drag kings in various poses in close proximity to the real mirror and its assortment of props and makeup. These photographs catalogued several different approaches and "looks" of masculinity adopted by the models, which Hubman hoped would serve as examples for installation participants:

> In a way, the photographs are modeling how society teaches people to be themselves. You can show someone how to be a drag king, and you can show them different methods or different steps to go through. People could look at these images, and see things they could model. (Hubman 2000b)

DRAG KINGS: THE NEW WAVE AND BEYOND

Drag king performance and presentation has evolved considerably over the last decade, moving into new venues beyond the lesbian bars and nightclubs that first presented king shows as entertainment. Many kings performing today are conversant with theories of performativity and gender identity, and this is reflected in their multi-layered acts. In addition to variations on earlier types of drag king performances such as the strip act, visual artists, dancers and thespians are exploring kinging in new and interesting ways, often incorporating participation as a key element of the act.

In this chapter I argue that the contemporary drag king is a figure emanating from a specific cultural history, which has shaped both audience response and the critical readings surrounding king performances. Butch-femme identities within the lesbian community have provided a "real-life" framework for the performance of masculinities against which to measure drag kings, giving rise to debates about king authenticity and their potential for subversion of gender norms. As Volcano and Halberstam have observed in their study of drag kings, butch "realness" has traditionally received high marks from audiences, as well as from judges in competition settings, even when not categorized as such for contest purposes.

The relationship between the drag act and gender identity "in real life" has persistently resurfaced in analyses and discussions of king performances, particularly regarding the claim that "gender is fluid." Paradoxically, the extent to which drag king performance is touted as subversive often hinges on the stability of the performer's "true" gender identity underlying the drag. If at the conclusion of the show (or in the Torr example, at the end of the day), the king's masculine presentation is erased in a return to the feminine, the performance is seen to be an example of gender fluidity, but one that fails to subvert binary gender categories. On the other hand, if the staged masculinity is understood to be an extension of the performer's own female masculinity, the performance is a counter-demonstration of the fluidity of gender, but a transgression of the conventional sex/gender system, which maps masculine to male, feminine to female. Yet each of these scenarios relies on an understanding of the performer's prior gender identity as stable and recognizable as either masculine or feminine (butch or femme), which seems to carry us further away from Butler's description of drag as a parody of "the notion of an original or primary gender identity."

For Butler, the possibility of subversion in drag performance lies in the revelation of "the imitative structure of gender" (Butler 1990, 137), imitation I argue is made even more visible in the multi-layered performances of drag kings in the new wave, as they engage in double-drag, androgyny, and further complicate their performances with non-normative sexualities. Participation also plays a key role in the expansion of drag king performance, functioning as yet another form of imitation, as audience participants become drag kings themselves in events like the Science Fair or the "Performing Masculinities" installation. Remarkably, by "mixing it up," the kings in Columbus and Minneapolis are challenging reductive readings of female-to-male drag, and bridging gaps between the academic, the artistic, and the "man" on the street.

NOTES

1. Although Fischer likely intends this as an indictment of performers breaking character onstage, it should be noted that femininity is hardly less constructed than masculine drag, and many conventionally gendered women would not find it "easy to strip and be a girl."

2. The University of Minnesota is one of the largest state universities in the country, yet in this election the total number of votes cast was only 1,520. According to the May 1, 1998 edition of *The Minnesota Daily*, the winning candidates secured 450 votes, which represented approximately 1% of eligible student voters.

3. Lillian Faderman explores this in more depth in *Odd Girls and Twilight Lovers: A History of Lesbian Life in Twentieth-Century America*. 1991. New York: Columbia University Press.

4. See *http://www.butch-femme.com/Stonebutch/sbguide.htm* for specific reference to "butch-femme renaissance." Butch-femme.com is a popular contemporary Website serving the butch-femme lesbian community.

5. That there is recognition of such a historical trajectory from early male impersonation to contemporary drag kings is evident in the invitation Minneapolis' GLBT theater company Outward Spiral extended to Heather Spear (the aforementioned
Gentleman King) to serve as a movement consultant to actresses playing the nine-
teenth-century male impersonators Annie Hindle and Ella Wesner in the April 2000
production of Emma Donoghue's play, *Ladies and Gentlemen*.

6. The evolution of sexology and its cultural implications are discussed in greater
length in *Third Sex, Third Gender: Beyond Sexual Dimorphism in Culture and History*,
ed. Gilbert Herdt. 1993. New York: Zone Books.

7. Rosemarie Garland Thomson dates the end of the public spectacle of the freak
show at 1940.

REFERENCES

Applegate, Julie, and Donna Troka. 1999. Letter to *H.I.S. Kings First International
Drag King Extravaganza* participants. Columbus, Ohio. (October).

Blanchard, Jayne M. 1996. "Separated At Birth." *St. Paul Pioneer Press* (17 March): 1E.

Bogdan, Robert. 1996. "The Social Construction of Freaks." Pp. 23-27 in *Freakery:
Cultural Spectacles of the Extraordinary Body*, ed. Rosemarie Garland Thomson.
New York: New York University Press.

Butch-femme.com. Internet site dedicated to the butch-femme lesbian community.
Available online at *http://www.butch-femme.com*.

Butler, Judith. 1990. *Gender Trouble*. New York: Routledge.

_____. 1993. *Bodies That Matter: On the Discursive Limits of "Sex."* New York:
Routledge.

Clare, Eli. 1999. *Exile and Pride: Disability, Queerness, and Liberation*. Cambridge,
Massachusetts: South End Press.

Cohen, Leonard. 1989. "I'm Your Man," *I'm Your Man*. Columbia Records, compact
disc.

Faderman, Lillian. 1991. *Odd Girls and Twilight Lovers: A History of Lesbian Life in
Twentieth-Century America*. New York: Columbia University Press.

Feinberg, Leslie. 1996. *Transgender Warriors: Making History from Joan of Arc to
RuPaul*. Boston: Beacon Press.

Halberstam, Judith. 1998. *Female Masculinity*. Durham: Duke University Press.

Hennessy, Rosemary. 1993. "Queer Theory: A Review of the *differences* Special Issue
and Wittig's *The Straight Mind*." *SIGNS* 118, 4: 964-973.

Herdt, Gilbert, ed. 1993. *Third Sex, Third Gender: Beyond Sexual Dimorphism in Culture and History*. New York: Zone Books.

Hubman, Melinda. 2000. "Performing Masculinities: Take a Chance on Gender." Senior Thesis, University of Minnesota. (May).

_____. 2000. Interview by author. Tape recording. Minneapolis, Minnesota. (June).

Minnesota Daily, 1998. 28 April.

Olcott, Ryan. 1998. "I Wish You Were a Girl." *Split Personalities*. 12 Rods. V2 Records, compact disc.

Renaud, Rudy and Sarah Petersen. 2000. "The Crème de la Crème: Results of the 2000 Twin Cities GLBT Readers' Choice Survey" *Lavender Magazine* 6:135: np. Available online at: *<http://www.lavendermagazine.com/135/135_leisure_51_4.html>.*

Rodger, Gillian Margaret. 1998. "Male impersonation on the North American variety and vaudeville stage, 1868-1930." PhD dissertation, University of Pittsburgh.

Savage, Eleanor. 2000. Interview by author. Minneapolis, Minnesota. (December).

Spear, Heather. 2000. Interview by author. Tape recording. Minneapolis, Minnesota. (June).

Thomson, Rosemarie Garland, ed. 1996. *Freakery: Cultural Spectacles of the Extraordinary Body*. New York: New York University Press.

_____. 1997. *Extraordinary Bodies: Figuring Physical Disability in American Culture and Literature*. New York: Columbia University Press.

Torr, Diane. Home page describing Torr's drag performance *Drag Kings and Subjects* and experience with kinging. Available online at: *<http://www.franklinfurnace.org/caa/diane_torr/torr.html>.*

Troka, Donna. 1999. Interview by author. Tape recording. Columbus, Ohio. (October).

Volcano, Del LaGrace and Judith "Jack" Halberstam. 1999. *The Drag King Book*. London: Serpent's Tail.

DESIRE AND THE AUDIENCE

A Voice from the Audience

Ann Tweedy, JD

for S.W. aka S.D.L.

from the depths of a desire
i did not plan
to reckon with, i hear
the outline of a lie

from that first night in the bar—
and what can that word offer
except unadorned purpose?
from that first night onward

i loved you. (and i can say 'love' because
this is only a poem—even in a court of law
it would not stand up
as a proxy for adultery

and anyway, in the world that has
been given, this love is no more than
a sadness the heart carries
in its river.) and so i will say

i was a changed woman
though i had imagined
cross dressing was a game

[Haworth co-indexing entry note]: "A Voice from the Audience." Tweedy, Ann. Co-published simulta-neously in *Journal of Homosexuality* (Harrington Park Press, an imprint of The Haworth Press, Inc.) Vol. 43, No. 3/4, 2002, pp. 189-190; and: *The Drag King Anthology* (ed: Donna Troka, Kathleen LeBesco, and Jean Bobby Noble) Harrington Park Press, an imprint of The Haworth Press, Inc., 2002, pp. 189-190. Single or multiple copies of this article are available for a fee from The Haworth Document Delivery Service [1-800-HAWORTH, 9:00 a.m. - 5:00 p.m. (EST). E-mail address: docdelivery@haworthpress.com].

and remembering the boy george
wannabe at jr. high dances

believed it involved a distance
i was powerless to travel.
then you came onstage with a look
that said *this is the way it is*
to dance the way a man fucks.

the lines of your torso made
no pretense at artfulness
but something shone in the elegant bones
of the face, the way the soft skin
stretched taut over them.

let them say the sex
is the most vulnerable point
on the human body. as your eyes
scanned the audience, i caught them.
even knowing how i must be looking at you,
i wouldn't turn away.

One Body, Some Genders:
Drag Performances and Technologies

Alana Kumbier

SUMMARY. This chapter examines the ways in which one body becomes the site for multiple and varied gender performances through Alana Kumbier's performances as drag king Red Rider and drag queen Red Pearl. Using theoretical frameworks provided by Judith Halberstam, Ira Livingston, and Teresa de Lauretis the essay also calls for a consideration of material technologies and artifacts as technologies of gender. *[Article copies available for a fee from The Haworth Document Delivery Service: 1-800-HAWORTH. E-mail address: <docdelivery@haworthpress.com> Website: <http://www.HaworthPress.com> © 2002 by The Haworth Press, Inc. All rights reserved.]*

KEYWORDS. Drag, drag king, drag queen, queer, technology, glam, performance, masculinity, femininity

[S]exuality is a dispersed relation between bodies and things: some bodies (such as male lesbians, female cockwearers, baby butches, generationalists, sadofetishists, women with guns) and some things (dildoes, pistols, vegetables, ATM cards, computers, phones, phone books). Some turn-ons: women in suits looking like boys, women in suits wearing dildos looking like and being men, virtual body parts, interactive fantasy. . . . How many races, genders, sexualities are there? Some. How many are you? Some.

[Haworth co-indexing entry note]: "One Body, Some Genders: Drag Performances and Technologies." Kumbier, Alana. Co-published simultaneously in *Journal of Homosexuality* (Harrington Park Press, an imprint of The Haworth Press, Inc.) Vol. 43, No. 3/4, 2002, pp. 191-200; and: *The Drag King Anthology* (ed: Donna Troka, Kathleen LeBesco, and Jean Bobby Noble) Harrington Park Press, an imprint of The Haworth Press, Inc., 2002, pp. 191-200. Single or multiple copies of this article are available for a fee from The Haworth Document Delivery Service [1-800-HAWORTH, 9:00 a.m. - 5:00 p.m. (EST). E-mail address: docdelivery@haworthpress.com].

"Some" is not an indefinite number awaiting a more accurate measurement, but a rigorous theoretical mandate whose specification, necessary as it is . . . is neither numerable nor, in the common sense, innumerable.

–Judith Halberstam and Ira Livingston (1995)

Gender is not a property of bodies or something originally Existent in human beings, . . . it is the product and process of various social technologies, institutional discourses, epistemologies, and critical practices, as well as practices of daily life.

–Teresa de Lauretis (1987)

This chapter takes, as its cornerstones, these challenges to a dominant binary-gender, heteronormative discourse raised by Halberstam, Livingston and de Lauretis. As a drag performer, alternately king and queen, I inhabit the intersection of some genders (in my daily female embodiment, in the excessive masculinity that I perform in my sleazy macho king persona, Red Rider, and in the excessive femininity I performed as Red Pearl, member of genderqueer/performance art group The Pearl Girls in 1999 and 2000) and some things (fake facial hair, mascara, Ace bandages, fake eyelashes, tube socks, pomade, control-top nylons, glitter, a Miracle Bra, stereo systems, video cameras). If, as de Lauretis claims, gender is the product of various technologies, discourses, and practices, how do these "things" (these gender "technologies") challenge the production and perpetuation of heteronormative gender systems? How does their deployment as part of public drag performances contribute to the process of making gender and sexuality multiple, innumerable? I believe drag performances are useful locations from which to consider these questions, and to look for some answers. In this chapter, I take a highly subjective approach, drawing from my own experience to explore drag performance and drag technologies as they relate to my overarching questions. This approach has its limitations, but allows me to proceed while not pretending or assuming to speak for others, whose investments in their gender performances on- and offstage, are likely different from my own. Through my experiences as a drag performer (and avid drag king fan), I have learned a great deal about my own gendered subjectivity, my desire, and my relationship to my body. These multiple drag performances also allow me to make specific arguments supporting the denaturalization of gender and desire (as they relate to biological sex) to my audiences. Before moving on to the discussion of these performances, I am interested in articulating the conceptualization of gender technologies that informs the rest of this chapter.

TECHNOLOGIES

In my performances as a drag queen and as a drag king, I employ what I here term gender technologies. These technologies are both social and material. I consider drag to be a social technology that challenges discourses and practices which perpetuate the "naturality" of binary systems of gender and sexuality, and I consider the technologies of drag performance (from the low tech: wigs, dildos, fake eyelashes; to the high-tech: video cameras, stereo systems, stage lighting, e-mail listservers) instrumental in the process of embodying and appropriating multiple genders. While these two sorts of technologies, the social and the material, might seem at first to be separate (from each other, from the human subject interfacing with them), I would argue they are mutually implicated. In the introduction to *Processed Lives: Gender and Technology in Everyday Life,* Jennifer Terry and Melodie Calvert offer a fitting definition of technology, positing that technology may be defined "in terms of machine/human interface, that is, in terms of how particular machines and mechanisms accomplish tasks of configuring, effecting, mediating, and embodying social relations . . . machines do not necessarily determine social relations but are situated in networked social relations, subject to uses and creative misuses by the humans (and other machines) that surround them" (Terry and Calvert 1997, 4). We can extend this definition to think about technology as what Terry and Calvert refer to as "an integrated system of programmed structures, organized mechanisms of management and control, and processes of production and reproduction," in which "technologies function as systems that shape our lives, structuring not just what we do and how we do it, but even fashioning our vision of social relations and what it means to be human" (Terry and Calvert 1997, 5). This definition is in alignment with de Lauretis's notion of gender as the product of certain technologies and as productive of them, while also allowing room for the "some things" that operate as sex/gender technologies in Halberstam and Livingston's work.

SUBVERSIVE FEMININITIES

I made my drag debut at my senior prom. Then, I wasn't thinking about my prom night as a drag performance but when I look back at the photographs from that evening, it all makes sense. I spent the four years of my high school career dressed in combat boots, flannel shirts, a variety of t-shirts emblazoned with various activist slogans, and paint-stained jeans and cutoffs. I worked hard to perform my gender-neutrality. On school hiking trips, I tried to be one of the boys (when I was the only girl), and was happy when I became privy to my companions' jokes and sex talk. While I enjoyed friendships with several girls, my closest friends were male. By the time I went to the prom, I'd started to understand that my desire was multi-directional, as I'd found myself crushed-out on boys and girls, and was quite pleased to take a girlfriend as my date.

Now, if this were a proper drag king narrative, I would have donned a suit and tie for the big night, and the photos documenting the evening would have marked my proclivity for masculine performance. Instead, when we arrived at the event, my date was wearing a periwinkle dress that was a ballet costume in its previous incarnation. She was tall and willowy, and looked more graceful than I could ever hope to be. Next to her I looked compact, and, while you'd never guess her dress was a costume, you might think mine was. My dress was fuschia, off-the-shoulders, had a puffy skirt and was covered with sequins. It was the most girly outfit I'd ever owned, and I had spike-heeled shoes dyed to match. Like an amateur drag queen, I looked like I hadn't quite pulled the whole dressing-like-a-woman thing off. My desire to wear the dress wasn't as much about looking good (because, in retrospect, I could have found something much more flattering), as it was about performing a specific part of myself for the prom and for my date. By wearing that dress, I embodied and performed my femininity in contrast to my usual gender-neutral presentation. I experienced myself as aggressively, publicly queer *and* feminine, and felt empowered that I could be both at the same time. For one night of my teenage life, my spike heels and sequins were my mechanisms of subversion, and I had fun using them. My classmates were more shocked by my choice of dress than they were about my choice of date, a reaction that confirms my suspicion that traditionally "feminine" accoutrements and modes of presentation, when used in particular ways, can be as disruptively queer as other modes of genderqueer presentation. As the authors of the *GLAM Manifesto*, the Fabulous Lady Misses Julia and Jessica observe, "Girls fucking girls or boys fucking boys in any manner at all is a subversion of the gendered lives our culture plans for them. If we can communicate this choice . . . in a visually accessible but complex and possibly confusing way [e.g., as a biological female dresses like a drag queen or king while out with her girl/boyfriend for the night], we are publicly altering the definitions of gender" (*GLAM Manifesto*, online, 2001).

This glam logic informed my actions as a member of a performance art/genderqueer gang, The Pearl Girls. We (my friends April West, Erica Manville and I) didn't plan on starting a gang when we made our first appearance. We had been wanting an excuse to get glammed up in queen drag, and when filmmaker John Waters came through town for a film screening and book signing, our prayers were answered. April and Erica and I decided to get dressed up in homage to Divine, Waters' drag queen star. We donned fire-engine-red wigs (which would later become our key marker, the Pearl Girls' primary signifier), boas, cocktail and vintage dresses, fishnets and more makeup than any of our tastes would normally allow. Unlike my prom venture, I knew I was a drag queen that evening, and carried out my role with a vengeance. The three of us provided the event's photo-op, and the results were printed in the university newspaper, the local lesbian/gay/bi/trans paper, and in the Wexner Center for the Arts' tenth-anniversary catalog. We took our glam selves out into the streets (literally), riding the city bus downtown, having dinner and returning home in our regalia. While I'm not sure we did much to disrupt the gender binary during our first outing, we did discover an unexpected effect of our "performance": we all ended that first evening feeling like sexy, glamorous, powerful women. We had no shame about the fact that our hips were wider than 36 inches, or that we had scars or other markers of bodily "imperfection." This was my first conscious gender performance. Even though I was a woman performing femininity, the femininity I was performing was not my daily version; it was an excessive, sexy femininity I appropriated and bent to my will.

As Red Pearl (my queen persona), I was able to occupy that subject position I first attempted to explore on prom night: one in which I take dominant cultural forms of feminine attire and behavior and queer them for my own purposes. My Pearl Girl performances were not about measuring up to a culturally established standard of femininity (e.g., putting on heels and makeup to "pass" as a beautiful straight woman). Instead, these performances were about taking that standard and challenging it, so that the same combination of tools (lipstick, mascara, nylons, lingerie) would produce wildly different results. Again, I think the Fabulous Lady Misses say it best:

Glam uses symbols that pop culture creates for the expression of the desires that pop culture does not anticipate, endorse, or provide space for. The very expression of these desires in a public way is subversive. . . . People who are GLAM are sexy not because they desire to be used as sexual objects within the predefined relationships presented in pop culture, but because they wish to free themselves of these predefinitions by expressing their sexuality in a powerful way. (*GLAM Manifesto*, viewed online 2001)

In some ways, I recognize that my queen performances may not always be read as subversive, and that is a critique of the performance I'm willing to accept. I am less afraid to perform this particular version of gender disruption in public spaces (the mall, in galleries, in restaurants and on the street) than I am when I am in king mode. The Pearl Girls were never harassed or ridiculed on the street, in fact, we were often complimented and admired. When I appropriate an excessive femininity in this way I do not present the same immediate threat or disruption to mainstream notions of gender and sexuality that I do when I appropriate masculine presentation and behavior as a drag king. While my Pearl Girl performances may have had some subversive public effects, I do not count them as my most radical acts. This aspect of my gender agitative behavior is important to me, however, because it allowed me to access a specific dimension of my gendered subjectivity; to claim a femininity and embody a sexual persona that most women are denied, and that I had denied myself for most of my life. I do not believe my performances as a Pearl Girl mocked or imitated femininity in a shallow way (this is a claim that has been levied against drag queen performance in general); rather, I believe they allowed me to parody certain culturally scripted gender roles and to bolster my own sense of myself as a desiring, desirable subject on my own queer terms. Returning to the overarching concerns of this chapter, I argue my performances as a Pearl Girl make apparent the ways in which femininity is an apparatus, a social technology that can be appropriated and resignified in service of Halberstam and Livingston's call for the multiplication and proliferation of gender identities, sexualities, desires and performances. These processes of appropriation and multiplication also inform my drag king performances, which engage issues of gender technologies, their deployments, and their effects on subjectivity in quite different ways.

SOME TURN-ONS

While feminists, cultural theorists, queer activists, and some drag performers have engaged in the process of making apparent the technologies that shape femininity, these groups have recently begun (in the past decade) to denaturalize masculinity, to explore its technologies, and recognize its separability from biological males (e.g., as masculine women and butch lesbians embody and perform female masculinity) (Halberstam 1998). As Judith Halberstam has argued, drag kinging is one mode of making "assaults upon dominant gender regimes" (Halberstam 1997, 187). This is the way in which I think about my drag king performances, and is part of the agenda that shapes them.

I was a drag king fan for almost a year before I made my debut performance at an amateur drag night. I had fallen in love with the spectacular H.I.S. Kings of Columbus, Ohio; at each of their performances I found myself wonderfully confused. At least two of the kings had me fooled, in the best possible way. I was convinced one king was a gay man performing as a dreamy crooner (offstage, he was a tranny dyke), the other was the fabulous emcee, Lustivious, who I believed was a MTF drag queen (Lustivious/Lusty is actually Sile Singleton, a woman who gives powerful performances as both king and queen). Watching the Kings, I experienced for the first time what cultural critic Jennifer Maher calls the "starfucker blues" (Maher 1999, 32). Maher, writing about her reaction to watching Greg Dulli (lead singer of the band the Afghan Whigs) perform, describes the doubled desire experienced by some female fans while watching their male rock star idols:

> Our desires for and desires to be like the male rock star are all tangled up because we want so many things at once. We want the same entry into unrestrained sex as he has, we want to have sex with him. We want to sleep with the performer and we want to be one ourselves, to be both sex objects and performing subjects. We want carnal agency without sexual violence. (Maher 1999, 30)

As I watched my first drag king performance, I simultaneously wanted to be them and fuck them (or, be fucked by them). I would argue that the experience of the queer female fan watching and desiring a drag king act is different from that of the female fan watching the male rock star, because for the drag king fan, the possibility of desiring and owning that phallus, that masculine energy (carnal or otherwise) is much more real. Watching women perform convincingly as men, working their dicks and getting tips stuffed in their pants by adoring audience members, female fans are empowered with the knowledge that (with practice and some technological assistance) we, too, can possess that dick, can become the performing subjects of our desire. To put it much more simply, we fans *can both* watch the king and be him.

The sublime confusion I experienced upon watching my first king show was exacerbated months later, when I tried out my own king persona for the first time. That preliminary experience as a king, and all that have followed as I've begun performing in public, makes the strongest argument (to me, and I'd hope to my audiences) that the relationships between technologies of gender are intimately implicated in our subjectivities and our desires. After attending the "science fair" (a collection of drag king how-to booths and demonstrations) at the *First International Drag King Extravaganza* in Columbus in October 1999, I went home and put what I'd learned into practice, sticking socks in my pants, binding my chest, creating sideburns and a mustache with mascara, and slicking my hair into a greasy attempt at a pompadour. I was immediately surprised by how much I liked myself this way, how "right" and sexy my masculine presentation felt, and how ready I was to get in on some action (onstage and off). I had previously had difficulty understanding the practical appeal of strap-on dildos, and their effects on their wearers. While I could imagine the pleasure that could be derived for both parties using the strap-on, I had also imagined this pleasure would be limited by the fact that the dildo still wasn't the "real thing." Trying on an even farther-from-real version of the phallus (a pair of anklets from my sock drawer) for the first time was enough to convince me that my previous understanding was limited. Even though I knew that what was in my pants was not a dick, it was not difficult to imagine it as such. My enjoyment of the fantasies I then started to devise (both sexual and non-sexual, about performing with this new cock, going out, passing as male) confused me further. I had never felt any of the things I'd mistakenly assumed drag kings felt (I had confused transgender identity offstage and king identity onstage, thinking that most kings were performing FTM identities in both spaces). I enjoy myself in my own skin, don't feel as if I'm in the "wrong body" or living a falsely gendered life, and have never wanted to become a boy or man. But there I was, all of a sudden loving the way the pair of socks between my legs and some fake facial hair made me feel. I felt ready to strut my stuff, to be the sort of sleazy, sexually aggressive man I would hate in real life. I felt like a supreme, badass genderfucker, and I loved it. Ultimately, I decided to start enjoying the confusion these experiences produced; if anything could freak me out in the wonderful way this experience had, I figured it was evidence that doing drag as a king was an avenue worth exploring.

In my performances as Red Rider, I have done both "traditional" drag numbers (e.g., performing/lip-synching to the music of the Afghan Whigs, Beck and others) as well as performances informed by my own sense of gender-multiplicity, which I would not categorize as traditional drag acts (by performing as a drag queen Madonna to the song "Material Girl" or as Hedwig of the movie and off-Broadway musical *Hedwig and the Angry Inch*). In the most relevant case, I performed a routine choreographed to the Folk Implosion's "Natural One" single, to my mind a seductive song in which Lou Barlow references his "natural" sexual, masculine status as part of each of the song's verses. For this performance, I was accompanied by April West and Erica Manville (my Pearl Girl collaborators, still in high femme mode but without the red wigs). The performance began with a mutual pick-up scenario, followed by the mutual seduction of all participants, for which our trio provided a means of presenting multiply directed desires and combinations of partners. The culminating moments of the performance came at its end, as, while continuing to reference his status as the "Natural One" Red (I) was stripped of his shirt, ACE bandage, and phallic-substitute sock by the women (by this point also stripped of wigs and outer layers), who then split the pair of anklets and stuffed them into their pantyhose. While this performance obviously wrecks any attempt to perform a convincing masculine illusion, that's part of its appeal for me. I wanted to perform my sense of self as king and femme, as someone who enjoys the empowerment of moving among genders as I perform, and to establish some sense of continuity between these positions.

Through my performances as Red Pearl and Red Rider, I have come to better understand my relationship to multiple expressions of femininity and masculinity: my own, my male partner's, and those embodied and/or performed by women I admire. In significant ways, this understanding has helped me embody my queerness, and has offered me some clues as I explore the ways in which my desires relate to gender and sex at this point in my life. Finally, I know how one body can be the location for some genders (many more than two), that there is room for this multiply gendered subjectivity in one life, and that drag performance is a very real way of making gender multiple, of achieving the "someness" Halberstam and Livingston desire in their vision of our posthuman-queer future.

REFERENCES

De Lauretis, Teresa. 1987. *Technologies of Gender: Essays on Theory, Film and Fiction*. Bloomington: Indiana University Press.

The Fabulous Lady Misses Julia and Jessica. *GLAM Manifesto* [online]. Available from World Wide Web at <*http://www.rhizomes.net/Issue1/glam/GLAM_Manifesto.html*>. This site presents the *GLAM Manifesto*, its theorization, and implementation. The site also includes the *Manifesto*'s Appendices.

Halberstam, Judith. 1998. *Female Masculinity*. Durham: Duke University Press.

_____. 1997. Techno-Homo: On bathrooms, butches, and sex with furniture. Pp. 183-193 in *Processed Lives: Gender and Technology in Everyday Life*, ed. J. Terry and M. Calvert. London: Routledge.

Halberstam, Judith and Livingston, Ira. 1995. "Introduction: Posthuman Bodies." Pp. 1-19 in *Posthuman Bodies*, ed. J. Halberstam and I. Livingston. Bloomington: Indiana University Press.

Maher, Jennifer. "Starfucker Blues." *Bitch: Feminist Response to Pop Culture* 11 (Spring 1999): 28-32.

Terry, Jennifer and Calvert, Melodie, eds. 1997. *Processed Lives: Gender and Technology in Everyday Life*. London: Routledge,

Drag King Magic:
Performing/Becoming the Other

Kathryn Rosenfeld, MA

Roosevelt University

SUMMARY. This chapter seeks to theorize drag king practice through the lenses of alterity, liminality, and performance theory, while attempting to complicate and reinvigorate discussions of identity raised by drag. I examine the ways in which drag king performance plumbs the concept of "the Other," and forces confrontation with a complex field of desire. Contemporary "queergirl" existence negotiates a range of desirable and desiring Others, from the polarities (i.e., butch-femme) unique to queer structures of desire, to the desire of those on the cultural margins for the power of those at the center, and vice versa. I employ anthropological theories of performance, mimesis, and liminality to establish a framework through which drag kings may be viewed as crucibles of this desire and agents of this power exchange. By performing maleness, drag kings expand and redraw the definitional boundaries of the male, interfere with the cultural power of mainstream maleness, and simultaneously transfer some of this power to themselves as queer women. At the same time, drag king existence forces a renegotiation of queergirl desire to encompass a range of masculinities. By performing/becoming the Other, drag kings engage in a practice of magic which transforms both margin and center. *[Article copies available for a fee from The Haworth Document Delivery Service: 1-800-HAWORTH. E-mail address: <docdelivery@haworthpress.com> Website: <http://www.HaworthPress.com> © 2002 by The Haworth Press, Inc. All rights reserved.]*

[Haworth co-indexing entry note]: "Drag King Magic: Performing/Becoming the Other." Rosenfeld, Kathryn. Co-published simultaneously in *Journal of Homosexuality* (Harrington Park Press, an imprint of The Haworth Press, Inc.) Vol. 43, No. 3/4, 2002, pp. 201-219; and: *The Drag King Anthology* (ed: Donna Troka, Kathleen LeBesco, and Jean Bobby Noble) Harrington Park Press, an imprint of The Haworth Press, Inc., 2002, pp. 201-219. Single or multiple copies of this article are available for a fee from The Haworth Document Delivery Service [1-800-HAWORTH, 9:00 a.m. - 5:00 p.m. (EST). E-mail address: docdelivery@haworthpress.com].

KEYWORDS. Drag kings, performance, magic, masculinity, lesbian, bisexuality, gender, anthropology, social power, desire

This is where we must begin; with the magical power of replication, the image affecting what it is an image of, wherein the representation shares in or takes power from the represented . . .

–Michael Taussig, *Mimesis and Alterity*

INTRODUCTION: QUEER ISN'T WHAT IT USED TO BE

Even my parents went to see *Boys Don't Cry.* Director Kimberly Peirce's 1999 fictionalization of the real-life story of Brandon Teena–the female-to-male transsexual who was raped and murdered in 1993 by two of the young, poor Nebraskans among whom he lived and passed–had surprisingly broad success, winning an Oscar for lead Hillary Swank, and running in art houses far longer than could be sustained by the predominantly lesbian and transgender audiences one might have expected the film to draw. *Boys Don't Cry* seems to be one of the first American lesbian films (if it can be called that) to depict multidimensional, diverse characters negotiating an equally complex and messy world. Despite being young, confused, and constrained by his culture of origin as well as his own bad choices, Brandon (Swank) is not naive in his awareness of himself as a transsexual. He packs a prosthesis, collects literature on sex reassignment, and insists to his gay male friend that he is not a lesbian; to read his attempts at passing in the straight world as innocent folly is inaccurate. Brandon's girlfriend Lana (Chloe Sevigny) exhibits a similar mounting self-awareness as she realizes who he is and what it will mean for her, as a straight woman, to love him. *Boys Don't Cry* is a film about gender identity that lacks the blow-to-the-head didacticism the word "identity" has come to imply. But has the broad critical and popular reception of the film been merely a question of fine acting, subtle direction, and a well-executed script? Or has a shift occurred, and if it has, is it a shift in queer culture, visual culture, pop culture, or all of the above?

The year 1999 saw the publication of *The Drag King Book* by theorist Judith Halberstam and photographer Del LaGrace Volcano. A lush and glossy coffee table paperback, *The Drag King Book* is the culmination of four years' participant observation by the authors in the drag king scenes of London, New York, and San Francisco. At the very end of her chapter on locality Halberstam comments that as the book was going to press, she learned of the "active and exciting new drag king scene" crafted by the performance troupe H.I.S. Kings in Columbus, Ohio, indicating that drag kinging has spread to the provinces (Volcano and Halberstam 1999, 86-7). In actuality, H.I.S. Kings have been around since 1996, when they were founded by a group of women's studies grad students from Ohio State University. They were also the force behind the *First International Drag King Extravaganza*, yet another manifestation of the exploding popularity of drag kings to hit the cultural field in the fall of 1999.[1] As Halberstam asks, "Why drag kings? Why now?" (Volcano and Halberstam 1999, 32).

To theorize drag and gender is not a new proposition; that anyone could have existed during the past decade as a queer person or feminist academic and avoided these topics is inconceivable. Is the drag king, then, basically a late bloomer, or a postscript to a mostly spent trend? Or do drag kings posit new, underinvestigated avenues of inquiry? This chapter is about the changes in queer reality that have both made way for and been precipitated by the drag king explosion, and about the divisions that remain and proliferate in that reality. From my position as audience member, critical observer, and fan, I seek to complicate and reinvigorate drag-induced discussions of identity by theorizing drag king practice through the lenses of alterity and liminality. I have borrowed these concepts from anthropology, not to conflate a contemporary Western popular performance idiom with those of more usual anthropological subjects, but as useful tools for framing the ways in which drag kings do social magic by traversing states of being and boundaries between mutually constructing others. I particularly draw upon anthropologist Michael Taussig's writing on mimetic performance because of his close analysis of social and political power and the reversal of or interference with its operations in this sort of performance.

Proceeding from the premise that gender and race function intersectionally, so that where one is performed the other is also necessarily performed, I will claim that drag kings confound the power differentials embedded in these constructs by "becoming" the powerful other in performance.[2] The assumption that contemporary Western drag king practice exists against and within the framework of a mainstream patriarchal culture, while perhaps obvious, also necessarily underlies my discussion. As socially "weak" but performatively strong operatives (a designation which will become important below, in light of anthropologist

Victor Turner's theories of performance), drag kings represent three significant forms of alterity, or otherness: they (or, at any rate, the performers who "create" them) are women, queers, and members of at least one subculture. I want to show that by performing maleness–by performatively/mimetically "becoming" men–drag kings simultaneously alter the nature of power-over as it operates in the general culture, and claim power for themselves.

Within drag kinging as a queer cultural phenomenon are embedded several potent and contested understandings about the nature and structure of queergirl desire–for ourselves, for one another, and for the figure of masculinity. Yet desire is both visceral and intellectual, and also includes the political desire of marginalized subjects for freedom of movement within the fields of identity and power. Then there is mutual desire between margin and center–the margin's desire to simultaneously possess and intervene in the center's power, as well as the center's desire for the margin's perceived edginess and illicit, exotic appeal. Particularly on the first level, it seems most effective to think through the ineffable topic of desire by plumbing my own desire in the realm of drag kings.

The centrality to drag of costuming and style leads back to questions of mimesis and desire. Style carries implications of individual self-representation as well as group identification that underscore its broad importance to marginal cultures or subcultures (Hebdige 1988). If queerdom is both a subculture in cultural historian Dick Hebdige's sense, and a community of desire, then style–which is mimetic in that it is produced through mutual modeling by individuals within a cultural field–becomes a montage of signs of desire, and aesthetic trappings become capable both of identifying potential objects of desire, and of invoking desire itself. For these and other reasons, the importance of supposedly superficial aesthetic and stylistic elements cannot be underestimated. The whole comprises the parts of the mimetic representational function, on which my later discussion of drag kings as mimetic and liminal figures will depend.

Being a queergirl is not what it was ten years ago, when I was helping run my campus LGB group (and we had to fight for that "B"; no one even thought about "T" then). To get through the door, girls and boys alike had to display the proper uniform: combat boots, baseball cap, leather jacket festooned with Queer Nation stickers. Given this stylistic history, I can only imagine how barely recognizable *today's* multifarious, multigendered Lesbian Nation would be to its Second Wave founding mothers. If anything lies at the heart of these shifts, it has been a slowly dawning acceptance of gender variance: over the past years, it has become increasingly admissible that some of the girls want to be boys. First there was a rebirth of butch-femme (and the mainstream's initial loud astonishment, subsumed rapidly by "lesbian chic," that some lesbians liked to wear make-up–some of the girls also wanted to be girls), then a new visibility of and increased interest in female-to-male transsexuality, and, more recently, an explosion in the popularity and practice of drag kinging.

Such developments seem to reflect the slow evolution of an overall rejection of homogeneity. Butch dykes in facial hair (apart from being the ultimate bi-girl wet dream) reveal a multivalent queer female desire beneath the specious, if heretofore common, assumption that queer desire equals the eroticization of sameness. Contemporary drag king performance literally spotlights the diverse range of pop-cultural templates available for queergirl gender expression. In this and other respects, drag kinging is important for the ways in which it differs from gay male uses of drag. Both forms emanate from queer cultural history: as H.I.S. Kings member Julia Applegate pointed out in her opening remarks at the *First International Drag King Extravaganza* (IDKE) in 1999, the current fascination with drag kinging is most accurately viewed as a revival of the tradition established by both entertainers and patrons in the working-class butch-femme bar culture of the mid-twentieth century. However, while drag queens have remained a vital and definitive aspect of queer culture since Stonewall, drag kings represent a dormant tradition rediscovered. Drag queens are now a widely recognized object of general popular culture: RuPaul does television ads, and even hyper-heterosexual movie stars Wesley Snipes and Patrick Swayze donned the campy, sparkly uniform of the drag queen in 1995s *To Wong Foo, Thanks for Everything, Julie Newmar*. But the drag queen, at least at her most emblematic, represents a highly particular conception of performative male femininity: she is not the analog of a "real" woman, but the distillation of a surrealistically exaggerated, outrageously flamboyant femininity that most "real" women neither embody nor aspire to. While there are certainly varying "flavors" of drag queen performance, the showgirl aesthetic typically associated with drag queens is uniform in comparison to the broad range of masculinities performed by drag kings.

Drag king archetypes range from Elvis to Chuck D., from biker to Mafioso, from average working-class stiff to effete dandy. Some drag king acts adopt an aggressively hetero male sexuality, as when performers flirt lasciviously with femmes in the audience, or interact onstage with drag queens. Other kings favor gay male styles of desire: as a fellow audience member once said to me, following a performance by two kings in a leather-inflected, military-style officer-and-underling scene, "It was nice to see some faggotry." Drag kings tend to perform subtle reconfigurations of maleness; their outrageousness comes from blatant sexual bravado and a genuflection (in common with drag queens, although its objects are quite different) at the throne of pop culture iconicity, rather than the performance of a single conception of hyperbolic maler-than-maleness. Or, as Halberstam puts it,

> If the drag queen takes what is artificial about femininity (or what has been culturally constructed as artificial) and plays it to the hilt, the drag king takes what is so-called natural about masculinity and reveals its mechanisms–the tricks and poses, the speech patterns and attitudes that have been seamlessly assimilated into a performance of realness. (Volcano and Halberstam 1999, 62)

It may be simply that the general culture offers more ways of being male than female. Yet drag king macho, when it appears, tends to be more layered and nuanced than macho in the mainstream.

PLAYING ON OUR DESIRES

I have been somewhat deliberately conflating female masculinity and drag king performance, because I think the latter is both symptomatic and exemplary of the former, and that together they say something crucial about queergirl existence and desire. But because I am interested in mimesis, I want to note the specifically performative state of drag kings, and the difference between being and appearing to be that this state delineates. For Taussig, mimesis is the point of contact between the represented and its representation, between original and copy, at which the latter plays upon and influences the former, possibly even changing the original's nature as it changes its own. This theory of contact also underscores sympathetic magic (wherein remnants such as hair or clothing, or visual or performative representations of the intended object stand in for and thus affect the reality of that object), leading Taussig to claim that in mimesis social magic is done (Taussig 1993, 47-8). In such a performance, the copy "poses as" the original, in some ways becoming it but also not ceasing to be itself, remaining, in a case such as the present one where the margin undertakes a mimetic performance of the center, within alterity (otherness, outside-ness). Taussig writes, "Once the mimetic has sprung into being, a terrifically ambiguous power is established; there is born the power to represent the world, yet that same power is a power to falsify, mask, and pose" (Taussig 1993, 42-3). This power is the marginal mimetic performer's (in this case, the drag king's) foil to the power-over of the other he or she performs (in this case, the male).

Taussig's invocation of ambiguity also points to the other anthropological concept I apply to drag kings, liminality. According to Turner, the liminal–from the term limen, or threshold–is time out of time, space out of space, the anti-quotidian margin inhabited by performance and ritual, literally "limbo" (Turner 1986, 25). At the same time, the liminal is as much a space of play as of sacred and serious ritual. The liminal is "the betwixt and between," through which "liminal personae" (the actors in a liminal ritual or performance–often shape-shifting figures who specialize in turning things on their heads and making things not as they seem) pass on their way from one state of being or status to another (Turner 1969, 95). The function of these personae is to mitigate and counterbalance the dominance of the socially powerful, sometimes by placing them in a temporarily abject state within liminal space. Turner calls liminality the "subjunctive mood" of culture–the expression of what could be or what is longed for as opposed to what is. As such, liminal space, where ordinary social realities are literally "in play," is a space of desire (Turner 1986, 25).

Reviewing the *First International Drag King Extravaganza* for my local queer rag, I concluded that the rules of How to Be a Queergirl are changing before our eyes. Drag kings are reimagining and reconfiguring masculinity for a queer female audience that is increasingly unafraid to claim it as part of our sexuality, and to announce our desire as diametric, phallic, faggotish and polymorphous (Rosenfeld 1999, 32). The drag king extends the figure of the attracting opposite in the erotic inventory of the queer female beyond butch to include macho, hairy, hung, and masculine. For a next step, we might come clean about the percentage of lesbians of all ages who love to watch fag porn, or even give Camille Paglia, with her assertion that men are her role models, another chance.

As long as I've been watching, admiring, writing about, and fantasizing about drag kings, I have repeatedly, and always somewhat confoundedly, asked myself *just what it is about them.* Why are drag kings such a potent site of desire for me, for themselves, for queergirls, for transfolks; in short, why exactly do I find drag kings such a turn on? I knew they made me hot, but I struggled for a long time (and still do) with questions about the possible subtextual motivations, meanings, and significance of my desire. Certainly desire's ineffability accounts for a good part of its appeal, but attempting to formulate these connections has also provided me with a powerful reminder that desire functions on at least two distinct but inseparable levels. There is the visceral, sexual, sometimes elusive longing for sensory satiation and complex beauty, and then there is the socioeconomic longing for power, agency, and self-definition. Both remain categories of joy and problems.

The pleasure of genderfuck is in many ways dependent on the power hierarchy of gender, which explains what some view as the limited usefulness of male feminization as opposed to female masculinization. As bell hooks has pointed out, a man who deliberately "trades down" on the gender hierarchy by becoming feminized is seen from the dominant viewpoint as at worst pathological and at best laughable, an instance of and/or subject for parody (hooks 1996, 215). On the other hand, a woman who successfully masculinizes herself has access to a far more varied field of cultural play that might include practices of parody and pastiche, irony and critique, or personal and collective desire-fulfillment. The visceral queergirl desire invoked by the dissonant gender expression of drag kings is also, then, the desire of those on the margins of gender and sexuality for fluidity, movement, and freedom within these fields.

Speaking in character, New York drag king Mo B. Dick describes the experience of being an ambiguous object of desire:

> Somebody came up to me and said, "Are you a man or a woman?" I said, "I'm a drag king." . . . She was totally confused, and then she was all nervous and didn't know what to expect. And she was attracted to me so it made her nervous or uncomfortable to think, what is she attracted to? (Kashanski 1998)

The "what" in this question points to the heart of drag kings' sexiness. Is the person described nervous because she is a straight woman who finds herself attracted to someone female-bodied, or because she is a lesbian who finds herself attracted to masculinity? Much of the punch and potency of drag kings is that they represent that unattainable other side of the chasm of queer female desire: they enable the possibility of admitting queergirl desire for the phallus. Women who feel powerful when they pack a dildo and strut out into the evening, and women who lust after them, both manifest this desire. In other words, the complicated desire invoked by drag kings is desire for the self *and* desire for the other.

This formulation mostly understands "the phallus" literally, but re-articulated in psychoanalytic terms, desire for the phallus becomes desire for power–for the sexual agency available to the socio-sexual center.

But the "what" in Mo's question is also the gender dissonance itself embodied by drag kings (see Butler 1990, 123). Desire, dissonance, and irony all produce the same sensory "edge," born of the erotic appeal of ambiguity, of balancing on the brink between certainties. Drag kings invoke multiple experiences of irony: performance of a male character by a female-bodied person, critical parody of hegemonic forms of maleness by actors assuming but not "normally" embodying those forms, desire for a masculine figure on the part of viewers usually seen (by themselves and/or others) as eroticized to femaleness. These ironies both temper and complicate the seemingly straightforward experience of pleasure associated with drag. This irony/pleasure edge may be seen as analogous to the figure/ground edge produced by gender expressed in "opposition" to biological sex. Thus the desire drag kings inspire is also desire for fluidity and range of movement–for the power and freedom to be sexually unpredictable and undecidable.

DRAG RACE-ING

The complexity of drag king identity is perhaps related to its inevitable filtration through the tangled web of lesbian politics, or to the "reverse trajectory" along which current drag king practice has evolved: from the feminist academy's love affair with gender performativity to the bars and clubs, rather than from the streets to the schools. Within both feminism and lesbian culture, there has long been this tension between "the street" (grassroots activism, or working-class bar culture) and the academy (the advent of women's studies in the 1970s and the subsequent rise of academic feminism); the drag king phenomenon is especially interesting in its relationship to these often opposed spaces. While drag king performance was historically rooted in bar and cabaret culture, its current incarnation has its antecedents in academia; for example, that H.I.S. Kings were founded by graduate students suggests that scholarly interest in drag as an exemplar of certain forms of gender theory has in turn led young academics to pursue an active praxis of drag.

With this series of "street-campus" exchanges in its history, it is not surprising that the drag king community finds itself grappling with the sociopolitical implications of its practice, to the approval of some and the annoyance of others. At the *First International Drag King Extravaganza* (IDKE) in Columbus, Ohio in October 1999, the afternoon open panel discussion, whose topic was "Is FTM [Female to Male] Drag Political?" turned quickly to questions of race.[3] What does it mean for white drag kings to perform black music, or vice versa? Is one more politically problematic than the other? Does drag performance necessarily carry a racialized meaning? Where does tribute end and appropriation begin? Or, as many performers insisted, in a drag-specific version of "Can't we all just get along," is it simply about the desire to entertain and have a good time?

If drag kings signal a refraction of the menu of ways to be a queergirl, then this expanded field must encompass not only gender, but the equally volatile aspects of identity with which gender intersects. If one of the drag king's functions is to demonstrate or personify the performability of gender, then he must also necessarily embody the performability of race, as another identity construct that adheres to the body. It is important to add race as treated by drag kings to the discussion not only because it makes for a more complete picture, but because it further exemplifies drag kings' "power play." If drag kings both usurp and mitigate the social power of maleness by performing/becoming it, then they necessarily do the same to white maleness, when that is what they perform. Drag performers of color similarly intervene in the status of, for example, black maleness as they negotiate that terrain of power and disempowerment.

Where the subject is performed with the purpose of foregrounding the figure of identity in terms of its unfixed relationship to the ground of body, the intersecting facets of that identity necessarily become texts in the performance. The gendered body is, simultaneously and inextricably, the raced body. While drag is by definition gender performed, it must also by extension be race performed, *at least* inasmuch as the stylistic and performative characteristics that compose "gender" operate analogously to those which, if they are not one and the same, compose "race." To deny, for instance, that white drag kings who lip synch to black music and impersonate black artists reference fraught histories of minstrelsy and blackface, as well as point to (or even mark themselves as participants in) the contemporary phenomenon of "wiggers" (white kids who adopt hip-hop style and cultural identification), is to imply that drag kinging does or should exist in a cultural vacuum.[4] As Halberstam points out, white kings' "reluctance to connect [their] performance to racial drag speaks to some of the anxiety about identity that crops up when cross-racial performances are in question" (Volcano and

Halberstam 1999, 145). To insist that all drag performance is uniformly and unequivocally "just about entertaining and having a good time" is to erase the cultural and historical meanings of the styles, personae, and pop culture icons that are the source material of drag.

However, there are drag kings of diverse races who, to varying degrees, consciously perform race along with gender. Mo B. Dick (a.k.a. Maureen Fischer) has a thick Brooklyn accent, a heavily greased pompadour, and cheesy, chest hair baring, lounge-lizard duds. As a short white woman, Fischer performs a male character with a Napoleon complex. Mo flirts crassly with female audience members, always thinks he's right, and loudly and repeatedly makes it known that he "ain't no homo" (Volcano and Halberstam 1999, 114; Kashanski 1998). In Mo, Fischer performs a certain stereotype of straight, white male bravado, whose subtext is a comedic yet profound insecurity about his own sexuality. In a display of the parodic/admiring ambivalence toward maleness often embodied in the drag king, Mo is both charming and pathetic, offensive and endearing. Fischer's performance of the flawed nature of both whiteness and maleness reveals the failure of white males to completely live up to White Maleness (Volcano and Halberstam 1999, 118).

Mo seems to represent a fairly conscious performance of whiteness; his character at once reveals characterizations of the working-class white male as sexist, homophobic, and exaggeratedly macho for the stereotypes they are, and intervenes in these machinations of power as they adhere to the figure of white maleness he embodies. As the actor behind the character, Fischer in some way takes all of these characterizations upon herself, and with them their attendant power plays. Mo has rigid ideas about what men and women are, and gets confused when these are challenged, as when he finds himself in bawdy performances with drag queens, or even, as in one instance, performing in female drag himself. In these situations, Fischer seems to play Mo as mostly in the dark as to the queerness of his circumstances, and naively befuddled where it becomes clear to him that something is "not quite right" gender-wise. At the same time, Fischer's own savvy about these things and about the parodic irony of her character is always subtly present in Mo. The pleasure and sexiness of a drag king persona like Mo lies in his ability to claim some of the bravado of a certain flavor of white maleness for queer female subjects, while simultaneously mitigating the social power of that figure by proving that it can adhere to the very bodies and sexualities to which it tries to define itself in opposition. The power of the dominant other is thus made less potent and less threatening by mimetically becoming him.

Performances of whiteness, while not always fully deliberate, become evident much of the time in drag kings' fondness for pop-cultural male "types." For example, at the 1999 IDKE performative whiteness could be seen in the acts of kings who portrayed such figures as "the Cowboy" or the leather-clad, Harley Davidson logo-sporting "badboy." Two icons of white American maleness, these characters in the form of drag kings revealed two divergent but equally potent tropes of masculine sexiness: suave, chivalrous romanticism and fast, danger-seeking rebellion. Placing these familiar types in the queer context of drag kinging made their seductiveness available for queergirl use, and in so doing denaturalized it, thus calling these templates into question as adequate or neutral male ways of being. These performances also involved an element of tribute to these iconic characters that, while open to critique, have strongly shaped certain American ideas of romance and sexuality. This subtext of homage complicates arguments, discussed below, about differences along race lines in uses of drag.

Perhaps because of the more coherent and continuous tradition of butch/femme within lesbian communities of color, drag and butchness are there viewed less as performances and more as states of being. As Halberstam describes, in white clubs drag shows become elaborate, planned performances with emphasis on spectacle, theatricality, and production values, while in clubs frequented by women of color drag shows or contests tend to consist of entrants, many of whom may not even be performers or in costume, strutting their stuff to win the crowd's approval. In other words, the former is about imitation, the latter about the long-standing drag/queer criterion of "realness" (Halberstam 1998, 245). As connoted by realness, the ability to pass unnoticed in straight society in turn seems to reference the raced history of passing, particularly in relation to black female performers passing as a means of professional survival. Also, to the extent that some white drag king performances disparage men and/or act out anger at men and male sexism, the political history of black women's alliance with black men in anti-racist struggle, as opposed to white feminists' more wholesale political rejection of men, may inform black drag kings' apparent reliance more on being than on mimicking or parodying.

For Halberstam, some black drag kings' performances of black masculinities set them apart from white kings in specific ways. Their uses of classic hip-hop and R&B acts function, Halberstam believes, more as straightforward tribute, less as parody; rather than poke fun at the male personae they perform, black kings "appropriate black masculine style for a dyke performance" (Halberstam 1998, 257). New York performers Dréd and Shon, as interviewed by Halberstam, concur that their act takes a stance of respect toward the artists they perform, which have included both the Jackson Five and Run DMC (Volcano and Halberstam 1999, 142-3). Halberstam also aptly notes the social segregation that persists among lesbian communities, and describes the wide differences in uses of gender, both historically and now, between white and black queer women. However, her implication that black drag king performance is less likely to involve irony or self-reflexivity seems questionable, especially in light of her contention that the identity-layering in hip-hop performances by *white* kings "captures the performability of black masculinity" (Volcano and Halberstam 1999, 145). Her insistence that Dréd and Shon's act "appeals less to the crowd's sense of humor and more to their desires" (Volcano and Halberstam 1999, 143) seems to downplay the tension between parody and desire that inflects *all* drag king performance.

I am interested in the ways black drag kings *do* reconfigure maleness. For example, like many women hip-hop artists, they intervene in and reconfigure the hypermasculinized hip-hop aesthetic by infusing it with a blatant and effusive sexuality that is removed from straight maleness. Alternately, Dréd's ultra-slick, Blaxploitation-derived "Mackdaddy" persona shrewdly parodies not only a certain two-dimensional trope of black masculinity, but racist conceptions of black masculinity in general as hypersexualized. Or consider New York king Harry Krishna, whose performance of Prince at the 1999 IDKE inflected an outrageous black male sexuality with strains of male femininity. This deeply campy performance, in which Harry and a femme collaborator did Prince's raunchy tune "Darling Nikki," humorously and theatrically claimed the aggressive sexuality of the song and the artist for queer female subjects. As himself something of a throwback to a flamboyant "glam" mode of black male pop stardom (in the funk tradition of Sly and the Family Stone or Parliament), Prince, it may be argued, does not offer a standard masculinity for reconfiguration by drag kings, yet the use of his music by several different performers at the 1999 IDKE attests to the drag-specific appeal of his genderbending outrageousness and unapologetic sexuality. Yet even in Dréd and Shon's less parodic, more reverent tributes to classic rap artists, the reappropriation of these straight male-encoded figures by lesbian performers serves to intervene in, critique, and reconfigure hip-hop misogyny as well as to rescue the artists from racist condemnation.

If drag kings of color, or kings who perform to black music, are more likely to be seen or to see themselves as performing race alongside gender, I think it is primarily due to our culture's tendency to erase whiteness as race. White and black kings, I would argue, are set apart not by differences in the parody-tribute ratios of their performances, but by the necessarily different ways in which they play with power. Where white kings mimetically appropriate white maleness, thus reconfiguring its social power, black kings enter a subject position that both possesses and is denied access to that power. Their revelation of the performability of black maleness must also involve an element of the purely celebratory: power cannot be reclaimed, or wholly reclaimed, from a figure that does not possess it, or possesses it partially.

WHAT MAGIC LIES IN THIS?

When Taussig quotes anthropologist Gerardo Reichel-Dolmatoff's assertion that "in some way or another one can protect oneself from evil spirits by portraying them," he makes reference to mimetic performance's redress of social power differentials (Taussig 1993, 12). The use of drag performance to affect (in a double sense of the word–both to influence and to assume) the power of a dominant other constitutes the center of my discussion. If drag kings are not precisely replicas (of men, maleness, or masculinity), they nonetheless, as representations, engage on many levels in sharing power with and taking it from the represented, to paraphrase Taussig. Drag king practice, as we have seen, gives rise to multivalent representations of maleness and masculinity. At the same time, that drag kings reference men is unavoidable. Therein lies the threat of drag kings: they simultaneously introduce the possibility that there is no authentic gender, and tap a male fear of being replaced, a fear that someone other than men can be better men than men (Volcano and Halberstam 1999, 120). Taussig more poetically describes this uneasiness at seeing oneself performed/represented as other on the part of the other (in other words, a dominant subject's encounter with the marginalized subject's representation of himself): "What magic lies in this, my wooden self, sung to power in a language I cannot understand?" (Taussig 1993, 8)

It seems useful to establish two categories of drag king performance in order to treat it in terms of ritual, performance theory, and particularly Taussig's discussion of mimesis as "protect[ing] oneself from evil spirits by portraying them." Some drag kings privilege realness, aiming at least temporarily to become masculine, or in effect to be a certain type of male, while others deliberately emphasize a fluidity of gender, incorporating the disjunction between their female anatomies and masculine personae into their acts (Volcano and Halberstam 1999, 125). I want to call these categories, respectively, mimetic and liminal.

Unlike most of the mimetic performances of maleness I've been discussing, the destination of performances by drag kings such as Toe B. of Columbus is the charged gray area between masculinity and femininity, the site of gender's slippage and indeterminacy rather than gender itself. At the 1999 IDKE, Toe B. (a.k.a. Heidi Madsen) performed to Shania Twain's eminently drag-pervertible hit "Man, I Feel Like a Woman." The choice of music by a female artist was in itself a deviation from customary drag king form, in which performers generally lip synch to pop tunes by male artists. However, when Toe B. took the stage in cowboy drag complete with handlebar mustache, the song began playing at a slow enough speed that the vocal track was credible as lip synched by the performer's male character. But by the end of the act, the song was playing at normal speed, and Toe B. had stripped down to a lacy bra and tight stretch pants, pulling off hat and mustache to reveal feminine make-up and long hair. Similarly, "Dréd's act very often incorporates a strip tease of some kind and will culminate with her exposing her leather bra and pulling an apple out of her pants and taking a bite" (Volcano and Halberstam 1999, 120). Meanwhile, performers such as Lustivious de la Virgion (a.k.a. Sile Singleton), H.I.S. Kings' silver-lamé-, feather boa-, and false eyelash-clad emcee, demonstrate that women can also be drag queens.

These drag performers consciously float in a nether-region between states of (gendered) being–they are liminal. Turner holds that "genres of cultural performance"–of which drag kinging, whose culture is both queer culture and mainstream popular culture, is certainly an example–are "not simple mirrors but magical mirrors of social reality: they exaggerate, invert, re-form, magnify, minimize, dis-color, re-color, even deliberately falsify" (Turner 1986, 42). Such performances are, for Turner, instances of liminality. This performative "betwixt and between" is not simply or only time out of time, but specifically a space of role reversal between the socio-politically powerful and weak (Turner 1969, 99-100). Turner establishes a direct connection between the space of liminality and that of marginality: the quotidian weakness of the socially "low" or marginalized becomes, in liminality, "sacred power" (Turner 1969, 125). Drag kings are therefore liminal not only because they cultivate the "betwixt and between" of gender, but because their performance deliberately and pointedly confounds gendered structures of social power. For Turner, liminality's social function is self-reflexive, providing space in which performers "show ourselves to ourselves" (Turner 1986, 102). Thus, Turner's work can be used to illustrate the ways in which drag kings (and other liminal personae) execute social critique, while Taussig, with his emphasis on the transformative social/sympathetic magic of mimesis, frames the ways in which drag kings facilitate social change. Both mimetic and liminal kings negotiate a transformative power exchange with the powerful male other by representing, performing, becoming him.

Taussig's discussion of alterity as "a lot more performative and physical, a lot more realist yet fanciful, than implied in the way 'othering' is alluded to in discussions today" seems applicable to drag kings and their visceral rendering of gender theory, as well as their desiring and desire-invoking presentation of masculinity, through which this masculinity loses some of its alterity or otherness (Taussig 1993, 33). For Taussig, this sympathetic magic–the "notion of the copy . . . affecting the original to such a degree that the representation shares in or acquires the properties of the represented"–occurs at the point of contact between represented and representation (Taussig 1993, 47). If, as Halberstam contends, drag kings serve as barometers of "how thoroughly we as a society have learned to detach masculinity from men and to defuse the intensity and effect of male authority" (Volcano and Halberstam 1999, 150), then their performance of this authority operates according to the logic of mimetic magic. Drag kings are the contact points between maleness and its performative, mimetic representation through which maleness is transformed. Taussig puts it this way: "To exercise the mimetic faculty is to practice an everyday art of appearance, an art that delights and maddens as it cultivates the insoluble paradox of the distinction between essence and appearance" (Taussig 1993, 176). The author further contends that in a contemporary framework, rather than the fetish (representation) acting as an equivalent of the represented, the state of equivalence itself has become fetishized–a point that aptly frames the erotic charge of drag kings, why they are sexier men than men. Drag kings' assumption of the trappings of maleness converts, through performative practice, to a *sub*sumption of maleness by queerness. Hence, the importance of style and aesthetics to drag: facial hair, details of men's attire, packing, and so on function as the magically potent points of contact between the representation, drag kings, and the represented, maleness–the point at which the other lives inside the self and vice versa. By performing/becoming this alterity, this other, one can control him–which is to say transform him, desire him, and weaken his power over oneself.

My original interest in writing about, being a fan of, and driving eight hours in the middle of a semester, two years in a row, to attend a conference on drag kings stems from desire, so out of some sense of honesty that is where I conclude this chapter. I've spent a year struggling to theorize drag king practice because a dyke in facial hair turns me on. Yet the desire that resides in drag kings extends far beyond the capacity to admit the polyvalence of queergirl eroticism. Drag king desire is desire for the other, or more accurately put, the center's illicit desire for the margin, and the margin's desire for the power wielded by the center. By performing/becoming multiple versions of that center (some of which are, themselves, closer to or further from the center than others), drag kings subversively infiltrate and change it.

Asked to envision the world a thousand years from now, science fiction writer Samuel R. Delany said that peoples' response to the question of a time traveler from our own era–"How did you ever solve the race and gender problems?"–would be the same as ours to a visitor from the Middle Ages inquiring about demons: "We finally figured out those things don't exist" (Delany 1999). In Delany's fantasy world there is perhaps no need for drag kings, but for now, true to their butch chivalrous streaks, they're busy rescuing masculinity from the clutches of maleness, and being very, very sexy while they're at it.

NOTES

1. When I wrote this chapter there was no drag king scene to speak of in Chicago, where I live. That has changed dramatically since early 2001 with the advent of the Chicago Kings, a wildly innovative and, increasingly, tightly professional troupe founded by students from The School of the Art Institute of Chicago. In less than a year, the Chicago Kings have become an institution on the city's queer social scene. For its last Halloween window display, a well-known sex shop on the queer commercial strip of North Halsted featured mechanized cardboard cutouts of Chicago Kings stars like Max Hollywood, Billy T. Holly, and emcee Harley Poker, thus seeming to anoint the kings as the local rock stars they are. Regrettably, however, because of timing, the examples in this essay are drawn not from my home city, but from my observations as an audience member at H.I.S. Kings performances and at the 1999 *First International Drag King Extravaganza*, and from filmed performances and published accounts of kings in New York and elsewhere.

2. This is the claim made by Taussig concerning, for example, post-colonial cult religions whose members ritually perform the stylized roles of colonial governing figures as a way of both influencing these figures' power and claiming some of it for themselves. It should be noted that Taussig is talking here and throughout his discussion about the exchange of power through representation between colonized and colonizer, rather than between queer and straight, female and male, or subcultural and main-

stream. While I deliberately recontextualize Taussig by transposing anthropological theories of performance onto drag kings, I hope to avoid any sort of specious direct analogy between drag kings and postcolonial subjects, or between drag performance and religious ritual. It should further be noted that the popular comparison between drag and shamanism both erroneously ascribes certain religious beliefs and practices to contemporary Western queer culture, and erases the historical contemporaneity of actual shamanic traditions: see Pat Califia, *Sex Changes: The Politics of Transgenderism* (San Francisco: Cleis Press, 1997), 123-4. While I do believe that drag king performance engages and employs liminality, ritual, and magic, I do not believe nor wish to suggest that drag kings are shamans or can be thought of "shamanistically."

3. Certain objections to this panel title further illustrate the political intricacy of drag. Some female-to-male transsexuals and their supporters attending the conference took issue with the use of the term "FTM" to describe drag, arguing that this terminology implies 24-7 transgendered/transsexual existence, with its issues separate from those of drag kings. In short, they argued, you deal with a different set of problems and concerns, and operate from a less privileged position, when your moustache doesn't come off.

4. While all of these forms involve race-as-performance, the "wigger" phenomenon is especially interesting as an example of the absorption of the notion of performative race into contemporary popular culture. While this performativity is usually far less conscious with wiggers than with drag kings or historically with blackface performers, they nonetheless suggest that raced elements of style, language, and cultural conduct are as "transferable" and unfixed as gendered ones. At the same time, wiggers point to the dangers of appropriating culture without an awareness of the power differentials inherent in it. Like traditional drag queens, wiggers are more easily reduced to instances of critically uninformed parody. The well-known New York drag king and DJ Lizerace is an example of a white performer who appropriates a hip-hop identity both as a drag king and in self-presentation.

REFERENCES

Butler, Judith. 1990. *Gender Trouble: Feminism and the Subversion of Identity*. New York: Routledge.

Califia, Pat. 1997. *Sex Changes: The Politics of Transgenderism*. San Francisco: Cleis Press.

Delany, Samuel R. 1999. "Future Shock." *Village Voice* (29 December).

Halberstam, Judith. 1998. *Female Masculinity*. Durham: Duke University Press.

Hebdige, Dick. 1988. *Subculture: The Meaning of Style*. New York: Routledge.

hooks, bell. 1996. "Is Paris Burning?" Pp. 214-226 in *Real to Reel: Race, Sex, and Class at the Movies*. New York: Routledge.

Kashanski, Richard. 1998. *God Shave the Queen*. Video Ten, 1998. Videocassette.

Rosenfeld, Kathryn. 1999. "Hotter than Hell: The First International Drag King Extravaganza." *Windy City Times* (28 October).

Taussig, Michael. 1993. *Mimesis and Alterity: A Particular History of the Senses*. New York: Routledge.

Turner, Victor. 1969. *The Ritual Process: Structure and Anti-Structure.* New York: Aldine.

_____. 1986. *The Anthropology of Performance.* New York: PAJ Publications.

Volcano, Del LaGrace and Judith Halberstam. 1999. *The Drag King Book.* London: Serpent's Tail.

SUGGESTIONS FOR FURTHER READING

Califia, Pat. 2000. *Public Sex: The Culture of Radical Sex.* 2nd Edition. San Francisco: Cleis Press.

Chicago Kings, official Website: *http://www.chicagokings.com*

Feinberg, Leslie. 1997. *Transgender Warriors: Making History from Joan of Arc to Dennis Rodman.* Boston: Beacon Press.

H.I.S. Kings, official Website: *http://members.tripod.com/~fastfriday/*

Sweeney, Robin. 1997. "My Life as a Consort." Pp. 127-133 in *Bitch Goddess: The Spiritual Path of the Dominant Woman,* ed. P. Califia and D. Campbell. San Francisco: Greenery Press.

Taormino, Tristan. 2001. "Drag Kings Make Me Wet." *Village Voice* (21 November).

Taussig, Michael. 1996. *The Magic of the State.* New York: Routledge.

_____. 1999. *Defacement: Public Secrecy and the Labor of the Negative.* Stanford University Press.

QUESTIONS FOR FURTHER CONSIDERATION

1. What is magic, considered in the context of contemporary subculture, performance media, and/or sexual and gender minorities or fringes? How can magic be rescued from antiquarian or primitivistic associations; in what ways, and to what ends, if at all, is it useful to do so?

2. Is liminality a necessary part of any culture, in any time or place? If so, how does liminality manifest in contemporary Western, urban culture or subculture? Does it work in these spaces in the ways Turner describes; i.e., to place the power of dominant bodies *in play?*

3. How do queers and in particular drag kings extend the discourse set forth by Hebdige in the late 1970s, in his writings on punk?

4. Why and how is desire central to critical discourse? Is it important to foreground questions of desire–the writer's, the reader's, or the subject's–in scholarly thought and writing, and if so, how is this best done? Is this question more crucial for queer theory or other work generated by communities of/discourse around sexuality–or is it applicable in some way to all writing?

Erotic Arguments and Persuasive Acts: Discourses of Desire and the Rhetoric of Female-to-Male Drag

Tara Pauliny, MA

The Ohio State University

SUMMARY. This chapter analyzes the October 21, 2000 drag king performance by Mildred Gerestant, a.k.a. Dréd. Arguing that her act appropriates, embodies, and manipulates certain ideological discourses of desire and identity, the article studies the shape and force of Dréd's performative arguments and illuminates how a drag king act can not only tease and titillate the addressed audience (the actual people who watched the show) but also hail the invoked audience (the audience called upon, imagined, or made possible by the performance). Arguing that, as a rhetorical act, Dréd's performance offers a purposeful discourse about gender, race, and power, this chapter ultimately explores how a rhetorical analysis of FTM drag elucidates the complex relationship between the rhetor, performance, and audience. More specifically, it shows how a rhetor's performance of non-normative identity and engagement with discourses of desire has the potential to unmask the hegemonic effects of language and power and to unsuture the seemingly natural connections between sex and gender. *[Article copies available for a fee from The Haworth Document Delivery Service: 1-800-HAWORTH. E-mail address: <docdelivery@haworthpress.com> Website: <http://www.HaworthPress.com> © 2002 by The Haworth Press, Inc. All rights reserved.]*

[Haworth co-indexing entry note]: "Erotic Arguments and Persuasive Acts: Discourses of Desire of Desire and the Rhetoric of Female-to-Male Drag." Pauliny, Tara. Co-published simultaneously in *Journal of Homosexuality* (Harrington Park Press, an imprint of The Haworth Press, Inc.) Vol. 43, No. 3/4, 2002, pp. 221-248; and: *The Drag King Anthology* (ed: Donna Troka, Kathleen LeBesco, and Jean Bobby Noble) Harrington Park Press, an imprint of The Haworth Press, Inc., 2002, pp. 221-248. Single or multiple copies of this article are available for a fee from The Haworth Document Delivery Service [1-800-HAWORTH, 9:00 a.m. - 5:00 p.m. (EST). E-mail address: docdelivery@haworthpress.com].

KEYWORDS. Argument(s), audience, desire, discourse(s), drag king(s), ideology, identity, race, rhetoric, performance

INTRODUCTION

While Aristotle argued that rhetoric was "the ability to see the available means of persuasion" and Plato claimed it was the counterpart to dialectic and useful only when exercised to transmit the "good" (the ethical or the moral), feminist interventions into the history of rhetoric have called these definitions (and others) into question and have worked to revise the rhetorical canon and its logocentric underpinnings. As a project devoted to extending the aims and goals of feminist rhetorics, my dissertation, *"I Am Your King": Theorizing a Rhetoric of Female-to-Male Drag*, brings queer theory to bear on the history of rhetoric. By positing what I call a "rhetoric of female-to-male (FTM) drag," my work explores the multiplicity of gender and contributes a queer revision to the well-established feminist reshaping of rhetorical theory and history.

The following chapter represents one part of this larger project and focuses on a contemporary site of subordinate queer culture in which a modern female rhetor (in this case, a drag king–a woman who dresses in recognizably male costumes and performs "male" identities) destabilizes categories of sex, race, and gender. By engaging the constructs of masculinity and femininity and manipulating various discourses of desire, this performer critiques racial, sexual, and gender exploitation. Focusing on the October 21, 2000 performance given at the *Second International Drag King Extravaganza* by Dréd, a Haitian-American drag king, this chapter examines how Dréd's act appropriates and embodies certain ideological discourses of desire and identity. The intent of the paper is to study the shape and force of the performance's argument and to illuminate how a drag king performance not only teases and titillates the addressed audience (the actual people who watched the show), but also hails an invoked audience (the audience called upon, imagined, or made possible by the performance). I argue that as a rhetorical act, this drag performance is a purposeful discourse about gender, race, and power, and that it suggests a multiplicity of possible responses, engages varied subject positions, and presents an interactive encounter between a performer, her performance, and an audience that produces social, political, and theoretical meanings. The FTM rhetorical practice produced by Dréd thus amends the five canons of rhetoric, forcing both the addressed and invoked audience to "remember" the connections between sex and gender differently. It necessitates that a rhetor engage with style in an unorthodox and often paradoxical way, that she produce an often parodic delivery, utilize a new kind of invention, and arrange discursive codes and gendered behaviors in jarring or provocative ways. This chapter ultimately explores how a rhetorical analysis of drag elucidates the complex relationship between the rhetor, the performance, and the audience. More specifically, it shows how a rhetor's performance of non-normative identity and engagement with discourses of desire has the potential to unmask the hegemonic effects of language and power and to unsuture the seemingly natural connections between sex and gender.

In "Queer Spectacles," Emmanuel Cooper recalls the work of Roland Barthes and comments that "[w]ithin gay culture, much of the conflict between what is experienced and what can be expressed can be identified as the 'subtle state of amorous desire'" (Cooper 1996). It is this "subtle state," this point at which desire and expression coalesce, that this chapter examines within the context of FTM drag. It examines the role of audience and desire within the FTM drag performance, specifically examining the place of identification, ideology, and deviance in the construction of such desire (either expressed or silenced). The paper articulates the complex relationship that arises between objectification, recognition, dismissal, and celebration when a specifically lesbian audience gazes at the various performances of masculinity presented by a drag king.

THE TITILLATION OF DESIRE: SEDUCTION AND A DRAG KING PERFORMANCE

The club is dark and smoky. I am at the bar surrounded by a crowd comprised mostly of women who sit at small tables, stand in groups, and kneel on the floor in front of the stage where they wait, poised with cameras, video equipment, and crumpled dollar bills. As the song "All About the Benjamins" begins, a tall, black performer struts onstage. Handsome in a long tan leather coat, bell-bottom pants, and brightly patterned polyester shirt, he[1] sports a lavish Afro, neatly trimmed facial hair, and sunglasses. Playing to the audience, he strikes poses—standing tall with arms stretched out to his sides, slouching casually with one hand in his pants pocket, dancing rhythmically to the music. With his every move the audience whistles, dances, and claps. Captured by his

image, I cannot avert my gaze. As the music changes to "Shaft," he be-
gins to engage in a seductive striptease. Removing his pants and shirt
he reveals not well defined pectoral muscles, but a woman's curvaceous
body tied up in a red string bikini. Like Grace Jones, she now stands be-
fore us with slips of material cupping her breasts and a small sarong
draped over her bulging crotch. As the music shifts to Aretha Franklin's
song, "Woman," the noise in the club becomes overwhelming; cameras
flash and tips are tossed on stage and waved in the air. At the height of
the moment, the king removes her wig to reveal a cleanly shaven head,
reaches erotically into her briefs, and fingers a bright red apple. Ap-
pearing transfixed and mesmerized, the audience screams for more.
Finally, when the noise level reaches a fever pitch and the energy in the
club becomes palpable, the king removes the apple, accepts a tip, and
takes a bite. Shining with sweat and afterglow, she turns away from the
audience and leaves the stage.

This seductive and provocative performance by Dréd–a New York City-
based Haitian-American drag king, actor, singer, model, and gender
illusionist[2]–took place at the *Second International Drag King Extravaganza*[3]
held in Columbus, Ohio in October of 2000. As part of a three-day conference whose activities included panel discussions, presentations, and
drag performances, Dréd's act appeared in a showcase during which
thirty-three separate drag king performances took place. As I watched
this and the other drag king pieces, I was especially struck by the way
Dréd seemed to hold the attention of her audience. She was proficient at
playing both masculine and feminine roles and appeared to be extremely effective at engaging the crowd. Her performance was well ex-
ecuted and crafted; she commanded the stage and mesmerized at least
one audience member (me), and, if enthusiasm is a reliable gage, a great
deal more. As she moved from Sean "Puffy" Combs' song, "All About
the Benjamins," to Superfly's "Shaft," and finally to Aretha Franklin's
"Woman," her gender transformations and representations became
more complex and ambiguous and the audience visibly more respon-
sive.

Watching this scene as both a participant (audience member) and observer (rhetorical theorist), I was transfixed by Dréd's ability to manipulate such a wide variety of discourses surrounding race, sexuality, and
gender. For not only did I find great pleasure and entertainment in being
engaged by the discourses she deployed, but also, I found myself reflecting upon the possible significances of these configurations. Why, I
wondered, was I (and seemingly the majority of others in the audience)
so transfixed by her performance? What exactly was so enticing about

her act? And, to what devices or arguments was I responding? Was I being compelled by my desire for or appreciation of the masculinity Dréd performed? Was I desirous of the female body I "knew" to be under the markers of maleness? Did her parody and portrayal of a stock black male character titillate me, or was it the display of autoeroticism that excited me? In other words, I kept wondering about the rhetorical force of Dréd's performance. I wanted to know how Dréd's act could be read as making *arguments* about race, sexuality, gender, and discourses of desire. Because I understand rhetoric (at least for the purpose of this chapter) as the study of the ideological and potentially persuasive arguments made by texts, I am interested in how this particular text presents such types of arguments. My intention, therefore, is not to decipher how or why individual audience members responded to Dréd's performance. Rather, my interest lies in how Dréd's act appropriates and embodies certain dominant and subversive discourses and how her act can be read as making arguments about gender, masculinity, race, and desire.

I am not as concerned, therefore, with the "addressed" or actual audience, as I am with the "invoked" audience (Lunsford 1984)–the audience called upon, imagined, or made possible, by the performer: the audience "constructed and created in the discourse itself," that "informs the text and may be determined through the text" (Halasek 1999, 55). This is not to define the actual people in the audience as irrelevant, but rather to claim that the performance enacted by Dréd has an audience larger than its immediate or visible one. And while the individuals who watched Dréd that October night certainly contributed to her act and participated in the construction of the event, their actual reactions are not the only possible set of responses. Dréd's performance engaged the notion of audience on a number of levels, and the one I am interested in here is the implied, invoked, and even "informed" audience–the "ideal" audience–who has an "acute awareness of the formal features of all texts, and experience with the properties of every specific kind of discourse" (Seltzer 1992). My goal, then, is to examine how this performance suggests a multiplicity of possible responses, how it engages a variety of subject positions, and how it presents an interactive encounter between a performer, her performance, and an audience, that produces "social, political, and theoretical meanings" (Halasek 1999, 56). My discussion is meant to be a starting point for a rich cultural, academic, and political investigation into the rhetorical force and shape of FTM drag.

I name my following investigation an analysis of a "rhetoric of female-to-male drag" because I view Dréd's performance as a rhetorical argument that both utilizes and manipulates various discourses of desire. Constructing FTM drag in this way locates it within a tradition of female expression and argumentation and thus links contemporary drag kings to other women throughout history who have used masculinity to build their arguments and affect their audiences. As such, I define rhetorical analysis in this context as an investigation into the ideological discourses used by Dréd that produce particular effects and enact various arguments. And while the arguments and persuasive effects produced by this and other drag king performances may be ones unintended or unplanned by drag kings themselves, they are nevertheless present. Rhetorical analysis, therefore, does not rest finally upon the intentionality of the drag king, but rather concerns itself with the discursive forms of power enacted by the drag king performance. My intent, therefore, is to study the shape and force of the performance's arguments and to illuminate some of the ways a drag king performance not only teases and titillates the addressed audience (the drag king performance as entertainment), but also challenges the addressed audience and the invoked audience to confront their racism, sexism, and complicity with dominant, and perhaps problematic, discourses (the drag king performance as argument). Likewise, my aim is not to admonish real audiences for responding to pervasive cultural discourses, but to examine how drag king performances appropriate these discourses and refashion them into arguments alternate to their original construct.

Analyzing the above cited performance by Dréd, I will articulate how her particular "rhetoric of FTM drag" tempts us (or our subject positions, to be exact), teases us, and ultimately refuses to satisfy the very desires it so expertly elicits. Ultimately, my argument, therefore, is that drag king performances are rhetorical arguments made with and through discourses of identity—and as I will show later, of desire—that can be analyzed for the way they hail subjectivity, engage relations of power, and potentially work to revise dominant ideologies and subjects' connections to them.

Before I begin this analysis of Dréd's performance, however, I turn first to the most extended academic discussion of drag kings to date: Judith Halberstam's book, *Female Masculinity*. In the chapter titled "Drag Kings: Masculinity and Performance," Halberstam articulates the various masculinities drag kings portray as she situates drag kings and drag king culture within her larger argument about the history of female masculinities. Starting with a review of drag king culture and performances, she then describes the particular ways drag kings enact white heterosexual maleness, masculinities of color, and homosexual masculinities. Commenting on the relationship between kings and the larger culture in which they find themselves, she writes that: "masculinity does not belong to men" and that drag king performances "expose[s] the structure of dominant masculinity by making it theatrical and by rehearsing the repertoire of roles and types on which such masculinity depends." She continues this point, positing that a king's "active disidentification [. . .] with dominant ideology" is one way a king transfigures such ideology, and that this choice allows the drag king to "neither opt to assimilate within such a structure nor strictly oppose it" (Halberstam 1998, 139, 242-3). As a project devoted not only to the investigation of female uses of masculinity but also to the politics and issues of power surrounding such deployments, Halberstam's reading of drag kings pays careful attention to the kings' relationship to cultural movements and moments.

Given her emphasis on drag kings' use of masculinity and the construction of dominant and alternate forms of masculinity, Halberstam produces a "taxonomy of drag king types" and spends the second portion of her chapter delineating the types of masculine performance she sees evoked during drag king contests. Naming categories of "butch realness," "femme pretender," "male mimicry," "fag drag," and "denaturalized masculinity," Halberstam constructs an heuristic of female masculinity, not only identifying the kinds of performances and characters presented by kings, but also providing a method by which to read their work (Halberstam 1998, 231-266). Melding detailed, contextualized field research and a thorough analysis of the performers' presentation styles, Halberstam constructs a rich and productive base for academic discussions of drag kings and their culture.

Like any valuable critical work, however, Halberstam's investigations are not exhaustive. Although she discusses the strategies and cultural contexts of drag kinging, she does not address the specifically rhetorical ways drag kings engage with discourses of desire. Stepping into the spaces opened by Halberstam's theory, my analysis focuses on the rhetorical aspects of drag king performances and especially on the ways such a performance hails the subject positions of its invoked audience.

THE DISCOURSES OF (OUR) DESIRES:
A RHETORIC OF FEMALE-TO-MALE DRAG

The continuing emergence of FTM drag is inspiring and exciting [. . .] As cultural production fronted by women and made for women—with a built-in examination of gender roles that can be ex-

tended to interrogate matters of race, class, and body size as well–FTM drag presents a formidable challenge to the prevailing social order.

–Donna Jean Troka (Troka 2000, 47)

In *The History of Sexuality, Volume I*, during a discussion of the cultural transformation of sex into discourse, Michel Foucault writes that this transformation was subtended by the implicit command: "You will seek to transform your desire, your every desire into discourse." He claims that "[a] policing of sex: that is, not the rigor of a taboo, but the necessity of regulating sex through useful and public discourses," is how the West has come to define the parameters of sex (Foucault 1990, 21, 25). And it is this policing of sex via discourse and this transformation of desire into discourse that inform my rhetorical argument and analysis. I recognize desire as, at least in part, socially shaped and intimately related to the constructs that both mainstream culture and subcultures have determined to be "desirable."[4] As such, I proceed from a theoretical framework that conceives of desire through discourse. In other words, following Foucault, I recognize that what has been termed desire–such as lesbian desire, desire for the "other," desire to be dominated, desire to be dominant–has been at the very least, constructed by discourse. I want to focus on desire here (rather than pleasure, for example, as Foucault does), because subjectivity is, in part, both constructed and hailed through desire. What we learn to want, how we come to identify, and what behaviors we engage in are all related to those discourses that construct us as subjects. And because discourse supports and surrounds desire, and because desire operates through discourse–especially the power-imbued discourses of race, sexuality, and gender–this intersection represents a rhetorical palimpsest ripe for exploration and examination.

Working partly from this Foucauldian concept, Debra Moddelmog offers a definition of desire that further articulates the social nature of Foucault's characterization. Moddelmog writes that "desire [. . .] is formed within all sorts of identity structurings–including those of race, nationality, and able-bodiedness–and their intersections, and not simply within the category of sexual orientation" (Moddelmog 1999, 5). In terms of this theorization, desire exceeds sexuality, spilling over into a myriad of other identity categories. As a social construct, then, desire not only operates according to particular discourses about sexuality, but according to a whole host of identity-based discourses. In thus expanding Foucault's definition, Moddelmog has provided a nuanced reading of desire and a theoretical mechanism by which to understand the discursive elements of such desire. So while her work deals primarily with literary studies and the relationship among readers, authors, and fictional texts, her reading of desire is useful to an understanding of the relationship among texts, readers, and contexts, when more broadly defined. For example, when the notion of text is widened to include any cultural "text" and a "reader" is defined as an interpreter or audience of that text, Moddelmog's reading of desire may be applied to the relationship between drag kings and their invoked audiences. Because drag kings produce cultural texts through their performances, and because those texts necessarily engage with recognizable and recurring discourses about desire, the relationship between the king, her act, and the audience mimics that of the writer, text, and reader. Like the written text that uses "language as a means of establishing and maintaining [and I would add destabilizing to this list](social, political, professional, and so on) communities," the performed text also calls for "political, social, or cultural affirmations that transcend traditional notions of persuasion, proof, instruction, or pleasure" (Halasek 1999, 59). The performance thus becomes a text that not only engages existing discourses, but that also has the potential to disrupt or amend those discourses. It becomes a text that both makes an argument and makes multiple readings (and readers) possible. Audience, under this rubric, "expands across time, becomes diachronic, determined and contextualized by sociocultural situations and the inherent intertextuality of the utterance" (Halasek 1999, 65). The performance becomes a cultural text and the audience a participant in that text.

Given this context, when kings appropriate codes associated with masculinity (facial hair, tuxes, wide stances), femininity (bras, high heels, makeup), race (Afros, white pop music, hip-hop or Chicano clothing), and sexuality (butch haircuts, sexual interactions between "men" and "women," stylized or marked clothing), their performances engage those familiar signifiers in critical or even persuasive ways. Like the revision of the word "queer" or "queen,"[5] drag king performances can revise the associations typically connected to these codes. Their work has the potential to underscore the artificiality of such codes and to critique their normalizing function. When a drag king portrays a certain kind of masculinity, therefore, she is not simply repeating the naturalized connection between sex and gender, but is instead calling attention to the mobility and power of its markers. By performing masculinity she is attesting to the fact that gender (and therefore masculinity) is an accoutrement of sex; that sex is not inherently tied to gender, but produced through the reiteration and replication of such a connection (Butler 1990, 30-2, 79-149). Likewise, when she takes up dominant discourses on desire, her performance creates an argument—a persuasive text—that implicates race, sexuality, and gender. Using discourses already in place and juxtaposing them in such a way as to elicit critique, her work engages in two kinds of arguments: first, it makes an argument about the "original" force of such discourses, and second, it attempts to persuade the audience (at times both the addressed and invoked audience), to view these discourses critically and divorced from their typical contexts.[6] An important point I want to make here is that when the drag performance engages the audience it often does so at the level of their subject positions: in the words of Louis Althusser, it *hails* the audience. It is not that the performer necessarily orchestrates all her moves so that particular people in the crowd will see that sex and gender are separate or that masculinity is not naturally tied to the male body, but that the discourses her performance enacts do engage the identities and desires of particular subjects as they are (or aren't) represented by the actual audience.

By appropriating previously recognized discourses surrounding desire, then, the drag king performance relies upon the invoked audience's implicit knowledge of these discourses to elicit both pleasure and reflection. For example, if an audience is faced with a depiction of masculinity or femininity they readily recall from television, the movies, books, or "real" life (the suave and sexual "Latin lover," the potentially dangerous and wild young black man, the polite and responsible, if tepid, white professional male),[7] they simultaneously assume positions in relation to these frameworks. White women, perhaps, might recall white men's potential social, professional, and economic privilege over them yet, on some level, they may also remember the threat of rape and fantasy of domination they have been taught to imagine when faced with certain kinds of black masculinity. Alternately, black women could recall the physical and/or sexual intimidation they might feel in response to white men. Taken to another level, when drag king acts engage with less obvious and more embedded discourses of desire (the desire for the "exotic other," the desire to be "taken" by that which is supposedly dangerous, the desire to consume the deviant, for example), the performances not only entice their addressed and invoked audiences, but try to persuade the audiences to wrestle with those desires. When they first call attention to the power of those discourses and then argue for revision and critique, drag king acts drive toward the effect of laying bare the values, pleasures, and ideologies contained within these discourses. They make available a moment of exposure when discourse circulates and teeters in such a way that glimpses of its structure can be caught. Parodic and potentially disruptive in its play, the work of the drag king can encourage both complicit and critical readings of discourses of desire.

This interactive process of the audience's recognition of and (dis)identification with codes occurs because a drag king's performance relies as much upon context as it does upon discourse. It is, therefore, not only relevant what subject positions are engaged by the performance, but it is also pertinent where the performance takes place, in front of whom, by whom, and for what purpose. These "real" or immediate contexts are important because they also affect the arguments being made and the persuasive quality of those arguments. It matters whether the show takes place in a gay club or at a university function, whether it is performed in front of a crowd familiar with drag king culture who might be politically and socially aware of gender issues, or in front of people largely unaware of these issues. The actual onlookers, setting, and performers work in concert with the performance to create meaning; they are not separate from it. So while a drag king may indeed construct her act with particular audiences in mind, the king cannot anticipate all the varieties of audience members she will address nor can she control the reactions of those audiences. The effects of her utterances are not controllable, but at the same time, who speaks those utterances and who hears them are also not inconsequential.

The addressed audience and the invoked audience are all participants in this cultural text. As the performance constructs and hails their subjectivities, so too does the audience work to shape the arguments about desire being made by the performance. And since it is not only through sexuality and gender that desire is filtered, but through racialized signs and actions as well, race is also highly relevant to the deployment and reception of discourses of desire. It matters, for instance, that a black lesbian audience will most likely respond differently to codes and discourses associated with the portrayal of Marvin Gaye, for example, than a white lesbian audience will. bell hooks comments on this point when she writes that "race [and I would say specifically races of color] and ethnicity [have] become commodified as resources for pleasure" and that "the culture of specific groups, as well as the bodies of individuals, can be seen as constituting an alternative playground where members of dominating races, genders, and sexual practices affirm their power-over in intimate relations with the Other" (hooks 1992,

23). What hooks is discussing here is that bodies of color have been historically overburdened with meaning and that given this past, discourses of raced desire circulate in very different ways. Blackness, for example, has become an overdetermined marker for sexual pleasure and domination in the West, and when a drag king performance enacts or highlights this marker, it works both within and from dominant discourses about the black race. Consequently, not only will the addressed and invoked audience most likely respond differently to a drag show based given their varied identities, but also the racial identity of all kings will impact their performances. While this interaction between identity and performance is true for all kings, it is especially complicated for the work of kings of color because within the history of the United States, it has been bodies and identities like their own that have been commodified for pleasure and it is with those bodies that they construct arguments against this mechanism of domination.

Looking at this process through a rhetorical lens, we might say that drag king performances often arrange recognizable constructions and commodifications of masculinity and femininity in a way that relies on previous constructions of desire. Using an even wider rhetorical scope, it could be argued that drag kinging engages the five canons of rhetoric by "inventing" or creating the drag act, "arranging" the images to be emulated and reworked, crafting the "style" and format of the presentation, practicing the "delivery" of the performance, and finally compelling the invoked (and often times addressed) audience to draw on their "memories" of already established discourses.[8] Through this process of building and producing a staged performance, kings' acts construct rhetorical arguments: they call upon the available means of persuasion—in this case discourses of desire—and shape them to produce particular desired effects.

As rhetorical arguments, then, drag king performances function within particular social contexts and need, necessarily, to work with the frameworks and markers established by those contexts. Likewise, their audiences, too, become involved in these social contexts and the critique, parody, revision, or respect communicated by the performances. As participants in the rhetorical situation of writer (drag king), reader (audience), and text (performance), the addressed and invoked audience is compelled to respond to the discourses presented. Drag kinging is thus a process that engages both those in front of and behind the lights. Much like Foucault's conception of power, desire here exists *among* subjects and institutions; it does not reside *in* the drag king or the audience, or even within mainstream culture (Foucault 1990, 92-5). Rather, desire fluctuates among the on-lookers, the performers, and the various social and cultural contexts both within and outside the arenas in which they find themselves. As a result, the "frame of intelligibility through which we understand desire to come into existence, to be assigned value, and to circulate among bodies–affects our construction of the author [or king, in our case] and our reading of desire in author's texts." Furthermore, because "these frames exert political power in society, having the power to name and assign meaning," these performances can be read as aesthetic, seductive, and persuasive (Moddelmog 1999, 5).

THE OBJECT OF OUR DESIRES:
DRÉD AND THE TEMPTATION OF THE OTHER

I love doing drag. I have fun playing with my gender and I like to make people think about, and have fun with, their own gender/sexuality. It's a powerful statement and feeling for me, especially as a woman, and as a woman of color, doing this. It's important for women to not be afraid, and to feel free, to do what they want or need to do.

–Dréd (Gerestant)

As the opening section of this chapter relates, Dréd performed at the *IDKE 2*. I chose Dréd's performance as an example of a "rhetoric of female-to-male drag" that engages discourses of desire to a persuasive end because her performance foregrounds not only gender and sexuality, but race as well. As a black performer within an American lesbian scene that has primarily been theorized and discussed by white academics, journalists, and writers, Dréd's visibility not only represents an often ignored or unseen segment of the lesbian population, but it also allows her audience to contend with the discourses of power upon which she draws (Volcano 1999, 140-8).

As her Website explains, Mildred Gerestant, a.k.a Dréd, was

[b]orn in Brooklyn of Haitian parents, [. . . and] is a singer, actor, model and gender illusionist. Inspired after seeing drag kings at an East Village party, [. . .] Mildred decided to do her thing. Since 1995, Dréd has been the winner of several contests, [and her . . .] act can be described as a funky, funny, fly, and supernatural high, musical of gender fluidity. Dréd brings to life funky characters

like Shaft, Sly Stone, Isaac Hayes, Michael Jackson, Marvin Gaye, Grace Jones, Diana Ross, Busta Rhymes, Puff Daddy, DMX, Sylvester, etc. She also performs with other drag kings, recreating groups such as The Jackson Five, Run DMC, and The Village People. [. . . She morphs] from Busta Rhymes to Puff Daddy to Shaft to Grace Jones right before your eyes!!! [. . .] A woman of many talents, Dréd holds a Bachelor's degree from Pace University and works for a research institute creating computerized questionnaires and databases that study/examine statistical research of urban social problems. She also volunteers for The House of Moshood, a group which educates women who have sex with women about safer sex. (Gerestant)

Note the numerous markers and identity categories to which Dréd lays claim. She labels herself racially—as a Haitian-American; professionally—as a singer, model, actor, gender illusionist, degree holder, and researcher; critically—as funky, funny, fly and amazing; mimetically—as imitative of characters and celebrities (Sly Stone, Michael Jackson, Grace Jones); and politically—as a volunteer and activist. From her Website, which includes biographical information, full-text articles about her or in which images of her appear, and links to other drag king related sites, Dréd clearly locates herself in many subject positions. Furthermore, as her political work demonstrates, she is also aware of the social issues and power dynamics that complicate such positions. This is significant not necessarily because I believe Dréd is intentionally crafting her performance so that her audience will appropriately "respond or conform"—playing the femme to her butch or the lady to her man—to the images she portrays; neither performativity nor subjectivity work this way. Rather, it is significant because not only can her performance be considered rhetorical, but she herself can also be said to approach her act rhetorically: that is, she seems to make a conscious choice to portray certain characters, celebrities, masculinities and femininities in order to produce a desired effect. So her performance is both intentional and inadvertent; while it has been purposefully designed to produce potential effects, it also makes its own arguments, separate from those Dréd intended.

Like other drag kings, Dréd considers her performances both sexually and politically provocative. "It's a very powerful feeling and statement for me to be out there as a woman doing this," she says, "especially as a black Lesbian. I'm proud of my Haitian descent and it's important to celebrate and be proud of our cultures. [. . .] I realize how hard it is to be a black man and I also realize how important it is for women to not be afraid to do what they want or need to do." Dréd also notes that as a drag king she is not "making fun of those men that she impersonates," but rather, "paying homage to black masculinity with the twist of being a butch black Lesbian" (Gerestant).

Drag king performances, then, can be "both political and cultural" because performing the "fluidity of gender, whether it's performance or everyday life [. . .] is a political issue. [. . .] It's certainly a political statement [. . .] and it's also exhilarating and fun to be in the middle of all [those] women's sexual energy" (Gerestant). Dréd's work, like that of other kings, engages with discourses of desire because it utilizes codes of masculinity and femininity, race and gender, sexuality and power, in a persuasive manner. When Dréd performs various forms of gender that call specific attention to the markers of race and sexuality, she is drawing on the discourses of desire that shape identity and regulate power relations. Because her drag act hails her audience via these discourses–discourses they may not consciously recognize–but ones that are nevertheless compelling and ingrained within their subject positions–it presents arguments about gender, race, and power. As a cultural and critical text, such a performance attempts to co-opt and revise these discourses and their consequential effects.

To explore such an example of persuasion and engagement with discourses of desire, I now offer a more detailed description of Dréd's performance at the *IDKE 2*.

As the song "All About the Benjamins" begins to play, Dréd saunters on stage in a masculine outfit reminiscent of stock 1970s black urban masculinity (see Figure 1). Sporting a long leather coat, brightly patterned polyester shirt, large Afro, neatly trimmed facial hair, and sunglasses, she recalls the stereotypical pimp or disco king. The "devices" and "codes" of masculinity and race are readily apparent. As a gendered subject, Dréd is manly, suave, and sexy: taken out of the context of a drag show and transported to her "natural" place of a 1970s disco or city street corner, perhaps, she affirms the connections made by dominant discourses among sex, gender, race, and sexuality. Dréd conjures a stereotypical image of black-maleness, and as the addressed audience views her, they may be reminded of the portrayal of African-American men on television and at the movies, of the pimp and the ghetto cruiser. Admittedly, Dréd also offers a more positive image of "mackdaddy funk," yet her performance nonetheless recalls dominant culture's constructions of 70s black masculinity with all its negative connotations (Volcano and Halberstam 1999, 148). As a result, the invoked audience

FIGURE 1. At the beginning of her act, the song "All About the Benjamins" begins to play, and Dréd saunters onstage in a masculine outfit reminiscent of stock 1970s black urban masculinity that recalls the stereotypical pimp or disco king.

and addressed audience are urged to see themselves in relationship to all these portrayals. Furthermore, given that, as Halberstam and Volcano note, "many lesbian scenes are very segregated" and that "a split between white and women-of-color spaces does linger," it is important to recognize the context in which Dréd performs (Volcano and Halberstam 1999, 140-2). The facts that most of her audience in Columbus is white, that a great number of them have spent the day participating in the Drag King Conference, and that Dréd is one of a very few black performers in this showcase are significant. They are significant because Dréd, for better or worse, comes to represent not just a drag king, but a black drag king. Her presence in a predominantly white cultural space demands notice and raises the possibility that race as a category can be examined during this show. With her particularly critical presentation, race becomes a category of investigation. Set against her act, the construction of race presented in all the other drag king acts becomes visible.

As participants in this rhetorical situation then, the audience also participates (willingly or not) in larger cultural constructions. Their identities as raced (such as White, Black, Latina, Asian, etc.) and gendered people, as consumers of culture, and as already marked subjects cannot be left at the door. For example, the subjectivities of the white audience members of the drag show might be compelled to morph into some version of the white television audience for whom a character such as the one Dréd presents equals deviant and dangerous sexuality and power. Conversely, the subjectivity of black audience members might be transferred into that of black television viewers who are once again faced with images of their race that are flat, one-dimensional, threatening, and ludicrous. Ideologically, the white women in the audience are hailed to remember what would be their appropriately stereotypical fear of the black male and his potential to rape or rob them, as they are simultaneously tempted by their desire for difference, what hooks has called "eating the other." The white invoked audience is engaged by discourses of "power-over": black men may have physical or sexual power over them, but they have moral power over black men, and discourses of "power-to": the power to be sexually excited by the Other when they fantasize about devouring the black man sexually or having him devour them. Women of color in the audience, however, may ideologically identify with Dréd racially while they simultaneously dis-identify with her performance of black masculinity that connotes physical and/or sexual power.

When Dréd's performance recollects this image of black masculinity, then, it not only revises it and its signifiers, but also engages with its history. As well, while it may hail the invoked audience to inhabit certain subject positions, the audience can also resist these positions. Although Dréd's act may ask the invoked white audience to contend with their historical and racist desire for the Other even as it may ask the invoked black audience to recognize their continual place of marginality, for example, it also leaves room for these audiences to examine and reject these positions. Dréd's performance thus marks a point of opportunity–an opportunity to recognize the desires promulgated by dominant culture and by subcultures–as well as an opportunity to accept, reconfigure, critique, and/or confront those desires. Although the women in the audience who represent dominant culture–at least in terms of their race and class–most likely do not openly or consciously share these desires, they are, nevertheless, constructed by them and compelled to respond. As addressed audience members whose subjectivities are invoked, they are persuaded to make these connections and made to recognize the ways in which their own subject positions intersect with these identities.

As the first section of Dréd's performance ends, and the music shifts to "Shaft" by Superfly, the act begins problematizing and unsettling references to dominant racial, and sexual discourses. Removing some of the markers of masculinity–tailored men's slacks and a button-down shirt–Dréd's actions reveal that sex and gender in fact, do not always match (see Figure 2). Her seemingly "real" breasts and shapely feminine figure reveal "him" as a woman and the audience may be led to explore the relationship between masculine performance and the female body. With this provocative striptease Dréd begins to disrupt dominant notions of gender and sex. Although the audience is called upon to "remember" the 70s male icon in the first part of Dréd's performance and respond to the discourses of desire surrounding that image, they are now compelled to alter that memory. When Dréd deserts her portrayal of "super-fly" to reveal her breasts and shapely figure, she takes her audience from the 70s into the 80s and 90s by conjuring images of sexy, strong black women. As she shifts her image, so too are her audiences called to shift their responses. Their desire for other women, and especially black women, is called upon. Dréd juxtaposes female sexuality with suave masculinity. As an interaction of hyper-black-femininity and hyper-black-masculinity, her performance necessitates that the audience construct themselves as multiply desiring subjects. The object of their gaze and desire is varied. They cannot simply accept and enjoy these images, they must also interact with them and position themselves in relation to them, at least on the level of subjectivity.

FIGURE 2. With the completion of the first portion of the act, the music shifts to "Shaft" by Superfly, and Dréd removes some of the markers of masculinity—tailored men's slacks and a button-down shirt—and reveals that sex and gender in fact, do not always match.

Continuing with the striptease, Dréd drops her shirt and displays a very small sarong draped over a bulging groin (see Figure 3). What might be considered a simple masquerade is actually full of twists and turns–a woman is not merely appropriating or playing at masculinity–Dréd complicates matters far more than that. What one could assume to be a distinctive marker of male "sex"–the penis–clashes with a seemingly obvious marker of female sex–breasts. Gender becomes layered and multiple and defined always in relationship to race and sexuality. As a result, her performance begins to argue for a shifting and unstable definition of gender, and thus identity, as it gestures toward dominant discourses that produce and reiterate female heterosexual desire for the penis and especially the racist desire for the mythically large black penis. In this portion of the show, Dréd remarks and relies upon the commodification of both the black male and black female body. Through the erotic display of these Other bodies, she calls attention to the discourses already in circulation about them. Rather than simply rejecting such desires, however, Dréd exaggerates them so as to necessitate engagement. As subjects who are also constructed and limited by these discourses, then, her audience is forced to at once enjoy and interrogate their connection to and complicity in these structures of power.

In the final scene, the music changes again, this time to Aretha Franklin's "Woman," and Dréd removes her wig to reveal a shiny and smooth shaved head (see Figure 4). She then seductively reaches into her briefs and exposes her "penis," which is not a penis at all, but a bright red apple. With a final flourish, she accepts a tip from an audience member and bites into the fruit. By revealing the ultimate marker of masculinity and power–the penis–as consumable and prosthetic, Dréd does not return her audience to a place of "origin" where she reverts to her "proper" place as a woman. Instead, she reconfigures their past relationship with masculinity, femininity, race, and power. Now that they associate her body with a masculine identity, the idea that identity is stable and unalterable is troubled. Similarly, her final act of autoeroticism (the eating/consuming of her penis/apple/prosthesis) conjures dominant discourses about possession and control of the raced and sexed Other while critiquing those structures. When Dréd reveals her penis to actually be an apple, she highlights the power dynamics contained within such a heavily coded body part. The "apple as penis" comes to signify the power historically accorded to maleness. By not only wearing the apple/penis, but also revealing it as prosthetic, Dréd becomes, in effect, a queer Eve. She is the dildo/apple/phallus bearing Other who not only possesses the power of the phallus (at least momentarily), but who rede-

FIGURE 3. Continuing with the striptease, Dréd drops her shirt and displays a very small sarong draped over a bulging groin.

FIGURE 4. In the final scene, the music changes again–this time to Aretha Franklin's "Woman"–and Dréd removes her wig to reveal a shiny and smooth shaved head. Seductively reaching into her briefs and exposing her "penis" as a bright red apple, she accepts a tip from an audience member and, in a final flourish, bites into the fruit.

fines herself as more than just an object of raced and gendered desire. By recuperating the biblical image of the deceptive Eve and then castrating herself as she partakes of the fruit of knowledge, Dréd disrupts dominant discourses that code her as exotic and commodifiable, undercuts subcultural discourses that attempt to erase her difference, and subverts Christian discourses that code central biblical figures as white. As a black performer who plays the part of a figure traditionally coded as white, flawed, and feminine, her work offers an alternative to the whitewashed bible. It revises the tarnished image of Christianity's original female ancestor and exposes just how deeply raced, gendered, and sexualized all subjects truly are.

THE OPENING OF OUR DESIRES: RHETORIC, FTM DRAG AND NEW POSSIBILITIES

As women, we need to examine the ways in which our world can be truly different. I am speaking here of the necessity for reassessing the quality of all the aspects of our lives and of our work, and of how we move toward and through them.

–Audre Lorde (Lorde 1997, 278)

While my analysis has begun to deconstruct the rhetorical situation in which FTM drag occurs, it has only touched the tip of the proverbial iceberg. There are certainly other discourses of desire engaged by this performance and by the wide variety of contemporary and historical enactments of FTM rhetorical drag. Other acts, for instance, engage whiteness and class more obviously, while some take discourses of ability and size as their main focus. Dréd's performance, however, is compelling because it dramatizes the "incoherencies in the allegorically stable relations between chromosomal sex, gender, and sexual desire," and because it rejects heterosexuality, race, and gender as stable origins (Jagose 1996, 3). By intervening into the regulatory process of traditional identity formation and the often oppressive functioning of discourses of desire, Dréd's performance works to link subjects to a particular history of "normal" acts and responses by compelling those subjects to recognize and hopefully contend with those connections.

Kings like Dréd, therefore, whose work enacts rhetorical FTM drag, critique the referential real, while those performers whose sex and gender seem to match in some ways provide a fantasy of coherence and closure and a fidelity to a mythic past. Performances akin to Dréd's challenge the sex/gender binary and display its incoherencies and instabilities and, at times, revise racist and homophobic discourses. Sometimes parodically and sometimes seriously, these acts of drag loosely suture the openings produced when notions of sex, gender, race, and sexuality conflict. They highlight the fictionalized and unnatural connections between discourse and culture as they critique the rhetorical effects of such associations. Therefore, since masculinity and femininity cannot be enacted by either gender without consequences, and because masculinity, as Judith Halberstam notes, is not equal to the "social, cultural, and political expression of maleness or the male body," performances in which women effect masculinity should not only, I think, be bracketed under the heading of mere entertainment. They should, rather, be recognized for their potential to alter discourses, mediate subject positions, and trouble understandings of gender, race, and sexuality.

This performance of Dréd's illustrates that there can be an interaction between the dominant and the subversive when FTM drag is performed. As well, her work supports the claims that "masculinity and feminine gender cannot be neutrally attributed to bodies of either sex" and that "masculinity of the male body is not the same as masculinity of the female body," because it uncovers and critiques these associations (Grosz 1994, 58). For when women pair their culturally proscribed gender with gender performances deemed acceptable only for men, they awaken an awareness of a multiplicity of possible truths, rearrange and revalue the performance of sexuality, race, and gender, and engage in an activity that exploits the fissures inherent in such constructions. FTM rhetorical practice thus forces an audience to ultimately "remember" the connections between sex, race, and gender differently, necessitates that a performer engage with style in an unorthodox and often paradoxical way, and produces an often parodic and political interpretation of discourses of desire.

ACKNOWLEDGMENTS

First, the author wishes to thank Mildred Gerestant for being such a provocative and talented performer and for allowing use of images of her in this chapter. Next, for their invaluable advice, critique, attentive reading of drafts, and responding to conference presentations related to this chapter, the author thanks the following people: the audience (addressed) for her paper: "I Am Your King: Theorizing FTM Rhetorical Drag," delivered at the *IDKE 2*, and the audience for her paper: "Identity, Praxis, and the

'Original' Gendered Body," which she delivered at the Canadian Association for American Studies Conference (2000). (She owe special thanks to one audience member, Dara Byrne–Howard University, for her insightful comments about this second presentation.) Thanks is also owed to the members of Ohio State English Department's "First-Draft Group," for commenting on two different drafts of this paper and to members of the Winter 2001 Dissertation Seminar for providing helpful feedback as well. The author also thanks Jim Fredal and Thomas Piontek for responding to this paper and for continually challenging her thinking in productive (and fun) ways. And finally, the author thanks her friends and colleagues in the English Department: Rebecca Dingo, Melissa Ianetta, and Lisa Tatonetti for their tireless reading of drafts and their overall emotional and academic support, and her mentors, Kay Halasek and Debra Moddelmog, for their consistent academic and personal support of her, this paper, and other work of hers. One couldn't ask for better folks.

NOTES

1. Although I use the masculine pronoun at the beginning of this description for effect, in deference to Mildred's own use of the feminine pronoun, I use the female pronoun throughout the rest of this paper. (See her Website for a more comprehensive discussion of why she makes this choice.) The choice of which pronoun, or combination thereof, to use when discussing FTM drag is a subject of much debate by drag kings and academics alike. Although my decision in this paper no way solves the debate, it at least calls attention to the gender ambiguity displayed in the work of many drag kings.

2. Mildred has an extensive Website which includes information about her various professional selves, information about her shows, reviews of her work, photos, links to other drag king related sites, and an extensive bibliography of sources regarding gender, drag, and related concepts. Mildred can be contacted and her Website viewed at: <Dred Gerestant–Drag King/Gender-Illusionist, e-mail: dredking@hotmail.com>, Website: <*http:// www.dredking.com/*>.

3. *The Second International Drag King Extravaganza: FTM Drag In Voice/In Action* was held in Columbus, Ohio from October 20-22, 2000. It featured Dragdom, an amateur showcase of drag king performances, a day of practical and theoretical workshops, a professional showcase of thirty-three drag king performances, and a brunch. Bringing together people from thirteen states and two Canadian provinces, the conference was promoted (by its informational pamphlet) as "an international collection of performers, fans, photographers, activists and theorists of drag king culture" that was intended to "create an environment for creative, enjoyable networking and dialogue on a wide range of topics directly related to FTM drag."

4. Although I do not want to take a psychoanalytic approach to discourse, I do want to note that this approach has certainly been taken in quite valuable ways by many theorists. Here is a brief sampling of their work: Teresa de Lauretis. 1994. *The Practice of Love: Lesbian Sexuality and Perverse Desire*. Indianapolis: Indiana UP.; Heather Findlay. 1995. "Freud's 'Fetishism' and the Lesbian Dildo Debates." Pp: 328-342 in *Out in Culture: Gay, Lesbian and Queer Essays on Popular Culture*. eds. Cory K. Creekmur and Alexander Doty. London: Cassell; Elizabeth Grosz. 1991. "Lesbian Fetishism?" *Differences*, 3:2 (Summer): 39-54; and Diane Hamer. 1990. "Significant Others: Lesbianism and Psychoanalytic Theory." *Feminist Review*, 34 (Spring): 134-51.

5. I am referring here to the transition the words queer and queen have made from being mainly slurs used against homosexuals to being recuperated by some in the gay community. This can be seen, for example, in the phrases, "queer theory," "queer nation," and the popular use of the word "queen" in academic and popular books by gay writers.

6. I am purposefully mentioning particularly rampant and highly problematic stereotypes found on television to exaggerate the possibility that an invoked audience could connect a performance of masculinity to these skewed markers. I do not mean to imply that these are all the representations that could be conjured nor that these are without serious prejudice.

7. An abundant amount of research and critical work has been done on the related topics of black masculinity and femininity, the commodification and exoticization of the black body, and the representation of race in discourse, culture, and literature. The following texts are a small sample of those that have influenced my thinking on these subjects, but are certainly not all the sources that deal with these issues. Julian Carter. 1996. "Normality, Whiteness, Authorship: Evolutionary Sexology and the Primitive Pervert." Pp: 155-176 in *Science and Homosexualities.* ed. Vernon A. Rosario. New York: Routledge; Patricia Hill Collins. 1990. *Black Feminist Thought: Knowledge, Consciousness, and the Politics of Empowerment.* New York: Routledge; Angela Y. Davis. 1983. *Women, Race and Class.* New York: Vintage Books; Sagri Dhairyam. 1994. "Racing the Lesbian, Dodging White Critics." Pp. 25-46 in *The Lesbian Postmodern.* ed. Laura Doan. New York: Columbia UP; Evelynn M. Hammonds. 1997. "Black (W)holes and the Geometry of Black Female Sexuality." Pp. 136-156 in *Feminism Meets Queer Theory.* eds. Elizabeth Weed and Naomi Schor. Bloomington: Indiana UP; Londa Schiebinger. 1999. "Theories of Gender and Race." Pp. 21-31 in *Feminist Theory and The Body: A Reader.* eds. Janet Price and Margrit Shildrick. New York: Routledge; and Alan Hyde. 1997. *Bodies of Law.* Princeton: Princeton UP.

8. The five canons of rhetoric refer to the five parts of classical rhetoric: invention, arrangement, style, delivery, and memory. Invention is the art of finding persuasive arguments in any given rhetorical situation; arrangement refers to the dividing of a discourse into its parts and then ordering, omitting, or maintaining those parts according to the rhetor's audience and purpose; style refers to the selection of appropriate and effective language; delivery refers to the process of performing a speech using various gestures, tones, and vocal modulations, and memory includes devices and systems for recalling the points a rhetor wishes to make. Although these parts of rhetoric were certainly not originally meant to be as inclusive as I regard them here, I do think they are malleable, and, if utilized in the right way, can be expanded to encompass less traditional, more (post-) modern rhetorical activities.

REFERENCES

Butler, Judith. 1990. *Gender Trouble: Feminism and the Subversion of Identity.* New York: Routledge.

Cooper, Emmanuelle. "Queer Spectacles." Pp. 13-27 in *Outlooks: Lesbian and Gay Sexualities and Visual Culture*, eds. Peter Horne and Reina Lewis. New York: Routledge.

Foucault, Michel. 1990. *The History of Sexuality. Volume I: An Introduction.* Robert Hurley, trans. New York: Vintage Books.

Gerestant, Mildred. "Web Site" [cited November 2001-April 2001]. Available online at http://www.dredking.com.

Grosz, Elizabeth. 1994. *Volatile Bodies: Toward a Corporeal Feminism.* Bloomington: Indiana University Press.

Halasek, Kay. 1991. *A Pedagogy of Possibility: Bakhtinian Perspectives on Composition Studies.* Carbondale: Southern Illinois University Press.

Halberstam, Judith. 1998. *Female Masculinity.* Durham: Duke University Press.

hooks, bell. 1992. *Black Looks: Race and Representation.* Boston: South End Press.

Jagose, Annamarie. 1996. *Queer Theory: An Introduction.* New York: New York University Press.

Lorde, Audre. 1997. "Uses of the Erotic." Pp. 277-282 in *Writing on the Body: Female Embodiment and Feminist Theory*, eds. Katie Conboy, Nadia Medina, and Sarah Stanbury. New York: Columbia University Press.

Lunsford, Andrea and Lisa Ede. 1984. "Audience Addressed/Audience Invoked: The Role of Audience in Composition Theory and Pedagogy." *College Composition and Communication*, 35:2 (May): 155-171.

Moddelmog, Debra. 1999. *Reading Desire: In Pursuit of Ernest Hemingway.* Ithaca: Cornell University Press.

Seltzer, Jack. 1992. "More Meanings of Audience." Pp. 161-177 in *A Rhetoric of Doing: Essays on Written Discourse in Honor of James L. Kinneavy*, eds. Stephen P. Witte, Neil Nakadate, Roger D. Cherry. Carbondale: Southern Illinois University Press.

Troka, Donna Jean. 2000. "When We Were Kings. On Being a Midwestern Drag King." *Bitch: Feminist Response to Pop Culture* 12 (2000): 42-47.

Volcano, Del LaGrace and Judith "Jack" Halberstam. 1999. *The Drag King Book.* London: Serpent's Tail.

BIBLIOGRAPHY OF SUGGESTED FURTHER READINGS

Alderson, David, and Linda Anderson, eds. 2000. *Territories of Desires in Queer Culture: Refiguring Contemporary Boundaries.* Manchester: Manchester University Press.

Brody, Miriam. 1993. *Manly Writing: Gender, Rhetoric, and the Rise of Composition.* Carbondale: Southern Illinois University Press.

Case, Sue-Ellen, Philip Brett, and Susan Leigh Foster, eds. 1995. *Cruising the Performative: Interventions into the Representation of Ethnicity, Nationality, and Sexuality.* Bloomington: Indiana University Press.

Ekins, Richard, and Dave King, eds. 1996. *Blending Genders: Social Aspects of Cross-dressing and Sex-changing.* New York: Routledge.

Frankenberg, Ruth. 1993. *The Social Construction of Whiteness: White Women, Race Matters.* Minneapolis: University of Minnesota Press.

Goodman, Lizbeth with Jane de Gay, eds. 1998. *The Routledge Reader in Gender and Performance.* New York: Routledge.

Halberstam, Judith, and Ira Livingston, eds. 1995. *Posthuman Bodies.* Bloomington: Indiana University Press.

Hart, Lynda, and Peggy Phelan, eds. 1993. *Acting Out: Feminist Performances.* Ann Arbor: The University of Michigan Press.

Horne, Peter, and Reina Lewis, eds. 1996. *Outlooks: Lesbian and Gay Sexualities and Visual Cultures.* New York: Routledge.

Mailloux, Steven. 1989. *Rhetorical Power.* Ithaca: Cornell University Press.

McGarry, Molly, and Fred Wasserman, eds. 1998. *Becoming Visible: An Illustrated History of Lesbian and Gay Life in Twentieth-Century America.* New York: The New York Public Library Penguin Studio.

Muñoz, José Esteban, ed. 1999. *Disidentifications: Queers of Color and the Performance of Politics.* Minneapolis: University of Minneapolis Press.

Munt, Sally R. 1998. *Heroic Desire: Lesbian Identity and Cultural Space.* New York: New York University Press.

O'Farrell, Mary Ann, and Lynne Vallone, eds. 1999. *Virtual Gender: Fantasies of Subjectivity and Embodiment.* Ann Arbor: The University of Michigan Press.

Patton, Cindy, and Benigno Sanchez-Eppler, eds. 2000. *Queer Diasporas.* Durham: Duke University Press.

Queen, Carol, and Lawrence Schimel, eds. 1997. *Pomosexuals: Challenging Assumptions about Gender and Sexuality.* San Francisco: Cleis Press.

Sinfield, Alan. 1994. *Cultural Politics, Queer Reading.* Philadelphia: University of Pennsylvania Press.

Stam, Robert. 1989. *Subversive Pleasures: Bakhtin, Cultural Criticism, and Film.* Baltimore: The Johns Hopkins University Press.

Tulloch, John. 1999. *Performing Culture: Stories of Expertise and the Everyday.* London: Sage.

ISSUES AND QUESTIONS
FOR FURTHER CONSIDERATION AND ANALYSIS

- What are the dangers of a performance that utilizes and appropriates dominant discourses about desire, especially when those discourses might be considered racist, homophobic, or essentialist?
- How might the actual political or ideological effect of FTM drag on both addressed and invoked audiences be calculated? Can the effect, in fact, be calculated, and moreover, should it be?
- How might FTM drag be used to foster queer agendas in more culturally dominant contexts?
- What arguments, in addition to those forwarded by this paper, does FTM drag make (about sex and gender, race, desire, and cultural proscriptions)? How might a drag king's race, performance topic, and kind of masculinity shape these arguments?
- Once masculinity is theoretically and practically separated from the male body, what potential does it hold for women's personal and cultural expression? Besides FTM drag, how can masculinity be used by women to effect change or construct politically efficacious performances?

THEORIZING KINGS

Seeing Double,
Thinking Twice:
The Toronto Drag Kings
and (Re-) Articulations of Masculinity

Jean Bobby Noble, PhD

York University

SUMMARY. Through a close reading of the performances of masculinity by the Toronto drag kings, this chapter argues that drag king shows parody the hyper-masculine star at his most contradictory and dialogic. Given that drag king performances parody both the contradictions of masculinity on stage, and the productive technologies of the star, king performances are essentially both meta-theatrical (performances about performing where lights, music, body language, dance all make the man) and meta-performative (performances which are at once conditioned by the performative reiterations which enable a fiction of identity in the first place). Finally, I explore the rather abstracted question of what cultural work the category of "drag king" does. I argue that it is a term which articulates a series of productive but necessary slippages in and through the contradictory and dialogic practices of identification. The bottom line is this: drag kings are situated in and play with the ironic *no man's land* between "lesbian," "butch," "transman" and "bio-boy" where the self-evident is neither. *[Article copies available for a fee from The Haworth Document Delivery Service: 1-800-HAWORTH. E-mail address: <docdelivery@haworthpress.com> Website: <http://www.HaworthPress.com> © 2002 by The Haworth Press, Inc. All rights reserved.]*

[Haworth co-indexing entry note]: "Seeing Double, Thinking Twice: The Toronto Drag Kings and (Re-) Articulations of Masculinity." Noble, Jean Bobby. Co-published simultaneously in *Journal of Homosexuality* (Harrington Park Press, an imprint of The Haworth Press, Inc.) Vol. 43, No. 3/4, 2002, pp. 251-261; and: *The Drag King Anthology* (ed: Donna Troka, Kathleen LeBesco, and Jean Bobby Noble) Harrington Park Press, an imprint of The Haworth Press, Inc., 2002, pp. 251-261. Single or multiple copies of this article are available for a fee from The Haworth Document Delivery Service [1-800-HAWORTH, 9:00 a.m. - 5:00 p.m. (EST). E-mail address: docdelivery@haworthpress.com].

KEYWORDS. Camp, drag king, female masculinity, dialogism, Bakhtin, masculinity, Toronto, queer theory, performativity, race, whiteness, irony, transsexual

Irony is not a figure of self-consciousness . . . irony comes into be-ing precisely when self-consciousness loses control over itself. . . . It's a break, an interruption, a disruption [of consciousness]. It is a moment of loss of control, and not just for the author but for the reader as well.

–Paul de Man (quoted in Johnson xii)

SETTING THE SCENE

I begin with a story. Growing up in the age of the Beatles with their attendant hordes of screaming, fainting girls, my working class mother decided to take me to an afternoon performance by a Beatle-esque band at a local bar in our fairly small town. In my admittedly hazy memory of that afternoon–circa 1969–the audience was made up of mostly moms and daughters imagining themselves, not at this smoky bar, but in Shea Stadium instead, anticipating the dramatic and frenzied entrance by the Beatles, not the rather unknown group of boys warming up on the very small stage. As the performance ensued, many of the young girls in the audience duplicated the Beatles' frenzied female audiences by imitating screams, swoons, and other such behaviours that I, then baby butch, was both baffled and intrigued by. At some point, my mother leaned into me and asked: "Which one do you like?" Instantly embarrassed I awk-wardly ignored the question, concentrating on the girls in the audience instead. To be sure, I was drawn to the performance but it wasn't until much later that I realized, in one of those somewhat clichéd identity-for-mation narratives, that I didn't actually *want* any of those boys perform-ing on stage. Rather, *my* "want" was to *be* one of those boys, complete with guitars, lights, microphones and, of course, in my pre-adolescent boy fantasy, hordes of screaming, swooning girls hanging on my every move. To make a much longer story short, I chose academia instead of rock and roll, although it remains uncanny how they both spin around the same terms: desire and identification. Jump ahead by about 25 or 30 years and I'm in Toronto watching two different performances by two different waves of drag kings, still identifying with the boys onstage and still struck by a bunch of questions that continue to haunt my thinking about these shows in terms of identity, desire and identification.

I want to do three things in this chapter. First, I want to show off the Toronto kings. Second, I want to situate the drag king shows at the junction of three intellectual currents: (1) theories of "performativity," and by implication, identification; (2) the cluster of theatrical practices, relations and traditions known as performance; and (3) the imperatives of critical race studies to begin to think whiteness, and for my own work, to theorize white masculinity. My argument is that it is precisely the tension between irony, performativity and performance that fuels the intensity of the drag king shows. These shows "work" (and I'll come back to what I mean by that later) because they are at once the fruition and limit of each current. They are, in other words, what Sedgwick calls threshold effects, places where incremental movement along one dimension (say for instance, a king who passes both in- and outside of the performance) suddenly appears as a variable on an entirely different dimension (say that same king identifying as transsexual or transgendered). In terms of gender, it is sometimes necessary to cross over the threshold of one thing (butchness), or flip its switches from on to off, to register on another scale (transsexual). In terms of race, though, the opposite is true. It is necessary to move the switch from off to on, to invert what it is we think we see in order to see what we're not supposed to. This project is part of a much larger dissertation on female masculinity which attempts to theorize the operations of white supremacy as they speak through gender performance. Because Judith Halberstam and others concentrate on performances of racialized masculinity in their work, and because of time constraints, I've decided to limit my focus here to the ways a few of the kings racialized whiteness and queer masculinity. What I address here is by no means the extent of the performances of the Toronto kings. Drag king shows parody the hyper-masculine star at his most contradictory. Given that they also parody both the contradictions of masculinity onstage, and the productive technologies of the star, drag king performances are essentially both meta-theatrical (performances about performing where lights, music, body language, dance, all make the man) and meta-performative (performances which are at once conditioned by the identifications but which also enact or enable further identifications, say, for instance, my identifying and so writing about the drag kings). Finally, by the end of this chapter, I hope to leave us with the rather abstracted question of what cultural work the category of "drag king" does. My tentative hypothesis is that it is a term which articulates (and I'll come back to what I mean by "articulate") a series of productive but necessary slippages in and through the practices of identity. The bottom line is this: drag kings are situated in and play with the ironic *no man's land* between "lesbian," "butch," "transman" and "bio-boy" where the self-evident is neither.

IMPERSONATING A PERFORMATIVE

What intrigued me about the Toronto Drag Kings, both the earlier incarnation in 1994 and the most recent wave, was their staging of the dialogic and contradictory ambivalences which structure white and heteronormative masculinity. And one of those primary ambivalences, as I noted before, is that between its day-to-day hyper-visibility and its constitutive invisibility (that is, that it passes as the norm, as the un-marked, as the non-identity). As Halberstam has I think rightly argued where gay camp often foregrounds the performativity and excess of tra-ditional femininity through its 'over-the-top' parody, masculinity re-mains unmarked and underspoken. The drag kings on the other hand foreground precisely that cloaked status. Their parody forces masculin-ities' silences to speak, exposing contradictions which need to remain hidden for masculinity to accomplish its cultural work. As Judith Butler reminds us, "to the extent that gender is an assignment, it is an assign-ment which is never quite carried out according to expectation," where the addressee never quite inhabits the ideal s/he is compelled to approx-imate. In their parody of heteronormative masculinity as "failure," the drag kings flesh out Butler's assertion. When white heteronormative identities are parodied, what is revealed is that their parts don't always work together. What the drag kings articulate are the places where mas-culinity, especially white masculinity, speaks volumes, and that is, of course, through race and the operations of white supremacy.

I suggest that we understand whiteness as a racialized identity that understands itself functioning not necessarily as a race but as *the* human race, as universal mankind. White supremacy functions best by allow-ing whiteness to remain unmarked. It operates by cloaking itself as the universal and the norm, around which all other races, especially those marked by colour, circulate and define. On the one hand, white domina-tion is reproduced by the way that white people colonize the definition of the normal. On the other hand, if the invisibility of whiteness colo-nizes the definitions of other norms, it also masks itself as a category so that the representational power of whiteness comes precisely from its belief in itself as so thoroughly everywhere and everything that it fails to visually register at all. Two of the white kings target precisely that paradoxical hyper- and yet invisibility: Zach does an impressive angry young white boy in his salute to *Rage Against the Machine*. What makes this particularly effective is that Zach is wearing an "Anti-racism Action" ["ARA"] t-shirt that shows a young white boy jumping up and down on top of a swastika. The effect is to mark whiteness from inside and articulate it against the invisibility of white supremacy. Moner, too, stages whiteness and stages it as a subjectivity simultaneously hypervisible and invisible. Moner performs a song called "Pretty Fly (For a White Guy)." The lyrics of this song document the ways that white masculinity imagines itself in relation to men of colour who are read as "hip" and "cool." "Our subject" so the lyrics tell us, "isn't cool but fakes it." He dresses up, overcompensates, as it were, to fit the part and to disguise the emptiness of whiteness: he "listens to the right music, Vanilla Ice, cruises in a cool car, a Pinto," and finds himself "trying too hard" to imitate masculinity. The song inverts a white racist gaze back at itself, and shows whiteness to be both vacuous and hyperbolic. Moner's version of this song forces our attention onto the artificiality of the white subject in the song and both denaturalizes and ironizes that artifice even further. As Moner said to me in conversation, "it's important to work the white boy persona, that's what I am." Whiteness is marked and articulated, that is, made to work by revealing its own articulations. The verb *to articulate* means to divide into words, to pronounce or utter. But it also means to connect or mark with joints, that is, to be connected with sections. Thus, to articulate is both to express fluently but also to manipulate a site where component parts join (as in a knee or hip), to bring segmented parts together to enable functionality. These kings dissemble white masculinity, break it down into its parts, and then reassemble those parts to make them work differently, to render them dysfunctional, if you will. If white supremacy works best when it is hyper-visible and invisible, it cannot work in quite the same way when it is denaturalized, re-articulated and most importantly, decloaked.

In the same way that whiteness manifests itself and speaks through normative masculinity, gender is also spoken loudly through sexuality in these performances. A number of the kings stage the sexual failures at the heart of straight masculinity. For instance, during a skit where Kelly, Flare and Zach dress, well, down to look like stereotypical ill-kempt, working-class men with huge beer bellies and perform "*I'm Too Sexy*," the men at one point drop their pants to show their butts to the audience. Two of the three are wearing men's underwear which is what you might expect. But Flare's character is wearing girls' panties and subsequently gets chased off the stage for it. Chris and Stu do a similar routine only their characters are hyper-masculine soccer players, where one player (Stu) has a crush on the other (Chris) who at first refuses him but then returns his advances and finally carries him off the stage. The song is the *Cup of Life* by Mr. Contradiction himself, Ricky Martin. Ricky represents an entirely curious figure of masculinity. He's racially marked but sings in English; he's hypersexualized as a man of colour, but that over-sexualization is always already overdetermined as simultaneously in excess of heteronormative masculinity. What is parodied in these numbers is the sometimes very thin line between gay and heterosexual masculinity, where ironic reading practices articulate the contradictions that masculinity often disavows and yet is unable to contain. The first wave of drag kings in Toronto similarly played with these tensions. Not to be outdone by the 'original' Village People and their own parody of gay masculinity, the drag kings' Village People parodies a parody in a performance that simultaneously signifies masculinity, hyper-masculinity, failed heteronormative masculinity and white notions of queer diversity all at the same time. The current wave of drag kings staged queer community when Flare, dressed in a sailor suit, performed Kermit the Frog's *Rainbow Song* while the rest of the kings joined him on stage with rainbow flags in a group finale.

Moreover, the drag kings' impersonation of masculinity and parody of sexual desire between men relies on but also shifts away from what we might identify as butch-femme sexual identities toward a continuum of female masculinity, and then off the map completely to what might be called "something a wee bit different." Evoking those axiomatic epistemological tensions outlined by Sedgwick in *Epistemology of the Closet*, that same-sex desire is "understood" either as an expression of the essence of one gender (gender-separatism), or as cross-gendering (gender transitivity), I suggest that what overdetermines the male impersonation at the heart of the drag kings' show is a shift from the separatist to transitive trope, complete with its shifts in alliances and cross-identifications. To quote Sedgwick, "under a gender-separatist [trope], lesbians have looked for identifications and alliances among women in general [while under] . . . a [trope] of gender [transitivity] . . . lesbians have analogously looked to identify with gay men, or, though this latter identification has not been strong since second-wave feminism, with straight men" (89). In many ways, I think this latter turn, toward straight men, has finally been taken. Christopher Noelle, for instance, plays on the different expectations between looking like a girl and identifying as a boy in his number *Sharp Dressed Man*. Noelle comes out in a tight black slinky dress with hair down and proceeds to transform himself into a John Travolta looking man (from *Grease*) in front of a mirror onstage to the song "Sharp Dressed Man." The transformation from femininity into masculinity in some ways defies the premise I began with, that is, that femininity is about hyperbole, masculinity about understatement. Noelle puts on the man using as many accessories and props as he takes off. And Chris too, formerly Ricky Martin in the *Cup of Life* returns to do La Vida Loca Ricky Martin, also references this turn when he told me "I'm the straight man of the lesbians . . . its hard for me to do the gay stuff onstage." Mona and Jesse also do a song, *Mr. Roboto* by Styx, which re-articulates these identifications with straight men. The narrator of the song is a self-made man who allegorizes the natural and ultimately defamiliarizes the liberal humanist "man": "I've a secret I've been hiding under my skin . . . I'm not what you think / Forget what you know / I am the modern man who hides behind a man / so no one else can see / my true identity." Clearly, the drag kings' performance could be grouped under that category of gender transitivity, and the proliferation of butch-femme subjectivities. But fuelled by its referent "butch-femme of the 50s," female masculinity of the 90s in many ways far surpasses its own history, demonstrated by the proliferation of female and male masculinity in all their complexities: transman, straight man, butch-boy, butch-bottoms, soft butches, stone masculinity, gay masculinity, fag-butch, etc. The masculinities performed on the stage signify in very contradictory but remarkably rich ways, simultaneously as "butch," *and* in excess of "butch," an approximation of heterosexual masculinity, *and* queering of that masculinity, racialized masculinity and the longer overdue racialization of whiteness.

One postscript here: I asked nine of the kings one day if they identified or found themselves at all in the word lesbian. All nine of them said no including the one "girl" who identifies as femme; they offered me a bevy of other words but not one of them said lesbian, suggesting that the history of lesbian politics has been both incredibly successful and a failure all at the same time. Barbara Johnson anticipated this kind of paradox when she wrote on the failure of success: "If the political impulse of lesbianism and/or queer theory and/or performativity [and that's a giant 'if'] is to retain its vital, subversive edge, we must become ignorant of it again and again. It is only by forgetting what we know how to do, by setting aside the thoughts that have most changed us, that those thoughts and that knowledge can go on doing what a surprise encounter with otherness should do, that is, lay bare some hint of an ignorance one never knew one had" (84-85). In other words, and this is where I want to return to the quote on irony that I opened with, if de Man is right about irony, that it is not about controlled self-consciousness but about its failure instead, then these scenes of irony need to be read for what they reveal about ourselves and our identifications. To phrase this differently, what drag kings do is stage the things that whiteness and masculinity do not want to know and can not know about themselves, to use irony to make these subjects strange and make their ambivalences work against what they think they do know. As a mode of critical politics, the scene of irony has to be inherently noisy and dialogic in the Bakhtinian sense, that is, that it is engaged in many conversations all at the same time. As a discursive mode of the unsaid and the unseen, irony is the ideal form in which to stage ambivalences, ambiguities and contradictions. Meaning is made and confused, reduced and complexified all at the same time. Drag king performances are both inherently dialogic, in conversation with both conservative and oppositional politics of gender, with lesbian feminism, queer theory, homophobia, feminism, with race and racism, with transgendered politics, etc., but also with the contradictions that fracture each. Irony troubles correspondences, it removes certainty that we mean what we say, or conversely, that reality is somehow reducible to some appearances. It also betrays the continuous and inevitable failure of the visual as an epistemological mode and that, it seems to me, is precisely the point.

(RE-)ARTICULATING MASCULINITY

By way of a conclusion I want to gesture in a slightly different direction. In addition to my arguments that (1) drag kinging allows for the ironic *re-articulations* of whiteness and masculinity, especially of those things they can not know about itself and (2) that the culture of drag kings produces, indeed, necessitates new affiliations across gender and sexual orientations, my own interest as of late has been in those performances of more *abjected masculinities*: the guys who perform, for lack of a better term, and I use this term affectionately, "pond scum." I remember listening to a friend talk once about a king character she was creating and developing. In her non-drag king life, she's one of the best looking, most charming gentleman butches around: "He" she said, referring to her drag persona, "is nothing but pure pond scum. . . . He's gross to women. He's entirely flirtatious in a way that is completely disgusting. He's constantly grabbing himself and making those offensive noises to women. He's a pig!" How might we begin to make sense out of these somewhat paradoxical articulations of a kind of masculinity that, 15 years ago, we might have tried to intimidate into disappearing? What are the pleasures of watching say, "Josh," who did a stunning non-musical performance where he impersonated an incredibly homophobic man who picks up what he thinks is a woman in a fag bar, has sex with her, then, upon discovering she was a drag queen, beats her up? Josh held his audience spellbound while he performed this scene. The larger question at stake in a performance like Josh's is similar to one articulated by Stuart Hall. Hall rereads Bakhtin to ask the question: "Why is it that the thing we deem socially peripheral has be[come] symbolically central?" (1996, 303). Why did Josh's character–a homophobic man–hold us spellbound that night in a dyke bar? Part of my answer lies in reformulating the question to ask: What is the cultural work that the category of drag kings does? My tentative answer is that when drag kinging emerged it worked toward articulating an unspoken tension inherent in identity politics which continually asks what we are. I have to agree with Foucault when he suggests that our political task must be not finding out what we are but instead understanding the relations between what we say we are and what we deny we are. I'm not implying that we are actually Pond Scum at our core. But I do want to suggest that the power of the drag kings lies in their exposure of the impurity of categorization itself, especially those categories which have historically understood themselves to be bound, distinct, somehow discrete and separate (like, for instance, our history of lesbian separatism, and for some of us, the history of white supremacy). These lines that are crossed are there to differentiate, say, lesbian from straight man, black from white, but that line already allows "in" that which it is supposed to "ward off." It binds identities–those based on notions of racial or gender or sexual purity–in the very same gesture through which it supposedly differentiates itself. By way of a conclusion then I suggest that the drag kings remind us, with Bakhtin, that: "When one finds a word, one finds it already inhabited . . . there is no access to one's own personal ultimate word . . . every thought, feeling, experience must be refracted through the medium of someone else's discourse, someone else's style, someone else's manner . . . almost no word is without its intense sideward glance at someone else's" (1984, 202-203).

REFERENCES

Bakhtin, Mikhail. 1990. *Art and Answerability*. London: University of Texas Press.
_____. 1986. *Speech Genres and Other Late Essays*. London: University of Texas Press.
_____. 1984. "Discourse in Dostoevsky." Pp. 181-269 in *Problems of Dostoevsky's Poetics*. Manchester University Press.
_____. 1981. "Discourse in the Novel." Pp. 259-422 in *The Dialogic Imagination*. London: University of Texas Press.
Butler, Judith. 1990. *Gender Trouble: Feminism and the Subversion of Identity*. New York: Routledge.
_____. 1991. "Imitation and Gender Insubordination." Pp. 13-31 in *Inside/Out*, ed. Diana Fuss. New York: Routledge.
_____. 1993. *Bodies that Matter: On the Discursive Limits of "Sex."* New York: Routledge.
Case, Sue-Ellen. 1993. "Toward a Butch-Femme Aesthetic." Pp. 294-306 in *The Lesbian and Gay Studies Reader*, eds. Henry Abelove, Michèle Barale, and David Halperin. New York: Routledge.
_____. 1995. "Performing Lesbian in the Space of Technology: Part I." *Theatre Journal* 47: 1-18.
_____. 1995. "Performing Lesbian in the Space of Technology: Part II." *Theatre Journal* 47: 329-343.
Davy, Kate. 1994. "Fe/Male Impersonation: The Discourse of Camp." Pp. 130-148 in *The Politics and Poetics of Camp*, ed. Moe Meyer. London: Routledge.
_____. 1995. "Outing Whiteness: A Feminist/Lesbian Project." *Theatre Journal* 47: 189-205.
De Lauretis, Teresa. 1987. "The Technologies of Gender." Pp. 1-30 in *Technologies of Gender*, ed. de Lauretis. Bloomington: Indiana University Press.
Dolan, Jill. 1988. "The Discourse of Feminisms: The Spectator and Representation." Pp. 1-18 in *The Feminist Spectator as Critic*, ed. Dolan. Ann Arbor: UMI Research Press.
_____. 1990. " 'Lesbian' Subjectivity in Realism: Dragging at the Margins of Structure and Ideology." Pp. 40-53 in *Performing Feminisms: Feminist Critical Theory and Theatre*, ed. Sue-Ellen Case. Baltimore: The Johns Hopkins University Press.
_____. 1993. "Geographies of Learning: Theatre Studies, Performance, and the 'Performative'." *Theatre Journal* 45: 417-441.
Fuss, Diana. 1995. *Identification Papers*. New York: Routledge.
Gledhill, Christine, ed. 1991. *Stardom: Industry of Desire*. New York: Routledge.
Hall, Stuart. 1997. *Representation: Cultural Representations and Signifying Practices*. Sage: London.
_____. 1996a. "On Postmodernism and Articulation." Pp. 131-150 in *Stuart Hall: Critical Dialogues in Cultural Studies*, eds. David Morley and Kuan-Hsing Chen. London and New York: Routledge.
_____. 1996b. "For Allon White: Metaphors of Transformation." Pp. 287-305 in *Stuart Hall: Critical Dialogues in Cultural Studies*, eds. David Morley and Kuan-Hsing Chen. London and New York: Routledge.

Hart, Lynda. 1993. "Identity and Seduction: Lesbians in the Mainstream." Pp. 119-137 in *Acting Out: Feminist Performances*, eds. Hart and Peggy Phelan. Ann Arbor: The University of Michigan Press.

Johnson, Barbara. 1987. *A World of Difference*. Baltimore, MD: The Johns Hopkins University Press.

Martindale, Kathleen. 1995. *The Making of an Un/popular Culture: From Lesbian Feminism to Lesbian Postmodernism*. New York: SUNY Press.

Parker, Andrew and Eve Kosofsky Sedgwick, eds. 1995. *Performativity and Performance*. New York: Routledge.

Phelan, Peggy. 1993a. "Reciting the Citation of Others; Or, A Second Introduction." Pp. 13-31 in *Acting Out: Feminist Performances*, eds. Lynda Hart and Phelan. Ann Arbor: The University of Michigan Press.

_____. 1993b. "White Men and Pregnancy: Discovering the Body to Be Rescued." Pp. 383-401 in *Acting Out: Feminist Performances*, eds. Lynda Hart and Phelan. Ann Arbor: The University of Michigan Press.

_____. 1993c. *Unmarked: The Politics of Performance*. New York: Routledge.

Probyn, Elspeth. 1995. "Lesbians in Space. Gender, Sex and the Structure of Missing." *Gender, Place and Culture* 2: 77-84.

Sedgwick, Eve Kosofsky. 1990. *Epistemology of the Closet*. Berkeley: University of California Press.

Wallace, Robert. 1996. "Performance Anxiety: 'Identity,' 'Community,' and Tim Miller's *My Queer Body.*" *Modern Drama* 39: 97-116.

Whose Drag Is It Anyway?
Drag Kings and Monarchy in the UK

Annabelle Willox, BA (Hons), MA

University of Wales, Cardiff

SUMMARY. This chapter will show that the term "drag" in drag queen has a different meaning, history and value than the term "drag" in drag king. By exposing this basic, yet fundamental, difference this paper will expose the problems inherent in the assumption of parity between the two forms of drag.

An exposition of how camp has been used to comprehend and theorise drag queens will facilitate an understanding of the parasitic interrelationship between camp and drag queen performances, while a critique of "Towards a Butch-Femme Aesthetic," by Sue Ellen Case, will point out the problematic assumptions made about camp when attributed to a cultural location different from the drag queen.

By interrogating the historical, cultural and theoretical similarities and differences between drag kings, butches, drag queens and femmes this paper will expose the flawed assumption that camp can be attributed to all of the above without proviso, and hence expose why drag has a fundamentally different contextual meaning for kings and queens.

This chapter will conclude by examining the work of both Judith Halberstam and Biddy Martin and the practical examples of drag king and

[Haworth co-indexing entry note]: "Whose Drag Is It Anyway? Drag Kings and Monarchy in the UK." Willox, Annabelle. Co-published simultaneously in *Journal of Homosexuality* (Harrington Park Press, an imprint of The Haworth Press, Inc.) Vol. 43, No. 3/4, 2002, pp. 263-284; and: *The Drag King Anthology* (ed: Donna Troka, Kathleen LeBesco, and Jean Bobby Noble) Harrington Park Press, an imprint of The Haworth Press, Inc., 2002, pp. 263-284. Single or multiple copies of this article are available for a fee from The Haworth Document Delivery Service [1-800-HAWORTH, 9:00 a.m. - 5:00 p.m. (EST). E-mail address: docdelivery@ haworthpress.com].

queen performances provided at the UK drag contest held at The Fridge in Brixton, London on 23 June 1999. *[Article copies available for a fee from The Haworth Document Delivery Service: 1-800-HAWORTH. E-mail address: <docdelivery@haworthpress.com> Website: <http://www.HaworthPress.com> © 2002 by The Haworth Press, Inc. All rights reserved.]*

KEYWORDS. Transgender, queer, drag, camp, butch, femme, sexuality, performativity, performance, identity

This chapter will show that the term "drag" in drag queen has a different meaning, history and value than the term "drag" in drag king. By exposing this basic, yet fundamental, difference this chapter will further disclose the problems inherent in the assumption of parity between the two forms of drag. Theorists who have assumed that drag is drag no matter what is being parodied, or by whom, or for what reasons, have allowed a confusion of meanings that leads to inadequate and misleading conclusions about a multitude of cultural entities.

The assumption that both forms of drag have the same relationship to camp has led to further confusion over camp as a mode through which to theorise identities such as butch/femme without acknowledging the different historical and cultural relationship to camp that these identities have. Through an exploration of some theoretical discussions of camp and drag, this chapter will expose the flawed assumptions made concerning the inter-dynamics of these terms, before using the practical examples provided by the UK Drag Contest[1] to point out the greater subversive possibilities of drag kings. First, the interconnections between camp and drag must be expounded in order to facilitate understanding of the differences between drag queens and drag kings.

SETTING UP CAMP

Drag queens became visible outside the gay subculture throughout the 60s, during which time psychologists and doctors had attempted to explain homosexuality as a medical, mental and psychological "illness," to be cured, or fixed, through methods such as aversion therapy and electric shock treatment. Effeminate men were assumed to be the epitome of the homosexual, the logic of this being based on the assumptions of heterosexuality as norm, and a necessary link between biology and gendered expression. It was assumed that as men were masculine, and women feminine, a man who was too feminine would desire masculinity, and therefore desire men. In other words, someone who was too feminine must desire men sexually; otherwise heterosexuality would not be a pre-requisite of human desire. The notion of homosexuality was thus viewed as a gender inconsistency, not a sexual inclination, and drag queens could be seen as an extreme subversive exaggeration of this stereotype; "I decided that if I was going to be labelled a queen, I would be the biggest, best queen there was" (Thompson 1995, 450).

Using their camp sensibility as a weapon, drag queens challenged straight society through a defensive, offensive strategy that disarmed the insults and labels thrown at them through appropriation.[2] As Esther Newton points out in her still influential book *Mother Camp: Female Impersonators in America* (1979), "[c]amp humour is a system of laughing at one's incongruous position instead of crying," and that "[b]y accepting his homosexuality and flaunting it, the camp undercuts all homosexuals who won't accept the stigmatised identity. Only by fully embracing the stigma itself can one neutralise the sting and make it laughable" (1979, 109, 111). As Andy Medhurst points out, however, this is not to say that camp is drag, but simply acknowledges that "drag is merely one incarnation of camp, just one room in camp's mansion" (1997, 282).

This link between camp and drag queen performance, as well as the subversive possibilities of camp, are acknowledged by many theorists, including Medhurst who explains that, "[c]amp, above all, is the domain of queens. It is a configuration of taste codes and a declaration of effeminate intent. . . . It both vigorously undermines and rigorously reinscribes traditional gender roles" (1997, 276). To describe what exactly camp is, however, has proved an elusive and constantly challenging project. Esther Newton points out that "There is very little agreement on what is camp because camp is in the eye of the beholder . . . because of the spontaneity and individuality of camp, camp taste is always changing" (1979, 105).

Having made this observation, Newton does attempt to narrow down the possibilities of a definition of camp, stating that "[w]hile camp is in the eye of the homosexual beholder, it is assumed that there is an underlying unity of perspective among homosexuals that give any particular campy thing its special flavour. . . . The three that seemed most recurrent and characteristic to me were *incongruity, theatricality* and *humour*" (1979, 106 emphasis in original). While it could be argued that it is not necessary to be gay to understand camp, or to find camp humorous, it is important to acknowledge that the historical creation of camp as a comic rebuff came specifically out of the stigmatisation of gay men as effeminate.

With academic representation of camp, however, came a misrepresentation and effacement of this historical and cultural genesis, as well as one of the most fundamental aspects of camp, namely humour: camp is above all else funny, at least to those who are in on the joke. The removal of this important subversive element of camp has arguably been caused by the very theories that attempted to define camp itself. Through her essay "Notes on Camp" (1969), Susan Sontag made camp a commodity that lost its subversive power through its appropriation and use outside of the gay male subculture that created it. Even though Sontag acknowledges the difficulty of theorising adequately about camp, stating that it is "embarrassing to be solemn and treatise-like about Camp. One runs the risk of having, oneself, produced a very inferior piece of Camp," she nonetheless portrayed camp as devoid of humour (1969, 278). Within her definition she claims that camp is apolitical and innocent; however, what this does is make camp palatable to the general public, which is to say less powerful. By focusing on the effects created by it, rather than on its history as a subversive, offensive and comical rebuff of charges levelled against homosexual men, Sontag removes the most powerful element of camp humour.

In contrast to this, Newton affirms and reaffirms the importance of humour, as well as the historical reciprocity between camp and gay men, explaining not only that one of the most prominent features of camp is its humour, but also that, by removing any homosexual inflection from the definition of camp, Sontag does great disservice and violence to those queens who explicitly use camp. Within her essay, Sontag does not mention until the fiftieth point that camp has any relation to gay men, and even then claims that "if homosexuals hadn't more or less invented Camp, someone else would," thereby undermining the subversive power of camp as used by gay men by claiming that it was just waiting to happen (1969, 292). Newton, however, argues that camp usually depends on incongruous juxtapositions, with masculine and feminine juxtapositions being the most characteristic form of camp. For Newton, in contrast to Sontag, the importance of homosexuality for camp is underscored, as she explains, "the homosexual 'creates' the camp, by pointing out the incongruity or by devising it," thereby giving the agency of camp back to the gay male subculture that created it (Newton 1979, 106).

Another way of understanding camp, and a good way of compre-
hending the fundamental link between camp and drag queens, is by critically reading the image of British romance novelist Barbara Cartland.
Cartland looked like a drag queen. She appeared to be a parody of femininity in her exuberance and tasteless overuse of pink; she looked like
an ironic portrayal of "woman" as constructed femininity, and her image proved the ridiculous concept of pink and fluffy = feminine. Yet she
was not a drag queen simply because she did not possess the camp sensibility; she did not get the joke. This is not to say that Barbara Cartland
could not be described as camp, but she was not deliberately camping
up her performance, nor was she self-aware of her camp visuality. [This
paper was originally written before the death of Ms. Cartland, and the
autor wishes to stress that this reading of her image is not intended to de-
fame her character in any way.]

Newton would probably describe the camp of Barbara Cartland as
"unintentional camp," a form of camp that she explains through her example of a Midwestern American Football player in high drag at a Halloween Ball. Newton explains that the football player, as with Barbara
Cartland, makes what he perceives to be a serious attempt at appearing
to be a lady, and as such his intention is not camp or parody. The effect
of this performance, however, can be perceived as camp by an observer,
thereby becoming unintentionally camp, as the protagonist does not
perceive the camp incongruity of their performance. This points out the
other fundamental point of camp, whether intentional or not, which is
that camp, "like drag, always involves a performer or performers and an
audience . . . It is only stretching the point a little to say that even in unintentional camp, this interaction is maintained" (Newton 1979, 107).

Camp is, therefore, able to challenge the dominant culture through its
staged parodic and essentially humorous effects, and the inversion of
the processes of appropriation means that camp can "be read as a critique of ideology through a parody that is always already appropriated"
(Meyer 1994, 18). In other words, camp, simply by virtue of being
camp, always already subverts ideology through its intrinsic ironic, and
parodic, humour. A tentative definition of camp could claim that camp
is an internally incongruous or self-contradictory sensibility that is used
to disrupt traditional categories, usually though not exclusively gender,
through over-conformity, parody and/or caricature.

While it is true that not everyone who puts on six-inch heels, false
eyelashes, and a wig is making a political statement about the construction of gender–some people just do it for the "sheer God damned glamour of it all" (Finch 1995)–it is difficult to see a drag queen in full

flamboyant glory and not find it amusing in some way. In the post-modern era, camp was seen as the ultimate tool of subversion, a specifically "postmodern strategy for the subversion of phallogocentric identities and desires" (Tyler 1991, 32), while drag was used to exemplify theories of gender.

DRAGGING UP THEORY

Judith Butler uses drag as an example through which to explain her theories about construction and performativity. Butler develops Esther Newton's notion that "drag is not an imitation or copy of some prior and true gender . . . drag enacts the very structure of impersonation by which *any gender* is assumed," stating that "*gender is a kind of imitation for which there is no original*" (Butler 1993, 312 emphasis in original). The performance that constitutes this gender is bound to fail due to this lack of an original; therefore the performance must be endlessly repeated in order to attempt to substantiate the identity.

Thus gender is performative in that the performance, which is necessarily and continuously repeated, constitutes the gender itself; the performance performatively creates the gender. This repetition produces a coherence of identity that constitutes the subject, therefore there can be no ungendered subject; gender becomes a matter of personal identity and "truth" about who a person is. This gender performance is further constituted through and by the dominant discourse, the heterosexual matrix, which produces a domain of "unthinkability and unnameability" beyond its borders. Therefore, for Butler, we cannot escape the gender system, we can only subvert it through (visible) transgression (Butler 1993, 310). In other words, imitation is always already present in gender, and vice versa: gender is itself imitation, but not of any real or true gender. It is the repetition of gender as performatively constructed that establishes the ultimate instability of gender categories, and drag is a physical manifestation, or representation, of this constant contradictory repetition. Butler uses drag as the example that proves the rule of performativity through its exposition of the constructed nature of gender categories.

The use of drag as the exemplar of performativity, however, has led to misreadings of Butler's theory not as performativity, but as mere performance; the basis of this misreading being the definition of drag. As Butler states, "I do not mean to suggest that drag is a 'role' that can be taken on or taken off at will" (1993, 314), but this is precisely the point of drag as exemplified by the statement made by British entertainer and drag artist Paul O'Grady when receiving a British Television comedy award for his on-screen persona, Lilly Savage. Paul O'Grady collected it, giving Lilly's apologies, and stating that he "couldn't be bothered to put her wig on"; when he won an award previously he had given Lilly's apologies again, saying that she was in a suitcase in the garage.

A drag queen is not, in my opinion, pretending to *be* a woman, nor is the performance merely about women, or femininity (not that the two are synonymous); the performance is ultimately that of a drag queen, and this performance is transient. Butler's theory is about the necessity of performativity of gender, but to use drag as an example I feel hinders understanding of her theory due to the problems of definition surrounding drag as parody.[3] The important difference between drag queens and gender is the ability to choose; one often has no choice over one's assigned gender, however, the drag queen not only chooses her performance, but can change it at will.

The question will still always remain, however, parody of what exactly; women, effeminacy in (some) homosexual men, or simply self-parody? After all, the most important aspect of drag queens is that they are "pretending to be a woman for the amusement of those who had better be expected to believe he is not a woman. . . . The impersonator's [sic] gestures are *about* women," they are not, therefore, merely representations *of* women (Danto 1981, 68, emphasis in original). "Is the drag queen a misogynistic put-down of women, a self-hating parody, or a complex cultural sign that defies any simple translation into 'meaning'?" is the question that Marjorie Garber puts to the reader at large (Garber 1993, 149). If woman as construct is necessarily one of mask and masquerade, as Garber suggests, then how can the Drag Queen be more than a self-imitating parody?

What Garber claims drag to be is "the theoretical and deconstructive social practice that analyzes these structures from within, by putting in question the 'naturalness' of gender roles through the discourse of clothing and body parts" (1993, 151). However this definition seems to rely, to some extent, on the necessity of the body beneath the masquerade. More specifically it appears to require the incongruity between mask and body in order to challenge the assumed gender roles meted out to individuals by the very clothes that they wear. This is not to suggest that Garber does not believe that there can be double drag, or women dressed as drag queens–although she does not explore this particular phenomenon fully in her book, *Vested Interests*–it simply shows that the body is inevitably the site of meaning; the mask cannot stand alone as the signifier of the subject. This view is in contrast to Butler for whom there is no site of meaning, no "truth" to gender, beyond the performances that performatively constitute the gender itself, but rather gender performativity is the pre-condition of the subject.

Butler also claims that the "performance of drag plays upon the distinction between the anatomy of the performer and the gender that is being performed" (1990, 137). Drag, therefore, questions our understanding of gender through a performance that we perceive as "real," and assume to be parodic or ironic. What is assumed here is that the humour inherent in drag queens is based on the incongruity between the body of the performer, and the performed gender. This again relies on the assumption that drag queens perform as "women," not simply as themselves, therefore their performed gender is incongruous with their physical sex, thus exposing the construction of gender as an image that has no necessary link to physicality.

The problem with this assumption can be exemplified through the instances of female drag queens that became fashionable during the mid-nineties, as well as through drag kings whose gender may well be indeterminate offstage. The assumed incongruity in such examples is not actuality, although the doubly parodic exposé of femininity as masquerade when performed by a woman may have given the drag queen an added subversive twist. Such a parody, when played by a person assumed to have the attributes being parodied, may provide a more subversive performance by questioning the assumption of incongruity between biology and performance, as well as pointing out the ridiculous within the masquerade. The problem seemed to be that academic abstractions could never sufficiently analyse the practical demonstrations or performances of drag queens and drag kings, and as drag artists adapted their performance to their life experiences theory failed to keep up. Not only did theory fail to adequately analyse drag performances, but "[p]aradoxically, this theoreticized vindication of camp [and, by inference, drag] threatened to destroy its specific subcultural vitality. For if we conclude that *all* gender is play and performance, then camp, which has long held that conclusion as its cherished secret weapon, no longer has any unique contribution to make" (Medhurst 1997, 282).

CAMPING UP ROLES

One example of camp being used to theorise gendered, and in this instance sexual, identifications, and an example through which the difficulties of misrepresenting historical relations between terms is foregrounded, is the article "Toward a Butch-Femme Aesthetic," by Sue-Ellen Case. Case explains that her aim is to explore the feminist subject position of butch/femme that she claims to be endowed with an agency for political change; "it would appear that the lesbian roles of butch and femme, as a dynamic duo, offer precisely the strong subject position the movement requires" (Case 1993, 295).

In order to allow the performance of such a subject position to be studied, however, Case suggests that firstly the lesbian subject of feminist theory must come out, secondly "the basic discourse or style of camp for the lesbian butch-femme positions would have to be clarified," thirdly an understanding of the function of roles in homosexual lifestyles must be developed (1993, 295). It is not only the second of her tasks that is problematic, but also her explicit assumption that "within this schema, the butch-femme couple inhabit the subject position together" (Case 1993, 295), thereby paradoxically removing the very self agency that she is attempting to reintroduce to the feminist subject.

It is the fusion of this assumed singular entity of butch/femme, coupled with the belief that camp can be ascribed to such a schizophrenic entity that causes problems. Case explains that "[t]he closet has given us camp–the style, the discourse, the *misé en scène* of butch-femme roles" (1993, 297), yet as I have shown, camp was the domain of queens and effeminate gay men, not butch/femme. While I am not denying that butch/femme can be camped up for comic effect, Case appears to be claiming that butch/femme couples are always already camp simply by virtue of their homosexuality. Case claims that "camp both articulates the lives of homosexuals through the obtuse tone of irony and inscribes their oppression with the same device" (1993, 298), making camp a "gay thing," rather than a "gay *male* thing." While I am not suggesting that camp can only ever be the property of queens, it seems that by implicitly assuming that camp can be ascribed to all homosexuals, regardless of cultural or historical reference, Case undermines camp by removing the very specificity that created camp.

This concern noted, however, Case continues to suggest that butch/femme couples, or as Case would have us believe the singular entity of butch/femme, embody the theoretical conception of woman as masquerade. The butch "proudly displays the possession of the penis, while the femme . . . foregrounds her masquerade by playing to a butch" (1993, 300). Case suggests that the fact that there is no penis, there is no referent, means that the butch/femme couple ironize the notion of the penis and "camp it up"; "these women play on the phallic economy rather than to it" (1993, 300). Further Case suggests that because the roles of butch/femme are acknowledged as roles to be perfected, rather than inalienable essences, "these roles qua roles lend agency and self-determination to the historically passive subject, providing her with at least two options for gender identification and with the aid of camp, an irony that allows her perception to be constructed from outside ideology, with a gender role that makes her appear as if she is inside of it" (1993, 301). In other words, the femme is non-passive as she subverts the heterosexual norm by playing to the butch, while the butch is non-passive as she plays with masculinity. It is this self-aware ironic portrayal of gender roles that subverts the notion of the passive subject upon whom gendered roles are ascribed, and the camp inflection that Case claims for butch/femme allows this parody to become evident.

The first problem that arises from Case's argument is the internal contradiction of imbuing the butch and femme subjects with agency through their parody of the phallic economy, while simultaneously claiming that butch/femme occupy the same subject position. In allowing such a paradox to exist, Case appears to deny the possibility of individual agency, precisely that which she is attempting to provide for the feminist subject, due to the necessary conjoinment of subjects. Furthermore, within Case's argument the femme disappears.

As Biddy Martin notes, "[d]istinguishing lesbian desire from heterosexual desire . . . requires not only two lesbians but the butch-femme couple, one that parodies masculine and feminine roles and heterosexuality by playing them to excess. It requires a femme who visibly addresses her desire to another woman, because as a femme alone, her lesbianism would be invisible" (1998, 25). The femme parodies and subverts the notion of femininity and heterosexuality by being a feminine lesbian, yet she is only seen as parodic because of her lesbianism, which becomes visible only through the existence of a butch partner. This tautology of the femme underlies Case's argument, and is summarised by Martin when she states that "femmes are parodic because they are lesbians and are lesbians because they are parodic" (1998, 22).

In other words, the femme is only different from heterosexual women because she is a lesbian, yet she is acknowledged as a lesbian only because of the existence of a butch through which her lesbianism is made visible; therefore the femme only has meaning, for Case, when necessarily conjoined with the butch. Thus Case must claim that the butch and femme occupy the same subject position in order for the femme to be imbued with any parodic, or "camp," power. Martin goes on to point out that within queer theory as an academic genre it is the visible transgression of the butch that is celebrated as subversive, while the femme is ignored or discussed only as an appendage to the butch.

The important point to be gleaned from this discussion, however, is that attempting to theorise the subject position(s) of butch/femme through camp and parody misunderstands the historical and cultural significance of both butch/femme and camp itself. While it may be argued that some 90s butch/femme couples may deliberately parody heterosexuality, or gender expectations, it is highly questionable whether butch/femme of the time that camp and drag queens first flourished was a deliberately camp subversion of ideology.[4] Without wishing to recreate the biases that facilitate the disappearance of the femme, it is important to our understanding of the cultural relevance of the drag king to explore the cultural relevance and history of the butch.

WHEN WERE WE KINGS?

At the same time as the pathologization of effeminate behaviour that gave rise to the drag queen was taking place, a parallel move was being made with regard to butch dykes who were seen as overly masculine by the medical establishment. The charge of homosexuality seemed to be gender based here also, and probably accounts for the transvestite laws in the United States of America that stated that everyone must wear at least three items of clothing appropriate to their gender (Feinberg 1996, 8; Faderman 1992, 185). The idea of clothes making the man has never been more explicit, with the assumption seemingly being that if the clothes were correct, then normality would follow. Again it appeared that butch dykes could subvert assumptions about gendered roles in the same way as the drag queen.

While it has been noted that "it is questionable whether lesbians in the 1950s were genuinely aware of the butch/femme roles as a politically subversive act which served to expose the constraint of the 'masquerade'" (Patterson and Le Blé 1996, 124), it is also important to acknowledge that self-awareness of one's political potential is not always necessary for a performance to be subversive. As with unintentional camp one may be subversive without intending to be and in this way butch/femme couples could be read as being subversive even if their performances were not deliberately intended to be so.

The reason why the butch/femme couple differed in (assumed) political ideology from the drag queen was that butch/femme was often seen as a survival tactic, at least during the early years. As has been noted, not all drag queens were politically motivated, but their visibility often made them the stereotype of the gay community. The butch/femme couple, on the other hand, could be argued to often appear invisible, both women passing either as male, or as heterosexual.[5]

Of the two of these cultural entities, however, it was the butch that became the stereotypical image through which society judged and comprehended the lesbian. A point that is worth noting here is that the drag king did not come about as a result of the specific stigmatisation of the butch that took place at the time that drag queens emerged. As Judith Halberstam notes, "[m]ale impersonation has been a theatrical genre for at least two hundred years, but the drag king is a recent phenomena" (1998, 232). Further is it generally agreed that "no extensive drag king culture developed within lesbian bar culture" beyond pockets of male impersonation such as Storme Delaverie (Halberstam 1998, 234).

The modern drag king is a theatrically deliberate parody of masculinities rather than the cross dressed entertainers who, while they may be regarded as one historical incarnation of male drag which could be seen as one possible genesis for the concept of drag kings, were nonetheless entertaining through drag rather than as drag kings. The drag king has emerged out of the recent moves towards gender blurring as a subversive act that denaturalises categories of gender advocated by queer theory, rather than out of the comical rebuff to straight society that the drag queen represents. It is the different genealogy of the drag king that should alert theorists to the need for any theory concerning drag to be informed of, and by, the cultural and historical differences between kings and queens.

REALITY CHECK

The advent of the drag king problematized the existing theoretical framework as the theories always presupposed that drag necessarily meant female drag, and as Andy Medhurst suggests, "the performativity theory of gender, seduced by its own conceptual elegance, lost sight of the everyday contexts in which gender is experienced" (1997, 283). More often than not the difference between female drag and male drag was glossed over, and ignored by theorists who claimed that drag was just drag whoever performed it, as long as it disrupted concepts of gender. The feeling was that "[i]f gay camp is seen as revealing the construction of feminine identity and its flaws, then butch-acting lesbians should have the same parodic effect of deconstruction–which is by no means the case" (Patterson and Le Blé 1996, 127). The differences between drag queens and drag kings stem from their histories, power relations and positions within society, as well as their differing relations to camp.

The drag queen, as we have seen, was born out of the stigmatisation of effeminacy both from the medical establishment, and from within gay male subculture. Through the parallel experiences of lesbians labelled "mannish," one would perhaps expect to discover the creation of the drag king; however, the existence of cross-dressed entertainers at this time, while important in understanding the history of male drag, does not automatically lead to the deliberately and theatrically parodic drag king of today. In other words, while butch dykes became visibly evident during this time, the drag king is a relatively new phenomenon, thus proving that, with regard to drag queens and butch dykes, to be parallel is not to be identical.

The image of the drag queen was also established, and remained relatively static since its conception, with the advent of female drag queens adding a twist to the mixture of gender assumptions and parody that constitute the image itself. The irony of a masculine woman such as k d lang performing as a drag queen merely seemed to reinforce the adaptability of the parodic and now doubly ironic effect of the drag queen.[6] This also exemplifies one of the assumptions that can be drawn from existing theories of drag, namely that one would assume that k d lang, being a woman, would perform drag in male attire thereby using incongruity as the basis of the performance. However, I am suggesting that the drag queen is a specifically historically and culturally created entity that differs fundamentally from the drag king, which has been created by different historical and cultural discourses, with the basis for this historical divergence being the concepts of camp and masculinities.

It has been noted by theorists that butch lesbians and camp have a troublesome relationship; as Halberstam notes, "camp has been a luxury that the passing butch cannot afford" (1998, 234). Halberstam also concurs with the assertion that drag queens and butches do not share easily comparable histories, even though the premise of their stigmatisation lies in gender deviance or variance from gender norms. The result of this differing history is skepticism of the use of camp when ascribed to butch sexualities, as postmodern notions of queer camp often ignore the historical lack of camp in lesbian visuality. Newton suggests that lesbian camp is a relatively new phenomenon (Halberstam 1998, 237), and therefore the same culturally and historically defined theoretical framework, namely camp, cannot be used to explicate gender parody across sex divides.

The main differences that undoubtedly exist are cultural location and relative power. As Andy Medhurst explains, "butches' social and cultural position as women cannot be lazily equated with queens' social and cultural position as men, and to use the word 'camp' as a blanket term for both . . . conceals this crucial difference" (1997, 285). Furthermore, Medhurst claims that "[l]esbian camp is as impossible as gay male butch-femme" (1997, 286). This is not to say that lesbians cannot use camp effects to disrupt and destabilise gender norms, the point is that this cannot be theorised *in the same way* without acknowledging the historical and cultural differences of the term as ascribed in each circumstance. Halberstam suggests that camp, historically and practically, is concerned with an outrageous performance of femininity rather than masculinity (Halberstam 1998, 238); therefore the use of camp to describe butch sexuality, without femme sexuality explicitly conjoined, would fail in some way. This is not to say that butch and femme sexualities are necessarily conjoined; on the contrary, this points out that to ascribe camp to butch/femme sexuality, as some theorists have done,[7] ignores the visual performance of the butch.

This seems to be a paradoxical statement in the light of objections to theorising about butch/femme sexuality that almost always seems to privilege the butch within the couple, after all, "at no point in lesbian history has an excess or caricature of femininity symbolised the lesbian" (Patterson and Le Blé 1996, 135). However, privileging the "camp" femme performance of femininity, while paradoxically allowing the butch predominance in the field of vision and theory, allows the incompatibility of camp and butch sexuality to be ignored by theorists. While this area is in need of more consideration, what is fundamentally important is that *if* camp is attributable to drag king performance it is only so if the history and contemporary situation of the drag king is taken into account.

In order to attempt to clarify the position of gender and parody in drag performances Halberstam proposes the term "kinging" as masculine alternative for camp. The history of butch lesbians and their relationship with visual masculinities must be acknowledged for comprehension of the use of "kinging" in drag king performances, as "[m]asculinity within the drag king act is always inflected by race, class, and gender and by the histories of different lesbian communities and their different relationships over time to butch-femme styles and to female masculinity in general" (Halberstam 1997, 106). The use of a different and new term such as "kinging" would allow these inflections to be taken into account when theorising drag kings, rather than effacing these inflections by using a term that seems incompatible with the historical and cultural location of female masculinities and male drag.

While I applaud the reasoning for proposing a new term such as kinging, I am hesitant about the ease with which the division between kinging and camp may unfold. To argue that camp is to femininity what kinging is to masculinity seems to evade some of the more difficult and intriguing areas of drag performance. I am wary of such a neat and easily definable territory for camp, and kinging, and would point towards the intricacies of clone drag, butch queens and gay skins as some areas that would problematize such a distinction. Further I would question whether it is so easy to divorce drag king parodies of masculinities from camp.

> When femmes or feminine straight women perform as Drag Kings, they . . . produce a camp mingling of femininity and masculinity. When butches perform as Drag Kings, they build a new, flashy masculinity upon their own carefully cultivated masculinities. . . . When transgender Drag Kings put on male drag, they thoroughly detach masculinity from men and even maleness from men. (Halberstam and Del LaGrace Volcano 1999, 150)

It becomes obvious from this quotation that drag kings have a complicated relationship to camp, drag and kinging, and the possibilities for drag king performance are as multiple as masculinities are themselves. How to theorise such a multifarious and intricate cultural entity is difficult indeed, and to make a lazy equation between drag kings and queens effaces some of the subversive potential of this conundrum.

THE KING AND "I"

The history of the queen shows their defiance of derogatory labels, and reduction of power through these labels, through their defensive, offensive, playful and ultimately powerful approach. The parallel history of the butch dyke, however, shows an apparently dangerous appropriation of power through assimilation and mimesis that has threatened society in a different manner. While, as I have suggested, drag kings did not evolve directly from the butch dyke, the fact that some drag kings do not see themselves as parodic, but as duplicate images of masculinity signals another difference between drag queens and kings. Take the example of Dianne Torr, one of the forerunners of the current drag king scene, and the Web page that explains how she first "passed" as a man, implying that her final image was not a parody, or an exaggeration of masculinity, but a believable *impersonation* of a man. The workshops that she runs "for women only" exist to teach women to pass as men, and are therefore more concerned with cross-dressing than they are with drag. The Web also asks whether the user wishes to "enter the male domain," which I would suggest is not the requirement of drag queens, as they merely enter the drag queen domain.

Having made this objection, however, it must be made explicit that Torr is only one example of a drag king, and the performances that are given by and through this workshop format should not be assumed to be the epitome of drag. The drag king is a more complex and variable entity that Halberstam attempts to define as widely as possible, stating that the drag king is "a performer who pinpoints and exploits the (often obscured) theatricality of masculinity" (1997, 105). Halberstam goes on to suggest that "[t]he drag king may be extremely self-conscious about her performance and may have elaborate justifications and theories about what she is doing, or she may just think of her act as 'having fun' and make no further claims for it" (1997, 105). In this manner drag kings are akin to drag queens as they may well just be doing it for pleasure, however the subversive possibilities of drag king performances make them infinitely more intriguing now than drag queens.

Halberstam suggests that there is an essential difference between theatrical and non-theatrical performance of gender/masculinities (1997, 105). This point is exemplified with the example of Torr who, I would argue, performs a non-theatrical form of drag that is more akin to male impersonation than drag. This emphasises the importance of the performance itself, without which, as Halberstam points out, the entertainer in question may be read as being "just butch" (1997, 107). Halberstam further notes that "some male impersonators carried over their cross-dressing practices into their everyday lives," suggesting that being butch may, or may not, be an aspect of drag king performance itself (1998, 233).[8]

This suggests that the performances of masculinities on display in drag king acts may extend beyond simple theatricality, resulting in the multiple categorisations of drag king acts outlined by Halberstam such as Butch Realness, Male Mimicry, Denaturalised Masculinity, Femme Pretender and Fag Drag (Halberstam 1998, 244ff). Here again we can see the subversive potential of drag kings as the categories themselves

point out the multifarious nature of masculinities, deliberately plural-
ized to undermine the notion of masculinity as a fixed, central and fundamental gender through which others are defined through deviation.
The performances also undermine notions of race- and class-based
masculinities through excessive parody and, in some cases, respectful
mimicry: "although white masculinity seems to be readily available for
parody by the drag kings, black masculinities or queer masculinities are
often performed by drag kings in the spirit of homage or tribute rather
than humor" (Halberstam 1998, 235).

This experience of homage to black masculinities underlines one of
the interesting twists that has occurred within the recent history of drag
king performance in that there was initially a high proportion of women
of colour taking part in drag king events, whereas now there is a predominance of white performers. Halberstam suggests that this is because "black masculinity tends to be represented as always in excess of
some white ideal of self-restraint" (1997, 107), and therefore it was easier, in first instance, to find images of black masculinity that lent themselves to parody as they could be argued to be always already parodic
when compared to white masculinities. However, the recent "white
drag kings have found the soft underbelly of white masculinity"
(Halberstam 1997, 107) and are exposing its own self-parodic possibilities thereby undermining the very image that was assumed to be original, stable and unquestionable, thereby subverting the presumed core of
gender identity itself.

The main question that is raised by drag king performance concerns
the assumptions about the construction of masculinity and femininity.
"We know that femininity is socially constructed, there is no 'real' feminine essence which is biologically determined" (Simpson 1996, 136),
therefore can we assume that there is a male essence which is similarly
constructed, and is therefore able to be imitated and parodied? The basic
question is whether you can parody that, which in society is unname-
able, as it is the basis or original from which all else is distinguished.

As has been pointed out by Butler amongst others, that which is the
origin is always already defined by that which is its derivative; "[t]he
origin requires its derivations in order to affirm itself as an origin, for
origins only make sense to the extent that they are differentiated from
that which they produce as derivatives" (1993a, 313). Therefore drag
kings serve the purpose of pointing out the constructed nature of masculinity assumed to be an origin, giving impetus to the questioning of a
"natural" reciprocity between masculinity and male embodiment that
Halberstam's work on female masculinity provides. After all, if the cen-

tre is proved to be a construction in itself, then all eccentric entities are proved to be just as (ec)centric as the "original," and the drag king's parodic display of masculinities can expose the constructed nature of masculinity, the original origin.

Furthermore, by parodying the presumed original of gender, from which femininity as Other is a derivative, drag kings do not simply question masculinities, they question what can be parodied. This is a fundamental difference between drag kings and queens in that drag queens simply parody the masquerade of femininity through their performances, yet femininity as masquerade is always already parodic as it is only ever a performance. Drag kings, on the other hand, question the distinctions between masculinity and femininity, camp and masculinity, performance and masquerade, by parodying that which society presumes to be a pre-given: masculinity.

This makes the drag king infinitely more subversive than the drag queen, making any drag king performance always already subversive whether this is acknowledged by the performer as an intention or not. The politically aware basis of drag king contests and performances means that I would question even non-theatrical drag kings having no investment in parodic readings of their performances. In a manner akin to "unintentional camp," one could argue that drag king performances are unintentionally subversive, even if the protagonists claim that they are performing for fun. They must be aware of the possibilities of readings, even if only because of academics taking explicit interest in their performances.

THE QUEEN IS DEAD, LONG LIVE THE KING

Drag kings and queens are essentially different cultural entities due to their historical, cultural and genealogical differences which current theories of camp and drag do not adequately tackle. If we assume the same theoretical framework for both forms of drag, then male drag may arguably lose the subversive element of the performance as it appears to be a failed copy (of a copy). This is not to say that male drag does not exist, nor does it claim that male drag does not have multiple and powerful subversive possibilities, it is just that the two forms of drag cannot be theorised, *in the same way*. To claim the same theoretical framework would be to deny the social, cultural and historical differences that define and create the two forms of drag and would deny the greater subversive potential of the drag king. It would be as impossible as to use an uninformed theory of camp to explain butch/femme lesbians, or vice versa. To do so would deny the important differences between the academic abstractions that attempt to define and explain the practical demonstrations of drag kings as opposed to drag queens whose performances are different visually, culturally and historically.[9]

Without taking into account the fundamental differences between the performance and significance of male and female drag and "in the absence of theoretical models of drag, the drag king scene can be quickly dismissed by popular media as a glorification of male masculinity or as evidence of a lesbian fascination with men. Theories of drag king performance are able to mobilize the assault on male privilege that is implicit in many of the acts and to transform this assault into discourse" (Halberstam 1997, 109).

The recent Drag Contest held at the Fridge in Brixton, London pointed out the subversive potential of the drag king, while directly comparing it to drag queen performances. The drag kings were exciting, individual and passionate, encompassing multiple masculinities and emphasising the difference of class and race through their parody. In contrast the drag queens, while no less entertaining, appeared to be remarkably similar visually and their performances could be argued to be flat in comparison to the drag kings.

The winner of the drag king contest, Vincent, provided the (almost) perfect spectacle of the drag king. The performance blended masculinities through the backing band, who were also in drag giving a visual perspective that allowed an engagement with the main king, while Vincent himself performed as a blues singer thereby questioning both the assumed class-based status of the protagonist but also giving a certain undecidability to his race, encouraged by his appearance. Vincent became the eccentric of the eccentric contest, being through his performance undecidable, intriguing and undeniably sexy (which probably won him the contest). The drag king, as John Waters points out, does seem to possess possibilities that are no longer apparent in the drag queen; "[t]o me they're much more exciting than drag queens, but it's really just a new take on it. When we have families loving drag queens, then we need something new" (op cit. Bailey 1997). After all, when drag queen Lilly Savage took over from Judy[10] for a brief spell on British daytime television in the late 1990s, who could claim that the drag queen was still truly eccentric, subversive or a powerfully camp, gay image?

Assimilation and appropriation of subversive elements renders them powerless, and perhaps the centre of "normal" society has finally engulfed the drag queen. The drag king is one of the few eccentrics left that can subvert and denaturalise our notions of gender, race and class through parodic performance, and without doubt a new hybrid theory that encompasses the cultural, historical and power-based construction of the King is needed.

This chapter has shown that assumptions made by theorists can render the most subversive identities obsolete due to misrepresentations of the lived experience of individuals in question. By assuming that current theories can be applied wholesale to embodied and fundamentally lived experiences, theory ignores the subversive potential inherent in subjects such as drag kings, femmes and those individuals rendered invisible by theories such as performativity. My suggestion, then, is that theory needs to re-approach these identities with a view to learning from them, rather than overlaying theory onto them. With such a project in mind, then, perhaps the last word of this paper should go to Judith Halberstam and *The Drag King Book*, which suggests that "[t]he Drag King, in a way, does not simply expose so-called abnormal desires or abnormal genders, rather he revels in what is already perverse in the normal" (1999, 152).

ACKNOWLEDGMENT

The author wishes to thank the editors of this volume for their helpful comments on earlier drafts of this paper, and their patience when dealing with overseas postal services. This work is adapted from part of the author's PhD thesis, which was supported by a University of Wales scholarship obtained with the assistance of Professor Catherine Belsey, and supervised by Dr. Alessandra Tanesini.

NOTES

1. The Drag King and Drag Queen contest was held at The Fridge in Brixton, London on 23 June 1999.

2. Similar to the Queer tactic of appropriation employed in the 1990s.

3. Butler does argue later that drag has its own melancholia, but the use of drag as an example can be, nonetheless, confusing for her theory due to its voluntaristic nature. If Butler were to claim that "drag queen" is a gender in itself, that there are multiple genders of which this is merely one manifestation, then the performer could be said to be performatively constructing "drag queen" through the performed actions. The drag queen, therefore, is only subversive if we assume the traditional binary configuration of genders, and if we assume the parody is about women and not simply a self-parodic performance.

4. It is worth mentioning here that the femme may be able to subvert notions of heterosexuality and gender. For a more detailed exposition of how the femme could be subversive without being necessarily associated with a butch, see Martin, Biddy. 1998. "Sexualities Without Genders and Other Queer Utopias." Pp. 11-35 in *Coming Out of Feminism?* eds. Mandy Merck et al. Oxford: Basil Blackwell.

5. This is obviously a simplistic account of butch/femme dynamics, however the main point is valid, the drag queen could not fail to be noticed.

6. This is a reference to PETA anti-fur trade protest held at the Hard Rock Café in New York, February 1993. See Bennahum, David. 1995. *k d lang: In Her Own Words*. New York, London, Rosebery: Omnibus Press, p. 13 for image.

7. See Case, Sue-Ellen. 1993. "Toward a Butch-Femme Aesthetic." Pp. 294-306 in *The Lesbian and Gay Studies Reader*, eds. Henry Albelove et al. London: Routledge.

8. The different approaches of New York and London Drag Kings exemplify this difference with London Drag Kings often seeing their onstage persona as an extension of their female masculinity, many of them being transgendered themselves. See p. 64 Volcano, Del LaGrace, and Judith Halberstam 1999. *The Drag King Book*. London: Serpent's Tail, especially pp. 75 and 83.

9. The terms "academic abstraction" and "practical demonstration" are unashamedly lifted from Halberstam's article in *Social Text*. My thanks must go to her for getting me out of the theory/reality trap.

10. Judy Finnigan and husband Richard Madley present a magazine style British daytime television show, *This Morning*, that, due to the informal chat style and kitsch content, has become cult viewing for students.

REFERENCES

Abelove, Henry, Michèle Aina Barale, and David M. Halperin, eds. 1993. *The Lesbian and Gay Studies Reader*. London: Routledge.

Bailey, Andy. 1997. "Hair Apparent." *The Face*. October. Available online at <http://www.pipeline.com/~jordinyc/face/face1097.htm>. Accessed November 1999.

Bennahum, David. 1993. *k.d.lang: An Illustrated Biography*. London: Omnibus Press.

Butler, Judith. 1990. *Gender Trouble*. London: Routledge.

_____. 1993. "Imitation and Gender Insubordination." Pp. 307-320 in *The Lesbian and Gay Studies Reader*, eds. Henry Abelove, Michèle Aina Barale, and David M. Halperin. London: Routledge.

Califia, Pat. 1997. *Sex Changes: The Politics of Transgenderism*. San Francisco: Cleis.

Case, Sue-Ellen. 1993. "Toward a Butch-Femme Aesthetic." Pp. 294-306 in *The Lesbian and Gay Studies Reader*, eds. Henry Abelove, Michèle Aina Barale, and David M. Halperin. London: Routledge.

Creekmur, Cory, and Alexander Doty, eds. 1995. *Out in Culture: Gay, Lesbian and Queer Essays on Popular Culture*. London: Cassell.

Danto, Arthur. 1981. *Philosophy and Art*. Cambridge: Harvard University Press.

Faderman, Lillian. 1992. *Odd Girls and Twilight Lovers: A History of Lesbian Life in Twentieth-Century America*. London: Penguin.

Feinberg, Leslie. 1996. *Transgendered Warriors: Making History from Joan of Arc to Dennis Rodman*. Boston: Beacon Press.

Finch, Nigel, director. 1995. *Stonewall*. USA.

Fuss, Diana, ed. 1991. *Inside/Out: Lesbian Theories, Gay Theories*. London: Routledge.

Garber, Marjorie. 1993. *Vested Interests: Cross-dressing and Cultural Anxiety*. London: Penguin.

Halberstam, Judith. 1997. "Mackdaddy, Superfly, Rapper: Gender, Race, and Masculinity in the Drag King Scene." *Social Text 52-53 Special Issue: Queer Transexions of Race, Nation, and Gender*, ed. Phillip Harper, Ann McClintock, José Muñoz and Trish Rosen: 105-131.

————. 1998. *Female Masculinity*. Durham, NC: Duke University Press.

Hilbert, Jeffrey. 1995. "The Politics of Drag." Pp. 463-469 in *Out in Culture: Gay, Lesbian and Queer Essays on Popular Culture*, eds. Cory Creekmur and Alexander Doty. London: Cassell.

Martin, Biddy. 1998. "Sexualities Without Genders and Other Queer Utopias." Pp. 11-35 in *Coming Out of Feminism?* eds. Mandy Merck, Naomi Segal and Elizabeth Wright. Oxford: Basil Blackwell.

Medhurst, Andy. 1997. "Camp." Pp. 274-293 in *Lesbian and Gay Studies: A Critical Introduction*, eds. Andy Medhurst and Sally Munt. London: Cassell.

Medhurst, Andy and Sally Munt, eds. 1997. *Lesbian and Gay Studies: A Critical Introduction*. London: Cassell.

Merck, Mandy, Naomi Segal and Elizabeth Wright, eds. 1998. *Coming Out of Feminism?* Oxford: Basil Blackwell.

Meyer, Moe. 1994. *The Politics and Poetics of Camp*. London: Routledge.

Moore, Suzanne. 1998. "Life's a drag and then . . ." *The Independent Features Magazine* (7 February): 28-29.

Newton, Esther. 1979. *Mother Camp: Female Impersonators in America*. Chicago: University of Chicago Press.

Simpson, Mark. 1996. *Anti-Gay*. London: Freedom Editions.

Sontag, Susan. 1969. *Against Interpretation and Other Essays*. New York: Dell.

Tassell, Colleen Van. 1997. "King for a Night." *New Haven Advocate*. Available online at *<http:/www.newhavenadvocate.com/articles/dragking.html>*. Accessed November 1999.

Thompson, Mark. 1995. "Children of Paradise: A Brief History of Queens." Pp. 447-462 in *Out in Culture: Gay, Lesbian and Queer Essays on Popular Culture*, eds. Cory Creekmur and Alexander Doty. London: Cassell.

Torr, Dianne. 1999. *Diane Torr: Drag King Ambassador to the World*. Available online at *<http://www.pipeline.com~jordinyc/torr/home.htm>*. Accessed November 1999.

Tyler, Carole-Anne. 1991. "Boys Will Be Girls: The Politics of Gay Drag." Pp. 32-70 in *Inside/Out: Lesbian Theories, Gay Theories*, ed. Diana Fuss. London: Routledge.

Volcano, Del LaGrace and Judith Halberstam. 1999. *The Drag King Book*. London: Serpent's Tail.

Waters, John. 1997. "In the Company of Drag Kings: An interview between John Waters and Mo B. Dick." Available online at *<http://www.blueperiod.com/Dreamland/dragkings.html>* (15 August). Accessed November 1999.

Williams, Frances. 1995. "Girls Who Wear Moustaches." *Independent on Sunday, Real Life Magazine* (17 September): 4.

Drag Kings "Down Under":
An Archive and Introspective
of a Few Aussie Blokes

Vicki Crowley, PhD, BEd, Dip Teach

University of South Australia

SUMMARY. The mid 1990s saw an explosion of Drag Kings in many major and smaller cities throughout the world. While documentation of this has largely occurred through publications in the USA and UK, the Internet and smaller publications have demonstrated a phenomenon that has arguably re-ignited feminist debate. In Adelaide, Australia, Ben Dover and His Beautiful Boys set the annual lesbian and gay festival alight. This chapter describes this performance to set the stage for exploration of some of the workings of 'race' and ethnicity in the creation of persona, choice of name and naming that is brought to Drag King performance. Drawing on interview material the chapter suggests that just as Drag Kings and kinging has been a useful and provocative site for closer and deeper understandings of genders, bodies and sexualities, Drag Kings and Kinging may also provide a useful site for unraveling some of the minefield that is race and racism. *[Article copies available for a fee from The Haworth Document Delivery Service: 1-800-HAWORTH. E-mail address: <docdelivery@haworthpress.com> Website: <http://www.HaworthPress.com> © 2002 by The Haworth Press, Inc. All rights reserved.]*

KEYWORDS. Drag king, female masculinity, race, identity, sexuality, performativity, queer, lesbian

[Haworth co-indexing entry note]: "Drag Kings 'Down Under': An Archive and Introspective of a Few Aussie Blokes." Crowley, Vicki. Co-published simultaneously in *Journal of Homosexuality* (Harrington Park Press, an imprint of The Haworth Press, Inc.) Vol. 43, No. 3/4, 2002, pp. 285-308; and: *The Drag King Anthology* (ed: Donna Troka, Kathleen LeBesco, and Jean Bobby Noble) Harrington Park Press, an imprint of The Haworth Press, Inc., 2002, pp. 285-308. Single or multiple copies of this article are available for a fee from The Haworth Document Delivery Service [1-800-HAWORTH, 9:00 a.m. - 5:00 p.m. (EST). E-mail address: docdelivery@haworthpress.com].

PART I:
ANTIPODEAN INDULGENCE:
AN ANTIPODEAN RECORD

Date: 23 October, 1998.

Time: 10:30 pm.

Place: Adelaide, Australia–regional city, population one million. More specifically, The Lion Arts space in the forecourt of the University of South Australia. A very crowded party space on a warm near-summer night.

Context: Opening night of *Feast*, Adelaide's annual "lesbian and gay arts and cultural festival." Palpable is the excitement and celebration of the opening event for a cultural festival significant to its varied communities, their friends, supporters and families.

Final Act: Ben Dover and His Beautiful Boys[1] (amongst themselves also sometimes affectionately referred to as "Ben and his Sixteen Sexy Boys"). The single most amassed Drag King performance in the southern, if not the northern hemisphere. With all the flourish and *panache* of theater they are–reputedly–attempting an unofficial breaking of *The Guinness Book of Records* for the most amassed Drag Kings in a single performance.[2]

The evening of free entertainment draws close to its zenith and culminates, it is thought, in the emblematic epitome of a queer life, the performance of Drag Queens. In high costume, high heels, high hair and to Drag icon Cher's "I Believe" an array of Drag Queens celebrate and perform Cher's iconicity through a delicious and queer spectre including seriously hairy Drag Queens whose appeal is to a certain benign masculinity and the conscious and political playfulness of traditional and contemporary Drag.

Then, in contrast to the glitz and glamour comes the understated overstatement–Ben Dover steps through the rainbow curtains, back to the audience and turns to the tune of Ricky Martin's "Ole, Ole, Ole." Again, through those very same rainbow curtains, step first eight Drag Kings, followed by another eight Drag Kings as the audience grows wilder and wilder in their entertainment, amusement and for some, bemusement. The audience laugh and dance more and more frenetically

as Ben and his boys strut their stuff and stroke their egos. The audience
is utterly seduced by this explosive and vertiginous admixture of the
convincing and teasingly unconvincing. There is parody and pastiche,
mimicry and impersonation. There is butchness, queerness, masculinity
and female masculinity. There is derision amid affection, identity and
identification. There is most certainly connection, and at least in part,
that connection is to the public and private desire for a re-gendered and
multi-gendered world in which the binary of male/masculinity and fe-
male/femininity loses it vice-like grip on the body. Like Drag Kings
elsewhere, there is unequivocal display and repudiation of any pure
space of bodies aligned to sex and sexuality in absolute, clear-cut ways.

I wax lyrical about the Opening Night of *Feast* and the appearance of
Ben Dover and His Beautiful Boys for a number of reasons. First, it was
an extraordinarily pleasurable, exhilarating and triumphant moment,
where for some four or so minutes the atmosphere was totally electric
and where the hit of performing to an adulating audience is hard to sur-
pass! The chances of experiencing such intense, shared public pleasure
focused on sex, sexuality and the perversity of gender are not easily
found in this deeply homophobic and racialised world. In Adelaide we
experienced and continue to experience the kind of moment Judith
Halberstam (1998) and others[3] relate and capture as wildly ecstatic engagement between audience and Drag King performers. Secondly,
somewhat cheekily and provocatively, I want to place Kinging in the
antipodes amid what is a very broad political space of the emergence of
Kinging–a political space that is not America-centric–despite my delight in, but of necessity at this time, an over-reliance on North Atlantic
literature and analysis. Thirdly, being a part of Ben Dover and His
Beautiful Boys has provided me with an exceptional opportunity to im-
merse myself in the pleasures of "research" that allows a more fluid
sense of connection between the "ivory tower," my sense of self in all
his/herselves, my commitment to disturbing and troubling practices,
and to not allowing any of my worlds to box me in. Fourthly, and perhaps most difficult and importantly, Drag Kinging has provided the
possibility to enter more deeply into some dangerous and vexed ter-
rains, namely what Paul Gilroy (2000, 14)[4] now terms "raciology"–the
idea of "race"–the brutality and inhumanity that it has wrought and the
"tacit rules governing the expectations" (Gilroy 2000, 18) of how
publics understand and mobilize "race," including contemporary sensitivities embraced by anti-racism. Put more simply–and I will return to
this below–while Kinging has been exhilarating and brilliant fun, it has
also been a site of curiosity, challenge and ambivalence. This is espe-

cially acute when I reflect on the uses of "minority masculinities" in creating persona and performance. In mobilizing the term minority masculinity, Halberstam (1998) refers to the ways in which masculinities do not appear "natural" and are Othered such as are racialized masculinities, homosexual masculinities and some working-class masculinities. The ambivalence about minority masculinity, performance and persona is nowhere more apparent than in Halberstam's awkward, though important navigations of race, class and gender.[5]

Kinging has not been uniformly embraced or celebrated in Adelaide and other Australian cities. In Sydney some performers have been booed off the stage.[6] In Adelaide there is much discussion and criticism of Kinging and any performance deemed "trans" because they are seen to equivocate around 'testosterone,' its actual and symbolic effects and meanings to feminism. Some of this criticism is from butch sympathetic, even butch-identified lesbians and is thus not necessarily part of "butch-phobia" (Volcano and Halberstam 1999). Criticism also comes in the form of aspects of the kings being offensive to men (by women on behalf of men) and to women who care for men. It is also argued that the interpretations and representations of masculinity are primarily of a tediously repetitive, crotch grabbing, scratching and stroking kind that says nothing political. In appreciating Kinging, some gay men also believe that the performances are offensive because they demean the kind of masculinity they routinely live as intentionally challenging the heterosexist excesses, display and practices of masculinism. There is much in here to be explored and argued, but it is beyond the scope of this chapter. I would note, however, that many of the objections and criticisms hinge on and return to an understanding of there being only two kinds of masculinity–good masculinity and bad masculinity and these as having an intrinsic connection to the male body. This does not mean that the issues raised should not be thoroughly dissected and examined–for me it means that they can be taken up elsewhere.

Another level of objection comes from lesbians within the academy and includes assertions that it is okay to perform as a Drag King, but not okay to make it part of a/my public and institutional research activity. Again there are many different reasons for the objection including butch-phobia, a fear and unease about the question of "lesbians just wanna be men," as well as the positivist research assumption that being a real "participant observer" in the research means a loss of objectivity. I suspect, however, that it may also be associated with my repeating Drag King Frank Lee's summation of Ben's Boys as including three academics/three PhDs in the chorus–"They must be Pretty hard Dicks," he said. I imagine that this perhaps touches a few raw nerves.

My curiosity and ambivalence, however, at times, and in some ways approximates the criticisms. Ben Dover and His Beautiful Boys could, at first reading of the opening of *Feast*, be read as almost entirely mimicking working-class men. For all intents and purposes here was yet again a group of relatively privileged, white women taking the piss out of men by drawing on reductive stereotypes and at times questionable appropriations of ethnicity. However, having been a part of the development of Ben's Beautiful Boys, I knew across many ways of knowing, that much, not little was going on. Indeed, the play, playfulness, excesses, and minimizations of rehearsals and performance generated complex discussions and debates about politics, identity and Kinging. I also knew that there were more private discussions and, as always, those interior musings and engagements with the self that mean more is going on than meets the eye. For this reason and disturbed by a repetitive inability to move into the deep fissures of the surface contestation, I approached Ben and His Boys about interviewing them for the purposes of establishing an archive and researching the tendrils of Butler's notions of performativity and the citational practices of gender (Butler 1990, 1993). Ben and His Beautiful Boys agreed that this was okay and I applied to my university for ethics clearance to proceed. In early 1999 I conducted interviews with Ben Dover and all but two of His Beautiful Boys. In these interviews I particularly pursued questions of persona, identity, identification and the meanings of gender.

Interviews do not elicit absolute "truth" or deep secrets and indeed I do not approach them with either the desire for, or expectation of, either a singular truth or an attempt to access deep psyches. I approach interviews as a means of possibly accessing worlds and realms beyond my readings and understandings and in the hope that these will push the limits of my thinking and indeed the limits of the theories, practices and issues that I deal with, teach about, and live. It is an introspective approach–one that takes my own thinking as text juxtaposed and intermingled with the ideas in play in recorded conversations. My ability to see and hear is constrained by my histories of knowing and will always be filtered through these. Interview information and transcript is always a representation. It is always a derivative re-presentation in which layers of the interviewer and writer are inescapably imposed and frame the presentation. This is, I would argue, the context of all research. Indeed every researcher and every conversationalist sees and hears through their histories of knowing–some of which may be shared, some over-lapping, but equally some histories of knowing are disparate. Approaching interviews in this way does not mean that I am inattentive to what participants have to say. It means that I can be explicit about mobilizing selected elements to expand upon issues and niggling doubts and that, hopefully, they can help open up better ways of reading, writing, understanding, and representing our worlds. The interviews included only three set questions: How do you identify? What is your everyday profession? What is your age or age group? From these we launched into conversation about becoming one of Ben's Beautiful Boys. It almost goes without saying that Ben's Beautiful Boys have much to say, insisting that I listen and go on working and performing, with an ethic of pleasure and play across an incisive and disruptive politics–especially for those that dare to see.

In what follows I briefly return to some descriptive representation of Ben Dover and His Beautiful Boys. From there I will move into some of the intimacies, intricacies and complexities of persona, the uses of minority masculinities and particularly the question of "cross-ethnic performance," alongside what I see as the willful intention of Ben Dover and His Beautiful Boys. Within this I tread some difficult territories of race, class, and gender to suggest that Kinging is tricky but its trickiness holds important opportunities for exceeding some of the stalemates and effects of raciology and in particular, ethnic absolutism and notions of discrete cultural identities.

PART II:
BACK TO THE PERFORMERS:
KINGS ON DISPLAY, KINGS IN THE HOT-SEAT

The cast:
Front Man: Ben Dover.
Chorus: Don Smallgoods, Mikki (poster boy), Michael, Eugene, Mario, Max E. Shield, (Cool Hand) Luke, Mr. Mark Up, Fabian, Tom (dropped out because of work and study commitments), Rick, Hugh G. Rection, Chip, Chuck, Prof. Anton D'Ik, Bazza, Frank Lee.

This is a group of Drag Kings that are not necessarily "beautiful boys" in terms of "gay"[7] iconicity about youthfulness, gym-toned, pierced, tattooed flesh, and exposed bodies. Indeed the performance at *Feast* in many ways masked actual bodies with loose-fitting suits, yet impressed and gestured towards the centrality of the body through choreography and theatre, the application and stylization of hair (head, face, chest, and hands in some instances). Ben was costumed in his black cape and red satin shirt, purple laser sequined cummerbund, black trousers, and flashy jewellery. The chorus was costumed in versions of the black dinner suit, white 1970s-style frilled shirts, glittery cummerbunds, gold neck chains and black shoes. Other jewellery such as bracelets, rings and watches were left for individual embellishment and each chorus member had to develop a persona for a brief cameo moment at front of stage. Notable about this front man and chorus is the effect of a mass performance of masculinities. With so much to look at and so much subtle and unsubtle variation, it is impossible to fix the gaze and fix gender in any singular way. The chorus, for instance, was manned by bear-man Mario, the suave and stylized Luke, Rick and Fabian, the utter understatement of Mikki and Michael, 'ozzie' blokes like Bazza, crooners like Eugene, sleazes like Anton, and your best mate Frank as well as your cabaret star, Ben. While it is possible for me to characterize some of the personas, the choreography was able to both build a sense of collective gender identification and seemingly to simultaneously subvert it. Individual characters slipped between the explicit and inexplicit of Australian masculinities. It is precisely the slippage between the explicit and the inexplicit that is so seductive and troubling. Ben and His Beautiful Boys make a point of being counter intuitive, of moving into something additional and other, just as the observer thinks they have a handle on what is before their eyes.[8]

In terms of identity, many of the Drag Kings identified as lesbian, some as lesbian and feminist, some rejecting feminism as a problematic and outmoded concept. There was identity as heterosexual, there was a response that refused an identificatory category without any explanation being offered, there were responses that qualified an identity and identification with things like "butch," "queer," "maybe trans," even "poofy, butchy girl" across some insistence that the categories used and available were extremely limited and limiting. This was amid an expressed desire by most for Drag King performance and practice to be seen as a political intervention as well as the expression of the more that we always are.

In terms of employment and profession, Ben and all of His Beautiful Boys were employed at the time of interview. Some have their own businesses, some are in private practice of various forms of therapy, others work in government institutions. Three were academics (Frank's PhDs—"Pretty hard Dicks" even though they may not have had such qualifications). Several of the troupe work in the arts, in theatre as directors, administrators, costumers and actors. Several have professional performance experience as actors and singers, musicians and band members. There is a DJ, school counsellor and several health workers of various kinds.

The age range is from 24 to 50 with a considerable cluster of "middle-aged men" (some of who are having a mid-life crisis, and many of whom are reinventing themselves for their own and others' amusement). Because of the age cohort, it is not surprising that many of Ben's Beautiful Boys have a long history of various forms of engagement in feminist politics and many have, at periods of time, even called themselves lesbian separatists. Everyone was committed to some form of sexual politics and to what might loosely be termed "social justice."

What stands out in this summary is an identity in sexual politics framed as a "race"/ethnicity-neutral sexuality although mention of whiteness did occur in some of the interviews. As a group we had informally discussed what Drag Kinging might mean to us in terms of genders and selves but we had not expressly broached issues of whiteness, "race," and ethnicity. Yet, everywhere, feminist and queer politics are a messy intermediary across questions of difference and the Other as "race," ethnicity, sexuality, gender and class (Mercer, 1994).[9] During rehearsals and preparations and the development of persona, including my own, I had paused to think about the degree of representativeness and forms of representation we present given that Australia is a nation of Indigenous/First Nation peoples and one of migrancy and multiculturalism across a British imperial and colonial enterprise.[10] The very act of pausing to consider the politics of our representations speaks to the ways in which "race," ethnicity and whiteness are issues in cultural and queer politics framed in the local (Adelaide and Australian) as well as global particularities, preoccupations and important concerns. These are issues that members of the troupe include in their political repertoires, yet when together failed to mention. Again, this speaks to the prevailing discursive frameworks of understanding and knowing. It also speaks to acute sensitivities and the limited ways we have of speaking about certain anxieties, wariness and awareness. Thus, at first glance, it is reasonable to ask the question: were we simply replicating the racial hierarchies and power structures of Australian and many western societies?

The troupe had come together through a published open invitation in the only local gay newspaper in Adelaide and through word of mouth. On the one hand this meant a certain degree of openness. On the other hand its dependency on word of mouth meant it relied on already established networks. Perhaps too, in the early days of establishing this troupe there existed a vulnerability about Kinging and how it would be judged as dubious in an often harsh environment of critical politics. The troupe did turn out, at least for the *Feast* performance, to have a significant cohort of a long-standing criss-crossing friendship, sporting and political networks that might be described by some, as a lack of openness. However, more difficult and nuanced questions are embedded in these issues–how were we navigating identity and identifications and what do these navigations suggest about how we, as Kings and political performers, hold, understand, and represent racial and ethnic (including white) particularities? As the troupe expanded and shifted, did the color and ethnicity of new Kings necessarily alter how these navigations operated? What are the limits of ethnic appropriation and where are lines drawn between reverence, homage, tribute, entitlement and the right to be read as approaching "cross-ethnic acts carefully?" (Volcano and Halberstam 1999, 149).

In criticizing some of the scholarship about masculinity in *Female Masculinity*, Halberstam points to queer communities as containing the "messy identifications that make up contemporary power relations around gender, race, and class" (1998, 149) and this as an ongoing problem across much of the public face of queer politics, particularly in the west.[11] Unlike US counterparts, the Adelaide lesbian scene does not have a club or pub scene "split" or segregated across color, "race" or ethnicity. For the most part this is because the pubbing and clubbing lesbian population of the city is insufficient to support more than one club or pub but does not mean that space is occupied in the same way. The public face of lesbian presence in Adelaide, however, very often continues to mirror the face of Australia's whiteness. To simply label the public face as racist would be both crude and too easy. A simple label of racist is an assertion unable to elicit the machinations of struggle that occur within, through, and under such representations and representational readings. This is not to say that racism is absent. It is, rather, to suggest a need to shift away from quick dismissal and move into a cultural practice that routinely demands deeper and trickier engagement. How can we read surface and underbelly with a critical generosity that creates a more open, caring and careful approach to the workings of oppressions? In applying this to Ben Dover and His Beautiful Boys–were there networks of practices in the development of persona that suggest that racial and ethnic identities are not near so discrete as they are read to suggest from surface and historical representations? Is there a really useful moment in Drag Kinging for redefining or sharpening our political sensibilities about our capacity to work towards freeing ourselves from what Gilroy (2000, 15) refers to as "the bonds of all raciology in a novel and ambitious abolitionist project"? How are questions of "race" and racism explored through Drag Kinging and how could they be examined differently?

Judith Halberstam raised the question of "race" in *Female Masculinity* (1998, 235) and it is further mentioned in *The Drag King Book* (1999, 140-149) and in an on-line interview between Jagose and Halberstam. Halberstam's work is positioned within a practice of queer identity and politics in which subjectivity is always-already the complex corporeal of instability—a conjunction of tensions of "race," class, gender, sexualities and representation. Halberstam draws readers into the question of "race" through interviews and analysis of Dréd and Lizerace by contrasting representations of masculinity through African-American and white Drag Kinging. Within this Halberstam found that "white drag kings" tended to perform "conventional heterosexual maleness" that seemed "to be readily available for parody." In contrast she found, "black and queer masculinities" as often performed, "in the spirit of homage and tribute rather than humor" (1998, 235). In relation to Lizerace, Halberstam writes that, "Lizerace, curiously, seems to fear being accused of trying to perform something that she is not *entitled* to and her reluctance to connect her performance to racial drag speaks to some anxiety about identity that crops up when cross-racial performances are in question" (Halberstam in Volcano and Halberstam 1999, 145, emphasis added). Halberstam goes on to write that "Obviously cross-ethnic performances raise specific issues about race and authenticity for kings" (1999, 145). Several things strike me about the attention that Halberstam gives to this issue. First, she appreciates the salience of "race" and many lesbian scenes as very segregated. Secondly, the comparative attention given to white masculinities and black and queer masculinities points to tensions that deserve scrutiny. Across these, Halberstam asserts an "obviousness" about the tensions and entitlement that does not do justice to the complexities that are intimated through the uneven application of descriptors such as "curiously" to Lizerace. The positioning of the issues, however, opens up a site of complexity that is deserving of the attention that Halberstam can be read to argue for. The emergence of persona and naming practices of Ben Dover and His Beautiful Boys provides an intriguing site for examining some of the nuance, convolutions and difficulties involved in traversing "race," ethnicity, whiteness and entitled representation in Drag Kinging.

WHO IS THAT (!) AND WHAT'S 'IS NAME?
GETTING CLOSE TO THE TRICKY BUSINESS OF PERSONA,
AFFILIATIONS, AND THE QUESTION OF RACE

After donning some facial hair at our first rehearsal we went onto the stage and were asked to select a name, walk around and introduce ourselves. This meant, unless already pre-planned or pre-known, that the choice of Drag King name was "off the cuff." The two Vicki's, for instance, had a discussion about being Victor–a name that neither ended up using for Kinging, but one that sprung to mind through the gender binary and masculinizing of femininized names. The practices of name and naming are critical to gender. In Kinging name and naming is also significant. If we return to Derrida's (1995) notion of the performative as those kinds of lawful and powerful institutional practices such as sentencing, baptism, conferral, then names and naming can be seen to be at the very heart of the making and maintaining of gender. Being named and called a name is also one of the conditions by which a subject is constituted in language. Names such as Elvis Herselvis, Justin Case, Pencil Case, Mo B. Dick, Ben Dover (USA and AUS), Lizerace, The Downe Brothers, Dréd, Murray Hill, Jesus Wept, Jack, Harry, Vinnie, Don, Luke, Pedro, Mario, and Roger That demonstrate that Drag King names theatricalize, suggest, overstate, understate, assert, signify and mask certain kinds of masculinities within particular cultural contexts. In the comedic–names parody. They demand recognition. They claim space and they defy absolutes.

The name in Drag Kinging becomes an evocation around which certain practices can be hinged. As a hinge names signal not mere replication or secure attachment, but enable a pivotal practice and are perhaps a fulcrum around which actions, intimations, accuracies and inaccuracies can move and be mobilized in the performance of drag. When Drag Kings' names are read or uttered–they invoke and evoke a series of possibilities including certain cultural locations that are at once perhaps historical as well as contemporary. A Bazza is or a Mickey (Mikki) might both be understood as in part the Australian tradition of abbreviation, a matey, mateship thing. They may be 'nick-names' and nick-names can be and are a means of supplanting the authority of a conferred full-name–they mediate relationships. Sometimes an abbreviation such as Vick for Vicki can be an equalizer, an attempt to enter a more familiar space and relationship, but it is always to position. The person who applies the nick-name sets in train a chain of relational responses some of which may be desired and others not. Nick-naming, too, is more often than not a practice among blokes, men, fathers to sons and tom-boys. Abbreviating or nick-naming can be an affectionate transferral. Nick-names and abbreviations, however, are rarely nominated or initiated by the addressed or named. Names and naming mediate social and cultural context. In Drag Kinging there is often an intentional overstatement, an explicit emphasizing of certain masculinities. The names also provide a means of access to persona and it is in here that affiliative, associative and cultural webs of meaning dance around the delicate (for important and problematic reasons) issues of representation and the tricky business of "race."

At surface and to an Australian audience the names of Ben and His Beautiful Boys can be read racially. In the Australian context, Fabian, Anton, Chip, Chuck, Bazza and perhaps Mickey and Don Smallgoods[12] can be heard to connote national and ethnic identities that are "non-Australian," whereas names such as Michael, Luke, Max and Ben remain relatively "race"-neutral and are more likely to signal a naturalized white Australian middle-class masculinity. Bazza, however, connotes a working-class Australian, and to an Australian audience, Chip and Chuck are likely to connote North American (USA) identities. The names Fabian and Anton signal the possibility of European identity read in Australian contemporary terms and racial trajectories as ethnicity ("Australian" not being an ethnicity in national racial politics or in the Australian racial imaginary). Such are the racial formations in Australia that none of the Drag King names would be read by Indigenous or non-Indigenous Australians as connoting Indigeneity. The absence of Indigenous performers in this troupe would, at first glance, go unnoticed by many, but certainly not all.[13]

Names resonate with affect and effect and as Judith Halberstam importantly points out, it is through minority masculinities that masculinity is denaturalized and becomes visibly performative, performed and performable. Names can assist in this process but they are drawn from circuits of meanings that are always-already gendered, raced and classed in particular ways. Drag Kings, however, do not just appear or perform as names on a blank sheet, though clearly names may appear on fliers and billboards and are intended to be provocative signifiers that appeal to cultural imaginaries and a queer sensibility. Yet Drag Kings are an amalgam of designed and desired persona. Names are meaningful and chosen names and stage names become something malleable, something able to be sculpted and remodelled. Names and their collaborations with invented and imitated masculinities are matrices of exchange. "Race" is part of those matrices and exchange. A few selective examples from Ben's Beautiful Boys illustrates just how uneven and unstable is the position of "race" within matrices of exchange particularly in a highly charged politics of identity and anti-racism.

Chip chose his name because he was trying for something, "very American that was somehow related to my 'real' identity in some way." The name Chip clearly had cultural specificity and in describing the persona,[14] Julia talked about Chip as being more "elegant" than "doofussy or geeky." The name was also chosen to press into the ambivalence that Julia at times experiences from Australians about being an American from New York in Australia. In an Australian context Chip's American-ness is a minority masculinity, one that is noticed and observed across difference. For Julia, it is linked to lived experience and is a site able to be mined for performability. Despite it being a minority masculinity and Other than Australian, it is for the most part a masculinity that is sufficiently outside the cultural imaginary of "Australian," but not so far so as to be positioned as Other in an Australian racial imaginary. Arguably, whiteness is such that it tempers Otherness. Amid the banter and jokes of Ben's Beautiful Boys, Chip's American-ness was a site for teasing and stereotyping but was not sufficient to be problematic in a field of representation, not sufficient for Ben's Beautiful Boys to read as being "representative" in anti-racism and social justice terms.

Vicki selected the name Fabian after a client she works with in part because "his name really suited him," in part because, "he is really gorgeous" and in part because, as Vicki says:

> I've always sort of quite fancied a name that didn't have a last name like Fabian the actor from the 60s . . . it was a bit of a good gay boy's name that wasn't too effeminate but also wasn't totally butch . . . I wanted to be a bit fluid if I wanted to–depending on what I did with Fabian.

Drag King persona is drawn from many elements and arenas of knowing. Drawing on Fabian the actor, his larger than life smoothness and screen fame combine to diminish the "race" content and to set the persona/performance outside of the highly charged readings of "race" as racism. This is in part because the fame of a screen identity is elevated beyond "the real" to the realms of the fictive and imaginary. Yet the masculinity of Fabian the actor in the 1960s has very clear "racial"/ethnic resonance and connection. Indeed Fabian's appeal to women was the evocation of a smouldering, "Latin," sexuality Other to the repressive, undemonstrative, masculinities of wholesome, predictable, white husband types. With the absence in Australia of a latina/o political presence and consciousness, Fabian is a name of erotic-exotic possibility relatively safely positioned as unproblematic in the politics of the Australian racial imaginary and the racial realms of anti-racism.

Also importantly evident in Vicki's description is the issue of drag as an actively fashioned and created practice. The performed persona of Fabian depended on, "what I did with Fabian." Thus, performance may accentuate or minimize histories and selected elements. It is the performance attenuated in some instances to a name that may bring name and persona into the arena of racism. What I want to emphasize here is that racial formations and trajectories are present regardless of their apparentness. In some ways this is so obvious as to be near meaningless. What it can importantly point to is, however, the narrow and selective ways in which racism is popularly understood. Ironically it is the very hybridity of Drag Kinging and its ability to draw on the subsurface matrices of exchange that makes it so seductive and exciting. What is refused and repudiated continues to determine the subject.

Within Ben Dover's Beautiful Boys, ethnicity is worked in terms of identity, identification and persona along two other trajectories. Firstly, across ethnicity as a category and identity recognized in Australian racial formations as ethnicity and where there is seemingly equivalence between body, culture and ethnicity. Secondly, where ethnicity appears as an appropriation and lack of entitlement in terms of an absence of alignment between body, culture and identity–where Australian is not an ethnicity but the natural Australian.

Eugene and Michael fall into the first trajectory. Eugene selected his name as the masculine form of Eugenia. Jenny describes her selection of name and persona in terms of, "That's my name, my name's actually Eugenia in Spanish so I thought that I'd use the male version. My own name is short for Eugenia." The persona, however, is not necessarily connected with ethnicity as Spanish and as Other might be read in Australia's racial and ethnic typologies. Eugene is "definitely blokey, very macho, a bit of a Stewart Granger, a bit of a swashbuckler, and he definitely goes for the girls rather than the boys." In developing Eugene's walk and mannerisms, Jenny talked about the men in her family, her and her father's way of walking. In developing Eugene's persona, however, Jenny talked more about observing men in general and very closely to develop posture and mannerism. In this instance Jenny calls on a repertoire of affiliations and observations. From Jenny's description and Eugene's performance, Eugene takes on no ethnicity that is apparent through Australian constructions of ethnicity yet he is drawn from minority masculinities–ethnicity, matinee idols, lived actualities and observation.

Unlike Eugene, Michael's persona does not draw on Michelle's Dutch identity and heritage. In the interviews Michelle mentioned that she had noticed the use of ethnicity in the performance of certain drag king personas and masculinities. More striking to Michelle, however, was the class factor. It was striking to her because of the highly developed persona of Michael who is part of an elaborate story of city life. Michelle says of Michael:

> He is probably the Australian equivalent of some English upper class type of ex-Eton schoolboy type of thing but just cruises around. He has a lot of contacts though I am not quite sure though what he does for money. . . . He has got a dark blue latest model Volvo. It's a bit of conservatism coming out of him . . . Michael is not a working class bloke at all. He probably has a Masters in English or something or maybe some politics or something like that. He's very knowledgeable in the arts and literature I think. And yes, he is a musician (he plays the piano and it is a very good piano). It's in his house–he is very proud of it–it's in a special music room. Unlike the person who performs Michael, he is Anglo-Australian.

Michael and Eugene are Drag personas drawn from a range of personal experiences, including an ethnicity that is in some ways Otherized in Australian racial politics. The personas are also exaggerations and fictive extensions of self. Where Eugene through name draws on ethnicity as self, Michael also masculinizes Michelle's name but performs an ethnicity that Michelle is not an appropriation that does not draw particular attention within the popular discourses of anti-racism. The apparently clear relationship between actor and Drag King in the workings of ethnicity and identity in these instances is unlikely to be disturbing in the politics of representation and racism–especially a politics of ethnicity as absolutely belonging to particular bodies.

In contrast to Eugene and Michael and along the second trajectory are Anton and Mario, both of whom are explained in terms of affiliations with ethnicity that is not embodied, in 'ethnic identity' terms by either Vicki or Ellen. Like Michael, both Mario and Anton have highly narrativized personas. Mario is the proprietor of an Adult Only Book Shop. He is described as having "started his life as a travelling salesman. He was such a novelty with his female clients he decided to introduce them to a range of specialty marital accessories . . . Mario . . . has been accustomed to dealing predominantly with lonely women."

When interviewed Ellen worked through the affiliations and associations that helped bring Mario into view. Ellen talked about the times she had as a teenager with one of her brothers and his friend Mario which were "remembered as fabulous times." In explaining this and when asked about questions of ethnicity, Ellen paused to consider that some people might read her borrowing from her friendship with her brother's friend Mario to be problematic. Yet the man that is Mario is a flamboyant, jovial, larger than life *bon vivant*. His connection with Ellen's adolescence and her friend Mario's Italianness is a point of referral–the remembering of an experience with a male that was particularly fun. Use of Mario in developing persona falls within Halberstam's understandings of minority masculinities. Mario's appearance is not a naturalized white Australian masculinity. His ginger whiskers, and generally hirsute appearance echo masculinities that have been the site of white racism in Australia. In terms of questions of ethnicity attenuated to authenticity, Mario presents a challenge. In some ways he may be read to represent a visual stereotype yet the affection and the utter charm in which he is performed present a congruity that destabilizes the visual stereotype. Indeed, arguably, the performance of Mario brings the incongruity of stereotype into open purview. In this way Drag Kings are also able to bring the discourses of racism and an anti-racism built on notions of authenticity and ethnic absolutism to center stage. Given the prevalence of notions of authenticity and ethnic absolutism in anti-racism discourses, it would not be surprising or curious that a Drag King such as Mario might display some unease about persona and performance.

Perhaps most deliberate and potentially contentious of all Ben's Beautiful Boys is the Drag King persona, Anton. He is

a Drag King that developed in part through conversations with friends. The name Anton, however, was chosen after a childhood neighbor who was a source of curiosity in outer urban, 50s Melbourne. Anton and his wife, Annie, were WW2 Dutch migrants. Their household was an endless source of difference, the children were 'wild', there was always fun and action–we slept over in their backyard in an old army tent that was put up for the kids to have a holiday in. I remember Anton as a small, fiery, witty, energetic and generous man who, despite working hard and being terribly busy, always had time to say hello. Drag King Anton needed to be a small man and

I wanted him to be from parts of my past that do not often get an airing. The persona of Anton is, however, also drawn on affections and affiliations for my former Sicilian husband and his family.

The highly narrativized story of Anton positions him as being from Dutch-Sicilian heritage–an unlikely combination in the Australian racial imaginary. His mother worked in WW2 resistance and Anton is the product of an affair with a Sicilian anti-fascist also working on the resistance lines. Anton does not know his father and his mother has never seen Anton's father since her affair with him. Anton actually lives in another city (Melbourne) where he is a visiting academic with a keen interest in observing his research assistants. Arguably this story is an elaboration made possible through the fantasmatic that is a characteristic contour of the western cultural enterprise of Othering. Within racism understood as authenticity, absolutism and congruity between heritage and body, Anton is deeply problematic. Within identity and persona understood as hybrid, engaged, borrowed, appropriated and performative, Anton may be both less and more troubling. He may be less troubling where lines of identity and identification are considered able to be transversed. He is more troubling when rigidity and purities are seen to be destabilized in ways that we are yet to create a language for.

Through the issues of name and naming, issues of identity as "ethnicity," through questions of authenticity, memory, appropriation and affiliation I have attempted to approach the issue of entitlement in performance that Drag Kinging enters into in terms of "race" and racism. The question of appropriation and racism, and therefore entitlement is curiously positioned in Drag King performance. After Butler and in rejection of the gender binary masculinity is not and cannot be considered the sole province of the male body. If as Halberstam argues there are female masculinities then there are ways of being that defy binaries and exemplify fluidity. Given that there is no such thing as "race," only the effects of "race,"[15] is it possible that there are ways of being that defy binaries and exemplify fluidity across the constructed categories of "race," ethnicity, nation and nationality? How and in what circumstances is the defiance of ethnic absolutism and a practice of fluidity available to Drag King performance?

Travelling across the issues of name and persona, minority masculinities, performance and explanation through an onstage performance and the behind-the-curtains musings and thinking is an attempt to hold onto the delights and pleasures of Drag Kinging. It is also to travel across the machinations that constitute the politics of "race" and anti-racism in local and perhaps some global contexts. Ben Dover and His Beautiful Boys are "Ozzie Blokes" in as much as they come into being through Australian cultural contexts.[16] The question of "race" and racism will continue to be a part of the politics and performance of queer/kweer,[17] lesbian gay, intersex, transgender and transsexual identity practices. If, however, we agree that there is no "race," only the effects of "race": naturalization and denaturalization, it stands that Drag Kinging emerges within the practices of naturalization and denaturalization. It will also stand that the shape and shaping of the kings will be within prevailing discursive possibilities and political actualities. What I want to emphasize is the instability of categories and that the practices of Drag Kinging are ambiguous. They are ambivalently situated in the available yet vexed possibilities. I am also wanting to insist that Drag Kinging provides a possibility for a more nuanced and careful reading of "race" and the processes of naturalization and denaturalization. Like Drag Kings all over, Ben and His Beautiful Boys illustrate the absurdities of gender and, while there are no parallels between the forms and practices of oppression, they demonstrate contingent, context bound specificities.

CONCLUSION

Drag Kinging is about performer, performance, performativity and performability. It is about theatre, excess and politics. Without exception, a sense of abiding affection and connection with masculinities runs across conversations, in-person and on-line interviews I have had with US, Canadian and Australian Drag Kings–every Drag King at some point reflected on their family and the men within them in affectionate, affiliative and connected ways. Access to Kinging, at least in some small part, comes from within repertoires of connection and bonding. I'd suggest that these affiliative repertoires of connection do not work in binary ways be they "race," class or gender. If new masculinities are being formed across genders being understood as the province of no particular bodies, then these masculinities must also be understood as outside of ethnic and "race" purities. What precisely this means in Kinging and Drag King performance is an open question, especially if we understand identity as produced "within, not outside of representation" (Hall, 1997). While moments of bonding, affiliative connection and mutual love do not mean that we experience or know what is discursively and culturally overlaid as Other, as if we were ourself to be the Other, it does mean that we know in inflected and complicated ways. While this does not give us necessary insight or provide a guarantee of consideration, it can point to the limitations and limits of the ways in which we routinely practice our understandings and politics of Othering. Perhaps most of all it contributes to identity as flux and flow constituted by myriad complexities that are beyond singularities. It is too easy to read certain kinds of "raced," sex-gendering and classed bodies as more likely to hold truth and virtue than are others because of their histories of oppression. It is too easy to dismiss beyond exploration certain kinds of reluctance as problematic in "known" ways as, after-all, problematics also have their histories.

What I hope to have opened up through the use of names and persona is the deeply ambiguous, delicious and ambivalent movement that takes place in creating and mobilizing persona. I do not want in any way to suggest any position or practice is more or less virtuous or soundly situated than others. I particularly do not want to diminish experience, affiliations, connections and loves that are part of the self that is brought into Kinging and Drag Kinging as an expression of deep, abiding pride and self-love, and is I think, manifest in a desire for connection in Drag King performance. Nor do I want to diminish the practices of reverence, recognition and remembrance that occur through sometimes particular and significant histories of cultural expression and celebration. The workings of "race," its contemporary practices in racialization are everywhere uneven. There is no ease of reading or natural flow of reading performance locally or transnationally. Kinging in Drag Kings is theatre, and theatre–like carnival–provides myriad possibilities for drawing attention to the practices of oppression through exaggeration and appropriation, respect and homage. It does take some skill to navigate these delicate, risky and complicated paths and we ought not to blithely accept all venturing into the vexed domains of minority masculinities as a useful political intervention. But, I think, I believe, that Drag King performance holds delightful prospects for inching towards better kinds of worlds that celebrate intimacies, intricacies, idiosyncrasies, complexities and a willful desire to bring about the end of normalcy, homophobia, racism and poverty. I have to say it, "Long Live the Kings!"

ACKNOWLEDGMENTS

With adoration and gratitude to Ben and all His Beautiful Boys listed above and to Catherine, Helen, Mystery, Sally, Jenny, Michelle, Fiona, Ellen, Julia, Susan, Michelle, Vicki, Barbara, Ollie, Kylie, Fiona, Jaye, and Karen. The author would also like to record the inspiration and joy that comes in particular from Catherine and Ben,

Helen and Frank, Eugene and Jenny, Mario and Ellen, Chip and Julia, Tom–though she rarely sees him–and Susan, as well as to newer Kings and mates, Jesus Wept and MayLou, and Mack, Pedro and Kate. Special thanks also goes to Julie Mariko Matthews for comments and editing and to her fabulous family for providing the resting and reading space that meant the author could get to write this paper. Most of all she wants to mention the loves of most of her lives, the to-die-for Fiona and the simply gorgeous Mikki. (And a special smooch for Lilian Crowley and Georgie Ryan-Crowley who make up their intimate family, . . . and a thistle for Bob who lives outside but is also a great little crooner.) None of these people is in any way responsible for the content of this paper–a paper that in no manner represents or attempts to represent their views. The controversy, limitations and errors in thinking are entirely the author's and her responsibility.

This paper is developed from "Exceeding Femininities: The citational practices of gender and performativity in the body politic" presented in The Body Seminar, Hawke Institute, University of South Australia (8 July, 1999) and presented at the University of London (August, 1999) and Mount Saint Vincent University, Halifax, Nova Scotia (September, 1999).

NOTES

1. The opening night performance was followed by an appearance of the same song/act at the *Vitalstatistix* fundraising night and later performances at Queer Lounge at the *Cargo Club* and at the *Nexus Club* for the *Queer Collaborations*, the 1999 *Feast* Pool Party at "Mega Drag," a night of drag performances at the Adelaide Festival Theatre. Unlike counterparts in London, San Francisco and New York, Drag Kinging in Adelaide has not emerged in clubs or Drag King competitions. The phenomenon of Drag Kinging has, however, continued to grow in Adelaide. Drag Kings now appear at fund-raisers, special events, and clubs. Some of Ben's Beautiful Boys have appeared in solo and duet performances and some have birthed a new group–The Queers Boys of Quebec. The line-up of Ben's Beautiful Boys has also included Troy, Roger That, Mack and Pedro. Phil Anderer regularly appears at events and venues around Adelaide and recently appeared in a duet with Drag Queen Shimmer Chernobyl (a DQ who has from the outset taken a keen interest in Drag Kings). Likewise the Downe Brothers recently performed and various Elvises have materialized at various events. Blak Elvis, an Indigenous singer-guitarist also performed in Adelaide but as an Indigenous artist, not as a Drag King. Drag King workshops are run in Adelaide by DJ and Drag King and sometimes trans identified, Del Barzac. Drag Kings were the subject of papers presented at the National Union of Students *Queer Collaborations* conference in July 1999 and earlier this year, the Adelaide University Pride Group brought together a panel of Drag Kings and Drag Queens to discuss the issue of the political status and meaning of drag. The discussion grew out of tensions surrounding the appearance and performance of some Drag Queens in Orientation Week. Drag is alive and thriving in Adelaide. While the Drag Queens across Australia have long engaged in issues, questions, associations and affiliations with MTF, trans issues and identities, unlike the major east coast cities of Sydney and Melbourne, FTM remains a relatively muted and moot point in Adelaide.

2. Ben has previously appeared on several occasions as a stand alone Adelaide Drag act and it was Catherine Fitzgerald (a.k.a. Ben Dover) who wanted to present

Drag Kings *en masse*. Very loosely the idea grew out of Ben's own history, conversations with Margie Fischer, a meeting to see if there was interest, an afternoon workshop that got straight into the hair thing, a series of rehearsals where the performance was worked out and up to the appearance at *Feast*.

3. Personal communication Mo B. Dick and Lizerace and seen for instance in Websites in the USA such as *Fast Friday Productions, Club Casanova, Lizerace* and in various popular lesbian press.

4. I cannot do justice to the significant work on analyzing the uses and practices of "race" that Paul Gilroy has developed over the past two decades. His work is significant in that it charts a meticulous path through the emergence and effects of racial typologies, its historical mobilizations and alignments including contemporary appeals to essentialized identities particularly as they relate to the North Atlantic (see for instance, *There Ain't No Black in the Union Jack* (1987), *Small Acts* (1993), *The Black Atlantic* (1993), *Between Camps* (2000) and his work on anti-racism, particularly, "The end of antiracism" (1992). In *Between Camps* Gilroy argues that we face a significant opportunity to move towards a practice and positions able "to free ourselves from the bonds of all raciology in a novel and ambitious abolitionist project" (2000, 15). I take his project to include engaging with the slippery practices of popular, emergent, and intentionally transgressive cultures, which now includes Kinging and Drag Kinging.

5. See also Volcano and Halberstam, *The Drag King Book* and Jagose, Web Site, <http://www.gender.org/g29/g29_halberstam.html> "Masculinity without men. Annamarie Jagose interviews Judith Halberstam about her latest book, *Female Masculinity*."

6. I am not precisely sure why this is so. One article in a Sydney magazine described a performance as tasteless dick jokes and revelling in jock culture. Of interest to me was the issue of forms of masculinity being performed especially as some of the women adopted ethnicities other than their own–an element that was bypassed in the reporter's analysis, perhaps either escaping her view or being too sensitive an issue to mention.

7. Here I use "gay" to include a local vernacular sense of "gay" that includes "gay ladies," camp scenes, gay men and some gay clubs (limited though the latter are in Adelaide). As elsewhere, terms of identification and for identifying are continuously contested, treasured, asserted as absolute and/or in a state of flux. Elsewhere I use queer as an intentionally open and fluid recognition of multiple, shifting, inventive identifications and identities that include for instance current debates about trans, transsexual, transgender, xxy, intersex, the "nature of drag" and developing the notion of "a queer sensibility."

8. This is where I most clearly depart from the importance of, or necessity for, new identity categories such as those developed by Halberstam in *Female Masculinity*. While some of Ben's Boys would agree with Halberstam's argument for the importance of creating new categories, I remain unconvinced by her argument. I am more persuaded by arguments that categories and typologies are technologies of surveillance–a point interestingly not pursued by Jagose in her interview with Halberstam (Web Site, <http://www.gender.org/g29/g29_halberstam.html>.) I would also want to persist in arguing that while certain singularities may be evidenced in the performances of Ben and His Beautiful Boys, they are also simultaneously subverted through the deliberate and readable layering and shifting into and across diverse masculinities that defy categorization or conversely can only be categorized when complexity is refused.

9. Mercer, "Skin head sex thing: Racial difference and the homoerotic imaginary," 172-220. See also Hammonds, "Black (w)holes and the geometry of black female sex-

uality," 136-156, Samuels, "Dangerous liaisons: Queer subjectivity, liberalism and race," 91-109, and Zhou Xiaojing, "Web Site," "Denaturalizing identities, decolonising desire: Videos by Richard Fung."

10. As is abundantly evident in literatures on racialization and racism, the language and languag-ing shift. This "shiftingness" demonstrates the importance of Omi and Winant's (1986) notions of trajectories, racialization and racial formations. The language and categorization of "race"/ethnicity/Indigeneity in Australia occurs across local and global practices. Language and categories used in Australia such as "ethnic" are elsewhere held to be racist in a way that is often not read as problematic in Australia. This does not mean that local terminology that shortcuts racial formations is "race" neutral; it means for the purposes of this paper that categories and typologies have shifting meanings.

11. It is important to note here that the issues raised by and through Halberstam's work are more complicated and intricate than I am able to do justice to in this particular chapter. I am currently working on a paper, "Performer, performance, performativity, performability: Drag Kings and the question of 'race' " in an attempt to unpack and examine the issues in greater depth.

12. In Australia "small goods" (salami, cheese, pickles, etc.) are often prefaced by, or equated with, the word 'Continental' which in post-war Australia was also a term used to signify 'new-Australian,' 'European,' 'foreigner,' 'migrant,' Other.

13. Where the highlight of the 1998 *Feast* Opening Party was the Drag Kings, the highlight of 1999 was another absolute blast and first, a mass performance of Indigenous Drag Queens, *Sista Girls*, who came from all over Australia to perform together. They too sent the audience into frenzied celebration.

14. I interviewed performers about their Drag King. The interview data is reported as "she" to indicate that I did not interview Drag Kings to whom I refer as "he." Other authors in this collection note the extensiveness and importance of debates about the use of the personal pronoun in queer politics and drag kinging. See Pauliny in this volume, "Erotic Arguments and Persuasive Acts: Discourses of Desire and the Rhetoric of Female-to-Male Drag."

15. I make this statement on the basis of "race" having symbolic currency based on historical exigencies and practices rather than having any "scientific," physiological, biological, gene-oriented basis. "Race" and race-thinking are as Gilroy states, "destructive patterns that were established when the rational absurdity of 'race' was elevated into an essential concept and endowed a unique power to both determine history and explain its selective unfolding" (2000, 14). Such a framework means that it is historical and contemporary practices attenuated to "race" and the effects of its emergence and re-emergence that are of ongoing critical concern. The naturalization of its facticity is one such effect.

16. I have a far from complete sense of Drag Kings performances and Kinging in Australia, but faithful to Sydney Mardi Gras style, Drag Kings appeared *en masse* as LAPD and as George Michaels. Like elsewhere, Kinging in Australia is galvanized by and galvanizes popular culture and especially screen and popular culture.

17. Kweer is the preferred spelling of many Australian Indigenous peoples, see for instance Rea and Brook Andrew, *Blak Bebe(z) & Kweer Kat(z).*

REFERENCES

Butler, Judith. 1990. *Gender Trouble: Feminism and the subversion of identity.* New York: Routledge.

———. 1993. *Bodies That Matter: On the discursive limits of sex.* New York: Routledge.

Club Casanova. Available online at *<http://www.users.nyc.pipeline.com/~jordinyc/ccnews01/dn970220a.htm>*.

Derrida, Jacques. 1995. *On the Name.* Thomas Dutoit, ed. Stanford: Stanford University Press.

Fast Friday Productions. *DragDom.* Available online at *<http://members.tripod.com/~fastfriday/show.html>*.

Gilroy, Paul. 2000. *Between Camps: Nations, cultures and the allure of race.* London: Allen Lane/The Penguin Press.

——— 1993. *Small Acts: Thoughts on the politics of black cultures.* London: Serpent's Tail.

——— 1993. *The Black Atlantic: Modernity and double consciousness.* Cambridge, Mass.: Harvard University Press.

——— 1992. "The end of antiracism." Pp. 49-61 in *Race, Culture and Difference*, eds. J. Donald and A. Rattansi. London: Sage.

——— 1987. *There Ain't No Black in the Union Jack.* London: Hutchinson.

Halberstam, Judith. 1998. *Female Masculinity.* Durham: Duke University Press.

———. "Mackdaddy, Superfly, Rapper: Gender, race and the Drag King scene." *Social Text* 52-53 (1997 fall/winter): 104-132.

Hall, Stuart. 1997. "Old and New Identities, Old and New Ethnicities." Pp. 41-68 in *Culture, Globalization and the World System*, ed. Anthony D. King. Minneapolis: University of Minnesota Press.

Hammonds, Evelyn. 1997. "Black (W)holes and the Geometry of Black Female Sexuality." Pp. 136-156 in *Feminism Meets Queer Theory*, eds. E. Weed and N. Schor. Bloomington & Indianapolis: Indiana University Press.

Jagose, Annamarie. 1999. "Masculinity without men. Annamarie Jagose interviews Judith Halberstam about her latest book, *Female Masculinity*." Available online at *<http://www.genders.org/g29/g29halberstam.html>*.

Lizerace. Available online at *<www.lizerace.com >*.

Mercer, Kobena. 1994. "Skin Head Sex Thing: Racial Difference and the Homoerotic Imaginary." Pp. 171-220 in *Welcome to the Jungle.* New York & London: Routledge.

Morrison, Toni. 1992. *Playing in the Dark.* Cambridge: Harvard University Press.

Newton, Esther. 1996. "Dick(less) Tracy and the Homecoming Queen: Lesbian Power and Representation in Gay Male Cherry Grove." Pp.162-93 in *Inventing Lesbian Cultures*, ed. E. Lewin. Boston: Beacon Press.

Omi, Michael, and Howard Winant. 1986. *Racial Formations in the United States: From the 1960s to the 1980s.* New York & London: Routledge.

Rea and Brook Andrew. 1998. *Blak Bebe(z) & Kweer Kat(z).* Exhibition at Gitte Weise Gallery, 12 February-7 March and as part of the 1998 Sydney Gay and Lesbian

Mardi Gras Festival Catalogue produced by Boomali Aboriginal Artists Co-operative, Chippendale, New South Wales.

Samuels, Jacinth. 1999. "Dangerous Liaisons: Queer Subjectivity, Liberalism and Race." *Cultural Studies* 13 (1): 91-109.

Searle, John. 1968. *Speech Acts: An essay on the philosophy of language.* Cambridge: Cambridge University Press.

Volcano, Del La Grace and Judith "Jack" Halberstam. 1999. *The Drag King Book.* London: Serpent's Tail.

Zhou Xiaojing. Denaturalizing Identities, Decolonizing Desire: Videos by Richard Fung. Vol. 4, No 3. 2000. Available online at <*http://social.chass.nscu.edu/jouvert/v4i3/zhou.htm*>.

PICTURE THIS:
KING PHOTOS

Personae

Pierre Dalpé

"Julien, Colleen & Mary"

[Haworth co-indexing entry note]: "Personae." Dalpé, Pierre. Co-published simultaneously in *Journal of Homosexuality* (Harrington Park Press, an imprint of The Haworth Press, Inc.) Vol. 43, No. 3/4, 2002, pp. 311-315; and: *The Drag King Anthology* (ed: Donna Troka, Kathleen LeBesco, and Jean Bobby Noble) Harrington Park Press, an imprint of The Haworth Press, Inc., 2002, pp. 311-315. Single or multiple copies of this article are available for a fee from The Haworth Document Delivery Service [1-800-HAWORTH, 9:00 a.m. - 5:00 p.m. (EST). E-mail address: docdelivery@haworthpress.com].

"Erika and Frederic"

"Saul, Sarah and Johanne"

"Tony, Andrea and Zack"

CLOTHES MINDED
photos par
PIERRE DALPÉ

du 18 septembre au 12 octobre 1997

vernissage
samedi le 20 septembre à 19:00

G A L E R I E   P I N K
1456 rue Notre Dame O., Montréal QC H3C 1K9
(514) 935-9851
jeudi au dimanche 13h à 17h
www.total.net/~anaka/clothes.minded

diptyque: *Julie and Colleen*, 1996

Ephemera (postcard)

Eugene Does His Nails

Stephanie Rogerson

[Haworth co-indexing entry note]: "Eugene Does His Nails." Rogerson, Stephanie. Co-published simultaneously in *Journal of Homosexuality* (Harrington Park Press, an imprint of The Haworth Press, Inc.) Vol. 43,
No. 3/4, 2002, pp. 317-318; and: *The Drag King Anthology* (ed: Donna Troka, Kathleen LeBesco, and Jean
Bobby Noble) Harrington Park Press, an imprint of The Haworth Press, Inc., 2002, pp. 317-318. Single or
multiple copies of this article are available for a fee from The Haworth Document Delivery Service
[1-800-HAWORTH, 9:00 a.m. - 5:00 p.m. (EST). E-mail address: docdelivery@haworthpress.com].

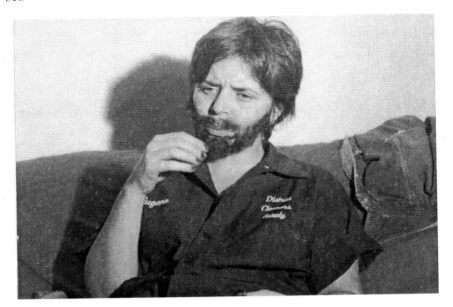

Autoportrait

Aaron Kimberly, BFA

[Haworth co-indexing entry note]: "Autoportrait." Kimberly, Aaron. Co-published simultaneously in *Journal of Homosexuality* (Harrington Park Press, an imprint of The Haworth Press, Inc.) Vol. 43, No. 3/4, 2002, pp. 319-320; and: *The Drag King Anthology* (ed: Donna Troka, Kathleen LeBesco, and Jean Bobby Noble) Harrington Park Press, an imprint of The Haworth Press, Inc., 2002, pp. 319-320. Single or multiple copies of this article are available for a fee from The Haworth Document Delivery Service [1-800-HAWORTH, 9:00 a.m. - 5:00 p.m. (EST). E-mail address: docdelivery@haworthpress.com].

Drag King Workshop Advertisement

Tania Hammidi

University of California, Irvine

The Drag King Workshop in Davis came out of my desire, as a student and later community member, to have a space in which to do drag, improve on drag, share resources, and have some bona fide fun. Davis has a seven-year recorded history of drag: the annual "Davis Is Burning" ball put on by the gay male fraternity. It features largely queens, but in the last few years has had a growing number of kings. I've been doing drag in Davis almost ten years, and "walked" in those Balls. They have been, of course, Queen style; in terms of context, prize (I got the Silver High Heel Award for second place. No silver boot), and style.

These experiences made me question what lesbian camp and lesbian or drag king Balls would look like. And to add, I was getting lonely, bored, and in great desire of creative compatriots for drag.

Davis has a strong lesbian community. A local net list boasts over 250 lesbian-identified women in Yolo County. Looking around town, like any community, a newcomer can't find the lesbians; but upon closer look we are everywhere. It's a town filled with dykes. Lots of room for drag and other lesbian camp. And yet, we didn't have much. So, this class was an attempt to find the dykes.

I've done a number of classes in Davis: shorter ones for the local list, evening slide show on drag in the bisexual café; they appeal usually to college students, usually 10-15 come. The Davis dykes workshop had about twenty in total. The six-week class had four. I have, following, had women come up to me saying, "I wanted to attend, but didn't."

There's an interest in drag kinging here. We just had the Ball, and I heard there were a fair number of kings. Now the fraternity gives away prizes to Kings.

[Haworth co-indexing entry note]: "Drag King Workshop Advertisement." Hammidi, Tania. Co-published simultaneously in *Journal of Homosexuality* (Harrington Park Press, an imprint of The Haworth Press, Inc.) Vol. 43, No. 3/4, 2002, pp. 321-322; and: *The Drag King Anthology* (ed: Donna Troka, Kathleen LeBesco, and Jean Bobby Noble) Harrington Park Press, an imprint of The Haworth Press, Inc., 2002, pp. 321-322. Single or multiple copies of this article are available for a fee from The Haworth Document Delivery Service [1-800-HAWORTH, 9:00 a.m. - 5:00 p.m. (EST). E-mail address: docdelivery@haworthpress.com].

321

Drag King Workshop Advertisement, designed by Tania Hammidi, was used to advertise the Drag King Winter Workshop of 2000 held at UC Davis.

Performing Masculinities

Melinda Hubman, BA

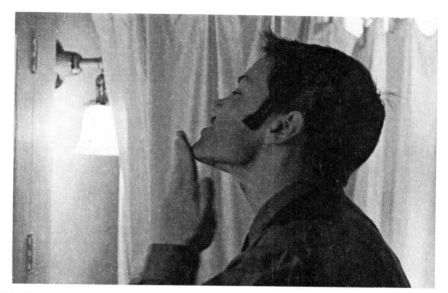

"Karl"

[Haworth co-indexing entry note]: "Performing Masculinities." Hubman, Melinda. Co-published simultaneously in *Journal of Homosexuality* (Harrington Park Press, an imprint of The Haworth Press, Inc.) Vol. 43, No. 3/4, 2002, pp. 323-327; and: *The Drag King Anthology* (ed: Donna Troka, Kathleen LeBesco, and Jean Bobby Noble) Harrington Park Press, an imprint of The Haworth Press, Inc., 2002, pp. 323-327. Single or multiple copies of this article are available for a fee from The Haworth Document Delivery Service [1-800-HAWORTH, 9:00 a.m. - 5:00 p.m. (EST). E-mail address: docdelivery@haworthpress.com].

"The Retro Hetro"

"The Gentleman King"

"The Retro Hetro"

"Karl"

About the Contributors

Colleen Ayoup is a Montréal-based filmmaker/videographer and photographer. She received a BA in Psychology and a BFA in Film Production from Concordia University (Montréal), and studied photography for three years at the Dawson Institute of Photography (Montréal). As a photographer, Colleen's background has been mostly commercial and editorial. Her first film entitled *Oral* (1998) has played at film and video festivals across Canada, the United States, Australia, Brazil and Europe. Her second, and most recent film, *Kings* (2001)–produced in part with a grant from the National Film Board of Canada–traces the four-year span of a local Montréal performance group called the "Mambo Drag Kings." To date, the film has also been shown at festivals in Canada and the United States as well as in France. A ten-minute work in progress of *Kings* (1999) was initially shown at festivals in Canada; London, England; and Berlin.

Sarah Bay-Cheng, PhD, is an assistant professor of English and Theater at Colgate University. Her essays on drama and performance have appeared in *The Journal of American Drama and Theatre*, *Studies in the Humanities*, and *Essays in Theatre*. She is currently completing a book on the drama of Gertrude Stein.

k. bradford, a.k.a. Johnny T., is a poet, filmmaker, performance artist and drag king living as a working artist in Austin, Texas. bradford directs and teaches *It's a She-Shoot,* a feminist film program for women and girls, and is an editor of *Borderlands: Texas Poetry Review*. In 1999, she received a Masters in Creative Writing from UT-Austin. With a Fulbright scholarship, bradford directed *White-Out: The Outing of Whiteness* (1996), a documentary about racism in Southern Africa and the U.S. She has performed her one-woman show *Horses & Suits* in Austin and San Antonio and is at work on her next piece, "The Tales of a Gypsy Cowboy, or the Road on the Show."

Vicki Crowley is a senior lecturer in Gender Studies and a research fellow with the Hawke Institute, University of South Australia. She has published on issues of identity and is currently working on a collection of essays on cultural memory as it pertains to 'race' and racism in Australia. Vicki is also the Chairperson of Feast, the Adelaide Gay and Lesbian Cultural Festival, and actively involved in Drag King performances and other queer politics.

Pierre Dalpé is a Montréal-based photographer. He completed an undergraduate degree in film studies and photography at Concordia University in 1993. Since completing his BFA he has participated in several group shows throughout Canada and has had two solo shows in Montréal. In 1997 Dalpé began fusing his photography with digital imaging and in 1999 he received a grant from the Conseil des Arts et des Lettres du Québec to allow him to attend the Banff Centre for the Arts. It was in Banff that he began producing his latest body of digitally manipulated work entitled *Personae*. His images have been published in *Hour Magazine* (Montréal), the *Montreal Mirror*, and have appeared in *Now Magazine* in Toronto.

Tania N. Hammidi is a performance artist and writer living in Southern California. She has performed as a drag king and worked to build a critical, playful, pro-drag king, transgender-friendly community in Davis, California for the last 8 years. She has presented academic cultural theory on queers and clothing in the *Tulsa Journal of Women's Studies*, the *International Textiles and Apparel Association Journal*, the *Journal of Homosexuality* and two independent film projects. She is currently pursuing her PhD in Visual Studies at the University of California, Irvine.

Melinda Hubman graduated from the University of Minnesota in the fall of 2000 with a BA in Women's Studies. Soon after graduation Melinda moved to New York City where she is currently pursuing various interests. The images presented in this collection are selected from an interactive multi-media installation titled "Performing Masculinities: Take a Chance on Gender." This piece received honorable mention in the undergraduate arts awards by The Steven J. Schochet Center for GLBT Studies.

Aaron Kimberly received her BFA at the Nova Scotia College of Art and Design, supported in part by a bursary from the Manitoba Arts Council. Her paintings, drawings and photographs have been exhibited in

Halifax, Toronto and Winnipeg, Canada. *Autoportraits* were first shown in *Dressing Down* (1998), curated by Robin Metcalfe for the Oakville Galleries, Ontario and have subsequently appeared in *C Magazine*'s "Artist Project" (2000) and in *Portraits: Unsettled Subjects* (2001) at the Mount Saint Vincent University Art Gallery, Halifax. Aaron currently lives outside Vancouver, British Columbia, Canada where she continues a painting practice and teaches art and art history at the Fraser River Art School.

Sheila Koenig, a graduate of the University of Alberta, is co-founder and producer of the Fly Bastards Drag King Troupe. She is also the co-founder and former editor of the grassroots journal *4Corners: A Feminist Review*, and has performed and given lectures on drag throughout Canada.

Alana Kumbier, MA, is a library assistant and writer working in Columbus, Ohio. She currently performs as a member of the Royal Renegades drag king troupe in Columbus, and was a founding member of New Orleans' drag king troupe, Fe-Male Trouble, in 2000-2001. She has been involved with sex-positive sex education performances with the Safer Sex Sluts and served as the television section editor for PopPolitics.com, and has published articles in *Bitch: Feminist Response to Pop Culture* and *Bust Magazine*.

Neeve "Amy" Neevel, a.k.a. Pat Riarch, is co-founder of Feed the Fire Productions with spoken word artist Alix Olson. Within this organization, s/he is the director of Youth Aloud, a project that provides queer youth with spoken word workshops and resources. S/he is a nationally touring drag king and an artist who aspires to see the kingdom come. Hir first book *Transnational Geographic* came out in the fall of 2002.

Jennifer Lyn Patterson is a teaching assistant pursuing a Master's degree in the Department of Art History and Archaeology at the University of Maryland, College Park. Her interests include contemporary art and popular culture, 1970s feminist art production, gender studies, and critical theory. In 1998, she received a BA in Philosophy from Marshall University in Huntington, West Virginia. She graduated Summa Cum Laude and is an alumna of the Society of Yeager Scholars.

Tara Pauliny is a PhD candidate in Rhetoric and Composition at the Ohio State University. She is presently finishing her dissertation, " 'I

Am Your King': A Theorization of Rhetorical Female-to-Male Drag," which bridges the currently disparate fields of feminist rhetoric and queer theory by theorizing women's persuasive use of masculinity. Her publications include " 'Outing the Institution': Composition, the University, and the Rhetoric of FTM Drag," forthcoming in the collection *Labor, Writing Technologies, and the Shaping of Composition in the Academy.*

Thomas Piontek, PhD, is an assistant professor of English at the Ohio State University, where he teaches classes in contemporary literature, gay and lesbian studies, queer theory, film, and cultural studies. The author of articles and reviews on contemporary American culture, representations of AIDS, gay literature, and pedagogy, Professor Piontek is currently completing a book on the impact of queer theory on the field of gay and lesbian studies.

Julie Podmore, PhD, is a geography instructor at John Abbott College and Concordia University in Montréal. Her research on lesbian space in Montréal has appeared in *Matrix* and *Téoros.* After hours, she is Julien St-Urbain, a suave but shy king who dances in the chorus line of Montréal's Mambo Drag Kings.

Stephanie Rogerson was born and raised in Toronto, Canada. After moving to and from six cities, four countries and an unfathomable amount of apartments, she currently lives in Los Angeles. She had a lecture series at Antioch College, Ohio in October 2002 that coincided with her photographic work *Sexing the Inanimate.* Currently, she is working on another drag king series *Sabotage: Another Scenario* and a photographic project based on Los Angeles architecture.

Kathryn Rosenfeld recently had the privilege of offering the first-ever course on pornography at Roosevelt University, where she is an adjunct professor in the Department of Liberal Studies, teaching courses in women's studies, queer studies, and art history. She is also Assistant Editor of *New Art Examiner.* She holds a BA from Antioch College, an MA from the University of Cincinnati, and is completing a second MA from The School of the Art Institute of Chicago. A native New Yorker, she leers at queers of all genders and sells healthy anarchy in her adopted home of Chicago.

Steven P. Schacht, PhD, is an associate professor of Sociology at Plattsburgh State University of New York. His primary areas of research and teaching interest are race, class, gender and sexuality. He is co-editor of *Feminism and Men: Reconstructing Gender Relations* (with Doris Ewing) and *Forging Radical Alliances Across Difference: Coalition Politics for the New Millennium* (with Jill Bystysdzienski) and presently working on two books entitled *A Feminist Phallacy: The Failure to Include Men* (with Doris Ewing) and *Gay and Lesbian Royalty: Inside an Imperial Sovereign Court.*

Jay Sennett, MA, is a writer and filmmaker living in Michigan. His film *Phallocy* has screened in over 30 festivals nationally and internationally. Sennett is the first female-to-male transsexual to receive the prestigious Cultural Award from the Detroit Gay and Lesbian Pride Awards. He is currently at work on his second film, *The Transition Zone*, and his first novel, *Terror.*

Kim Surkan is a PhD candidate in English with a Feminist Studies minor at the University of Minnesota, where she is finishing her dissertation on gender passing and the performance of identity. She teaches GLBT studies courses and works as the site administrator for Voices From the Gaps (*http://voices.cla.umn.edu*), a literary Website dedicated to women writers of color.

Ann Tweedy is a poet and lawyer and an avid fan of drag kings. Her poetry has been published in *Clackamas Literary Review, The Yalobusha Review, Berkeley Poetry Review*, and elsewhere. Her legal writing has appeared in *Buffalo Public Interest Law Journal.* Originally from Massachusetts, she graduated from University of California, Berkeley School of Law (Boalt Hall) in 1999 and was inducted into the Order of the Coif. Ann currently lives in Northern Washington, where she works for an Indian Tribe. She credits drag kings with having helped her discover her sexual orientation.

Annabelle Willox has a BA in Philosophy, an MA in Sexual Politics, and she is currently a PhD research student at the Centre for Critical and Cultural Theory, University of Wales, Cardiff. Using phenomenology as a theoretical basis, her thesis examines the apparent contradiction between the experience and the ideology of queer embodied gendered subjects. Her research interests include queer theory, phenomenology, transgender, sexuality, and field hockey.

Index

The Pursuit of Sodomy: Male Homosexuality in Renaissance and Enlightenment Europe, edited by Kent Gerard, PhD, and Gert Hekma, PhD (Vol. 16, No. 1/2, 1989). *"Presenting a wealth of information in a compact form, this book should be welcomed by anyone with an interest in this period in European history or in the precursors to modern concepts of homosexuality." (The Canadian Journal of Human Sexuality)*

Psychopathology and Psychotherapy in Homosexuality, edited by Michael W. Ross, PhD (Vol. 15, No. 1/2, 1988). *"One of the more objective, scientific collections of articles concerning the mental health of gays and lesbians. . . . Extraordinarily thoughtful. . . . New thoughts about treatments. Vital viewpoints." (The Book Reader)*

Psychotherapy with Homosexual Men and Women: Integrated Identity Approaches for Clinical Practice, edited by Eli Coleman, PhD (Vol. 14, No. 1/2, 1987). *"An invaluable tool. . . . This is an extremely useful book for the clinician seeking better ways to understand gay and lesbian patients." (Hospital and Community Psychiatry)*

Interdisciplinary Research on Homosexuality in The Netherlands, edited by A. X. van Naerssen, PhD (Vol. 13, No. 2/3, 1987). *"Valuable not just for its insightful analysis of the evolution of gay rights in The Netherlands, but also for the lessons that can be extracted by our own society from the Dutch tradition of tolerance for homosexuals." (The San Francisco Chronicle)*

Historical, Literary, and Erotic Aspects of Lesbianism, edited by Monica Kehoe, PhD (Vol. 12, No. 3/4, 1986). *"Fascinating . . . Even though this entire volume is serious scholarship penned by degreed writers, most of it is vital, accessible, and thoroughly readable even to the casual student of lesbian history." (Lambda Rising)*

Anthropology and Homosexual Behavior, edited by Evelyn Blackwood, PhD (cand.) (Vol. 11, No. 3/4, 1986). *"A fascinating account of homosexuality during various historical periods and in non-Western cultures." (SIECUS Report)*

Bisexualities: Theory and Research, edited by Fritz Klein, MD, and Timothy J. Wolf, PhD (Vol. 11, No. 1/2, 1985). *"The editors have brought together a formidable array of new data challenging old stereotypes about a very important human phenomenon. . . . A milestone in furthering our knowledge about sexual orientation." (David P. McWhirter, Co-author, The Male Couple)*

Homophobia: An Overview, edited by John P. De Cecco, PhD (Vol. 10, No. 1/2, 1984). *"Breaks ground in helping to make the study of homophobia a science." (Contemporary Psychiatry)*

Bisexual and Homosexual Identities: Critical Clinical Issues, edited by John P. De Cecco, PhD (Vol. 9, No. 4, 1985). *Leading experts provide valuable insights into sexual identity within a clinical context–broadly defined to include depth psychology, diagnostic classification, therapy, and psychomedical research on the hormonal basis of homosexuality.*

Bisexual and Homosexual Identities: Critical Theoretical Issues, edited by John P. De Cecco, PhD, and Michael G. Shively, MA (Vol. 9, No. 2/3, 1984). *"A valuable book. . . . The careful scholarship, analytic rigor, and lucid exposition of virtually all of these essays make them thought-provoking and worth more than one reading." (Sex Roles, A Journal of Research)*

Homosexuality and Social Sex Roles, edited by Michael W. Ross, PhD (Vol. 9, No. 1, 1983). *"For a comprehensive review of the literature in this domain, exposure to some interesting methodological models, and a glance at 'older' theories undergoing contemporary scrutiny, I recommend this book." (Journal of Sex Education & Therapy)*

Literary Visions of Homosexuality, edited by Stuart Kellogg, PhD (Vol. 8, No. 3/4, 1985). *"An important book. Gay sensibility has never been given such a boost." (The Advocate)*

Alcoholism and Homosexuality, edited by Thomas O. Ziebold, PhD, and John E. Mongeon (Vol. 7, No. 4, 1985). *"A landmark in the fields of both alcoholism and homosexuality . . . a very lush work of high caliber." (The Journal of Sex Research)*

Homosexuality and Psychotherapy: A Practitioner's Handbook of Affirmative Models, edited by John C. Gonsiorek, PhD (Vol. 7, No. 2/3, 1985). *"A book that seeks to create affirmative psychotherapeutic models. . . . To say this book is needed by all doing therapy with gay or lesbian clients is an understatement." (The Advocate)*

Nature and Causes of Homosexuality: A Philosophic and Scientific Inquiry, edited by Noretta Koertge, PhD (Vol. 6, No. 4, 1982). *"An interesting, thought-provoking book, well worth reading as a corrective to much of the research literature on homosexuality." (Australian Journal of Sex, Marriage & Family)*

Historical Perspectives on Homosexuality, edited by Salvatore J. Licata, PhD, and Robert P. Petersen, PhD (cand.) (Vol. 6, No. 1/2, 1986). *"Scholarly and excellent. Its authority is impeccable, and its treatment of this neglected area exemplary." (Choice)*

Homosexuality and the Law, edited by Donald C. Knutson, PhD (Vol. 5, No. 1/2, 1979). *A comprehensive analysis of current legal issues and court decisions relevant to male and female homosexuality.*

DATE DUE

APR 2 9 2005			
GAYLORD			PRINTED IN U.S.A.